Paul Whilbey

Into

Captivity

"When you get where you are going
Where will you be?"
What will you be?

All Scriptures are taken from the King James Version of the Bible

ISBN: 1-933899-94-8

Published by:
Holy Fire Publishing
Unit 116
1525-D Old Trolley Rd.
Summerville, SC 29485

www.ChristianPublish.com

Printed in the United States of America and the United Kingdom

Acknowledgment

Our "evolving" in faith must needs be ever changing – as we allow God to add to our own knowledge in Him.

The truth in the Bible has "never" changed and "never will" …whereas my "every day" is changed (hopefully) by the preceding day.

"Every" thought into captivity …is going to take some serious searching …and may we not fail in the task …right?   (somebody say – "right")

Special thanks to sister in Christ, Teresa Job …and to brother in Christ, pastor Dave Benson …but far above all else, thanks and praise to God for His Son and then thanks for His gift also of my son.

Editor's Note

In the process of the author's spiritual walk, out of love for his son, has written of the things we all face in this world in our own seeking and our questions that are all answered in God's Word. He writes straight from his heart with both serious concern and humor and clearly does so with the help of the Holy Spirit, indwelling there. Several new Christians that have read the author's pages have found enormous positive encouragement there, and are very much aware of the power of God.

Introduction

What has been written here is from the first half of the year 2005. (hence Into Captivity series 051) 052 …is from the 2nd half of 2005

Much of our life circumstances are dateable, even cultural …but God's truths have been somehow made available to us since God first created man in His likeness.

Regardless of how simple we maintain our lives or how complex …we allow our lives to become, God has always been available and capable of meeting man's every need if we place our trust in Him.

Our "thoughts" (maybe "millions" every day) define our attitudes and actions as "pleasing to God" …or not.

I would strongly encourage Richard (and everyone) to "daily" make written note of what's on your hearts.

Christ is our "Mediator" without whom there is no God for us.
(1 Tim. 2: 5)

In "our own" hands are interesting days (and eternities) ahead for us and for those we profess to love.

(January 21, 2007)

Preface

This writing is dedicated to my parents, Jean and Stan and to my son, Richard (who is about a third of my age)

…Hi Richard …much of this is "dedicated to" you but also "directed to" you in the earnest hope that you continue to pursue a close walk with God through Christ.

…there's much truth in the Bible that I now "get" but which I didn't get up until maybe five years ago and there's much I probably could have gotten (of life more abundant) had I, at a younger age, "smartened up."

…if, and as you read this stuff, I hope you "mark it up" with a high lighter pen or pencil and that we, together, might one day revisit some issues I've pondered herein.

…while I "don't believe" we have evolved from amoeba (or whatever) I "do believe" we evolve from a starting point of "trusting" (without fully understanding) God's instruction to mankind through the Bible and I hope anything I might say (herein or hereafter) that's displeasing to God…be stricken from your eyes, ears, mind, heart, etc.

…if what I present, now, is at variance with what I have previously presented it's due to growth in faith, and please know that the journey between was joy.

…what I say towards you, is towards myself also and before God also.

…I sort of like to think that what I write is (hopefully) from a loving Father through His Son …then forwarded to a loving father to his son …and whether I've used God's word well or not …at least the Bible passages herein are "sound and profitable" unto all things. (every thought)

…anyway, what will be, will be and we each are either on "God's team" …or "musts needs" find ourselves on "an opposing team" (enmity against God) (James 4: 4)

…having spent much time away from God (in worldly darkness) I pray I never again return therein. …I've "thrown books away" that didn't suit me …and whatsoever you do with this rambling of thoughts is your call. …the unconditional love God holds for all is the love I hold for you.

Love,

Dad

Without faith and God's word …we have only the world to draw from.

…the "world" will never be enough. …the "soul", in submission, will not only be ample …but will in addition have ample to share. …sort of like with the fishes and loaves.

…I suppose ….if we soften and allow Christ to touch us with His Holy hands …or His Holy Spirit ….well ….that must at least be faith as of a mustard seed! …so why so little growth in Christ's following? …I sure hope the fact that so little appears to be happening, isn't a testament to the softness of our faith. ….but what else could it be? …are we blindly praying for the filling of His joy, His peace, His rest, His love …even though the vessel to hold that filling is already full of junk?

…coming from a house in the suburbs to this bachelor apartment has somehow been a blessing. …in moving, I left behind, probably, half of my little "pleasing to my eye and mind" unnecessary treasures and tools. …the "few" that I've retained will require wall to wall – floor to ceiling shelves or else storage somewhere! ….something has to change! …to enter my door, your eyes immediately go to one large window with a writing desk in front of it and a large Bible, writing material, dictionary, etc. …it even still impresses me! …but three short strides into my place and incredulity sets in.

…this man's "Bible focus" falters gravely in distraction upon distraction of interesting items far removed "from faith". …treasures all but distractions all, also. …I know God sees it and I hope anyone who is of God's flock sees it …and hope they will always ask …"what's with all this stuff?"

…I suppose that's the "exhortation" in "not" forsaking the assembly of ourselves together." (Heb. 10: 25)

…I like to hear others say "this is cool stuff!" …but the Bible says God doesn't want me to hear that. …if I can't truthfully explain how this stuff is "of faith", then it's taking up space in this vessel that in turn impedes God's filling me with faith. …how can it be otherwise?   …for me …it's in that light that

(Rom. 14: 23) …"for whatsoever is not of faith is sin ….makes perfect "sense".

...so, isn't it our own choices that puts a "cap" on what we can potentially receive from Christ?

...it occurs to me ...(this first day of 2005) ....that to wish God's blessing on another for the coming year is not necessarily to wish them happiness ...in that ...God's blessing may come in the form of a struggle ...but a "struggle that draws us closer to God" is the greater blessing". ...whereas "happiness of the world" is "of death". ...it may be a death of many cuts or simply decay ...but it will be far from "life more abundant in Christ." ...some distractions from faith are less pleasant than others. ...hunger or pain vs. entertainment or escape from conscience ...some are painfully apparent while others are deceptively innocent. ...to separate "faith" from sin will always entails serious (not casual) inner searching and "identifying" those areas that are clearly not of faith. ...that's something we can never do in our own strength. ...it's our nature (only natural) to be constantly bombarded with thoughts (or voices) of self motivation and "self" ...ishness" ...unfortunately most family and friends also encourage us along that road of "self".

(Micah 6: 8) ..."seek justice, love mercy, walk humbly with God."

...there's no benefit to "self" over another in our seeking objective justice nor benefit to those close to us.   ...there's nothing of "self" in our being merciful ...nor any focus on "self" in our walking humbly with our God. (...other than the surety that God will, in His own way, reward us through His added presence in us.) ...we generally accept that "prayer" is of our lips ...eyes closed ...maybe hands together, etc. ...and we call it a part of worship ...but perhaps "prayer" is more rightly "our daily walk with our God". ...eloquence and well meaning words are not required for worship of or trust in God. ...but obedience is. ..."obedience" is what God sees, hears and knows in us and of us.   ...I wonder what the worth is of "unavailing prayer"?

...before accepting communion, the Bible exhorts us to give strong thought to our individual "walk with our God." ....the Bible even warns us to pass up taking communion if something is perhaps amiss in our walk.   …same with tithing ….the tithe is His already ….there's no question of "can we afford it?"

…it's not ours to afford or not afford.   …and so with prayer, our righteousness is through God ….it's nothing of us.   …our prayer is to be effectual and fervent and of His will if we are to expect answer by Him.

(James 5: 16) .."the effectual, fervent prayer of a righteous man availeth much.

…what do we suppose the "availing" is …of casual prayer by lukewarm Christians? (….it boggles the mind.)   (Rom. 8: 26)   …and further …"likewise the Spirit also helpeth our infirmities (weakness) for we know not what we should pray for as we ought: the Spirit (His Spirit in us) itself makes intercession for us with groanings which cannot be uttered."   ….nothing there that speaks of casual or spur-of-the-moment petition to our Heavenly Father. …to pray for the filling of God's Spirit in us is probably of no merit to us unless we share with others of that "filling". …unless we use the gifts He has already given us …to His Glory …then how can we expect further "life more abundant" into a stagnant vessel? …unless we're of His flock, how can we be comforted even in great tragedy or great loss? …even our being comforted is to bring glory to Him through our choosing to believe on Him and trust His word.

…my parents passing was (is) a great loss to me but I'm assured through faith that none of His flock will know death. …my parents, while dead to earthly struggle, are yet alive in Christ. …and if I smarten up, then so will I be, too.

…without reservation, I trust God's word and trust in the Spirit to reveal the truth and light of His word to me, be it the King James Version or another close to it.

…what I don't trust is any part of me that might be apart from faith.

…I need mentors and prefer stern mentors …and better yet, stern mentors who themselves have stern mentors! …(maybe even unto four generations!)

(Isa. 55: 8) …the Bible warns …"for my thoughts are not your thoughts, neither are your ways my ways, saith the Lord." (Luke 13: 24) …Christ said …"Strive to enter in at the straight gate: for many, I say unto you, will seek to enter in and shall not be able."

…I have no intention of being among those who "shall not be able." …if my family or friends choose to casually wander to and fro in faith …then I'm not to be amongst them. …too bad if it doesn't make for "peaceful" living. …maybe I'm selfish …but my own salvation comes before peaceful existence. …being accepted, even by those I love …pales in priority to my striving to "enter at the straight gate."

(Heb. 12: 11) …"Now no chastening for the present seemeth to be joyous but grievous: nevertheless, afterward it yieldeth the peaceable fruit of righteousness unto them which are exercised thereby." (Heb. 12: 14) …if we can attain Godly humility, then, can we "Follow peace with all men and Holiness without which no men shall see the Lord." …"without which." …go figure. …I have no idea …what exactly, God has appointed to man vs. what He has appointed to woman. …if God's word suggests that there is no difference then I invite someone to cite me those passages in scripture. …my mother and grandmother were, of course, mentors by association …but weren't so stern (vigilant) in scriptural obedience as were my Dad or Grandfather.

…a woman's heart, which was once accepted and honored as a home for the man's heart has become a place of unrest and demands and equality. (I wonder if every old thing is to pass away and become new? ….and does man's heart no longer find an earthly home?)

…I wonder at the "falling domino" effect as each new generation claims advanced liberties (?) …and am reminded of the scripture …"All things are lawful unto me.

(1 Cor. 10: 23) …but all things are not expedient nor edifying." …what the Bible proffers is edifying unto all generations but seldom desired by our hearts. …and having declined God's will for marriage …we cast our fate to the wind. (…an "ill wind" at that.)

…at nearly any cost, we promote peace in our gatherings but at the price of forgetting why we are gathered! …perhaps glee-clubs are popular but why do we attach them to Christ's church? ….does church affiliation lend respectability to borderline programs? …over history, religion has been used to front many nefarious causes …some best described even as "heinous". ....there is never any crass or otherwise, self gain to attach to Christ and yet remain guiltless. ...all that is "of faith" will bring all glory to God the Father ...none to man. ...I always feel a warning ...when a friend says that they're happy with where they're at in their faith and would rather not open any sensitive areas just now. ...when we cap our "pursuing" then the Bible says we cap our "receiving" of God. ...I don't envy anyone who "caps their receiving" of God. ...without growth in

faith, we either stagnate ...or lose ground to satan ...and our troubles will surely compound and grow.

(Psa. 90: 10) ....we are given, at best, 70 - 80 years ...most of them in pain and trouble then ....we're gone to our reward. (verse 12) "So teach us to number our days that we may (choose) to apply our hearts unto wisdom."

(verse 17) "And let the beauty of the Lord our God be upon us: ...."

....we are blessed with a bit of time ...and from a young age we are accountable for our eternity. ...we're even accountable for how we impact one another's choices as regards their eternities also. ...our children's, our friends'...our neighbors' ...and all we come in contact with. ...do we uphold Christ? ...or do we fail Christ? ...it may not be the "cup we want" ...but every Christian (at least those who aspire to salvation) must join the fray in the carrying of Christ's burden of the souls of men, women and children ...both those close to our hearts ...and those distant also. ...the shy ...or the lay-low Christian must question and grapple with whether or not Christ's Spirit is with (in) them. ...if there is no passion for more of Him and barely discernable evidence of the fruit of His Spirit ...then would we not question our claim of faith? (Matt. 7: 20) :Wherefore by their fruits ye shall know them. (verse 21) "Not everyone that saith unto me, Lord, Lord, shall enter into the Kingdom of Heaven but (only) he that doeth the will of my Father which is in Heaven." ...we say that, in reciting the Lord's Prayer ...we just fail to say "Thy will be done on earth (by us) as it is in Heaven....." "...and whoever it is done by ...hopefully it won't interfere too much with us!" ...(scary, mom.)

…it's discouraging to see vast variance of content in the different versions of scripture …and I expect that to worsen in coming years. …yet I trust Christ's Spirit, in sincere seekers, to reveal the truths found in God's word while dismissing the chaff of liberal interpretation. …the "living Bible" translation was a fun and easier read for me, early on …but I'm thankful to now see it's weaknesses (infirmities) when compared to the King James version. …it was nevertheless a good starter Bible (baby's milk) for my turning to a more determined walk in faith ….but became a hindrance for me (Heb. 5: 12) …by leaving no room for the "strong meat" (vegetarian or not) God wishes for us. …"diet" foods have their place but limiting certain "intake" will sometimes cause "disorders." …nothing "of God" encourages disorder according to His perfect will.

…a "worldly" element of having many different (user friendly) Bible translations or versions is the time spent (no doubt to satan's pleasure) on semantics …in the seeking of God's truth and meaning. …while we claim "oneness" and "unity" …it's not supported by our reading from the same page …there are men's Bibles …and ladies Bibles, student Bibles, study Bibles, Bibles for scholars …and Bibles for dummies …gender neutral Bibles, Good News Bibles (haven't seen the Bad News Bible …yet.) …I suppose our desire for novelty will soon generate a satan's Bible which will promote every potential 21st century pleasure not "specifically" or "blatantly" denied us in Greek, Latin or Aramaic.

("Buy your stock shares now! in hustler or playboy publishing!!")

…it's not unnatural to want a "road map" that suits where we "want" to go …and we certainly have it within our willpower and capacity to open the door to that descent. …only through the strength of His Spirit can we turn from the temptation. …we dare God to show His wrath and anger and when he does we decry "where was God when this tragedy or that devastation occurred!?" …it's the pits when we reap what we sow. …those of "His Flock" need not fear nor be anxious as whether in this life or the next ….we remain "of His flock" …if we are advancing His cause. …our joy and our rest (freedom from worldly bondage) is but a foretaste of "glory divine."

…many worldly people may claim to not care if they live or die …but it's through apathy towards the life they know …and not through comforting assurance of a Heavenly home at their end of days.

…the word "carefree" usually has pleasant connotations but to be "without care" is akin to death also. …the Bible says that in caring for others we are more able to receive from Him. …voila …"life more abundant!"

…with Christmas just passed, the Dickens character of Scrooge probably well exemplifies the "death" in self focus. …few of us (hopefully) descend to such depths. …I don't know that Dickens ever shared "how" Scrooge "came to be" the way he was portrayed. …I, today, know people who through circumstances beyond their control could easily be Scrooge-ish, yet they are more "Christ-ish."

…as with Job …to be tested, is …to be honored in God's eyes. …to "praise" God for physical or emotional pain …seems absurd …but there is " a light" in which "praise" is an appropriate response. …Job, in the end, was restored to even greater prosperity then was his previously. …I don't think the Bible says that …Job's "pain in the neck friends", came to faith through Job's ordeal …but how could they not be faith positive-ly affected by what Job endured and overcame? …yet they too were not carefree but were perhaps somewhat true friends, in that they did not abandon Job nor flee his travail. …Job was a Godly man, so I doubt his "friends" were "ungodly" but rather had not the depth of Job's faith.

….in the winter dark of delivering morning newspapers there's a moment every day where the headlights of my car alight a warning of "DANGER…HIGH VOLTAGE" … I was pondering the various Bible versions this morning when that warning came into view and it occurred to me …that same warning should be a label on every King James Bible. …there may be a Bible I'm unaware of that is of yet "stronger meat" …but I gather that subsequent and more liberal versions are based (loosely?) on the King James version. …or even a label of "suitable but probably not desirous (suitable) for all adherents " ….or even "undiluted". …I think it's well for new believers to be warned (especially as regards the "yet to come even more liberal versions) that paraphrasing offers only a limited walk of faith ..."elementary" even. ...I certainly don't know what degree of our leniency the Holy Spirit finds acceptable apart from what my (choice of) Bible says it to be. (..sometimes questionably ...but I hope I'm beyond the "children's version.) ...so ...after "children's" ...what's the next "light" version? ...by and by, I

expect I'll eventually want my Spiritual walk to reflect the "true grit" of the most potent instruction and enlightenment of God's will for my life. ...else, exactly what is my "treasure"? (Phil. 2: 12)...for how long can I remain content in "working out my own salvation" by my choosing to blend my obedience to His will with treasures of the world? .....all the while expecting a greater outpouring of Christ's Spirit in my life? ...I'd be remiss to say other than: "woe is me" ...wouldn't it be something ...to learn that all my pursuit of quasi – faith is actually more pleasing to satan than pleasing to Christ?

(...I'd better "watch it!" ....or I'll start scaring myself here.) ...what's scary is when I say "why can't God just leave me alone for awhile?" ...but then I consider "my life" if He ever did! ...no thanks! (Psa. 84: 10) ...better is one day in His courts than a thousand out of His courts (house?) (Psa. 84: 11) ...while God's blessings fall on the just and the unjust "...no good thing will He withhold from them that walk uprightly"

...even Job ...far beyond his understanding, was honored by God and what better thing than that!?! ...I look on any suffering I may endure in light of how it impacts me. ....God's test is rather in light of how my suffering impacts others.

...the Apostle Paul suffered constant affliction and impacted (impacts!) thousands for the cause of Christ. ...the Bible suggests to me ...that although we, ourselves, may avoid personal suffering ...we are, nonetheless, to take on any suffering by our Christian brothers or sisters as though it were ours also.

...in Christ we are not given relief from suffering only so that we may enjoy relief but rather that through our relief do we have the added capacity to uphold the needs of the less fortunate. ...our escape from personal suffering may well be short lived, after which, we ourselves can find some comfort in the kindness or charity of others who might avail themselves to help carry a burden we have come to bear. ....it's not us who helps ...it's Christ who helps.

...better to not deceive ourselves through praying that Christ help those whom we suspect are in need ....as one who claims to be "of Christ" ...You go and be with them ....You seek His will, then just do it! ...how difficult can it be!?!

...to read what Jesus said ...to claim that as our treasure, then get off the couch or computer or writing table ...(wait a minute ...not writing table)

....and "go out" to share our "claimed treasure" with those who are likeminded, yet burdened? ...in the Bible ...(at least in the King James)

...the book of James ...speaks strongly to "walking the walk" ...as opposed to "talking the talk". ...if "it" (He) is in us ...then the word "difficult" becomes a non-word.

...what was once "difficult" ...now becomes "eagerness" to serve a risen Savior in the manner His Spirit dictates.

(Psa. 34: 8) .."Taste and see ....." ...maybe "taste" will leave us confused ....but to not taste is oblivion (the condition or fact, of being forgotten) ...so taste ...then eat! ...all of what is offered by God is good. ..."we are what we eat" ...is true Spiritually.

...we should want all that we do (our conduct) to be easily defendable from scripture if Christ's Spirit is really with us.

...if what I'm doing, at any time, is not drawing me closer to God ....then it's a barrier between me and God. ...I wonder what the Bible says regarding "how much" I'm to be about God's word ...and His will? ....Psalm 1: 2 ??

...I would guess somewhat more than "occasionally" ...right? ...funny the Bible doesn't say what I'm suppose to do the rest of the time??? ...probably stuff like golf ....right?

... see (Col. 3: 17) ...through Christ's Spirit we give deference to Christ.

(without His Spirit, why would we??) ....having "tasted" and seen that indeed God is good ...we begin to surrender many creature comforts (pleasures) of the world to comply with His requests and gain assurance that we have now changed from our old ways and have been "born again" into His Body (church). …yet we retain a few old treasures which are perhaps deeply rooted and require His strength in the bearing out and digging up of whatever may hold us back from our adding to our faith …God's truth, revealed through His Spirit in us, will help us realize the burden of continuing to carry these resistant treasures (baggage) around in us.   (Jer. 17: 9) …the Bible says "the heart is deceitful above all things and desperately wicked": …who can know it? (verse 10) I the Lord search the heart, I try the reins, even to give every man according to his ways and according to the fruit of his doings." …it appears that to the extent that we are "about" Him …that is the limit to our receiving "from" Him. …God doesn't deny as His presence …we deny ourselves His presence.

…Tom Jones made a recording in the late 60s called "All I want is just a Little You." …never mind what our lips say …do our lives reflect exactly that, towards God?

…I used to really like that song yet I don't think I've recalled it for longer than my son's been alive (18 years!)   …a couple of lines in that song say "there's a little truth in every lie you tell me …a little right in all the wrong you do."

…is that how God sees my heart? …moderately deceptive? …the Bible says God will have "no part" in a heart like that.   (Mark 12: 30) "…all thy heart …all thy soul …all thy mind …all thy strength."   …why couldn't the Bible say …some …or most…??? Right? …there must be …or soon will be a Bible version that cuts us some slack …right?

…are we "Christian enough" to "wait-it out"?   …this is the 21st century, age of nanosecond technology …surely God won't leave us wandering in the vast wastelands for 40 years! …God is forgiving and merciful …right?   …so …what's to fear? ….right? "(excuse me!! ….how about a little support here, from the Christian community!)

…we are …"one in the Spirit," ….right? …"wha'd ya mean, whose Spirit ??? …get with the program!!"   …the "Holy Spirit" …ya know? …like …in "part of the trinity"!?! " …yes! Yes! Yes! …that one! …the one we claim is in our church services!" "…yes!

…of course we'd all have our noses buried into the carpet if Christ or God made their presence known. …and no …I can't explain how the Holy Spirit seems to be the lesser partner …just do whatever the person on the platform says …and could ya try to lighten up a bit with the questions? …this is supposed to be joyous and fun!!!" (…last Sunday they said to bring a friend!!) (that's the last time I'm bringing that dolt to meet my Lord and Master! …some people just can't leave "well enough" alone! …I don't go out of my way and come here, to get raked over the coals as to why things aren't different!

…let sleeping dogs lie! …right? …besides, I've never killed anyone and I'm not an ex-convict! …so what's with all the talk from this pastor about being convicted!?! …maybe this is some kind of church for prisoners?? …I don't "feel good" about this church …where's the next closest one?" ….I actually have a church acquaintance/friend for whom the proceeding theatric might ring somewhat true! …he doesn't seem to be an avid seeker of a closer walk with God. …(maybe I'm wrong or maybe that attitude will change) …he's the member" …I am not as yet and in a shocked way I enjoy speaking

with him. (..although …I might find myself concerned should the church put my friend's name forward as potential elder.) …my friend may even be rightfully affected by Sunday morning medications that I know nothing about?? …then what??

…best to trust the Lord and through Him, my friend's dear wife.

…I'm quite interested in how and why it is that some Christians seem to be plugged into a different strength, joy and power source …than do others.

…it's the same unchanging God ….so the variations must be in attitude. …so what's that all about? …my vigilant and enthused Christian friend Dave and I sometimes joke at how there must a kind of dead Christians society.

…comparatively! …I'm maybe new to faith …so have these quiet, somber folk already arrived at their pinnacle of faith? …or does the bloom wear off over time? …some seem happy …or excited ….but to listen to them …it's nothing to do with Christ ….but rather other stuff!   (2 Cor. 5: 17) …maybe not quite "all things become new" …maybe we change as best we can then just incorporate the rest into our faith. …maybe Christ doesn't give us quite enough strength or vigilance …right? …that would account for a limited joy in the Lord …right? …how do I best explain that option to my son and others? …maybe I don't have to …maybe it just comes natural! …when I head out these days at 5 a.m. to deliver these newspapers it's most often cold, dark and wet outside …I start out with every world comfort I can …layered clothing, wool hat, gloves, scarf, rain jacket, etc. ….loaded for bear…so to speak. …but about ¼ into the route I start to warm up ….at which point many of these comforts I had enjoyed having …now they've become uncomfortable and more of a hindrance rather than a help. …faith is like that ….as we warm up to it or mature …whether through conviction or awareness we somehow realize more and more that our old ways are keeping us from something far better. …I suppose we try for both worlds …but what God offers is too big to handle with just one hand and we have to release whatever of the world is in our other hand. …(that's a good thing.)

…that's when the problems and concerns of earth start to grow strangely dim.

…it's like when it finally clicks for the dog who's been chasing it's tail and it can now devote full time to chasing cats! .

…our worldly pursuits will by and by confound us with all manner of anxiety.

…they all hinge (depend) upon ever changing circumstances and ever changing people.

(Prov. 3: 5) …the Bible says "lean not to your own understanding"

…that seems impossible but for the Christian who accepts that "fearing God is the beginning of wisdom" …then we respond to the "understanding" He shares with us …the understanding is of Him and "not of us." … and it will be confirmed through His word. ….conducting our lives under the direction of God's wisdom is a huge burden lifted from our cares …unless our ego and our emotion and our pride gets involved in trying to bend God's wisdom and God's word to our own self desire.

(Matt. 11: 29) …Christ said "Take my yoke upon you and learn of me for I am meek and lowly in heart and ye shall find rest for your souls" (verse 30) "For my yoke is easy and my burden is light." …each of us has a soul even if we don't believe we have one,

we do. …you may not even want one but too bad. …given God's content in Psalms 139.

…I believe even the fetus has a soul …which the violating of makes a huge issue of abortion …and even Birth control …from what I understand the Bible to say …neither can have any attachment to "faith". …I disagree strongly with the Living Bible's support of the tenet that if you feel that birth control or abortion is right …then it's apparently okay and pleasing to God. …how dangerous is that!?!

…you can bet when satan's Bible arrives at the bookstores there'll be no change needed from the Living Bible, as regards (Roman 14: 23!) …I have Christian friends who tell me I'm very "negative"…but to me, I'm not negative but rather just opposite! ….what's truly negative is to support what the Bible speaks against! …right?

…sensuality "need" not lead to birth control …nor abortion. …sexuality and sensuality can be a fantastic gift from a wonderful giver …but it need not control us to the point where we do wrong in God's eyes …and for every Christian and non-Christian alike ….all sex is before God's eyes. …and we're wise not to pretend that God sees through a glass darkly!

…the further we stray from God's truth (no matter which Bible you or your church advocates) …the more likely we'll pretend that God's ways are our ways. …and the heavier our hearts will be, weighted down in bondage and self deception. …a heavy heart is not God's will for us …a heavy heart is a result of our own determinations. ….basically, the reaping of what we sow. …there was a time I would have said "that must be ludicrous!" (hard to believe I was once even dumber than I appear to be now!) …what's ludicrous …is that I enjoy life now more than I ever have …and strangely …it doesn't even seem to be my life that I'm enjoying! …go figure! …"my life" …when I think about it …is probably best defined by "what I'm familiar with" at any particular time. ...beyond purely existing ...what else is "my life"? ...it's comprised of my past (good, bad or indifferent) ...plus my present (good bad or indifferent ...plus my hopes for tomorrow. ...apart from faith or religion, probably our greatest influences (positive or negative) will be our choice of companions (primarily - spouse)

...I suppose if our choice of church generally defines our God (as it should?)

...then our companions generally define our church. ...by "church" here, I mean, "that which we support " with our voluntary discretionary money and also our regular attendance. ..."our church" may be a Sunday morning pew or a Saturday night blackjack table ...the horse track or the golf course, the Azores, the opera or arena ...whatever we support is essentially our church. ...we may boldly claim our choice before our children and others. ...or we may prefer there be no record of our attendance anywhere. ...whatever our "church" ...it's likely a good place to meet likeminded people ...even a potential spouse! ...but also a place to meet potential mischief or worse.

...to become a sincere Christian one must also maintain that there is no (zero) privacy from God. ...in the light or in the dark, all we do and think is known to Him and recorded by Him.

(The large print giveth ...and the small print taketh away" ...Tom Waits)

..if only God could be like Santa Clause (ya know ...close his record book and go to sleep at 9:00 or 10:00 o'clock at night) ...then just about everybody might become Christian! ...there's probably a "Santa" Bible translation available already ...no small print. (I guess I'd better "watch-it!") (seems my Mom's "peaceful" influence is fast catching up with my Dad's "gloves off" influence. ...actually, they were both saying "watch-it!" ...they were just talking about different things.) ....did I mention they lived on Harmony Road when they retired? ...pretty cool ...right??)

...my folks had the same church and their folks had the same church ...that's a good start for a good match ...I imagine "harmony" comes more easily from mutually honored backgrounds.

…back to "God sees all ….." …if we are content to knowingly keep a few doors (hopefully) shielded from God's view …then we resign ourselves to a "form of Godliness" or a "form of faith" from which we really can't expect much "life more abundant".   …pretending to want the "straight goods" is always a recipe for disappointment. …I think, to receive Christ's love, we need to pursue loving others as Christ loves. …those who choose for something or someone other than Christ as their "first love" cut themselves off from receiving His comfort.   …I guess they in effect choose other forms of comfort.

…the hard part is that the Bible says specifically that whoever is not "for Christ" is "against Christ" …and the Bible often describes the grim ending for those against Christ.   (Matt. 12: 20)

…to encourage those close to us towards faith …without alienating them, is a tenuous struggle for sure …but the course is just and if tenacity is required …then it is! …ambivalence can't be an option for us. …nor can nagging …guess that leaves constant, gentle imploring by those who are gentle …and strong exhortation by those who aren't . …right?

…"the fruit of the Spirit" cited in (Gal. 5: 22) …in context are contrasted against "the works of the flesh (world)" …would that we all could confine our Christian walk to just these attributes …were it exclusively so, we could hunker down, peacefully, in some little enclave with little concern for the eternity of our fellow man.

…but the "whole Bible" calls us to disciple far beyond the envelope of this group of nine ….what of the requirements of service? …the discerning, the upholding of truth? …what of the "suffering" we are called to in the carrying out of Christ's cause? …the endurance without resentment? …the discipline to "hold fast to that good which remains" even against the coming Apostasy of church leaders!
(2 Peter 2) …what of the call that we hunger and thirst for His righteousness?

…why is it we're neither reviled nor persecuted for His sake? …even though the blessing and reward would be great yet use (1) decline that "front line" position.

(Matt. 5: 13) "Ye are the salt of the earth but if the salt have lost his savor, wherewith shall it (the earth) be salted? It is thence forth good for nothing, but to be cast out and to be trodden under foot of men."

...nowhere, to my knowledge, does the Bible suggest our Christian walk is to resemble the "box social" that the church (His people) seem to be fast becoming.

...the "fruit of the Spirit" isn't to be a comfort zone of "refuge" but rather, perhaps, God given ammunition and supplies for battle against a prevailing darkness!

...I don't know my "post judgment" status ...but please, at least, let me be in the line-up!!! ...let me do something worthy of His notice that warrants a checkmark in the "plus column"! ....maybe a few notable positives to offset my failings on His behalf.

(1 Peter 1: 23) ...the Bible says "the word of God" is the "source of birth" ...and also the "means of growth" (1 Peter 2: 2) ...and that "knowledge of Christ, through His word," will help us make our calling and election sure. ...I wonder at how closely "surety" and "vainglory" are related? ...my experience has been that I no sooner remove the hand from my ship's rudder and cross my arm upon my chest in surety ...but what doesn't a gust of wind immediately send me off course.

(1 Cor. 14: 23) says God is not the author of confusion ...but I wonder about "pranks" ...God knows I'm bad for knee-jerk reactions ...He made me this way! ...so I guess it's for me to figure out why. ...I expect it's something I'm missing from His word. (mind you ... I'm not so bad as I used to be.) (less fear of everything ...but not quite fearless ...yet.) ...I suppose "fear" is really just an extension of worry and imaginings. ...there's no comfort, or little at most, in simply saying "everyone has similar fears." ...better to identify the root cause and put that to rest and without faith in Christ we're at the mercy of the same world which is the source of fear also. ...it's a bit self defeating ...right?

(Luke 18: 22) ...The Bible says to "lay up treasures in Heaven" and while one probably doesn't wish to die ...neither is there fear of this life being "the end of the line"

...to deny ourselves "hope" is, for sure, cause to fear.

…just like if we deny ourselves exercise then we'll question our capabilities and our world becomes smaller for fear of what we can't do. …to not exercise our faith is to invite doubt to attach itself to our faith. ….and while doubt will never defeat Christ's Spirit …it will, however, crowd out Christ's Spirit from our lives.

…I personally have come to accept that whatsoever is not of faith is sin." (Rom. 14: 23)

…we can fudge the semantics of differing Bible versions but from my own experience that scripture (as does all scripture) rings more and more true.

…and as Christians I believe we're called to more and more seek out the Bible's truth personally and grow to rely more and more on His Spirit to fulfill us.

…how else can we "continue" to "work out our own salvation?"   (Phil. 2: 12)

…as well, that I haven't yet experienced the "with fear and trembling" is of my own shortcomings …but if it's a part of growth in faith, then I hope for that also and expect it. ….(although it doesn't sound so good to me just now) …I hope it's a different "fear" than what I've been trying, in faith, to overcome.

…it's interesting how churches seem to want to appear upbeat and happy.

…it sometimes reminds me of a balloon that fills with air (us) every Sunday morning …and then deflates except for the social part until the next Sunday. (….I often feel inflated "of the Spirit" until I go to church! …either a wrong attitude ….or a wrong church ….right?   …I was particularly blessed (and convicted) by this morning's church service, …although I didn't leave the apartment.

…my favorite pastor, in Cloverdale , B.C., broadcasts a service Sunday mornings.

…his name is Rev. Ian Goligher (the 'g' is silent …but if the 'g' represents God, His presence is in no way silent in this particular preacher.) …one of my treasures is to hear a voice that appears utterly fearless in lambasting anything that is a distraction from faith. …his message this morning was taken from Joshua …"as for me and my house" we will serve the Lord."   ("house" expanded to include our "effectible environment") …I don't know why it is that the Bible continually cites "man" as being answerable for what happens under his roof or for "his" being responsible to provide for his family …nor do I understand the extent to which "woman" doesn't seem to be equally accountable.

…I only know I suffer if I ever try to bend God's word to better suit my will or my capacity to understand.

…man is not to relinquish the respectful authority given to his care as cited in scripture. …it's not an option …nor an avenue of rest or peace or escape just because it's a complex world. …next to Christ …he's the man and the burden falls on his shoulders as regards where he turns to find the strength to help him carry it.

…for the Christian, God's plan is just as shared with us through His word. …we may not understand it nor even like it and until we conform ourselves to it we will continue to suffer separation from Him and probably considerable separation from one another also.

…to pretend equality so as to appease another is very thin ice on which to travel …better to accept that, apart from Godly focus, men and women are vastly different and to praise God for it. …our needs are different and our purposes are different even beyond our sources of reference (life experience) being different.

…I can don a hospital jacket and stethoscope and appear to be a doctor

…but I've no experience and would be a fool to expound on medical practice.

…likewise, I suppose I could shave, put on rouge, a wig and a dress and appear, somewhat, as a woman …but have no experience or source of reference to relate to women. …I can kindly listen to their concerns and make limited suggestions but that's my allowable extent of support according to the Bible. …men cannot be doctors for women …men can be friends …men can be as caring brothers …but men who try to appease women can also be the cause of women needing doctors …and visa versa. …best for men to comply with God's instruction ..and women to do so also.

…it's not in our wisdom that we'll find peace or harmony together but rather only in His wisdom. …I know, that for me to part from God's ways is stupidity. …does not stupidity beget stupidity wherever it can find support?

…any man or woman who wished to stray to the forefront of un-chartered rights or ground ought to look at the potential extended affects of failure. …I don't know why God asks that the wife submit to the husband …I only know there's a reason despite it often seeming unreasonable.

…and I know that today (21st century) barely half of our marriages last very long.

…(and that family law is a thriving profession) …go figure.

(Phil. 2: 3) …the Bible says to "consider (put) others, of those who are likeminded, ahead of ourselves (then general well-being in faith) ….not only ought we not create or cause any others to stumble …but rather ever encourage them towards their pursuit of God's truth and light. …the extent (or degree) of my faith is just that ….I need not expect it to be the same as others. …God reveals to the extent we are prepared to be filled.

….math is taught in elementary school but there are parts of math

…i.e. Calculus etc. that require more preparation.

…some of us are on baby's milk and that's good and yet some on strong meats …"according to God's giving" (Eph. 4: 7)

(Matt. 12: 20) the Bible says …"and smoking flax He shall not quench …'til He send forth judgment unto victory" …if our hearts are softened away from worldliness …and His seed is struggling to take root in us then we can have hope for what is yet unseen …but if I have airs of righteousness over humility …then from such I can pretty much ascertain that I've bitten the bullet. …it's no small task for conventional churches to both plant seed and also nourish the devout or established. …actually, I think the "devout and established believers are suppose to "go out" and make new starts to further the Kingdom of God here on Earth. …if they don't …then who will? …again …perhaps the "fruits of the Spirit" are our reward to be shared and not our "calling" to disciple for Christ …perhaps His Spirit calls us to something further …something more demanding. …nowhere does the Bible call us to live as though Christ's return might be in twelve months time …or six months …or even tomorrow! ….it calls us to believe His coming may be today! …do we not deprive ourselves a measure of His presence and His peace and joy by thinking or conducting ourselves otherwise?

...a lady at work mentioned how stores do better with continual "background noise/music" ...and added that she also always has music playing in her home.

...I wonder if music couldn't become like a drug or placebo ...I only know that for me it's far more distracting than it is productive ...some people claim to not even hear it after awhile. ...I hope I never get so used to distractions that I neither hear nor see them anymore ...sounds dangerously close to "unaware".

...Christ died to defeat "unawareness" that we might enjoy His light and His truth. ....without truth we resign ourselves to live in fiction and there's nothing solid or reliable in fiction ...much of life outside of faith is the seeking of fun and meaning through fiction. ...even to settle for moderate faith will supply little more than baby's milk or thin porridge at best ...nothing of the "strong meat" or "life more abundant" that the Bible promises.

...I think I would that every greeting by a brother or sister in Christ be not "how are you?" ...but rather "how is your treasure?" ...if I am to "die to self" then the security and surety of "my treasure alone" will dictate "how am I" ...likewise, it occurs to me that the parting statement of "God be with you" might better be stated (exhorted) as "be with God".

...who am I to hope or wish or pray that God be anything! ...apart from what He is and has always been? ...it seems presumptuous to infer that anything from my mouth or my heart (which the Bible says is deceitful) has the slightest bearing on God's will.

...but what comes from my mouth or my heart can have a bearing on the will of my son or spouse or friend. ...do I suppose God might not be with another except I or others wish it so? ...I need to plant seed ....not that God be somewhere but rather that my son or spouse or friend be somewhere. ...better to pray (ask) not that God give another comfort ...but rather that another take comfort that God makes available to all through Christ Jesus. ...the onus is on us to prepare "receivable" hearts ...not on God to have a "givable" disposition.

(Matt. 18: 20) "where two or three are gathered together in my name. ....means "in my will." ...how many "fly by the seat of your pants cults" have claimed to be gathered in Christ's name? ...yet have ignored Christ's will? ...how many lukewarm churches have watered down (diluted, moderated) Christ's will to a "form of Godliness?" (2 Tim. 3: 5)

...a "form of Godliness" isn't that much different from "worldliness"

...we, in the west, live in an apparently wonderful world ...although not an overly benevolent world in time of crisis (self crisis) ...will faith and hope avail itself for selfish (personal) ends? ...the Bible says "no" ...in the greatest ever crisis to come ...many will say "Lord, Lord" ...yet be denied because their cry is of desperation.

(Matt. 7: 21) ...so why would it be different in an even lesser crisis?

(James 5: 16) ......if only the "fervent and effectual prayer of the righteous, availeth much"...what hope for the lip prayer of self desperation? ...were a Tsunami to hit us, would we not exhaust every "worldly" hope before eventually conceding to Godly appeal? ...great is our weakness. ...how many of us are driven to our knees only by crisis beyond worldly remedy? ..."self" is a great motivator but "self" holds no sway in God's Kingdom ...His word, says so. ...if the sting of death is removed from the faithful ...then what worry has those who remain for those departed?

(Luke 12: 51) ...the Bible says Christ will bring strife and derision even among those close to us ...pending our choices for or against Him. ...we see that statement at odds with Christ's bringing peace on earth and eternal life for us but the Bible says throughout that the price of disobedience, compromise and lukewarm ness...is division and strife ...we just don't want to hear it. ...rather than our treasure and cause being honor to God ...it becomes our own fight for peace among ourselves, whatever it takes and admonishment on the back burner while our emotional needs and support take prominence. ...away from the "strong meat" in God's word can we do other than grow weaker in faith? ...weaker in relationships? ....weaker in the hope of peace on earth? …our interpretive license, over the 20ᵗʰ century, has perhaps reduced God's "strong meat" to a confusing "thin broth". …rather than churches being united in the Body of Christ …they're rather competitive and weakened …struggling to save face and yet save souls also. …to a new believer …the "Body of Christ" must look like an octopus …multiple clingy arms reaching out to draw them into an indefinable mass of ever-changing rights and wrongs.

(that may sound a bit negative …but at least I didn't use the word "slimy")

…if we are to let our conscience be our guide in faith rather than obedience to God's word (as suggested in liberal Bible translations) then I am surprised there aren't hundreds more faith denominations! …we can just tell ourselves that what we want is right, overlook the small print in scripture and hang our hats on the church of "God wants us to have it all!" …that's the church that will draw people in! …the "new and improved church of self-belief." (Romans 14: 23)

…coming soon to your town! …"step right up!" …"poke the octopus …that inky blur just means everything is fine …hunky dory!" …"don't worry …be happy!"

(I'd better "watch-it.)

…my sister recently shared of her praying for the right man to enter her daughter's life …don't know why …but I was thinking this morning of the "Gone with the Wind" sisters …whether in dating or in marriage …there's probably not a "right person"

…if we're outside a disciplined walk with God then all is pretty much a crap shoot (roll of the dice) but if our hearts are "of God" then there is, for sure, another heart "of God" if it is His will for us. …I'm convinced that if our hearts are of God then there are probably dozens of potential likeminded mates …but patience and vigilance are also of God. …as much as possible, in good faith …we might do well to separate from unreliability …be it in relationships, vehicles and situations …at least until such time as our faith is sufficient to withstand the fractures and fears of a house built on sand. …my niece, as I understand it, is not attending church, so probably isn't likely to encounter too many Christian fellas (Luke 12: 34) …wherever her heart is, is where her treasure is also. ...where we invest interest is where we can expect a return and to be comforted ...we ought first to be a comforter.

...if we seek quick remedies for our loneliness, we'll likely attract others seeking quick remedies. ...patience is hard to master. ...although the Bible says Christ "came not to bring peace but rather strife and division" ...that's because of our own selfishness ...however ...for those who choose to follow Him ...He gives His Spirit to comfort us in times alone and times of trial. ...many aren't too comfortable when alone. ...they maybe don't like their thoughts or feelings.

...if they don't like their own thoughts and feelings then I wonder why they suppose another would like them? ...maybe they're just looking for background noise or background people to distract them from their own lives (existences) ...sounds grim if they latch onto another. ...through Christ's Spirit, we can't ever be alone nor have ugly thoughts or intentions that we shouldn't share with others. ...nor are we called as Christians to wear an ear to ear grin as though we've discovered the fountain of youth and fun. ...what we are to have found is Christ's burden to take onto ourselves.

...in return we don't receive His fun ...but rather His comfort and His presence to lighten the gravity of His calling. ...actually, it seems that, according to scripture ..."fun" isn't even an issue! ...not one way ...nor the other ....so why introduce it!

...is Spiritual gratification fun? ....is it a kind of fringe benefit? ...or is it a form of "bait" that we perceive the lost as being in want of??

...I don't think bait is required if Christ has drawn one to Himself as the Bible says must happen. ...we know fun and pleasure are, for sure, tools of satan ...are they also tools of faith? (if I were you ...I'd be asking me ..."what do you propose, that's better?") ...harsh as it may sound ...is it not better that we stew in our discontent until we are broken to the point that we can honestly admit to ourselves that the world is insufficient for our needs?...the downhill skier won't advance his or her skill by continually, narrowly escaping disaster but never determining the reason for their folly ...they can thus only remain mediocre ...and will regretfully content themselves with unnecessary limitations.

…a lukewarm, fun skier but no passion for the steeper slope that may well be within their grasp. …if we want a "fun church" …just chill (hang out) with people who are "sort-of-Christian! …non-demanding, not zealous, not given to desiring His pure light but are rather more into "fun". …to be rebuked and chastened is a blessing. (Rev. 3: 19) …"be zealous therefore and repent (be contrite, or self reproachful)." …if we're "of Him" we need not wonder where His joy or His comfort or His peace of mind is. (although we may wonder why we've wasted so much time applying for it.) (Luke 11: 9) …"ask, seek, knock" …not casually or in self desperation or with our lips.

…but rather with a sincere and contrite and humble heart . …like a servant's heart.

…I don't know what the predominant faith is in Sri Lanka or Asia, recently devastated by Tsunami …nor that of Sodom or of Noah's time …nor of any locale that experiences catastrophic tragedy (including the 911 devastation). …throughout history thousands have cried out "where was God!?!

…"why wasn't He watching !?!" …who knows God's ways? …or His "whys"?

…I believe every trial ..large and small …either pushes us closer to Him

…or else comes between us and Him. …in the Bible …Job would be a good one to ask …we can't ask Job yet we can learn from him. …we can learn from everyone but when it comes to injustice, Job is a good example. (James 5:16) …the Bible says "the fervent, effectual prayer of the righteous, availeth much" …Job was such a man …yet look at what load was placed on his faith. …Job's steadfastness and patience brought glory to God …and defeat, to satan. …how much of our activity today brings just the opposite?

…we all stray and will continue to stray further unless we honestly identify "the reason for our straying." …we may "claim" that we don't want to stray but the fact that we do belies our claim. …"faith" is never the culprit …"self" is always the culprit.

…it's sometimes helpful to define …not how the "world supplies for us …but rather "what faith" doesn't supply "for us.

…maybe for us "faith" isn't fun …isn't pleasant or appropriate or conducive …..the discipline may be intolerable or even unbearable!

….the Bible warns us to prepare for every enticement that will weaken our individual faith and thus separate us from God and His provision.

…many "Christians" hold to the theory of "once saved – always saved" but belief is empty without "experience". …and experience is empty except we continue to "self-examine" and continue to grow apart from the "worldly".

….it seems from scripture that there's no "middle of the road" or "moderation" available to those who are for Christ. …we can busy ourselves with kindly and charitable efforts …yet if they're not to "God's" glory …then "whose?" (Phil. 2:3) …"Let nothing be done through strife (contention) for vainglory but in lowliness of mind …..."

…how often does God get "second billing" in our efforts on this behalf?

…that our churches are rife with personal agendas and personal recognition is poor testament to our faith. I don't know what the attraction is in our petty peeves but it's substantial …given how often we like to "pet them …and have others "pet" them also.

….of three churches I attend, two have had peculiar leadership change and the third is seemingly close to matinee. …God hasn't changed …His word (at least, His truth) hasn't changed …I guess that leaves "us". ….so, even supposing that maybe we've changed over the past 2000 years …how would that reasonably be reflected in our faith??? …is less expected of us by Christ that we may yet maintain our salvation and eternal life? …is God more merciful because of our 20-21st century hectic pace of life" …has He finally come around to appreciating our needs to be entertained? (watch-it!)

…our lives can quietly become much like a large ball rolling down a gentle slope.

…we don't like stones or impediments to our natural inclinations. …what we want, is smooth sailing. …yet it's the frequent interfering obstacles that toughen us and help develop character. …it's humble character that will see us both in need of God and in praise of God for His goodness, in seeing us through every hurdle in life and in death.

…to trust God is to unburden ourselves of the need to understand everything and control everything.

…He may not supply for our wants but He'll supply for our needs …and through us, He can supply for the needs of others also ….even foremost the needs of others, as His cares become our cares (long-term cares or eternal cares). …when our "wants" diminish …(thanks to His presence) …our needs also diminish …both are a portion of our bondage to this world, in that our wants often determine what we perceive our needs to be …both material and emotional.

…faith in Christ provides not for the fulfilling of our wants but rather for the relieving of our worldly needs …which, long term, is by far preferable. ….not we …but rather He is able to suffice for us ….and through that we may see clear to help another.

…normal people are rarely Christian. ….normal people's priorities are tied to "self" interests which are self perpetuated.

…whereas the Christian's (sincere Christian) weird interest is towards what they can "do without" so that another can have at least a little.

…whether Christian or not, my interest is always piqued in meeting someone who appears to have broken out of the mold of "normal". …I guess my "expectations" get short-circuited. …I appreciate that everyone is different …but some people are really different! …and I wonder at the road they've traveled to develop the way they have. (they're not like me ….so, are they getting proper help? …will they soon?)

(1 Cor. 13: 12) …expectations = "seeing through a glass darkly"

…a funny and humbling thing happened on the paper route just recently.

…every Christmas some (most) folks give cards or tips …so it's an added treat in those dark early mornings to see white envelopes taped to newspaper receptacles.

(I'm not perfect but I make a real effort to offer good service)

…at this one house I found a white envelope securely taped which appeared to have nothing to do with me. …without my glasses, in the dim light ….it read "Dear Bella

Brecken, please knock" …after about a week I wondered why they didn't just phone this Bella person and tell her to "knock"!?! …this is the 21ˢᵗ century….right?   …then we had one of those rare snowfalls in Victoria. …the additional reflected light off the snow enabled me to properly read "Door Bell Broken, please knock" …quite a reach from my "expected card or tip. …expectations can be a source of bondage …as well as a source of security …depending on the glass we're looking through.

…wisdom doesn't seem to come to us naturally …it's something we have to seek out amidst everything else we're "seeking" …she doesn't come to us when we're on the "treadmill" of life but rather when we're at "rest" …rest requires time …time requires effort to make time …making time requires separation from the treadmill.

…inside all of the games that we play in the courses of our lives, there's a unique and individual me and you …striving to be realized …void of all the appearances and hypocrisy of "when do I fit in?" …you …"with God" are a part of His design and purpose. ….you or me …without God are a part of a problem. …I would say, it's a big

mistake to be a problem for God.

…you might escape being a problem for your spouse or your boss …but no-one escapes being a problem for God.   …many appear to escape …even from the beginning

…Cain probably appeared to do better than Abel …but Cain is now (or soon will be) wailing and gnashing his teeth …whereas Abel will be "home free"! …it's a short life we're given and the portion of His gift, that we hoard to ourselves, is in the books.

…video cameras are a great invention but we're glad there are no x-ray video cameras …except there is just one equivalent. …there's nothing we do …or think, that isn't recorded. …to "expect" that can be scary for any who "choose" to continue "seeing through a glass darkly"   …can be scary even for Christians who choose not to continue growing stronger in faith or no longer continue to "work out their own salvation", in truth and light.   (Phil. 2: 12) …all is recorded by He who made us and all that is recorded can be edited by Him also if requested by a humble and surrendered heart. …God sees our hearts …whether they be for Him or not. (1 Chr. 28: 9) "…for the Lord searcheth all hearts and understandeth all the imaginations of the thoughts:

…if thou seek Him, He will be found of thee; but if thou forsake Him, He will cast thee off forever." …it appears that if we continue to seek Him …to seek even more of Him …only then will we find the relief of our sins being on the editing room floor. …whereas vacationing from seeking more of Him appears to be a sin of itself! …if we're "of God" then our conduct (fruit) will evidence just that.

…I hope I never stall or get distracted to the point where God's eyes turn to the cutting room floor. …I would that others pray for my chastening against such.

…to me, there arises the question of pride when I hear a professed Christian speak of their "assurance: of salvation. …seems pretty sketchy to be rubbing our hands at the desert tray when we have a full meal yet to eat back at the table. ..chickens are chickens …eggs aren't chickens, they're only "potential" chickens …the farmer may have the benefit of past seasons to assess percentages of failure. …we just have the "one" ..go around." …can there ever be assurance? …apart from potential delusion?

…I don't see in the Bible where it says that a "clear conscience" cuts it. …nor where it says "to not feel guilty is sufficient unto salvation." (1 Thes. 5: 21)

…if we're not "holding fast to that good which remains" and also facing the foe who is constantly eroding it …then our eternity is for sure (assuredly) not sure thing.

…that thing about our "working out our own salvation" in Phil. 2: 12 …carries a caveat …that it's not be done in our rest or leisure but rather "with fear and trembling" …that's a sobering reminder that Christ's cause and the Christian's cause is not a "spare time" endeavor but rather a life focus. (2 Cor. 10: 5) …"and bringing into captivity every thought to the obedience of Christ" …can the honest Christian ascribe to the pursuing of anything less? ….without ascribing to lukewarm ness of faith? …I don't think "lulls in growth" are anything of God's doing …but I expect the reasons for stagnant growth are and will be accountable to Him.

...and the most honest and most probable reason is lack of desire or placing alternate treasures ahead of God. ...both of which He has warned us against. ...even if it's a very valuable treasure such as our marriage or family or work

...the Bible says we're to entrust even our valued treasures to His keeping.

(Isa. 26: 3) "Thou wilt keep him in perfect peace whose mind is stayed on Thee.

...to depart from trust in God to oversee anything or any relationship ...is to depart from faith. (Rom. 14: 23) ...and we know that to depart from faith is sin.

...do we suppose it's of any lesser sin simply because we've perhaps been baptized or because we're solid church members?

...we need only consider how many noted Christians or pastors have fallen from grace through their momentary lack of vigilance ...to remind us of our frailty and

the importance of that phrase "stayed on Thee." ...vigilance, strong thought, discernment and self-sacrifice aren't boring ...they're necessary requirements to salvation!.....if our salvation is of importance to us.

(Psa. 1: 2) ...the Bible says "Blessed is the man who meditates on God's law (word) day and night" ...are we up for that or are we up for a little pretense of that? ...through "pretense" we soon become our own worst enemy to our salvation or even just to those we associate with ...especially children.

(Isa. 6: 5) ...if a Godly man as Isaiah can state "woe is me!" at his potential unworthiness ...then what of us!?! ...I suppose I might be thankful that the churches I attend appear to be lukewarm else despite my self gall (boldness) I (and perhaps others) would be unable to attend. ...we've come a long way over the past 2000 years ...but have we come the wrong way? ..."we" cite the "Spirit of God" as being in our church service ...but have we not also made "His Spirit" into our own image? ...vs. the way round? ..."what a friend we have in Jesus" ...doesn't mean "He's just like us" ...it means "He's just like God." ...so maybe we are better to forget all the "touchy feely" thing of our worldly relationships ...and acknowledge "deity" ...and confine our touchy-feely inclinations" ...to His guidelines."

(Rom. 12: 2) …we are not be conformed to this world (nor confine God to this world)….we are to be transformed in rebirth. (become anew) that we might experience knowledge of that which is God's will and soberly apply ourselves to His wishes according to what aptitudes He has given us.

…God made us in His image …Christ exemplified what the Christian conduct ought be about doing. …the Holy Spirit, when sincerely invited, enables us to resist worldly temptation and our natural selfish will and leads us rather to be a part of Christ's cause to reunite us with God and thus be complete and fulfilled. …and though it sounds like "all for them and nothing for us" …the effectual truth is just the opposite …as those of us with children can more easily grasp.

…children are denied most of their "daily wants" by loving parents who know the dangers that lie ahead for their child …this call to obedience lasts for what amounts to a "lifetime" (given the child's source of reference) when in reality it's only maybe ¼ of their lives …after which they themselves assume the direct responsibility for their conduct …while the loving parent wills them to continue growing in knowledge and wisdom. ..lasting (eternal) reward comes from continuing in these. …emptiness, despair, even death ..come from turning away.

…"faith" may not be what is wanted …but far better to reform our wants in hope of something better than to reform faith and lose even that which we now have.

…I've never heard of a sincere Christian, on their death bed, saying "I wish I'd done it my own way as opposed to God's way. …for the Christian, even problems and trials are opportunities for growth in faith and death holds no sting. (1 Cor. 15: 55)

…that's a pretty amazing comfort! …and it's not just a comfort for when we're ninety-nine years old …it's a comfort even if our last breath is taken today? …and what great thing have we done for God to deserve such a comfort? …never mind did we sing in the choir …or play a tune or make a joyful noise before the people as unto the Lord …or did we create some new and fun programs or activities to draw the lost to church.

…what I do when I'm alone with God is what I can trust of my faith. …if the heart is deceitful and the Bible says it is (Jer. 17: 9) then our "public worship" is ever suspect as to motive. …whatever the appearance of our church affiliation, it probably bears little resemblance to our actual, personal, relationship with Christ through obedience to His calling …it's a little too convenient to claim (perhaps in apparent humility) that we are inadequate to be of any substantial service to His cause or His will.

…if we're inadequate …it's because we've rendered ourselves inadequate. …closed our ears to His word …closed our hearts to His Love (both incoming and outgoing) …stagnant. …baptized …saved …whatever …"stagnant" will result in our "demise".

…we hear rumblings at how the church is failing to stimulate spiritual growth …and so people are leaving. …the church's responsibility is to present God's will to those who will come to listen and for the pastor to be God's voice in explaining His truth. …maybe it's "fun" …maybe it's not. …conviction and chastening ..(that we might grow Spiritually) …doesn't sound like fun to me. Heb. 12: 6 .."whom the Lord loveth He chasteneth" …if we want "fun" we should maybe go to Disneyland …or Canada's Wonderland! …I went there …and it was fun but there was nothing of "Spiritual growth" there! …at the time I went, Spiritual growth" wasn't my treasure. …my young wide-eyed child was my treasure …he still is! ….but now that we've both grown it's time to put away childish things. ….right?

…the church's responsibility (pastors' responsibility) is to share what God has revealed to the church (pastor).

…my responsibility is to share, with all I meet, what God has shared with this desperate heart. …more of Him and less of me."

…no loving parent wants less than what's best for their child. …when my son Richard was a little guy …I recall my dad asked him who his heroes were. (whether it was intentional or not, I overheard the question)

…I think Richard rhymed off several "men" …like Batman, Spiderman and whoever the guy is who invented Lego. …I knew, at that moment, that Richard's heroes were my responsibility …and Jesus wasn't named. …"Jesus" was the name my dad was looking for and I had failed both my son and my dad. …worse yet …I failed a man who suffered greatly and dies a death more grievous than the worst cancer can deliver …so that Richard, my dad and myself might have life and have everlasting life void of pain and regret and grief and sorrow. …only through vigilance can Christ, through His Spirit in us direct our ways so that we can evade regret. (what if?) …we usually minimize our regrets by crossing the line of "not caring" …that's certainly an easier route but the repeated and compounded cost to us becomes horrendous. …to "not care" is to produce another nail for our own coffin (brings us closer to death) …whereas "in Christ" there are no nails ….nor even a coffin for those who choose Him. …with Christ there cannot be other than Spiritual growth and thus life more abundant unto eternity.

…without Christ there cannot be other than what's in our pocket and wishing for more of it. …petty treasure, familiarity and mundane …over and over. …and yet many choose it. …is "life" our focus? …or our rut? ….who or what controls us?

…fate or our given lot in life will remain just that unless we opt for greater things and risk the incurring change.

…for whatever reasons, it seems lots of people opt for a little taste of faith

…maybe in a time of crisis but grow impatient for a tangible reward and turn their back on God to re-embrace the world's treasures and comforts.

…maybe, had their crisis been of long duration it would be their better fortune.

…it would, perhaps, introduce them to peace in the valley of despair.

…I think "the world takes "more than it ever gives …and that "Christ gives" more than He ever takes. …financially, the Bible says that 10% is God's due …so for the "Christian" anything less is sort of robbery. (I don't think 10% over basic needs would satisfactorily suffice in "worldly" reward either. …there's never enough, it seems, and the recognition and moral support we require is a long term burden for those on whom we depend for self worth.) …satisfaction or contentment can never be realized through worldly treasures …yet Christ makes these available to all those who seek after Him.

(John 14: 27") "…my peace I give unto you, not as the world giveth, give I unto you. Let not your heart be troubled, neither let it be afraid."

…to be untroubled and without fear is to be free of want …and only freedom from want will free us of the requirement for great chunks of money needed to buy the placebos for "life" more abundant in Christ" …in Christ, inner joy and a restful mind are there for the taking like plentiful fruit from a tree. …in the world (void of faith) continual discontent is our portion and ever increasing demand of our time is crucial to maintaining our status (self worth) …not only is there no peace in the valley's …there's no peace even on the mountain tops as we vie to hold our own and repel those needy losers who have not likewise fought and suffered as we have.

(Luke 6: 22) "Blessed are ye, when men shall hate you and when they shall separate you from their company and shall reproach you and cast out your name as evil for supporting the cause of Christ." …the world honors and respects worldly success and personal characteristics which are the antithesis of Christ's. …apart form "food and music" the word "soul" is largely foreign to those climbing the social ladder. …if all we ever expect to have is to be crammed into an approximate four score and then years then the taking advantage of every person and every opportunity, regardless of long term repercussions, can well become our reasonable mantra. (…lucky us …from our high positions we can don our colored glasses and barely discern the havoc we've left, in our wake, for those follow after us.) …"the Lord helps those who help themselves" may sound like wisdom but it's actually the opposite of Bible wisdom or Christ's will! …the Bible does say "Bear ye one another's burdens and so fulfill the law of Christ." (Gal. 6: 2)

(…no mention of social status) …comparing ourselves with others is always a bad placed to go, plus it asserts our own weakness in that we allow others to control our lives whom we're trying to keep up with. (…those dumb "Joneses" have been in far too much control for far too long!…maybe it's not the Joneses but rather maybe the in-laws or the mates at work …maybe siblings or even our parents are still pushing our buttons in ways that discourage us to break free from "world" domination.

…fear of rejection is a large negative motivation. …it binds us every bit as much as do physical shackles or chains. …it holds us back from even the hope of finding "life" more abundant" in faith. …what "hope" can there really be for a people who (perhaps through our affluence) increasingly consider tolerance and acceptance of defying God's word to be positive growth?

…secularism has, throughout history, shown itself to breed contempt for good. …yet we embrace it in the name of freedom. …secular gains seem always to come at great (even horrendous) cost to a segment of the weak who, in turn, unite and rebel (non-racial apartheid with splintered focus and directions)

(I'm less concerned for "a segment of the lazy" …even the Bible says if you don't work you don't get to eat either! …but the Bible nowhere promotes our gluttony while others, who are making a sincere effort, go hungry.)…our ambivalence to the plight of others and our tolerance and acceptance of secular values (void of scripture) will, in short time, destroy "the good that remains."   (1Thes. 5: 21) …despondency is closer than ever …I suppose that next comes desperation. …desperation begets despos. …they are the extreme of not looking out for your fellow man! …there's probably a seed (measure) of despo in all who decline faith in Christ (and perhaps even in some who profess to be Christian!)   …it's been said, that in mankind, the cream rises to the top …it can probably also be said that money and power also can quickly "descend" to the top through self focus. …i.e. Adolph Hitler, Idi Amine, Sad am Hussein etc. …self interest …supported by self interest. (…almost sounds like democracy!) …to me that's a sobering thought. …I sometimes wish Christ would put a tattoo or something on the forehead of those who have surrendered sufficiently to Him

…to signify any given person as having Christ's Spirit in them and leading them.

…it actually boggles the mind that we even have cause to doubt or wonder if another's focus is of such deity. …whether Baptist or Catholic or Mormon or Mennonite or any other …if we have not "His Spirit" then we are none of His. (Rom. 8: 9)

...I believe even the "most devout" followers of Christ started (starts) out lukewarm ...(or on baby's milk) ....but at some point and usually a point of great need we much each make a decision either for trust in Him alone.

...else "ride out" "what the world offers." ...in both good times and bad ...we support our treasure and our treasure supports us ...but it's usually in times of sadness or anxiety that our treasures are most clearly defined. ...I suppose we can always harden or steel ourselves against potential negative influences ...but that's like voluntary death as well ...(i.e. machismo) ...to "build walls" against a potential enemy is vastly different from "arming ourselves" to effectively resist potential enemies. ...walls become prisons whereas armor (wisdom) becomes freedom to live more abundantly. ...Christ supplies for us such armor as we will ever need, through His Spirit being in us to direct our ways. ...in my own life experiences, whether good or bad in my own eyes ...Christ continues faithfully, through the Bible, to say to me "have I not told you it would be so?"

...God never promised blue skies 24 hrs / 365 ¼ days ...but He's promised more surely than "in the bank" ...that if we look to Him we need not be unduly concerned about the color of the skies (blue isn't even my favorite color!) ...nor unduly concerned about what happens under the skies ....provided I seek to know His will and make efforts to uplift what I know to be of Him. ...apart from faith in Christ, I don't know of any other "place" where we can both have our cake and eat it too. ...how could one discover perpetual energy ...yet not want to share it with the world!?! ...actually ..."perpetual "is small potatoes! ...we're talking "eternal" here! (2 Cor. 5: 17) ...nothing "of us" everything "of Him!" dead to self ..new life in Christ. ..."new life" in faith includes new receptors (ears, eyes, general awareness) that are attentive to His leading.

...it's often hard to part with the old, especially as it's been our source of reference and source of refuge (hiding) for so long.

...to commit to trusting in Christ is like turning around and finding our tent gone! ...our eyes may widen and our mouths for sure will say "what do I do now!?!" (I think this is where we're suppose to remember that we've struck out on a new adventure …for which our "old tent" has become burdensome and awkward. …in faith either we don't need a tent or if we do, Christ will supply the materials to make one. …essentially, as Christians ….we're not to look to the world to supply for our needs those things Christ has assured us He will provide for else we cut ourselves off from our capacity to receive from Him.

(…if we're lukewarm in faith then we'll maybe just get " like" a newspaper tent, which is probably what we deserve.) …in our greatest trials is where He is able to shine greatly. (that's a pretty good line …somebody should write that down!)

…Christopher Reeves (aka superman) who died this past year as a result from a tragic fall …yet through adversity became a most effective spokesperson for spinal cord injury.

…there is darkness for which all the money in the world is unable to put aright.

…the Bible says that, through Christ, we are to give praise to God even through darkest hours and afflictions and suffering. ….whether in glowing health or in terminal illness, we can advance the best of causes and gain (respect of) the whole world …yet lose our souls if it's not to God's glory. (and I wonder if I am sufficiently dependant on Christ to write these thoughts were I on a hospital bed, in pain, having been informed that I have but days to live. …I expect not. …that's my failure.) …to me the Bible can be very abrasive …yet I find, surrender to the more abrasive parts reveals God's truths.

(2 Cor. 10: 5) "every thought into captivity …" (Rom. 14: 23) …either of faith, or of sin.

…I turn around and see that my tent is collapsed …but not gone.

…why is that??? …is my commitment (semi-sacrifice) unworthy of trade?

…surely I'm not to be asked to surrender even my love of "golden oldies" music!

…Everly Brothers? ….Ricky Nelson? …Gene Pitney? …surely not the Righteous Brothers!?! …what of The Temptations? …maybe the temptation, is why I am asked of God, to hand it all over to Him. …as soon as I start to pick and choose for myself what is and what is not acceptable or pleasing to God …then also do I infuse my own translation of God's word?

(1 Cor. 10: 5) …."every thought into captivity " becomes "most thoughts …."

(Rom. 14: 23) …"whatsoever is not of faith is sin" …becomes "a reasonable amount of non-faith stuff is possibly not the best." (I think the respectable definition here is "artistic license") …we see, we hear, we taste …what we want to ….then we justify it. …the only way for the Christian to do that is to alter (dim) God's light (word) ….anti Christ isn't too strong a word for knowingly aligning our desires to so please a cause other than Christ's …the non Christian has no such qualms but neither do they "claim" to be of Christ's flock and so are at least free of the burden (guilt) of deceit.

…the Christian doesn't gain reprieve or the right to carelessness through the strength of Christ's Spirit being in them …we are to gain wisdom and vigilance (discernment) against temptation through Him …not ourselves. …our conscience isn't to be our guide else those without conscience will rule the world …the Bible is to be our guide. …Christ's Spirit isn't (cannot be) in those who choose to walk outside the light of His word….the Bible says so and the Bible will verify our daily conduct as being pleasing to God and we ought be able to cite where the Bible says so …whereby we can walk boldly in faith.

(Psa. 119: 105) …His word is a lamp unto our feet and a light unto our paths. …myself, I have no problem with those who, for whatever reason, don't get it. …but I have a big problem with those who profess to get it (claim to be Christian) yet remain a blight (insult) against the sacrifice of Christ. …they (we) claim to be a part of Christ's body (His church) while our joy (enjoyment) remains "of the worldly"

…I think the Bible says that "from such, we are to have no dealings." …it seems a simple matter of "honesty" and if we fear being honest then our fate is indeed cast to the wind and our only "assurance" is of where we won't be spending our eternity should our lives end today!

…being as my "old tent" is merely collapsed and not entirely gone …then I'm probably quasi-Christian and I pray I never become a plastic Christian (phony)

…a plastic Christian not only doesn't encourage others to faith …they rather discourage others from faith and that's the works of satan.

(Rom. 14: 23)   "Therefore whatsoever is not of faith, is sin" …sobering light!

…I would say, my son Richard and I are pretty solid as friends …yet he no longer lives with me and I miss that constant contact with his world. …I'm sometimes tempted to compromise even my moderate "faith vigilance" to more closely connect with him and his world …but any professed Christian husband or father who compromises or strays from his #1 treasure (Christ) …offers little security of his not compromising or straying from any other professed treasure which is by far the greater harm.

…Richard (18 years old) knows that not too much of his present pursuits or treasures are overly pleasing to me …so I don't suppose he's overly motivated to share them with me.   (…pretty much the same as myself at 18 with my dad)   …compromise is no remedy …he knows where I stand, so knows where he can count on me and for what …but he knows where I'm at as regards anything illegal and anything sketchy or even subjective. …18 is a tough age in which to find rest which accommodates peers, parents and self

…at age 18, I didn't know what to think …so I escaped thinking too much, as best I could, to hurt the least people. …18 is an age of searching but not finding

…I recall snippets of good in my parents' faith …and snippets of good apart from it. …contentment in a girlfriend and frustration in a girlfriend.

…I know Richard sees me as "weird" or "square" …but my primary concern is how he sees me when he's twice 18 years old. …if he picks up even a portion of my dad's faith through me then he'll be left with something to steer him aright.

…I don't fault teens who blame their dilemmas on their folks …if the parents have relaxed vigilance in God's truths then kids are left with the ever-changing trends or ways of the world. …we may as well, with foreknowledge, secure them tickets on the Titanic. …the Bible as much as says so! …except you discount the Bible entirely. I personally believe that if one discounts a portion of the Bible then the balance of it is lost to them also. ...no one can control compromise. ...I'm not certain what satan did to get tossed from God's presence. ...I seem to recall being informed that it involved his wanting equality with God. ...the God of our lives is the treasure of our lives. ...if there's no force to which we are subservient then it's we "ourselves" who are our treasure (God) ...and "ourselves" who we desire to please.

..."Please please me" was a Beatle's song but it's also the quiet mantra of self focus. ...we begin to seek experiences and friendships in which there is personal gain. ..."what am I" becoming?" quickly gives way to "how do I look (to others)?"

...the Bible says we are to be concerned for those who find misfortune

...but "self-concern", even in the socially upright, finds legal ways to profit or gain power through the misfortune of others. ...it probably takes a very narrow and introspective viewpoint to resist personal gain, albeit, through weakness in others.

...in the extreme ...the pornography business thrives on the weaknesses in people. ...likewise ...tobacco, alcohol, chocolate, junk food, soda pop ...even theatres, sports arenas, restaurants and I suppose tourist destinations ...television, music studios

...all are legal but are they edifying? ...the Christian needs to ask which are of faith and which are not. ...if our conscience is our guide ...then faith is no factor as even people of no faith have consciences. ...but for the Christian ...if not the Holy Spirit ...then at least "the Bible" is to be our guide until such time as we are convicted to surrender our conscience along with our self-concern ..."of faith" ...or "of sin" is the question (and hopefully, the dilemma) for the seeking Christian. ...Christ (the shepherd) gives us the freedom to enjoy His gifts beyond the paddock but the outskirts of sin are never far from us ...inducing us to wander further from God's words and light.

...I expect they've probably stopped counting the innumerable cults that abound in North America. ...those who perhaps wandered too far in God's freedom.

...in their beginnings, these cults were probably tolerated or even accepted by the general church body ...but by and by ...every church body must decide between faith and sin." …it might be a good time to ask, just how accepting or how tolerant is the church you attend? ….is it holding fast?

…I grew up with an old line from an old hymn "will our anchor hold in the storms of life …are you lost in the blood of the Lamb?" …and just now another old hymn comes to mind "I surrender all" …different music, different lines, same anthem.

…the Everly Brothers are good but they're not good like that! …maybe I can part with them after all.

…I think it was Fats Domino who sang "ain't that a shame". …but there's no shame in exchanging something good for something better. …what's not of faith …is keeping me from what is of faith. ….right? …so does that not also mean …that only my faith is keeping me from sin?

…and further that should I maintain little …or presumptive faith …then I would have little or no Spiritual help in resisting temptation to sin???

…obvious wrongs (murder, blatant theft, physical abuse etc.) can, for most, be reasoned on a legal and social basis. …yet it's lawful to: think evil; provided we don't break the law. …what a positive social encouragement it would be to hear of prisons or court houses closing because of lack of need. …in our own strength and morals we're obviously losing ground yet the world fights tooth and nail against any curtailment of freedoms to think and say what-ever we want. …only through Christ can we put to rest the source of all wrongdoing …that being: the initial "thinking" of wrong.

(Ex. 20: 5) …in the Bible, God speaks of "visiting the iniquities of the fathers upon the children unto the third and fourth generation……" …to us …that probably seems unfair …..so we discount God's word. …yet history bears out that each new generation suffers at the liberal hand of previous generations.

…a few separated pockets of people hold God's word in sufficient esteem to escape the onslaught of the world's temptations. …the Amish or Mennonites, perhaps, best hold fast to the old ways…the rest of western world maybe considers them "quaint" …but they, at least, seem to be able to resist playing with the fire that we seem to embrace. (2 Cor. 6: 17) ...the Bible says "wherefore come out form among them and be ye separate, touch not the unclean thing ..." ...it would appear ...for good reason. ...a fearful people, without faith, tax the doctor's time at the first sign of a sneeze. ...their brief time on earth is all they have and so they vigorously hedge against any shortage. ...whereas the sincere believer doesn't have that desperation nor fear a shortened life on earth. ...their treasure and prize is elsewhere ...just as the Bible says it is to be. ...there's a line in a song that says "fools rush in ...where wise men fear to go." ...isn't that the truth

...and doesn't the Bible say (Matt. 7: 14) "...narrow is the way which leadeth unto life and few there be that find it."

...in the movie "Witness" is portrayed the callousness of the world contrasted with a community of faith. ...even in today's world, faith is tolerated by the majority only if it doesn't interfere with worldly desires but rather keeps to itself. ...but few of those of "professed" faith wish to separate from the attractions and interests of the world. ...we prefer to blend in ...perhaps on the pretext of "to better share our faith" or several other suspect claims. ...to what extent do we actually share Christ?

...in reality, it appears the transfer is working the opposite to "our sharing" as we absorb more and more of the world into faith and into our family life ...which, no doubt, will impact negatively on 3 or 4 generations if not more. ...it's no easy thing to keep not only "sin" out of our homes but to also keep the little "seeds" of sin out also.

...it's been said "a little knowledge is a dangerous thing" ...and a "little" knowledge of God's word and God's will is, for sure, insufficient ballast to counter the surge of distractions that have nothing to do with faith. ...pastors no longer preach "hell fire and damnation" which is the "sure fire" way to a small congregation. ...the world has offered and the pastors have accepted the softer gloves of tolerance and acceptance.

(Phil. 2: 12) ...the "fear and trembling" of "working out our salvation" ...has become a "hand shake and a wink". ...aren't churches suppose to grow through God's workings in the hearts of people? ...pretty soon we'll be stumped if someone should ask where they can go to hear God's truth. …what's our part if we send them to a "lukewarm" church that serves "weak tea" as opposed to "strong meat"?

…how can we wonder why family after family falls apart and yet continue to water down or completely ignore God's rigid instruction to those who profess to seek Him?

…we frequently pray for God's "giving" …yet why do we pray for something that the Bible tells us is a "constant" either with or without prayer? …why don't we rather pray in thankfulness for what His Spirit has enabled us to rid ourselves of as regards worldly pursuits and attractions that impede our possessing all that He offers in Spiritual joy and peace of mind?

…what if our family member or friend is undergoing a trial or illness as a means of deliverance or just a test of faith? …is it our place to pray for the voiding of what God has appointed? (Isa. 55: 5) …the Bible says "God's ways are not our ways"

…so why do we resist that truth? …why implore God to satisfy our understanding of what He has ordained or allowed? …have we forgotten our place? …are we "big shots" now …because we attend church or tithe or do a few charitable acts? …what's not done in need of Him …or to His glory …perhaps (most likely) is of no consequence to Him but of great consequence to ourselves, especially, as it pertains to our eternity.

…we wanted control …God gave us control.

…we are each squarely in the wheelhouse of our own ships. …our only hope for calm seas are within the parameters of His seas. …if we choose to steer into the world's seas and the world's ways …then what has that to do with God? …God never said that we can't remove ourselves from His instruction. …He said we can't remove ourselves from His love or His caring about us.

(Rom. 8: 39) …just as my son cannot remove himself from my love and caring.

…yet he can go his own way and ignore me. …I can't force faith on him if he has no desire for faith. …only the honest depth of my faith and it's resulting fruit will encourage him to faith. …my prayer is that he see through any pretense or façade and be highly discerning. …he's pretty good at that already.

...I had a "tea hour" at Tim Horton's with a pastor friend today and he was emphasizing the parable of non-producing portions of the "vine" being pruned away ...and how it's not enough to consider ourselves "once saved-always saved" ...unless we continue our growth in Christ and continue being useful to His will (bear fruit for His cause).

...the children's Bible may say "once saved always saved" ...but the Bibles for those older than maybe ten years ...also state "the requirements of "always" ...there's always and "if" to keep us from getting pious. ...to be Christian and die to self isn't like high school where you get your diploma then do what you want. ...to be Christian is to so live and grow in faith and trust in Christ that you are never without the hope of His approval ...in the "world" we look for assurance.

...the need to claim assurance of salvation refutes both humility and also refutes His will that we continue to the end to seek more and more of Him.

...the only "assurance" we have is that we will be called to answer for our service to His cause clear through to our end. ...for us to claim "once saved always saved" is a bit of our putting the cart before the horse.   (Rom. 11: 33) ...the Bible says "...how unsearchable are His judgments and His ways past finding out!"

...we need be very careful of leaping to decisions that are not ours to make. ...who are we to pronounce ourselves or others as saved or unsaved? ...are we so foolish as to suggest we have been given the mind of God?

(Isa. 55: 8) ...the Bible says "For my thoughts are not your thoughts neither are your ways my ways, saith the Lord."

...are there some who would boast that what God says doesn't apply to them?

...I know of a couple of prominent "cult" leaders (now dead) who boasted of their having such status with God ...but I strongly doubt their salvation.

(..purveyors of misery, for probably thousands, directly and indirectly.)

...my Bible concordance doesn't show the word "gross" ...probably the closest is "abomination". (Prov. 11: 20) ...the Bible says "they that are of a forward heart (self willful) are abomination to the Lord ….” …what desperation must fall at a pastors doorstep to induce him to pronounce what only God can pronounce?

…to save souls is God's domain not the pastor's nor priest's (whatever title we accept) …man can only prepare the ground (work). …the Bible can rightly claim that “many souls were saved” …but the disciples of Christ can't “claim” a single one.

…Jesus saves …sometimes with the help of His flock …but it's He who saves. …we need be careful not to confuse “signed-up” …with “saved by Christ”.

(2 Cor. 11: 14) …if satan can “appear as an angel of light” …then all must be suspect …right? ….while satan may be like a horror film vampire wishing to suck us dry of the life God wants for us to enjoy …satan (unlike the vampire) is not repelled by the Bible.

…can the Bible not be a powerful tool in satan's arsenal?

…can't he encourage a liberal translation or the picking and choosing of isolated verses to water down God's truth? …what hope have we against these wiles …except through continual growth in the Spirit that Christ has planted in us?

(Eph. 6: 11) …the Bible says “Put on the whole armor of God that ye may be able to stand against the wiles of the devil”. ……good stuff! (better yet 1: 18)

…sometimes…just reading something in the Bible is like “smelling” a good healthy meal …but there's little real satisfaction in just smelling…the meal has to be “eaten” for it to supply nourishment to us. …only by getting “inside” us can it do good and protect us from the seduction of wrong teaching. (Mark 13: 22) …the Bible says “for false Christs and false prophets shall rise and shall show wonders and signs to seduce, if it were possible, even the elect.” (verse 23) “But take ye heed…” …without the Spirit of Christ and the armor of God we are prime pickings for satan's network of deceit and distractions. …we surrender so much of our lives to the secular world that we have little interest in any book that further tells us what to do. …yet if the book is the Bible …in it lies the truth to every self-imposed burden we carry and the remedy of each. (…“if we found more Bibles on the tables …more mother's singing Rock of Ages cleft for me.” …line from a Willie Nelson record.)

…the Bible is the only word of God given us but knowing the Bible is not enough to save us. …we need to ingest it's content, it's substance, in order to be nourished and fed. …eventually, as His seed in us grows, we become hungry for what only God can provide. …so hungry that we can't be satisfied. …culture, arts …everything apart from faith (…even the Everly Brothers) …becomes as junk food by comparison. …to be a "glutton" for more of the Holy Spirit is the "sole" positive addiction in this short life.

…some churches may try to supply for us what only the Holy Spirit can provide.

…no church can supply us with joy and peace of a personal relationship with God through Jesus Christ. …they may be able to sell us on a facsimile but when you leave the church …it evaporates. …no church can forgive your sins.

(1 Tim. 2: 5) …the Bible says "there is one mediator between God and man" …that being Christ Jesus.

…the church can forgive us wrongs against the church, if we ask.

…the Bible says we are to clear the air between ourselves and others before presenting ourselves (offerings) before Christ. (Matt. 5: 23)

….if our brother refuses our apology towards reconciliation we have at least tried to put off any prideful defense at his being offended by our conduct.

…if we are to be our brother's keeper then we share his burden of hurt as our own.

…through Christ's Spirit in us our brother is one with us …his hurt is ours also.

…a friend is also a gift of God. …to consider our friend is to treasure God and honor Him. …just as a gratefully married man doesn't look at other women …for protecting his wife from potential hurt, protects him from hurt also. …they are one under God. …what appears negative …can often be positive for growth in faith.

…the Bible, by speaking for something, is also speaking against the opposite.

(Jer. 17: 9) …that the Bible states that "the heart is deceitful above all things."

…sounds petty negative …and we might all claim "not mine!"

….yet that Bible truth is a warning for us to closely examine where our treasure lies.

…is "self deceit" one's own business?

…self deceit is claiming something, even to one's own self, that the facts differ with …regardless of whether it's willful or through neglect of strong thought (carelessness) …such people are of questionable character …people of questionable character are everyone's business.

(Heb. 10: 25) …the Bible calls us "to not forsake the assembling of ourselves" …for the exhorting of one another" away from self or other deceit.

…I know few Christians (including myself) who are beyond the need of strong exhortation before being encouraged to maintain their spiritual walk.

…I hope it's the desire of every Christian to be warned away from what a brother or sister perceives as potential straying. …we don't love our children or families with disregard ….we can, hopefully, exhort one another without offense being taken.

…if we're unsure of the status of another's faith (early faith or more mature faith) then should we not inquire? …so that we can better help carry each other's burden of need?

…it used to bug me that my pastor friend often asked me where I was at, spiritually. …now it's me who's always bugging him about what different verses mean according to his array of concordances. …and should he not be at his phone when I call …there are a couple of other pastors I'm happy to pester. …too bad if they all wish I'd move to the other side of the country. …they shouldn't have signed up if they don't want to be pestered by dumb sheep. …nor should anyone ask Christ to enter their lives …if they don't want to be "pestered" by His Spirit to "surrender" more and more that "the Spirit might give" them more and more. …it's not unnatural that we grow from childhood with the belief that we are important …that belief is nurtured by parents, family (grandparents – big time!) teachers etc. …by the time we reach our teens our ego has grown to respectable proportions. …we can fairly easily maintain it's perpetual presence throughout our lifetime …especially with a little deceit thrown in from time to time. …the Bible throws a considerable size wrench into our self-importance that requires a lot of dismantling (tower of Babel??) …the dismantling of ego requires much time spent in solitude …which we are unprepared for (no time for that !) ...so in response ...we say that "we do the best we can" ...just that phrase, of itself, is not a "seed" of deceit ....rather it's already a thriving, healthy "plant"! ...probably already producing fruit of it's own!   ...to this plant, spiritual conviction is like the sound of a gas-powered weed-eater!   ...luckily ...the plant has "chameleon-like" features that allows it to blend into the landscape and avoid standing out. (...the fruit of the "egg plant is very distinctive ...whereas the fruit of the ego (or egg head.) plant is barely discernable. ...but the "ego plant" wants nothing to do with "faith in Christ" ....nor does Christ have anything to do with it ...except it be grafted, by Him, into a plant that produces the fruit of His Spirit. ...some, who are (1) born into Christian families, (2) humbly receive Christ's Spirit and (3) resist departing ...to partake of worldly pleasure (...for me, I was blessed with the first of the (3) ...and the rest didn't come 'till not long ago. ...the "resisting" is still a struggle but I'm making steady progress ...and in no strength of my own either.) ...without belief in the Bible, can there be any "master plan" for our lives? ...or is it a case of adjusting to "whatever the wind of fate blows our way?"

...we often expect answers or explanations from books or teachers or pastors but we may not be sufficiently surrendered to accept the answers nor may they be sufficiently "surrendered" to provide answers but the Holy Spirit, abiding in a humble and contrite heart ...will provide "the peace of God which passeth all understanding". (Phil. 4: 7)

(Rom. 8: 27) ...and "He that searcheth the hearts (God) knoweth what is the mind of the Spirit."   (verse 28) "And we know that all things work together for good to them that love God, to them that are called according to His purpose. ...in His rest ...it's not required that we know all His (God's) purposes yet there is a joy in the "further seeking" ...by and by ...our only striving will be in our seeking more and more of His sharing ...through Him, will we gain more "salt" and more "light" enabling us to impact every area of our lives in the bringing glory to Him. ...should we encounter a non-believer, whether they be incarcerated in prison or sumptuously feasting and playing at a luxury resort. ...we know that only through God's grace have we been relieved of the bondage of either …and we know that the one suffering in prison with, perhaps, nothing …is closer to attaining Christ than is the one who appears to have it all. (Mark 9: 35) "…if any man desire to be first, the same shall be last of all and servants of all." …how much can we have without it affecting (risking) our salvation? …seems a reasonable question but it doesn't seem a question "of faith" nor of "giving" …so of what then? …of being only human? …or maybe being part human and part spiritual also? …is there an acceptable ratio we can embrace without our becoming an adversary of faith. …the Christian knows, from the Bible, the present and future status of "the adversary" (Phil. 2: 12) …as so, "with fear and trembling" is an apt description of how we're to "continue" to work out our own salvation." …whatever Bible version we choose ….(verse. 13, is for sure, a clear and present light to help us establish and confirm our faithfulness as regards "what is of faith" and what is "borderline" and beyond.

(verse 13) "for it is God which worketh in you both to will and to do of His good pleasure." …I don't think it's "God working in us" that leads our minds to "acceptable ratios" …rather, His presence leads us to greater desire to know His word and instruction

…in His word is the barely disputable conduct of all those who are one in the Spirit of Christ…..and while our "understanding" may vary …our "passion to understand more" will be consistent with one another. …it's perhaps impossible to be on the same "page" but we for certain want to be in the same "book" (source). …while the Holy Spirit reveals a single (unvarying) truth to us …the extent of His presence in our lives, determines the extent of our capacity to receive more and more truth. (i.e. child-teen-adult) …so "truth" may appear varied when it's just "us" who are present.

…Christ's Spirit enables us to calmly and humbly reserve judgment and avoid hasty, impulsive reactions based on emotion rather than discernment. …we've learned (thankfully) to eat food (consume) yet not void on impulse or initial urge but rather to think first that we not foul our present and future days. …likewise, can't we learn to consider what our eyes and ears consume to the same end. …to enter relationships and experiences may not lead to impetuous fun or too much excitement …but it should benefit longevity, sound rest and a pleasing demeanor (attitude) void of undue anxiety or stress. ("escape" from bad choices is seldom with the same ease as the "entering.")

…I spoke with a church friend today and he mentioned the possibility of a pre-service prayer group, to pray for the pastor and the pastor's message …that God's truth be revealed through him and it. …my knowledge of the Bible is limited …but I know it says that God wants His truth and light revealed by His faithful …so, I'm not sure why we pray for what God has told us is "a given?? …what isn't "a given" …is that we're surrendered sufficiently to be of service to His will and this is, perhaps, where I (and others) get a bit sensitive and yet it's exactly where I shouldn't get sensitive.

…that's where sensitivity leaks to deceit. …is Christ's Spirit sensitive?

…what has "sensitivity to self" to do with "boldness of Spirit"?

(Eph. 3: 12) "In whom we have boldness and access with confidence by the faith of Him" …there is no "hurt feelings" in Christ's Spirit. …isn't emotional hurt the product of pride? …especially among brothers or sisters of faith?

(1 Cor. 15: 55) …if through Christ, "the sting of even death" is removed …then of what context is our (perceived) emotional injury?

… to pray for our own gain in any matter, whether secular or Spiritual, is not considering others ahead of ourselves. …again, we need not pray that God open our hearts and minds when God has repeatedly told us to (get off the couch and) open our own hearts and minds to His filling for His purposes. …if we choose to fudge and hedge …then we should pray for sufficient cause to break us completely. …..right?

(2 Cor. 3: 17) …"where the Spirit of the Lord is, there is liberty (freedom)."

(James 5: 16) …if our demeanor and conduct are contrary to His calling for us then our prayer is hardly "fervent" or "effectual" …? …it becomes more like an insult ….right? …so don't do it and open your eyes quick (in protest) if you hear another doing it. …don't tie your horse to a lazy wagon. (my advice to my son.)

(Matt. 6: 7) …the Bible says "But when ye pray, use not vain repetitions, as the heathen do: for they think that they shall be heard for their much speaking…"

…there's probably not too much Spiritual growth in hearing or reading a Bible text and agreeing with it …that can be affirming, which may, indirectly lead to growth. …but I think the greater growth comes from our disagreeing with Bible test then being transformed or conforming ourselves through the Spirit to align ourselves with Bible truths. (Prov. 3: 5) …the Bible says to, "lean not to our own understanding

…in the secular world it's hard for us to get our minds around injustice and horrific happenings. …in faith, it's also hard for us to allow God's word to get around our minds.

…please read (Romans 9: 14-23) …God is the potter (sculptor) …we are merely His clay, even though we are given voices. …some vessels of His making are fitted to destruction as He deems appropriate to His own design and His own glory.

…what we don't understand, we fear …unless …we accept that our understanding is meant (designed) to be limited to what God and not we wish it to be. …to be humbly seeking and pleasing God, is to entrust our todays and tomorrows to His care.

…in His human darkness, Christ said "into Thy hands I commend (entrust) my "Spirit." …we are to do likewise, whether in our darkness or not …we are to "commend" our understanding to His wishes (through His Spirit directing us) if we truly wish His perfect peace to be with us.

…the events of 911 was a wake-up call to the reality that "much" is out of our control …yet it seems we generally prefer nodding-off to even those things which are in our control. …through faith in God it's not required that we control everything

…it's required only that we obey and trust Him. …through their belief, parents of children who died are comforted by their raising their child to obey God and by their belief that their child is now with God. …those adults who died, who effectually walked with God in their daily lives, are also with God, despite physical death.

...the Bible says so ...and all believers take comfort in that ...whether they be an immediate family member or a Spiritual family member. ...our attitude (life) is of our faith (beliefs) ...in faith our glass can be "half-full" whatever befalls us.

...I think God blesses an idle mind that is open to Him.

...while delivering papers this morning this "idle mind" considered that in 2009, I'll be 61 years old. ...6' 1" is the approximate height of my son ...and he's still growing. ...without transplants ...I'll never be 6' 1" ...but at a different 61, I'd better still be growing. (1 Cor. 15: 55) ...the Bible says "O death, where is thy sting?

...on most fronts I'm pretty weak (...actually, I can't name one I'm strong on) ...but I don't fear death. ...(being a grandfather might be cool but I'd probably be a pain. ...and I'd miss delivering newspapers at 5 am.) ...I'm blessed today to not knowing too much pain and sorrow. ...the Bible says (should I make the "cut" (golf term) that after my death "...neither shall there be sorrow nor crying nor any more pain ... " (Rev. 21: 4) ...sounds like Heaven! ...even the non believer might respond "duh!" ...but the Bible explicitly says death is not the "end" for neither believer nor non believer. ...the Bible says we all have an eternity, ahead, to experience ...a never ending eternity (don'cha just hate purveyors of doom and gloom that give us nothing positive to hang our hopes on? ...."fear mongers" at best ....right? ...do you remember feeling a bit hungry before dinnertime, as a child ...and passing through the kitchen and your mother saying "don't touch that (pretty red swirl) hot element on the stove? ...so imagine if you pushed the pot aside and not only touched but actually pushed your hand into that red (hot) swirl. ...I imagine that would make one "gnash their teeth". ...right?

...the Bible tells us ...that if we don't "make the cut" ...then that will be our "eternal (forever) experience" forever and ever. ...it's not Heaven or nothing ...it's Heaven or "that"! ...we (Christians) can dilute "fear" to "awe" ...or "respect" ...and that's good enough ...if it's sufficient enough to keep us from burning. ...but if not ...then better to take it deep enough to crunch the odds to "zero tolerance". (to me ...I have no problem with "fear" ...meaning fear as in "with fear and trembling") (Phil. 2:

12)   …God is not one to overlook (risk) anything to chance …whether Donald Trump …or an isolated forest dweller …He will not judge our response to awareness of Him, unjustly. …the Bible tells us He wants to be the sole lifeline to a greater life. …whether we embrace that or ignore that …is for us to live and for Him to judge. …the non-believer can only read that and (ironically) pray it isn't so …because for them if it is so, their doom is sealed unless they humbly change. …few pastors any longer preach the horrific consequences of eternal damnation. …so naturally, non believers see their eternity as: possibly Heaven (if they've never killed anyone) …or perhaps just a void (nothing) …or possibly some unknown proximity of both. …through His word, God gives us glimpses of Heaven and we like to clap our hands and rejoice in presuming that to be our destination.

….worry free driving …right? …we downplay that nuisance caveat of "if ye continue" which hangs soberly over our "presumptions." …most of us are unsure of what that really means and most of us are afraid to ask. …but God also gives us glimpses of the single alternative to Heaven. …God is good and He is just.

…no one, when facing a heinous eternity at "judgment" will be able to say "I was never informed."   …God has promised that all will be informed and He has warned of a fate far worse than death for any who choose to not fear Him, not honor Him and not obey Him. …in this secular world we find ourselves with aptitudes which seem to come more easily or somehow suit our natures. …obedience to God's word is rarely one of these. …any such aptitude which doesn't bring glory to God is like an arrow pointed at God.   (Matt. 12: 30) …"with me or against me" …is pretty black and white. ….what's not to understand?

(Matt. 7: 13)   "…for broad is the way that leadeth to destruction and many there be that go there." …we seldom need struggle for those things which come naturally to us. …we're not inclined to strive against our natures.

…yet Christ said "strive to enter at the straight gate: for many, I say unto you, will seek to enter in and shall not be able." (Luke 13: 24)   …I make no bones about my fear of my falling among those "many" …and I really don't want much tote with those who claim salvation then continue on their merry way with some distant assurance of having already passed their final exams. …check-out the word "strive" in your dictionary. …there is no "content" in the definition …rather, the antithesis of content is suggested. …interestingly, even the struggle (striving) towards greater faith holds more rewards than do the myriad of distractions presented by this secular world.

…it's hardly unreasonable …that if we sow little for His glory …then we should reap likewise of His blessings. …if we put our money (investment & trust) in the TD bank we can hardly expect dividends from the Royal Bank. …is not what God gives us to be invested to His glory? …and if not invested to His glory then is that not thievery? …is it acceptable to give most of the glory to God and keep just a little to ourselves? …how bad can that be? ….right?

…in the parable of the rich young ruler, no distinction is made in defining "rich" …the only distinction is in that Christ said "sell all that thou hast and distribute unto the poor and thou shalt have treasure in Heaven." (Luke 18: 22) …Christ further defines the "comparative" priority of advancing the kingdom of God over family, friends, house, etc. …those who put God above all else will receive "manifold more in this present time and everlasting life in the world to come. (Luke 18: 30) …in truth, putting God first will unavoidably benefit all those other areas inclusively. …but putting "self" first encourages others to put "self" first also.

(2 Tim. 2: 11) "It is a faithful saying; that if we be dead with Him we shall also live with Him. (verse 12) if we suffer, we shall also reign with Him. …if we deny Him, He also will deny us. (verse 15) Study to show thyself approved unto God, a workman that needeth not to be ashamed, rightly dividing the word of truth.

…I think that before confidence and boldness there needs be an underlying fear of God. …the "fear" is not of the Spirit, but rather of self deceit.

(2 Tim. 1: 17) "For God hath not given us the Spirit of fear but of power and of love and of sound mind." …it's with that fear of self that we invite and encourage exhortation from caring brothers and sisters in faith. …the more "exhortation" …then the greater our "confidence" and our "boldness" …the Christian "free" is not

free of burden but rather free of worldly burden or anxiety. ...the Christian burden, through the Spirit, is to continually give to others of what Christ; dying on the cross, has given to us. ...ultimately, being the hope of life eternal and the present reality of life more abundant on earth.   (1 Tim. 6: 6)   "But Godliness with contentment is great gain."

...if we desire that God's will be like our will then best to throw that recipe away.

...but if we pursue God's will daily through His word and are empowered by His Spirit ...then all things will work together for the good, to them that love God, to them that are called according to His purpose.   (Rom. 8: 28) ...it may not happen that we will be given more, materially but rather that we will expect less and desire less, materially. ...nor that our concerns will lessen but rather that we are enabled to carry the same (or even more concern) yet do so gladly.   (Micah 6: 8) ...like the Bible says ...we may find mercy instead of bitterness against perceived injustice (objectivity over subjectivity) ...and maybe find a little humility instead of the cloud of pride. ...we may find that what we want for ourselves is actually at some undue cost to another.

...unlike a thing (vessel) made ...we have the capacity to change from an object of no value ...into something cherished and of great value to the maker (potter) if we respond to the will of the maker ...but not in our own strength can we change rather only in surrendering our will to remain defective and instead respond to what is pleasing to the maker. ...we can't change our hearts but we can have the will to humble ourselves and repent ....whereby Christ can change our hearts and in effect wash our hearts free from the dirt of this world ...before which we are unable to see the extent of the dirt (contamination) that abounds. ...to many, this dirt looks relatively harmless ...except it's ills impact us directly

...but to the Spiritually discerning, having let go of self-motivation, a new and brighter light penetrates through the darkened glass through which we see.

(Psa. 119: 108)   "Thy word (the Bible) is a lamp unto my feet and light unto my path."   (verse 110) "The wicked have laid a snare for me, yet I erred not (wandered) from thy precepts."

...to my son, Richard and all others also ...I admit that I don't think I fully understand half of what I write down ...but it seems that through repetitive revisiting of God's word that more and more apparent understanding is available to me. ...it makes sense to me that a casual reflection of the Bible can offer us no more than a casual understanding.

...I think back several years ...having watched a movie in which the line "wherefore come out from among them and be ye separate, saith the Lord ..." was cited. (2 Cor. 6:17) ...that line stuck with me and soon afterwards, following a church service, I asked a dear and kindly elder ...if, in fact, that line was in the Bible ...and he said he didn't know but said he could find out for me. ...not to be picky ...but that's a pretty defining verse for a "Christian" to not know if it is in the Bible ...whether it's taken literally or not ....the "defining" aspect is in that the verse continues....."...and I will receive you." ...anytime the Bible states a plausible condition of being received of God ...is a time to commit to memory that condition ...else will we minimize the need of our personal submission. ...that 'cloud of pride' I spoke of earlier might lead us to think that God is lucky to have someone like us on His side ...which belittles our unworthiness at even our best times. ...a huge and seemingly continual error on my part ...is my assumptions of what a loving God would and wouldn't do or would or wouldn't allow. ...like allow satan to test Job's faithfulness ...or cause death to the first born of all Egypt ...even the animals ....many of those people were no doubt seemingly normal folks ...much like folks today and probably about as Godly. (Psa. 24: 1) ...""the earth is the Lord's and the fullness thereof ...the world and they that dwelleth therein"

...should I make something ...say a table or a painting ...whatever, if it's mine then I can destroy it at will without regard, especially if it displeases me.

...if I destroy something I've made, I can make another if I want to or not if I don't want to. ...I can give form to something ...or I can take form away.

...one of my brothers is a bit of a recluse ...he once had (and may still have) a gift for drawing and sculpting of wood ...he sculpted a woman's head which I thought was exquisite ...but then, soon afterward, he destroyed it. ...I imagine the making of that bust gave him great pleasure! ...but an end result didn't. ...I suppose he could have altered his creation to reflect something that caused him less grief ...but I guess that initial disappointment would always be present no matter what changes he made.

...best to start anew. ...I think that bust became something my brother never intended. ...I expect it, eventually, came to cause him grief. ...I doubt it was the works of his hands (which pleased him) that caused him grief but rather that "what he created" took on a life of it's own. ...maybe a life of high expectations upon the maker to do wondrous things ...or to serve the interests of others.

...I was appalled to learn that he had destroyed his work   ...I actually considered that act as sinful. ...in truth ...perhaps that act " of destroying" negated sin.

...there are many instances in the Bible where God destroyed in order to negate sin. ...average, yet ungodly, people would have been stunned and abhorred by God's wrath had they known, with certainty, that their devastation and death had been deliberate acts of God.   ...the flood, the tower of Babel, Sodom and Gomorrah. ...God's mercy towards the humble may be without limit but it seems His patience with the proud of heart, is for sure, limited. ...imagine a people too proud to acknowledge Christ as the Messiah and God's chosen route for us to attain salvation. ...what wrath, through what means, might God pour upon their heads? ...and still they resist (defy) God's will that we surrender to and honor Christ as the son of God. ...through Moses, God rained horror on Pharaoh and his entire army for his defiance. ...by and by will we learn not to tempt God's wrath? ...nor take advantage of His mercies? ...today we seem to have faith but it's in our religiosity rather than our Lord. ...we look to the "community of religion" to establish our beliefs ...knowing full well that the community is moderate ...which is just what the Bible tells us we're not to be. (Mark 12: 30)

...the "new covenant doesn't replace the "ten commandments ...it's "further to" the commandments of God to Moses.

…for those who seek truth and God's wisdom the Bible will continue to speak more than what the words may initially imply. …Christ's Spirit will confirm the essence of the words yet also open up our hearts to experience (reveal) greater understanding.

…God has used man to supply the world with His word but man can never supply the "light" within the words …that light is of Christ. …even the Spirit of Christ.

…man can lay to memory every word in the Bible, cover to cover…and yet not be given the light of understanding the words except he surrender to experience the light of Christ's Spirit in himself.

…Muslims are disciplined from childhood to memorize the Koran (their Bible)

…the western world …rather, the whole world, would profit from such a discipline in memorizing the Bible (or least extensive parts of the Bible.) …it's not treason to admire discipline and adherence to what one believes to be right and good. …we memorize civil law so that we not be imprisoned physically: …would that we memorize God's law so that we not be imprisoned to darkness which is the even greater imprisonment.

…yet even just in the memorizing of Bible passages lies the inroad (fast track) to the light (experience) of Christ's Spirit. …personally, I can't say that I've surrendered sufficiently in all areas to warrant holding much of Christ's light (many might say I haven't any!) …but I'm grateful every day for my walk (however limited) in faith.

…at age 56, I am ever so aware that I've gone about this process backwards …in that, the seed was firmly planted by my parents …but in my "worldly" wisdom, I transplanted that seed to a "rocky terrain" (only for about 30 years thought.) …dumb, dumb, dumb.

…I think there's a parable that says that only when the seed dies …can new life be propagated. …in my case it was when the "sowers" of the seed died …that the seed took root. …that's not in the Bible but I believe it's in the "light" of God's word. …there is no "salvation" through association" with the sower.

…Moses was a good and Godly man but there is no salvation through association or being descendant from Moses.

(John 14: 6) ….the Bible says there is but one way, one truth and one life (light) …and that no man receives salvation except by surrender to Christ. …only Christ is the son of God (even in the world …what son honors his father by bringing into the home what is father finds distasteful?) …and so "Christ" is the mediator between God and man and between mankind and Heaven …and please believe, that you and I do not want to risk the eventual "alternative" to being acceptable to Heaven. …there are only two "super powers" and the US isn't one of them.

…we're well advised to consider what Christ asks as the "minimum" requirements for salvation …never mind the short-cuts or the easy path …if that entails "fear and trembling" for awhile …then accept that and endure that.

…don't even consider for a moment that "God can't be serious" about the alternatives. …I believe He's deathly serious.

…we put great value on the works of men that please us according to our interests …the painter can destroy what we might consider a masterpiece …we can cry "foul" but then again it's not ours to cry. …the potter can create a beautiful vase which to him is imperfect …he may set it aside to repair the defect …or he may destroy it …it's his creation to do with as it pleases him.

…we are all broken people and unworthy of God's concern …yet through Christ we can be as new. …we can humbly ask that of our maker so that we no longer displease Him and risk being cast aside (destroyed). (cast aside or destroyed is perhaps a split second reprieve before eternal damnation and torment (gnashing torment) for those who have chosen to deny Christ). …better to pray for a taste of that torment here and now, that we be encouraged to change our ways …even to thank God for any torment that turns us toward Him. …do we think we have a pretty good life apart from faith in God?

…or in our lukewarm faith? (Malachi 2:2) …the Bible says, "if ye will not hear and if ye will not lay it to heart to give glory unto my name, saith the Lord of hosts, I will even send a curse upon you and I will curse your blessings. ….." …God was speaking specifically to a people who had departed His ways and His wishes (caused God grief or displeasure).

…all that we have and treasure of this world can be taken …without rhyme or reason, by God …and much worse than just that, as Job found out. …the Lord gives and the Lord takes away without explanation. …I don't know how one could be faithful to God, without having a history of obedience to God, to support him in his woes.

…in plenty, we are to give glory to God …and in pain and sorrow and injustice we are also to trust His providence …humbly acknowledging that His ways are far, far above our miniscule vision and understanding. …without faith, we are intent in this world to control the pushing of buttons, the pulling of levers and the turning of knobs to alter and tweak others and our environments, to our own liking.

…I suppose in short …we want what satan wanted (before he got the boot.)

…I don't know if satan was informed of what awaited him in his expulsion.

…I know we have been informed through God's word. …but we don't like "to fear" anything …so we err greatly by making light of what we ought fear most.

…most of us belittle "hell" …and so don't earnestly fear it. …Webster's dictionary says "eternal misery and suffering for the unrepentant". …the "hellfire and damnation God", of the previous generation, appears to have been tamed by mere mankind and is now our ever tolerant and accepting friend. …how benevolent and wise we have become to be so accommodating of God. …we probably think He's not such a bad guy now that He realizes how relatively harmless (accepting, fun-loving) we are. …we no longer blatantly murder (except abortion) nor steal (except pretty much what we figure can escape detection) …actually, we're maybe a bit weak on all the other commandments too …but …what a friend we have in Jesus! …if we sin …or if we're doing stuff we're not suppose to (which is hardly ever) …our friend Jesus bears our guilt and grief so as we don't have to. …..right? …only Christians get to have this "win-win" situation …right? …the Bible is so right when it tells us to hang out with people who think like we do (likeminded brothers and sisters, one in the Spirit) …right? …do I hear an amen!?! …I sure hope not! …that's what we're warned of in the Bible and of His Spirit …to guard against. …the Bible says to be not conformed but rather be transformed by the renewing of our minds, that we may prove what is good and acceptable and perfect will of God. (Rom. 12: 2)

…there's no good thing in singing (saying) "what a friend we have in Jesus" …unless all other friendships pale by comparison. …He is our rock …He is our deliverer from a fate far, far, far worse than death" …the friend that doesn't encourage us to "fear" God (c/w trembling) …be it spouse, parent or whatever …is an ill chosen friend.

(aside) …I now live in a very small apartment in which the living area blends with the kitchen. …I shopped yesterday and now notice, as I sit here …two jars of pickles, yet unopened, on a counter. …as a boy …one of my mom's nick-names for me …was "Mr. Pickle" …it occurs to me that perhaps I've always been inclined towards the "sour" tastes in life. …maybe that's my "faith" side …because I still love chocolate éclairs and nanaimo bars (…worldly side???)

…anyway, back to friends in faith. …the one good thing in any of us is the "seed of God" which I believe is in each of us at birth (and which, abortion kills) …with today's technology we have the capacity to learn, beforehand, whether a child is likely to be pleasing to us …or displeasing to us. (1 Cor. 10: 23) (all things are lawful but all things edify not) …within the law, we can choose our eventual destiny by our conduct. …if our conduct doesn't favor Christ's will …then it favors satan's will.

…the Sunday evenings church message was on the book of Malachi (O/T) and primarily …three ways that leaders can fail their flock …being: teaching God's whole truth, presenting the community of God's love …and upholding God's instruction for marriage and family. …the pastor (James) encouraged the congregation to hold the feet of the leaders …to the fire …re: the teaching of God's truth. …yet if a church leader has God's word in his hand and Christ's Spirit in his heart …then how can he go amiss?? …would not Christ's Spirit disallow it? …except that the leader turn and then desire to place the wishes of the people above the wishes (will) of God. …it's probably not so much a question of balance but rather of vigilance against balance!

…it's God's church …not the people's church …and the leader who proffers "strictly Bible" instruction can hardly go amiss. …it, for sure, will be a smaller church and hardly popular …Christ repeatedly said it would be that way.   (Luke 12: 51) Suppose ye that I am come to give peace on earth? I tell you, Nay …"

…faith isn't complicated…"indecision" on important issues is complicated.

(1 Cor. 14: 33) …"For God is not the author of confusion but of peace, as in all churches of the saints." …it's probably not the pastor's place (job) to attract the "worldly" to the "Holy" …that's Christ's place to do or not according to our hearts being softened to Him. …the pastor or leader's job is probably to hold fast to the Spirit's leading and to keep contamination out of God's church …so that those who sincerely repent through Christ's workings find a community (church) in which to grow in Spirit and truth. …I think the one good thing in any of us …is the seed of God, which I believe is in us at birth …even in us at conception.

…perhaps even in more primitive tribes and more primitive times …that seed struggles to take root by various means. …I shudder to think of some of the sacrifices once thought to be required (human even) …and far removed from Abraham and Isaac. …through Christ's death and resurrection we're no longer required to sacrifice our dearest and best (children) …or is it that our self will is treasured by us even above our children? …in any case …"self will" is the sacrifice now required …dead to self - but new life in Christ. …the voluntary exchange of garbage for gold. …there's a certain logic that says if we're called to tithe 10% then perhaps we need only sacrifice 10% of self also …but it's the logic of looking through a very small window or less.

…technology has provided for many ills of the modern world yet God can use all to His purposes. …film entertains but it has also documented human atrocity beyond comprehension …to view heaps of human corpses at the hands and will of the leader of a country is a horrific reminder of the depths to which a desperate mind can descend to. …that film footage gives us a glimpse of what hell might be likened to for those who decline Christ as savior. …and my fear of hell envisions those heaps of bodies, not as dead but as being alive and tormented for eternity …"gnashing their teeth" for deliverance that will never and can never come....all because they chose their own way over God's way.

...the testament of God's word is the "big" window ...the "big" lens and the "big" picture of each of our eternities.

...the tithe we give is a part of a package and when we give gladly and without hesitation

...the Bible says this pleases God and that He blesses us. ...the "package" that pleases God is our thankfulness to Him and our bringing glory to Him through an appreciative attitude. ...if we are blessed with more than we need, we are not to hoard (bank) the surplus but rather are to put it back to His use. ...a thankful heart can make our 9-5 work seem not like work at all ...if we can shed our focus on self wants and instead offer our positive and grateful attitude to uplift others. ...pleasing God becomes pleasing ourselves, our families and our communities. ...has God ever not blessed those who gladly give Him His due??? ...He can be trusted to provide what He offers in the Bible to the compliant heart attentive to His will on earth, done as is in Heaven.

...submissive vs. defiant. ...the defiant can only hope for some luck in the receiving of God's blessings ...whereas the submissive enjoy the continual "experience" of God's faithfulness to His word and the patience to trust His workings in His own good timing.

...my minute understanding of God's ways can fashion a limited view of what Heaven might be like ...where I'll once again see my folks and friends.

...the Bible says that probably won't be the case ...but rather it'll be even better than that! ...my same minute understanding can also fashion a limited view of what hell might be like ...I think my brother and others, whom I've loved or liked, might be there ...so I like to minimize hell to "nothingness". ...the Bible says that's not the case.

...in the ten commandments, God said what to do ...and what not to do. ...we're a thick-headed people ...Christ clarified the minimum requirements by further stating what we're to "think" and not to think.   ...God is of love and of mercy and of grace. ...Satan ...(and please don't accept that there is no satan) ...has an entirely different agenda. ...in ourselves (our own strength) we succumb to satan's agenda (Godless) ...anti-Christ ...anti-sacrifice of self focus. ...God isn't mean ...He's loving and He's strict

...and I think any father who isn't both is wrong ...even "sinning" through negligence. ...especially Christian fathers. ...no caring parent invites someone into their home when they have doubts about their trustworthiness. ...and they inform their children as to

what is and what isn't appropriate.

...if parents were to open their doors to just anyone ...they'd soon have nothing of value remaining. (material or moral) ...for the Christian, only negligence and unfaithfulness blurs what Christ has clarified to be unacceptable.

...eternal torment and regret is the lot for those who choose not to strive to enter Heaven's gates through experiencing Christ's Spirit in their (our) earthly lives. ...and "assurance of salvation" is like humility ...the moment you claim it, is the moment you've lost it. ...the Holy Spirit (the professed dominating force) in the Christian's life ...has no need to claim assurance. ...that should tell us something.

...I don't know that we can "humbly" claim an "exalted" status (...and "salvation" is the most exalted status) but what we depose the Holy Spirit to make the claim. ...to "verbally" claim salvation seems like evidence of doubt, more so than anything else. ...we don't want to be "perceived" as "not saved" ...otherwise we risk being perceived as bound for hell!

...I had an interesting (differing) faith talk with my dentist today ...I think he's an "all roads lead to Heaven" guy. ...pleasant, passive ...intelligent. ...he believes in Heaven ...but not hell ...philosophy without conflict has always been popular.

...where faith says "all things are possible with God" ...science says "all things are possible with quantum physics.   ...that young dentist has his whole life or whole existence ahead of him ...depending on his choices and his perception of fate ...but his "hope" is in the "here and now" …I've been there and the "here and now" (no matter how good it appears or feels) isn't through faith in Him alone. …eternity doesn't have to have the uncertainty of a box of chocolates where one never knows what they'll get (apart from cavities). …my dentist's hope (post-earthy life) is in anything better than nothing …"nothing" being the "worst" he expects. …I fear his "nothing" will be considered as "Heaven" compared to what the Bible says all who reject Christ are going to experience. …having been informed, I don't know what impels us to risk purgatory or worse without even tasting that God is good and true to his word of life more abundant. …we're a hard-headed people of our own making and our own stubbornness …and what a horrific price we'll pay.…I did graciously share and concede that my dentist (being an evolutionist as opposed to Christian) could trace his ancestry back to the worm or amoeba. …whereas I was limited, basically, to trace mine no further back than Noah.

…and he graciously, only hesitated a few moments, before agreeing.

…that both God and satan should harden the hearts of mankind …is not of either …but rather first of ourselves, through our own will. …God is merciful …but is also omnipotent …being that …as with Adam, Eve, Cain, the people of Noah's days, Pharaoh and Egypt, Sodom, Gomorrah, etc.

…God knows all who (through His good blessing of man's will) are going to defy him even to the end …and God knows also who will surrender to Him.

…satan doesn't know these things …and so, through evil means, will work on man's will to ally with whatever is anti-Christ. …there is no neutral or middle ground with God …but that there is ample middle-defiance or even doubt …is satan's victory. …weakness and deceit always seeks company and support. ….the challenge towards "life more abundant" …is to never align ourselves with those things. …unfortunately, the "lukewarm" Christian also seeks company and support but Christ's Spirit will direct us to "lift our eyes up to the Heavens where our help comes from ….every good and perfect thing is of (from) God. …Christ was challenged on this by scribes and chief priests and justly responded. (Luke 20: 25) …"Render unto

Caesar what is of Caesar and unto God, what is of God. …is it not possible to maintain a community of God seeking "company and support" that can exempt itself from watering down His word.

…I suppose in one sense it's "holding fast …yet in another sense, it's "not sharing" with the more worldly. …vigilance vs. risky sharing? …monks and preachers? …I don't know that vigilance is a Spiritual gift like preaching is …but there's for sure a need for it from some quarter. …perhaps, by and by, through Christ's Spirit …vigilance becomes a primal nature of our faith. (…there's been a lot of "by and by" since Christ but I wonder when the vigilant nature comes?) …is it in our churches and pastors and believers? …I can't recall the last time I was even exhorted by a fellow believer …yet I know I need it! …and I know someone is supposed to be doing it!

…I think I'm known to be insensitive, so that can't be holding someone back.

…maybe nobody cares much about my walk in faith …maybe, unless I ask for prayer, it's sufficient that I just smile and say "hello" …are we past asking the hard questions? …we've come a long way from past generations …have we come too far? …are we already past fearing hell? …maybe we should pray that "fear of hell" be re-established so that "fear of God" be a part of the "solid rock" on which the Christian stands to conquer every other fear …including fear of death. …in the family of God (faith and loving our neighbor as ourselves) every day brings a surprise final exam to someone we know or someone they know. …death visits both the old and the young …often unawares. …we're not prepared ourselves unless we're helping other be prepared.

…what an encouragement for the Christian when Billy Graham, in a TV interview, claimed he didn't fear death …but rather welcomed it in the hope …(not assurance.) of going to a far, far better place. …that hope comes from digesting God's word and complying with it. …Mr. Graham didn't save a single soul but he gave to millions the Spiritual truth that God shared with him …and in so doing …voided every escape, every petty complaint and every excuse for every ear that heard him. …my dentist and others may think we should get 50 …or even 100 chances to avoid hell (…just as every child may think they should get 50 or 100 chances to play with fire and not get burned)

…yet to those who listen and comply, the ear is a blessing, …but to them that hear and ignore, the ear is a curse.   (Mal. 2: 2) …the Bible says, "I will curse your blessings" …not the ignorant but rather those who "knowingly ignore" what the Bible says have placed their treasure and hop elsewhere. …as the "ear" is a blessing …so then is our "free will" also a blessing. …all blessings are ours (perhaps only on loan) to apply to righteousness or "other" …for those who advance God's will, their blessings will be multiplied in the here and the hereafter …for those who choose not to advance God's will while here on earth, their end here will be grim and their eternity forever heinous. …they of course are free to think "what kind of God would devise such a plan!" …earth, wind and fire are all blessings …quakes, hurricanes and burning forests give us

reason to pause. …God is truth and is true to His word …He will deliver (deliver us) every thing He has told us …of earth, of Heaven …of hell. …most want His sunny days but not His rain. …we want his blessings but not His conditions.   …His blessings, or at least many of them, are for all …whether of faith or not

…His eventual and final blessing is for only His faithful …those who refuse His conditions, refuse His Spirit …His Spirit is the only ticket to His final blessing of promise. …we have been informed of the grievous alternative. …God does not condemn us to hell …we do that ourselves of our own freewill. …He is just and gives everyone ample opportunity to change our ways.

…He is loving and grieves for all who choose to ignore His warnings and who will forever suffer their own burnings. …Heaven could never be Heaven if God let the likes of most of us in. (theory only)

…God didn't create hell ….satan created hell. …whether directly or indirectly …so, render unto satan what is of satan. …satan is a superpower and is the antithesis of God. (…how that all played out …I have no idea …nor do I need to know …I only need to believe and trust the Bible. …God has promised that through His Spirit …if we seek Him then He will reveal sufficient for our needs.

…the apostle Paul, even while being a thorn to Christ's cause …was converted while traveling to Damascus …his hardened heart being softened by Christ who directed him to speak to the people and minister to them for Christ.

(Acts 26: 18) …"To open their eyes and to turn them from darkness to light and from the power of satan unto God, that they man receive forgiveness of sins and inheritance among them which are sanctified by faith that is in me".

…I used to hate thinking about the power of satan …or about what hell might be like …but, thanks to several harsh verses in the Bible, I somehow no longer fear thinking or talking about it. …I don't know that we can deny or ignore the power of satan except we also deny or ignore the power of God. …they are both cited in the same source book. …to acknowledge both then separate from one will determine our eternity.

(Matt. 12: 30) …the Bible says whoever is not with Christ is against Christ.

…no amount of schmoozing or twisting and turning or headaches or discomfort or pain is going to change that edict of Christ's. …Christ wants you with Him …and satan wants you with him. (Rom. 14: 23) "for whatsoever is not of faith is sin." …why risk playing with serious fire? …if excitement and the pleasures of this world is our treasure then the "gross cost" is going to be beyond our worst nightmare. …to my son Richard or any others …if it takes "blatant fear" to earnestly consider God's provisions …then I'm good with that.

(Rom. 14: 22) the Bible says just once "Hast thou faith? Have it to thyself before God. Happy is he that condemneth not himself in that thing which he alloweth." …that verse appears to give a fair amount of license (leeway) to our Christian walk. …I expect most cults use such a verse to entice followers to hell …never mentioning the following verse (23) which states "whatever is not of faith is sin." …in the 60s, while "freedom" and "loving" are both widely used in the Bible, it's context was never intended to promote the "free-love" that became so prevalent. …every lesser love, other than the love for God …can easily come between us and God. …all "love" is from God and is to be exercised within the confines of His purposes (will) …and we are to continually and always thank Him for every form of love else our loves are of satan's devices.

…although recently divorced and not particularly "liking" my ex-wife, I nevertheless love her to the extent of the comfort I would know should I feel confident that her heart and (more importantly) her eternity …is with the Lord. …our failure is that whatever love we once shared was apart from Him. …I love my teenage son but find no comfort in his present spiritual walk …yet I have hope. (…I expect my dad, likewise, shared a similar dearth of comfort and a similar hope, concerning myself.) …am I overly vigilant:

…I have only one church friend in whom I enjoy the comfort of a confidence for his eternity should he "move on" this day. …I'm sure there are others whom I don't know well enough to establish that same confidence (definitely, another one of my hopes!) …to the extent that an 18 year old worldly young man can perceive love, my son probably "loves" me …but given the choice, I'd rather he hate me in exchange for his loving Christ. (that's fairly safe, because to love Christ voids hating anyone) …the greater hope of my writing is and has always been … that he avoid squandering all or much of the years his dad did, in futile escapes. …choosing faith in Christ impacts greatly and positively every decision, large and small, that we make. …consequently, the compounded result will be "life more abundant" in every area of life …and increasingly so, as we continue in the working our of our salvation …whether we open the door to salvation is a willful choice we each make regardless of excuse.

(Rev. 22: 11) …the Bible says "He that is filthy, let him be filthy still." …if we choose to willfully relax our further seeking of salvation so too do we set aside Christ's suffering and sacrifice for us. …the time comes when our character as regards our availing ourselves of His grace is fixed for eternity. …maybe today. …when the last train has left the station …then it's too late. …at that time… …He who we have turned our back on turns His back on us ...as we have been repeatedly warned He would.

...as the consuming fire of torment approaches, we will know regret ...continual torment and continual regret ...with no end to it ...ever. ...absolute separation between the faithful and the negligent. ...all bridges to safety vanish immediately and irrevocably ...even the escape of death is removed to be replaced by utter darkness and utter torment. ...would that we "gnash our teeth" just thinking about our potential, dismally excruciating, plight ... especially when compared to the beauty and comfort of Heaven.

...rightful idiots (absolutely no slight intended) need have no fear but those of us blessed with knowing ears and knowing choices are accountable. ...firstly, to God ...then our children, our spouse, family, friends, co-workers, etc

...our accountability is the test of our character, the test of Christ's characteristics in us. ...it's what established His church on earth. ...it's a great blessing to be tested daily and take opportunity to grow in character.

...there's a hymn that asks "we're you there when they crucified my Lord," ...physically we could never be there but spiritually we should always be there, lest we forget our future forsakenness should we stray from Christ's cause.

...after a couple of consecutive misses, I actually made it to morning church.

...good message on "the diminishing church:

...denominations may crumble and fall and congregations come and go but whatever the temptations the church built on Christ, will stand secure forever to accommodate all who sincerely seek His truth and light. (Matt. 4: 1–11)

...we're prone to comparative thinking and that's good ...(to the extent that we compare apples with apples) ...but Christ's "bread of life" is not to be compared with the "manna of Moses" (through God). ...they sustain different hungers. ...ever increasing sensationalism sustains a worldly hunger (i.e. cheer-leaders in sports events.)

…Christ's cause has little relevance in the world's terms. …the world chooses to follow the lion knowing full well if the lion runs out of easy prey …it will turn and devour those who have followed. …yet if …even having been warned that there is no escape …still we follow the lion and the lion's final destination will be ours also. …Christ constantly displayed the character of the Lamb of God …and does so even now through His Spirit

…whom it is our great privilege to follow after and thus reach a far different destination …provided we not waver or succumb to vain glory in these "churches" of our own creation. …we are "nothing of Him" except we glorify Him." …because it's God's wish that we return to Him, even our very lives are in essence but a loan of His grace …as is everything we have. …even our treasured families are solely of His grace and under our temporary care.

…the pastor at tonight's service cited his wife's saying "yes" to marriage as being the greatest kindness ever shown him. …cute …but an unfortunate miss at prioritizing God's place. …about 500 young ears may see a human relationship as their priority when it's their relationship with Christ that will open proper doors to every intimacy. …the pastor's public compliment to his wife was met with applause …it's what some present wanted to hear. …as are political statements and sports scores cited from pulpits. …"levity" has it's place and for sure the greater the levity the more plentiful the congregation. …a young congregation is very malleable and may trust that a pastor's every word is from God and therefore is a holy grail to adopt and guide themselves. …and most congregations attend a church where they hear what they want to hear. …there's really not that much levity in the Bible

…but there's lots in the world! …is the "Body of Christ" to be a balance?

…it's a critical question for the Christian and more so for the pastor.

…while God seems to compound (increase) blessings for His own …mankind compounds mistakes and the seed of error grows quickly.

…the parable of "the wheat and the tares" illustrates the similar appearance of "Godly" and "worldly" …sometimes right up until harvest (judgment).

...another of Christ's parables speaks to the soils on which the seed is sown, affecting the seeds capacity to take root and grow ...and best also to consider the limitations, should the sower not be vigilant, about not sowing weak seed. ...seed that is not prepared and inspected by the Holy Spirit should never be scattered (sown) ....and especially not be sown in our churches. ...and so the Bible says ...these sowers (teachers) will be held to a more stern accountability.

...the body of Christ (church) doesn't need more pastors, so much as it needs pastors who "hold fast" to the word and Spirit of God.

...pastors are to be devout (set apart from Christ) and have vowed to be so. ...yet they themselves can never be the friend or companion that only Christ is to be for each of us. ...I believe their calling is to direct us and encourage us, individually, to seek that personal relationship with Christ wherein He ...and no other "body" will direct our paths. (...it must be discouraging for a pastor to be continually babysitting ...month after month ...those whom claim the desire for faith yet hedge their surrender to Christ and the word (light) of God.) ... it's the same Holy Spirit whom indwells both the preacher and the listener. ...Christ's Spirit wishes nothing more for the pastor ...than He wishes for any other. ...the pastor's calling carries a higher accountability but all are called to use God's gifts to advance His will on earth ...there is no blessing pertinent to pastors, in faith ...that is not also available to the church janitor, if he is humbly fulfilling Christ's calling. ...there is no special dispensation given to those who lead ....over those who serve in any other capacity. ...the only criteria is the state of one's heart, as pertains to their walk in faith. ...as we embrace Christ's purpose ...so does He embrace our lives.

(James 4" 8) ..."draw near to Him and He will draw near to you"

...that sounds like the perfect picture except that while God is always available to me ...I'm rarely available to Him ...and so ...in the "drawing near" department ....the weak link is me. ...that's not an "honest mistake" on my part ...it's the equivalent of dismemberment of the body of Christ....and ample grounds for "rightful dismissal" from His flock. …where do I suppose that leaves me …except to be fair and weakened game for the other super power ..satan!

(Isa. 6: 5) …"Then said I, woe is me! For I am undone: because I am a man of unclean lips (fouled) and I dwell in the midst of a people of unclean lips …."

…"carelessness" and "negligence" is far different from an honest mistake …a "mistake" is knowingly doing a thing you believe to be right ….even though it may prove to be wrong or even fatal. …whereas "negligence" is carelessness with faculties that God has given us.

(Luke 12: 48) "to whom much is given, much is expected."

…to be born Muslim, practice Islam and die Muslim ….is not sin.

…the Bible says that prior to judgment by God …all will be presented with God's truth and given opportunity to repent and convert.

…they, Muslims, may not have had the opportunity …yet …but we have and so our hour of judgment has come. …God is merciful …and those who are of God, are merciful …but they are not to be taken advantage of.

…Christ is a bit like the prodigal son (of God) who was required to leave the father's side for God's purposes …suffered greatly and now has returned home.

…He is the "standard" for all who desire to enter God's Kingdom.

…we are to heed all He said and all He's done for us …so that we too can enter God's Kingdom (King-dom).

…democracy is flouted here on earth …but perfect monarchy is available for our choosing it. …perfect monarchy ensures that our needs are satisfactorily met, now and always, by One who loves us unconditionally …our response to God is potentially our life more abundant and is also potentially our death (unblessed) beyond recovery.

…our embracing faith or our willful negligence is totally of our own doing. (…it's interesting

how people who deny any belief in God …seem to find sufficient belief to blame or question Him in times of tragedy or great trial.) …there is, for sure, a source of confusion …even anguish …but it's absolutely not God. (Isa. 3: 9) "woe unto their soul! For they have rewarded evil unto themselves." …why do we with our tiny bit of understanding …demand of God, who is deity, regarding things that are of Him and His purposes?

…I think we do that because we're self-mode idiots.

(verse 11) "woe unto the wicked! It shall be ill with him; for the reward of his hands shall be given him."

…I'm curious of the process by which satan chose to balk at obeying God …was it instantaneous? …or more gradual, like us? …how is it that satan came to put his own wants above God's wants? …does satan, even now, realize his horrendous error? …what about me? …am I clever enough or deceitful enough to not recognize or else plain ignore my errors in obedience to God?

…can I then not expect a fate similar to satan's, …come the end?

…our "on earth" source of reference holds very little time as compared to an eternity of "gnashing teeth" torment and regret of "continual weeping" magnitude. …how close to the edge of the abyss, will I risk walking? …how do I determine if my times of "feeling good" are of satan or of God?

(Matt. 5: 3 -11) ….the beatitudes describe well the portion of my "feeling good" that is of God and of His blessings and of His will.

(Phil. 4: 8) …and the Bible tells us … where our thoughts are to be. …are we smart enough to step outside these envelopes (His fold) and yet remain covered by His protection? (….is a child smart enough to play in traffic?)

…satan has no problem with our "feeling good" …provided we don't attribute it to God …not bring glory to Him publicly. …satan probably can sustain a few losses, provided the majority of Christians just hang out in their churches on occasion yet for the most part appear like their worldly neighbors. …that's sufficient to assure their doom alongside himself. …I think both God and satan …have the power to see our hearts.

…what could please satan more, than a doomed heart, proudly claiming assurance of salvation and assuring other proud hearts likewise?   …and what could grieve God more?

…for the seeking Christian, it's a tough question as to how much of the world we can allow into our lives …(His church) …yet avoid becoming "lukewarm" to His cause while asserting our own agendas.   …there is one body and one Spirit to both support and be supported by …else all is lost. …the Bible says we will each be revisited by our faithfulness to the word of God.   …not our faithfulness to the Catholic church or Protestant church …nor denomination, nor specific address.   …we don't hear many churches inviting Biblical scrutiny …so are there thousands of mini-empires being built apart from His Body and His Spirit? ….are they being built with our tithes and offerings? …God loves a cheerful giver ….does He love cheerful undiscerning givers? …I actually think good hearted people know that the greater blessing is in giving and are happy to give …whether good hearted people be Christian or not. …yet to tithe or to give without discernment could be even detrimental! …i.e. to give to a cult or a lukewarm church is unlikely to please God or advance His will.

…it's convenient to entrust our Spiritual walk and our faith to a pastor …or priest …but they won't be mentioned (I don't expect) when we stand at the gate of God's eternal fold (Heaven) and we're called to answer. …will we be dumb struck as we see our "convenient homage" crumble and fall? …probably immediately prior to our doing likewise? …for sure, the Bible says… woe will be to the Christian who has conveniently ventured into forbidden faith by trusting the words of man over the words of God. …the body (church) of Christ is not going to falter or fail for lack of finances. … that would make it dependant on mankind. …will it's growth be stymied by lack of finances? …probably not even that! …..it may be that finances (money) have become more of an encumbrance to the church of Christ, in that it appears, to the greater extent, to have enhanced the churches of man.

…the Bible primarily states that what the church of Christ requires of us …is precisely what we're unwilling to give …that being … service in the manner prescribed in the

Bible. .....not service as a tithing church goer ...but rather service as a "dead to self ...Spirit indwelt ...what can I do for Christ" disciple.

...whatever our service or giving of self, it ought to be specifically cited in God's word and preceded by "Blessed be those who ....(whatever)"

...there are many blessings cited in the Bible and we should gladly and lovingly be greedy for every one available to us. ...the "world" in us may not perceive "the receiving" of the blessing, ...but the "Spirit" in us will.

...as it pleases the loving parent to give their child every good thing ...so it pleases God, Christ and His Spirit to give us blessing ....and it is for us to be thankful for Spiritual blessings and share as we are given to and return glory to the Father. ....which in turn avails us of even further blessings! ...good stuff!. ...right? ...perpetual blessings upon blessings come to those who choose to be born again of the Spirit. ...only through rebirth in Him can we shed the dirt and anxieties of where we live. ...we're a proud and willful people, yet even our righteousness (self) is as "filthy rags" (Isa. 64: 6) ...only through seeking Christ can we throw away (part from) our own self righteousness and allow His goodness to take root and control of our thought and conduct. ...whatever our age, we literally become as innocent children in the eyes of God because we become newly formed.

...as we lovingly take all necessary measure to protect our children from harm.

...so God uses His maximum deterrent (eternal torment in hell) to protect His children (whatever their age) from any people who might interfere. ...it's very unwise to belittle the shepherd and the sheep analogy. ...the world can make light (casual) of it ....but it's deadly serious stuff.

...Christ said in no uncertain terms "But whoso shall offend one of these (His sheep) better for him that a huge stone were hanged about his neck and that he were drowned in the depth of the sea. ...nothing ambiguous there!

..."he that hath an ear, let him hear. (Rev. 2: 7)

....if my cause (will) isn't His cause then I deserve, for sure, no goodness from Him ...if my cause isn't His cause then whatever my cause may be ..it's contrary (actually, against) to His cause.

...actually, if one is not Christian then I must question any apparent good that they propose because I'm suspect of that good being "2ⁿᵈ or 3ʳᵈ rate good" at best.

...my son, even at eighteen yeas, is still my child ...whether he listens to me or not has no bearing on my love for him. ...I think there's a TV show that debates "parental validity" through DNA tests. ...is Richard my child first? ....or is he God's child first? ...I can watch out for (love) him ...maybe another 20 or 30 years. ....God can watch out for him (and his) far better and longer than me ...but it's Richard who has to let God do that, having attained the age of accountability. ...I pretty much would just as soon that non-Christian folk just leave him alone. ...no offence ...but I prefer only 1ˢᵗ rate good for him and his future and there's but one source of 1ˢᵗ rate good. ...2ⁿᵈ and 3ʳᵈ rate good will only encourage him to lesser good ...and yes, it is a big deal because I am also accountable for him. ...whatever his age! ...I'm accountable in that I cannot (will never) cease being concerned for his ultimate (eternal) Spiritual well being. ..that concern is probably the greater part of my own well being.

...to fervently and effectually care for another .... be it child, spouse, friend ...

(I suppose even a pet) ...is a great blessing on it's own. ....but even that blessing can become complicated and confusing when we introduce elements from without God's envelope of what please Him.

...that may be what satan did to get ousted from God's provision???...God must have entrusted something of great value to satan's care which satan eventually fouled ...whether through intent or "mere" neglect. ...whatever it was ...God saw through the deceit just as He sees through ours.) ...to live for the "moment" seems to be the prominent recipe for most ...and maybe put a little aside for retirement. (although I don't think "retirement" is within the Bible's envelope of what pleases God). ...but suppose we take "retirement" out of our "life" recipe and (Heaven forbid) replace it with "continue" ("continue" is a prominent element of the Bible's ingredients (envelope) of what pleases God. ...our physical (earning) race may only be 65 or 70 years long ....the "spiritual continuing" has no earthly limits or bounds ....as we are graced by God with

the wherewithal then regardless of age are we to continue in seeking ...and then further sharing of His providence.

...especially sharing with the young if, through age or infirmity, we are restricted. (Titus 2: 4) "That they may teach the young ...." (verse 12) "Teaching us that denying ungodliness and worldly lusts, we should live soberly, righteously and Godly in this present world." (verse 13) Looking for that blessed hope of salvation". ...the importance of any church maintaining strict adherence to God's word and also inviting it's patrons to exhort the church to do so lies in our corporate tendency towards the lukewarm. ...once a church adopts the "lukewarm" ...then the "exhortation" (every Christian's calling) becomes "heresy" should one be out of-line with the lukewarmness of any given church. ...what a debilitating predicament to be bound by the doctrines of a lukewarm church.

(Rev. 3: 16) "So then because thou art lukewarm, I will spue thee out of my mouth." (Rev. 2: 29) "He that hath an ear, let him hear what the Spirit saith unto the churches." (Rev. 3: 6) (Rev. 3: 3) "Remember therefore how thou hast received and heard, and hold fast, and repent."

...if there's not many repentant churches then how can there be many repentant members...if and when we walk by faith then God's word will verify our walk. ....only with humble and repentant attitudes can all be well with our soul

...whatever befalls us, whatever our pain ...shock or anger ...God's will is good and perfect and in the end He will clarify that, if we remain faithful.

(Rom. 8: 28) "all things work together for good for those who love the Lord."

...I don't think they will for those who don't. ...much of what appears good isn't good at all if it's apart from God's word. ...without God's word there is no "lamp unto our feet" so how much more quickly or more serious will be our stumble?

…the Bible doesn't say that any particular denomination is a "light unto our paths."

…only that God's word is …through what His Spirit reveals to the seeking heart.

…and I don't think it's 'God's Spirit" that has me parked in front of a football game or soap opera or American idol …nor on a flight to Disneyland …that would more likely indicate His Spirit's absence.

…some Bible translations suggest (in Romans 14: 23) that whatever we think is alright is fine by God.   …maybe I should just be more confident in my own thinking …although the Bible also says to "lean not to my own understanding."

(Prov. 3: 5)   …I don't suppose it's a problem, provided my own understanding complies with God's word. …Spiritual growth can be a real challenge but it can be an enjoyable challenge.   …dead to self, yet alive in Christ, should position us in the world but not of the world. …quietly fulfilled with the bread of life and hungry for more.   …can the (commonly referred to) "good life" (of our neighbors down the street) ever be ours?

…to believe in God is much more than accepting that there probably is a God.

…rather "to believe" is to "experience such of His presence in us that all doubt is removed. …it's that experience that constitutes being born again in the Spirit …and never again share the "good life" of our neighbor down the street.

…it sort of sounds like the pits …right? ….it's the exact opposite of "the pits". …the Bible suggests it's more like "the sow becoming the lamb" …instead of groveling in the dirt of the world, one gets to appreciate the separation from worldly dirt. …for the Christian to say "I'll try this born again thing for now …as a general rule" …it's the lukewarm form of faith that will quickly descend to deceit.

(John 3: 3) …the Bible says …that except we be "born again (experience) of the Spirit" …then we are (of our own choosing and neglect) doomed to hell.

…it doesn't matter if we think …"if I were God - I would never impose that misery on anyone!" …I imagine every prisoner on every death row says the same thing …bit it's not exactly through a roll-of-the-dice that they've found themselves where they are …yet even those people can repent through Christ and live their lives (such as it is) without fear. ...I don't see where the Bible suggests there is a "gradient" hell. ...like it or not ...the unrepentant child killer and the unrepentant philanthropist (doer of good) share the same fate.

...we are not "of His flock" (His people) until we are "born again" through surrender to Christ's Spirit ...after which He directs our ways by His light and also at which point we no longer "resemble our" neighbor down the street ...but rather ...in our non-

resemblance ...care for his eternity. ...three times, in the Bible, Christ says (Matt. 16: 24) "if any will come after (follow) me, let them deny themselves, take up my cross and follow after me. ...and that those who don't will lose their life ..yet those who do .. will find life. ...a measure of that life is in the caring that others not commit Spiritual suicide.

...perhaps most have heard and yet declined God's plea ..and perhaps it's unfortunate that it's fallen on us to be a pest for Christ. ...I'm sure my son, Richard, thinks I'm a pest ...but I have no option! ....how can we love Christ yet not care that another burn in hell forever? ....it's not possible! ...do I know if another has 30 years to change their ways? ...or 10? ...or 1? ...or only even a few hours? ...am I only human? ...can I rest in "if only I had known I would have said something to that fella down the street." ...for the "dead to self" Christian, being only human is to be the far lesser (if any) part of their conduct.

..."only human" is to be what we've traded in for "life more abundant" in sharing Christ with those we meet.

...a song we sang in church this morning says "I've traded my sorrow ...I've traded my pain ...I've traded it all for the joy of the Lord." (interesting that the tune reminds me of a song called "It drives me crazy" by a group called "Fine Young Cannibals" ...maybe more bizarre than interesting)

...if we haven't "traded in" the same worldly pleasures that the non-Christian treasures then doesn't our verbal professing of "faith and new life" begin to look a bit thin and yet just as thin is our defense that, despite our interests reflecting those of non Christian, we are not addicted to those interests like the non-Christian is.

…it's like the smoker claiming he's not addicted to tobacco but rather just enjoys smoking. (…that logic only works until the listener reaches the age of 7 or 8)

…I don't quite know what a non believer sees when he comes to find out that his neighbor is Christian as opposed to an average (normal) guy like himself.

…would his "finding out" explain anything? …or would he simply think "yeh …so?"

…does the Christian want all the same worldly comforts and toys as the

non-Christian plus the hope of salvation besides? ….even though the Bible says it's not remotely possible? …its possible only if we reduce "God's word" to encompass "people's wants" …and recent translations are moving ever closer to that end. …there is a modest pie of Christian interest …and it must be easy for the generic church to get caught up in it's physical well-being and the size of piece it can carve out for itself. ….but that's not synonymous with "vigilance to maintain and grow "in Christ's church. ….in the Bible, it's called "holding fast" …salvation is free but not negotiable. …I wish churches could be in the re-assurance business but they can't. ….assurance of our eternities can be only "strong hope" at best but hope is an essence of our lives from youth. …other than negatives …what have we ever made effort to attain that we didn't first hope for? …school grades, presents, gainful employment, relationships, healthy children …the list goes on.

(John 3: 16) …God so loved the world that he gave (sacrificed) His only son so that whosoever believeth in Him should not perish but have everlasting life".

…that's not to say that those who simply say "I believe in God" are automatically saved for eternity. (Rom. 8: 9) …we have to be "Christian" to be saved

…and the Bible also says that except the Holy Spirit of Christ be in you (dead to self) then we're not yet a Christian. …I guess the long and short of it is

…no Holy Spirit = no salvation. …and if we have the Holy Spirit in us then we'll strive to know and advance the will of God …and even that effort doesn't warrant assurance of salvation …because satan easily fools us into false confidence.

…our assurance can't be in our salvation …but it can be in our hope of salvation. …in finally graduating high school, we don't write our final exam then go and sign our own graduation diplomas. …there is an authority that holds that power.

…salvation lies in continually preparing and gladly so for us, lest we fall short. …the Bible says "few are chosen" …many claim clean hands, pure hearts, humility and no deceit …yet not many are sufficiently refined by the refiner's fire, hence are few chosen. …I know I frequently take my eye off the prize (which is my hope of being among the few) …in this race I run, I even frequently take my eye off the finish line! …sometimes even off the track beneath my feet! …that "carelessness" is all going to change immediately! …(what I mean is ..immediately after the Super Bowl game and a few other important issues that are presently occupying my thoughts …plus, I think I may be coming down with a head cold …so that's also bound to cause some slackness in faith pursuing.)

(Phil. 2: 12) …when the Bible says to "continue working out our own salvation." …it means "under ideal conditions" …right? ….and because God knows our weaknesses …He has mercy on us …right? ….God doesn't expect us to seek more of Him if we're distracted ….right? …doesn't the Bible say "there's a time for every purpose under Heaven? …so, of course, when we're distracted isn't the time to be seeking more of Him. …God is pretty good that way in that He doesn't just whack us simply because we're distracted. (…I wonder what the record is for testing God's benevolence, yet escaping hell?) ….where I live, drinking and driving is .03 tolerance before we get zapped." …God's tolerance is probably higher …right? ….Super Bowl, Disneyland, Academy Awards, etc. probably elevated God's tolerance considerably …so we're probably okay provided the distraction warrants our departure from God. …right? …plus, if we go to church regularly and do some good deeds then God would look favorably on that …for sure! …but woe to those Christians who don't even do that! …right? …I wonder what the fascination of both sin and fire is …that we love to play with it even knowing full well the risk of being burned. (actually …I guess we don't know the "risk" full well …if we see someone with the scars of having been in a fire then we can generally turn away our grotesque imaginings of what they must have endured. …our protection is our disbelief and with our burning in sin, it's our disbelief that will eventually cause our burning but there'll be no turning away in that grotesque experience. …objectively, (with no family member or friend in sports) I usually pull for (support) the underdog or less advantaged team.

…in the Spirit realm, there are only two teams …being "faith" (God) and "sin" (satan) …the Bible says we have to support God, period! …and that even if we have no interest in the game we nonetheless support sin. …without objectivity ….we can soon come to

tolerate (support) what is not good. …even a kind heart sympathizes with apparent struggle, often without discerning that the struggle may ultimately be harmful or sinful (i.e. women's rights, abortion, gay rights, wars, casinos, etc.) …this reminds me of movies I've seen years ago (Day of the Jackal" …or more recently "Bridges of Madison County") where, because of struggle or adversity, we empathizes with wrongdoing. …without a firm Bible based stance of right and wrong, we are left in a fog of indecision …worse yet, it appears to be within satan's present power to change the Bible! …I don't think I know any gay people (that's neither of credit nor discredit to me) but I believe I've stated in the past, that "I don't care if gay is right or wrong, just keep them away from my son." …I now see that it's wrong for me to "not care" …both about the sin and about those who advocate it. …to "not care" is perhaps the root of sin. …is it not the root of death? …can "apathy" be any part of "life more abundant"? …are there lesser issues which are not attached to greater issues? …"either of faith or of sin" …understanding or not …it was sin that took off the head of John the Baptist …it was sin that nailed Christ to a cross …and sin that caused torture and death to so many of God's advocates (children) and does so yet today. …we ask "what kind of God would create a burning tormented eternity for us harmless, fun loving people even though we sin a little? …it's not us "people" for whom God has established a forever tormented hell. …it's a place of punishment for the "sin" that causes God such grief …and if that causes God such grief ….and if we have attached ourselves (through not caring (negligence) or self pride (ego) or choosing some other treasure above His word and His Spirit ...if we have chosen to attach ourselves to other than faith in Him ...then we go to the same judgment as the "sin" we have accommodated (housed). ...the Bible says Christ (mediator) is merciful up to a point. ...eventually, those who continue to choose sin will effectively, through their choices, invite Christ to wash His hands of them and just leave them alone.

...there are ample precedents in the Bible of such peoples

...opportunity, after opportunity, after opportunity, has gone unheeded?

(Rom. 8: 17) "Now it is no more I that do it but sin that dwelleth in me."

...if we choose not to be the dwelling place of faith ...we are the dwelling place of sin and wishing it weren't so ...is probably "sin" also. ...we have to do something about it. ...I'm certain that what we don't do is every bit as much of "sin" as those things we do that are not of faith. ...we may pay a tolerable price for it just now but no man knows the hour of his death and I expect that even at the end of this day, thousands, world-wide, will have too long delayed repenting and will have sealed their own fate. ...when it comes to our eternity, the world might be our oyster ...but its also a can of gasoline and we are a match. ...interestingly, given the state of many churches today, the pastor who is a "good fit" for the people of the church is probably not the best pastor for it. ...most congregations aren't looking to be challenged (exhorted) in their ways when that's rather what we probably need most. ...on papers this morning, I was thinking about the Apostle Paul and the blessing his near continual imprisonment has brought to the cause of Christ. ...without imprisonment, I expect he would have visited and spoken to the churches rather than write the letters from which we, today, can gain so much inspiration and direction.

...perhaps God spoke particularly strong to me this morning ...in any case, it was sufficient that for the first time ...I wished others could be me and enjoy that particular stretch of road that I was covering. (I haven't thought it through ...but I hope that's a good thing.) ...I particularly wished it for my friend that is in constant physical pain.

…a while back …when I saw through a glass even more darkly than I now do …I recall suggesting to Christians that religion was merely a crutch and an escape from reality.

…if a "crutch" is something apart from myself on which I depend …then I was right. …and escape from the world? …of course it is! …plus escape from hell in the next world to boot. …where I was wrong, was in suggesting "merely" …there is nothing in faith to which the word "mere" applies. …to be sufficiently broken to need Christ, is huge …to repent is huge …to submit to His Spirit and His leading is huge …the joy and peace of doing that is huge and the hope of eternal salvation is huge as the diminishing fear of death is given over to the One who gives life. …nothing is "mere" …everything is significant. (Matt. 11: 28) Christ said, "Come unto me, all ye that labor and are heavy laden and I will give you rest." (James 4: 8) "Draw near to God and He will draw near unto you." ….the sooner we tire of our own "mere ness" the sooner we can submit and connect directly to His overwhelming capacity to provide for our needs. …through Christ's Spirit we can open ourselves to pleasures and inner peace that remains unknown (and always will remain unknown) to those who turn away from God. …through sin, the wretchedness we experience through the unexplainable loss of a child or loved one, will perhaps be likened to the wretchedness of one's eternity in hell. …on earth, God's blessings fall on the just and the unjust. …the defiant and the unthankful have no idea (nor do I) what the termination of God's mercy is going to entail but the Bible attempts to warn us in many descriptive passages which even the modern churches largely bypass because of their unpopularity …and church leaders will be called to a greater judgment for so doing. …even so, you and I and every professed Christian are Christ's church …not Baptist nor Pentecostal nor catholic but just ourselves …those who carry Christ's Spirit in them. …our homes are our church …our children and visitors are our congregation. …what we promote, allow and tolerate under our own roofs is what we'll be called to answer for at judgment. …heck …come judgment (and it will come) we may not even have hands or fingers to point at anyone else! ….then, will we know fear.

…(aside) …there's a ditty or writing (by Max Sherman) called Desiderata.

…my Mom liked it and the writing hung in a small room in my folk's home.

…my Dad never liked it. (married life …..eh?) …it's very peaceful and I admire my mom for liking it and I admire my Dad for tolerating my Mom's wish and also for making known his protest. …a portion of that writing states "you are a child of the universe …you have a right to be here" which conflicts big time with scripture and in particular (Psa. 139). (I'm not a nosey person …but if I get to Heaven, I think it would be nice if God granted me access to the conversation "that preceded that saying being hung in my folks home. I realize that's not likely to happen even should I make the cut)

…anyway …that saying is an example of tolerance towards what is "not too distant" from God's word. …unfortunately …gravity most often takes over, wherein "a form of Godliness" moves to the upper room.

…when we accommodate the "Spiritually negative" then it's unlikely the "positive" will be regained. …what we tolerate and accommodate we generally propagate …and that's what both impacts us (and ours) negatively and it's also what we are answerable for. …there is no "Godly" negative …there's only "worldly" negative ….and it's the "worldly negative" that sucks us into darkness. (2 Cor. 6: 17) …maybe that's what the Bible means when it says to "come out from amongst them and be ye separate." …to the extent that we can, we ought wash our hands of the emotionally unstable and those we can't trust, lest we be drawn into their

downward vortex into darkness. …God's word is a light yet if one, having been told, still refused God's light (2 Tim. 3: 5) "from such turn away." …a "little" knowledge is a dangerous thing …and so is "assurance" of salvation beyond doubt. …I hope I always "fear" presumptuous assurance and rather always continue working out my salvation whether with "fear and trembling" or not. (Phil. 2: 12)

…then again …maybe there's a "cut-off" …where God doesn't give us any more stuff (concerns) to work out. …although that seems hard to believe.

…do some Christians get their diplomas in advance of their exams? …I think it's more likely that we maybe get shown our diplomas from a distance but we can't see that they haven't been signed yet …(a proud imagination is also a dangerous thing.)

(Rom. 8: 9) …the Bible says that to be Christian …requires that the Holy Spirit be in us (in our hearts and in our minds) …so we need to be aware of satan's (sin's) temptations to (in effect) soil that Holiness. I know that's not possible, so sin can, at best, separate us from God's gift of Holiness, and thus separate us from Him. (that can happen, unless we surrender control of our lives to Christ, then in His strength we can turn from temptation.) everything of faith is pleasing to God. …anything not of faith is not …because it's of sin. (Rom. 14: 23)

(Psa. 34: 8) …once we sincerely "taste God and see that He is good"(…after we accept His light for our path) then we become aware (knowledgeable) of what constitutes encroaching darkness

…as we encourage (feed) Christ's Spirit to grow in us, more and more, do we realize how prevalent darkness is in this world. (it's the very wide road …and it's inviting, almost beyond resistance.) (personally, as a somewhat novice Christian, if it weren't for fear of hell, I'd probably be inclined to go for the wide road …even despite my having been on it already and knowing that it's empty of completeness …nevertheless, the world calls out to me to follow the path of least resistance.

(Jer. 17: 10) "God searcheth the heart" …and He knows our desires and our treasures of the heart. …satan doesn't have the knowledge that God has …but satan can see our weaknesses and can feed our weaknesses if we allow him to.

…despite appearances to the contrary, not all that seems good ….is, in the end. …only Christ's Spirit in us can cut through any illusion that satan presents as good.

…in the parable of the shepherd and his flock, also lies a message of the new covenant. …although not all his sheep are identical in every way and though his provision and care is without partiality, there will be no hint of individual gluttony in his fold …nor will there be any who are lean because of want while others are fat because of plenty. …to love our brothers and sisters as ourselves removes that option if we are actually of Christ's flock. …and though Christ be, just now, out looking for His lost sheep, His church (flock) has been left with His comforter and His written word by which to conduct themselves until His return. …His "word" is the flock's discernment" should any deceitful sheep attempt to enter the fold and deceitfully influence the flock towards anything untoward or not of faith. …when we walk by faith, God's word will verify it …and our hands, eyes and ears will comply to it. …true faith, is like stepping off a ledge onto the sheer face of a mountain …yet being drawn upwards in defiance of gravity. …our own natures (sinful) would be like gravity drawing us down to certain death and worse. (Phil. 2: 12) "Fear and trembling" are not words to scare us …but rather words to warn us.

…if not for the looming precipice of hell, we might choose to remain apart from God (lost) or perhaps accept some other religion that promises re-incarnation or cosmic rebirth …then, after death, complain that God should have created some drastic alternative …whatever it takes, to impress upon us the importance of our complying with His will.

…as it is today …even God's mercy to us in His plainly describing hell has little to no effect. …would that He give us a greater taste now of what lies ahead.

…have we ever been so blessed …yet so unappreciative? …nearly all is taken for granted. …it may "just be our nature?" …but it's our sinful nature. …our past experience is our "source of reference" …but I sometimes think it's a sort-of disgusting source of reference.

…it's true that, today, we haven't a cure for cancer …but 500 years ago we probably didn't even have anesthetic! (apart from a 2 x 4 across the head) …speaking of hell and gnashing of teeth …imagine a root canal with no anesthetic or an amputation! …imagine the tormented death (perhaps of an only child) through gangrene or, even further back, leprosy.

…evolution hasn't given us minds to accomplish great gains in medicine or science ..God has given these to us …yet most don't give that a second thought but rather complain. ...even eyeglasses are a huge blessing! ...can you imagine hospital waiting lists or botched surgeries if doctors had no eyeglasses?

...these critical advances aren't just a matter of chance ...they're blessings and opportunity for all to give thanks to God.

...if I sacrificed to buy an early 60s Austin Healey for my son (mint shape) and he took it for granted ...I would, of course, be displeased (mad as stink!)

...(I doubt it's why God made trees ...but that 2 x 4 that I mentioned earlier might help me express to Richard my displeasure.) ...I know I have nowhere near attained God's measure of kindness or mercy. ...it's a good thing (a start) that I'm only impetuous in my thinking and not in my actions ...and I know Christ said I'm not even to "think" like that.

...I'm not above beating sense into Richard but I guess, in fairness ...I'd have to also supply him with a piece of wood of equal or even larger size. (...best just to continue to harangue him) ...I know I'm weak in many areas of life, so when I pray for Richard or others, I try to pray, not for what they ask ...nor what I want for them ...but rather pray that their heart receive a measure of encouragement in any area that is now or will be pertinent to God's Will being done on earth ...and I pray that all other efforts be befuddled.

...of the only two spiritual teams ...it's not enough that we only pick one team to support ...we have to rather support one team in defeating the other. ...neutral" is never an option. (Matt. 12: 30) ...we're either for Christ ...or we're against Christ. ...no bleachers to sit in ...and no side-lines to wander. ....if we draw breath (are alive) then we are in the game ...and accountable. ...as with every free will choice, God doesn't make (force) us acknowledge hell. ..."denial" is certainly a game plan but it's, for sure, not of God's game plan. ...so then whose? ...I don't know why but it seems we're too easily offended these days. ...so was Christ easily offended? ...if my friend Dave is a non smoking, non drinking vegetarian and I'm none of those, can I not put aside those things when I'm with him, if it adds to his comfort? ...none of those things defiles man. ...a friend is interested in your heart or your essence ....all the rest is superficial preference and of little consequence to "all being well with your soul". ...through Christ's Spirit, the treasure of our heart is to be the hearts of others. ...I watched some of a television program today where a popular media psychologist or psychiatrist vowed to offer every help at his disposal to aid the healing of a troubled young man. ....but I don't think he will. ...I do think he'll offer every help that he chooses to offer. (i.e. choices that are acceptable to the show's producers and the majority viewers) ...his choices could be very limited and perhaps of no avail whatsoever. ...apparent good can, actually, firmly establish great harm. ...creating employment is good ....right?

...(I can hear my mother's chair begin to move away from the dinner table) ...anyway ..."confusion" creates employment ...right? ...just as "efficiency" generally reduces employment. ...employment feeds families and families maintain the supply and demand required for commerce....right? ...so whatever the source of employment there will at least come some good. ....right? ...if our son's and daughters are doctors and lawyers then we want them to have sufficient work and do well ....right? ....for them to do well, a need of their talents must be present ....right? ...so a little harmless pain and suffering or a little confusion in legal matters will be required for our sons and daughters to advance in their work ...right?

...after years of sacrifice and training "no available work" would not likely be construed as a blessing, ...right? ...life's like a box of chocolates. .....right?

...a good friend recently suggested I might be interested in a seminar at the church on "communicating with an ex spouse" ...being given by a church lady.

...my mind immediately shifted to a book I'd read (pre-divorce) called Venus and Mars Together Forever. ....that's the book where one part says other than what they mean in hopes that the other party will spend hour upon hour presenting possible meanings until they hit upon the right meaning ...except that, in the interim, the original meaning has by now changed thus allowing the process to continue into infinity. (...I don't even like monopoly!) ...I do, however, appreciate my friend's (lady friend's) good intentions. ...we can't like everyone ...yet even with people whom we may dislike …if it's Christ in me and not the "emotional ME" in me talking …then where's the problem in communicating? …at least briefly and in a civil manner? …we know it's God's will that we all get along. …so although I may wash my hands of deceitful people perhaps the Christ in me hasn't …yet??? …as Christian, I may expire my own "limited" efforts at reconciliation but am I not to also represent Christ's bountiful efforts towards our getting along with each other? …only through Christ's salvation can we know inner peace and only in our sharing (displaying) Christ's kindness and forgiveness will others seek interest in His ways. …bitterness, hostility, self-pity and withdrawal are not of Christ nor of His Spirit on earth. …those negative things can all be healed …just not by us

…though we may be required to confront them on occasion …we are not to associate (be a part) with them …lest we get dragged down with them.

…I've heard just recently, that our bodies are either alkaline or acidic …and that cancer will not, cannot live in alkaline. …and further, that through diet and attitude, we can control these factors. …I don't know if that's all true or not but it made me think of our spiritual lives. …the Bible says that … not God nor Christ nor the Holy Spirit can abide (accommodate) sin. (offence against God)

…to get a kd (knocked down) table from Ikea, look at the instructions then assemble the table incorrectly, ignoring the instructions …isn't sin ….it's a mistake or error unless we wanted something apart from the manufacturer's intent.

…however …to seek faith and look at God's word (instructions) then ignore His word to acquire a "form" of His intent …that isn't a mistake …it's sin.

…it's knowingly choosing to offend God. …no church, no pastor nor spouse nor friend can identify sin in our lives …only Christ's Spirit can do that.

…we can minimize sin, I suppose, by putting out of mind, the more challenging aspect of personal faith …we just can't be "Christian" and do that.

…a popular faith would then be one in which a "personal allegiance to Christ" is side-stepped in favor of "allegiance to a less demanding body" or organization.

…a "middle man", so to speak, between us and Christ. …a church, of some form, would duly qualify as a worthy entity for such an enterprise.

…the beauty of a church …is that it's also democratic in nature …the "majority" can mold it to it's "respectable" will. …why get bogged down in a "personal challenge" when it can be shared by a "group" …to our mutual satisfactions. …churches like stability …just like we do ourselves …but too often stability entails maintaining the status quo in support of unity …but maybe against faith and truth. …does the status quo of a church have to be it's lowest common denominator? …must we "shut down" the encouraging of every area of growth so that a "few" not be offended or feel left out??? …then how long before any given church becomes about "being One" …as opposed to it's being "one in the Spirit"? …no person or group can fulfill in us that

which only Christ is meant to satisfy. …have we strayed so far from God that our striving is now reduced to be for just any form of peace? …peace in the world? ….peace among neighbors? …peace in the home?

… "inner peace" isn't the absence of conflict or pain or stress or anxiety …won't that just leave us with nothingness? …sleep? …apathy?

…we're no less dead just because we don't realize we're dead. …"inner peace" is not an absence of something but rather the presence of something for better …of "someone" far better than the best we can make of ourselves. …inner peace is going to bed saying "thank you God" and waking up saying "thank you God" even though it may appear that we don't have all that much. …thankful even for the many things (illnesses) we don't have that we don't want.

…to be focused on what the "world" can supply is also to invite the darkness of being blind-sided by a myriad of unknown side-effects that prowl about like a hungry lion, seeking whom it may devour." (1 Peter 5: 8) …without God's protection (armor) through His Spirit, we are without defense.

…the computer virus is perhaps a good analogy of our odds without God's protection through His instruction and mercy. …instead of humbling us, we proudly and defiantly alter His instruction to encompass the evil side-effects. ....woe is me!" (Isa. 6: 5) ...we are "undone", at our own hands.

...many of us don't give a second's thought to God nor even claim belief in God ...until a tragedy like 911 strikes ...then we cry out to the God we don't believe in, for explanation ...or to question "why wasn't He watching our for us...!

(...I was jesting with a friend on the phone last night ...how my secret to being bold ...is always having someone to blame when I'm wrong ...although I was only wrong just that once ...when I thought I'd made a mistake.)

...what is it that's at the very root of our undoing, through our own choices???

...I don't think we're just plain dumb yet we seem intent on despoiling every good gift from God ....even down to our children ...good intent is right up there with wishful thinking. ...I've read somewhere that the smallest good deed is better than the grandest

intention and it's free. ...without the "interest" and "effort" then "intentions" are useless ...even "net-negative" because of their lazy deceit. ...both our positive and our negative choices and actions are largely dictated by the company we keep. ...misery may love company but joy loves company also.

...we both choose friends and are also chosen as friends by likeminded people. ...neither God nor satan want us to be lonely. ...we are encouraged and discouraged by what surrounds us. ...the Christian is clearly advised throughout the Bible as to the character their companions and spouses are to emulate. ...if an anti-Christian or non-Christian implores us to read a certain book or see a certain film or go a certain place ...then it's probably best that we don't. ...with today's technology, the mere touch of a button can land us and those we love where we're not suppose to be. ...a lonely spouse or child can find their dream friend in an on-line chat room of unknown origin.

...where people with zero credibility can fill our ears with everything we wish was in our spouse or parent ...every encouragement to self-pity and devious ways to attain what we want. ...even with television ...it used to be that if we restrained our viewing to the basic dozen or so channels there was reasonable safety for families.

(1Thes. 5: 21) when we don't "hold fast to that which is good" then good departs. ...it doesn't just happen" as we may like to think ...it's caused by people not caring ...and the "bad" that fills the vacuum calls out to the majority to fight for every lawful freedom, whether short-sighted or not. ...when we begin forgetting to be thankful ...we begin selfishness and no good thing will come of that.

...personally, I have been dealt many high cards which I've squandered ...loving Christian parents, good health, etc. ...I'm blessed far beyond what I deserve yet even with my stumbles I'm able to help, a little, those who have been less blessed. ...I know very little anxiety or fear ...which frees me to be a friend (hopefully) to others who have been dealt fewer high cards.

...we are not all created equal and maybe it's God's test for those who have been given more ...to see what use we put our blessings (talents) to.

...it's usually us who are given much (that we might help others) that help ourselves to gain even more for ourselves. ...there's a good Bible parable that relates what "end" awaits people like that ...it's not friendly and it's not pretty.

(Matt. 25: 30) "And cast ye the unprofitable servant into outer darkness: there shall be weeping and gnashing of teeth". (verse 46) "And these shall go away into everlasting punishment: but the righteous into life eternal."

...I don't see anywhere in God's word where being "good natured" (of goodly nature) presents any reprieve from "everlasting" punishment (hell)

...no amount of "natural hope" is ever going to change that.

...my dad gave one of my brothers the boot (sent from the house) for exhausting my dad's patience with his defiance of authority. ....the remaining brood learned a valuable lesson in the "tempting fate" department. (...my dad and brother were about the same size when that happened, so I reckon it was fair fight.)

...my dad's actions weren't natural ..but they were right, given the circumstances.

...God's actions don't align with our natures but they're not only right

…they're perfect. …no amount of squawking or complaining will ever change that. …He made everything …so He is the authority. …do you have what you believe to be a better plan? …maybe replace God with Mother Nature? …save the environment? …hug the trees? …but what about the hungry …in third world countries? ….shouldn't they come first? …there are many many commendable causes …vegetarianism seems good, sustainable environment sounds good. …there is no good cause not covered in the Bible ….plus ..His plan carries His blessing …the surrender of our own agenda (pride) is the "natural" impediment. …there's no harm in saying "it's only natural that we want our own issues dealt with."

…that's actually a good thing because it's "honest" …but it's important to accept that others may differ and allow to them equal passion for their issues.

…I don't think any adult person goes long without "a" god. …if not God of the Bible …then some other focus. …ego would have ourselves as gods or whatever brings us greatest pleasure and sustains our needs …addictions could be gods.

…it seems our slowly maturing, finite minds seek "tangible" gods until we come to realize that they are inadequate to fill an inner void in us.

…at that point we may or may not seek to taste what is not tangible but rather what is "hoped" for. …it's generally our culture and parents who have or haven't provided options from which we might choose. …no matter …it's ourselves who are accountable for our choices and for any repercussions from our choices.

…if the world goes to heck in a hand-basket, then in a democracy it's the majority who are accountable for their choices. …for the Christian, each is accountable to God for what they have silently allowed or what they have failed to encourage. …one cannot be a sincere Christian yet not be a disciple (promoter) of Christ. …His Spirit in the Christian …not might ..but will absolutely compel the Christian to share all that God shares with them. …if the world is not blessed through the essence (Spirit) of your God being in you … untie your horse from whatever wagon you've previously chosen and seek that better God. …the true God doesn't offer the casual or empty or mundane route…but rather the "hold onto your hat, life more abundant" route …life even more and more abundant after death in this life!

…we don't need a magic genie, we just need God, if we want real life.

(Prov. 3: 5) …the Bible says for us to "lean not to our own understanding" ….except, of course, it be within God's word. …to the extent to which we surrender to Him …will He also give us of His wisdom and understanding …for which we, unavoidably, are grateful to Him. …through gratitude and praise to God, do also the petty things of this life grow strangely dim.

…interestingly, all the years I've spent away from the Christian faith (and people of Christian faith) I'd always thought that Christians were "kind of weird" …now I find I was always right ….we are "kind of weird".

…at church, last night, there was a noticeable number of empty seats (…I was a bit late but when I saw the empty seats I thought I must be early)

…when I opened the bundles of newspapers this morning I saw on the front page that the "Oscar Awards" was on television last night. …I'm sure I used to be interested in

those things! …I even have a televison! …now I have to face my 18 year old son and confess that "no, I didn't watch it." …and then once again he'll smile, shake his head and tell me how I'm "so out-of it." (maybe I can save a little face if I just don't volunteer that I was at church instead)

…I've been there and I know a young fella can only handle so much "weird" in his dad. (although …I'm still impressed that Richard invited me to "chill" with him and his buddies for an evening! ….(probably need a "get-away" driver)

…to be a sincere and seeking Christian …then probably the only persons you're not going to seem "weird" to …are other sincere seeking Christians. …(like-minded attracts like-minded). …there's a certain limited comfort …or at least a freedom from intimidation …in being in the company of like-minded people. …it may not be joy …but at least it's not fear and a little relief from fear means a lot to a lot of people.

…I would hope that the good (God) in all companionship is nourished and built up…if "good" is built up …it can lead nowhere except to God's will on earth.

(James 1: 17) …the Bible say, "Every good gift and every perfect gift is from above and cometh down from the Father…." …and so all credit is due Him. …sorry but that's just life (more abundant) that we don't get any credit. …poor us …eh? …it's funny that violins aren't more popular ….given how frequently we feel they should be heard. …my son endured a brief few years of school violin

…the home practice was sometimes excruciating! …being a home-dad, I didn't balk much at his request to quit. …but piano …I endured and pushed for 'til he cleared grade 8. …which I attribute greatly my premature white hair to, at age 39. (right… me and Jack Benny) …anyway …"piano" is in him now, for good …and God's seed is in him now, for good. …he may spend some time trying to shake off one or the other or both …but won't be able to. …that's a big part of my job done, as regards Richard. …hopefully we'll both progress on parallel paths rather than divergent. …one or the other of us always looking to see if the other needs help. …piano is a slow process …and trust in God is a slow process …but …like piano …if we persevere and practice just what the instruction says …the rewards are phenomenal.

…not overnight or over days …but for sure, over time. …and like piano …without practice the promise of life more abundant becomes frustrating. …satan wants us frustrated so he can come between us and God. …frustration is weakness and that's where satan thrives, in our weakness.

(James 4: 7) …the Bible says "Submit yourself, therefore to God. Resist the devil and he will flee from you." (verse 10) "humble yourself in the sight of the Lord and He shall lift you up." …when satan flees, then all the garbage that's a part of him is flushed out along with him. …imagine a serenity that's free from negative garbage! …if we're enjoying much of the "world" …then it'll be a big adjustment …but the alternative is short-term gain here and now and eternal (everlasting) pain, later. …I'm not the sharpest tool in the shed …but even I am not so dumb as to gamble on "the alternative".

…for professed Christians, who enjoyed the Oscar Awards ..did the Holy Spirit in them also enjoy the program? …I'm not even suggesting it's impossible ..only that as we go through life the focus of our eyes reveals the desires of our hearts.

…we see what we're looking for …had my son, Richard, been with me last evening, I too would probably have watched …maybe even defended my actions with "family togetherness!" but who is the control under my roof? ..do I need a big piece of "world" so that my son sees worth in me? …is Christ's Spirit planting "lukewarm" seed through me? …if so, then for my son's sake, I'm better to denounce my pretense of the Spirit's presence and also of Christian faith and tell Richard to look elsewhere for an example of what Christ died to establish here on earth. …can I trust my conscience to be my guide over the Bible's truth and light?

…the reason I bristle if a brother or sister exhorts or questions my spiritual walk is my pride or arrogance. …the very things I'm suppose to have died to in my seeking Christ's Spirit in my heart. …we can find ourselves with very selective memories when ascribing what is of faith and what is of ourselves.

(Rom. 12: 2) …the Bible warns "And be not conformed to this world but be ye transformed by the renewing of your mind, that ye may prove what is that good and acceptable and perfect will of God."

…how quick am I to absolve myself of lukewarmness and even sin? …self-deceit is the worst deceit …in that it smothers even a glimpse of Christ's light in us. …do other relationships jeopardize "my Christ relationship"? …do I allow that? ….support that? …even use that as excuse or defense against my lukewarmness in faith?

…I need remember …and be reminded …that the Bible says there is but one source of personal forgiveness …being Christ. …I can't forgive myself, except I claim Christ's status as mediator …and if I weaken to deceive myself then the Bible says, God puts away from Him the deceitful heart.

(1 Peter 5: 5) "….for God resisteth the proud, and giveth grace to the humble."

(Psa. 101: 7) "…he that worketh deceit shall not dwell within my house."

…I believe we should all be considerate of others and tactful in conversation …but I think we all know people either at home or at church or at work …who easily take offence at near anything but praise.…there's little comfort or free exchange in conversation with people like that. …personally, I'd prefer to avoid them than risk offending them by speaking to them. …over-sensitivity is a prison, regardless of whether or not it's justified by any person …yet someone still needs to approach and share that these people don't have to isolate themselves in a prison of fear and hurt feelings (pride) …if insulted for their efforts, the Christian ought be able to deflect any insult to their strength (Christ) and not be dragged down to self-pity.

 …humble Christianity, is what the Bible calls us to.

…a "proud Christian" is an oxymoron (as is a "mini-gigantic" sale, in a store).

…where's the gain in claiming Christ as our first love yet remaining sensitive to exhortation? …a humble "demeanor" differs from a humble "heart". …do we too quickly claim the "deserts" of salvation without having eaten our "meal" of humble pie (shepherd's pie)?

…I spoke briefly with an adherent of "once saved-always saved" last night …and came away thinking of mathematics. (Phil. 2: 12) …in our calling to "continue to work out our own salvation" …it seems the math part ought to be "myself plus Christ."

…in broad terms "what is of me …needs and wants "what is of Christ" …"work out" doesn't mean "be assured of" …and "continue" doesn't mean sign your own graduation diploma. …my friend shared that she doesn't want to go through her entire life fearing she may so something to cause God to blot her name out of His "book of life". (Rev. 3: 5)

…another old friend, Tissa …didn't want to go through life like that either.

…he was part Christian, part Muslim, part Buddhist and a good hearted man.

…he's gone now but he's left me with no rest or comfort as regards his eternity.

...Tissa loved flowers and in his final few years was establishing his own small nursery. ...he could plant seed and nurture that seed to eventually become beautiful hanging baskets which graced the outside of many local homes.

...and I believe Tissa was a strongly spiritual man. ...near his end, Tissa shared how he was a bit offended at the increasing time I spend with Christian friends and Bible study, etc. ....I'm not sure I apologized sufficiently for that ...nor am I sure I ever could have. ...I guess, in the end, we all believe what we want to believe. ...I only know that I wouldn't trade my Christian upbringing and my present Christian friends (encouragement) for anything I've ever experienced.

...no "spiritual" walk is without regret ...nor is any worldly walk either ...but there is little of any relief from worldly regret. ...whereas in faith our regret is carried by the higher purpose of resisting those things which might lead us or others away from God's light. ...that "higher purpose" doesn't just come in the mail nor land on our doorstep. ...we have to seek it ...or go without "higher purpose". ...many are content with "lower purpose" ...that's their choice.

...I suppose some are content with "no" purpose but I think it's best to push for something! ...even if it's not for a faith ...don't just lay about buffeted by nothing. ...I expect a passion for something ...(anything!) will lead us to the right thing by and by. ...and whatever your passion ...share it with your children and others you love or care about. ...through sharing, won't our own reward be increased?

(Gal. 6: 7) ...the Bible says "Be not deceived, God is not mocked: for whatsoever a man soweth, that shall he also reap." (verse 8) "... he that soweth to the Spirit shall of the Spirit reap life everlasting." ...I guess that means that whatever our passion or whatever we treasure, then that's who or what we can count on to supply for our eternity after death here....I don't see how any sincere and seeking Christian would fear their not graduating unless they stop trying. ...in high school, I think, it was either grade ten or eleven that I failed but I didn't stop trying and in the end got my diploma.

…it wasn't a "piece of cake" for me ….then again, a fella could "die" from being given too much cake" if he's not careful. …maybe "what we're given" isn't so important to God as is "what we do" with whatever we are given.

…I guess anytime we have doubts as to our spiritual walk then it's logical that fear should settle on us …but to claim some distant security diploma is hardly the answer …but rather to inwardly seek the root of our doubts and alter our conduct to more greatly please Christ's Spirit in us will (the Bible says) alleviate all fear. …only through His Spirit can we know His perfect will. …whether we choose to seek more of Him and only His word, is a choice we each make and is evidenced in all we choose to see or hear or do. …maybe with all our new toys and new thinking ….we no longer want the old values of past generations.

…apostasy isn't new and "doubt" has probably always been a breeding ground for it but have we thrown out the baby with the bathwater? …we can't have it all. …as with my friend Tissa, I can't have new life if I continue to cling to the old, except any "old" I cling to be of God. …otherwise the "old" is an anchor holding me back …perhaps in "doubt". …God's perfect will …is in His perfect love …and only His "perfect love" casteth out "fear". (1 John 4: 18)

…I haven't seen my older brother for awhile and while speaking to him on the phone recently he shared that he couldn't imagine me living in a little tiny apartment …despite my affirming it was "great!" ….what's "great" isn't what I'm living in …it's what's living in me! …we each accommodate what lives in us.

…arsenic (I understand) smells good …sorta like almonds …maybe even looks like garlic salt ….it might appear and smell like something good to maybe put on a salad! …but when it gets inside you …it's deadly. …satan has cleverly made sin like that. …we may believe that there's lots of stuff we do that although not "of faith" …is certainly not "of sin". …it's just innocent stuff we like to do that doesn't hurt anyone else …"so just leave us alone and don't bring up that monkey business about seeing through a glass darkly! ….that stuff is fine for priests or preachers but it's not for us normal people!" …a little pride or arrogance can be a crippling blow to faith.

...I'm curious as to how many "always-saved" Christians have in confidence shared with those of other faiths ..only to find themselves weakened and compromised by their own assurance.

...it isn't for nothing, that the Bible warns against being conformed to beliefs or treasures that don't encourage growing in the "Spirit of Christ". ...my good friend doesn't want to feel she's always being tested ...but I don't see what's wrong with that challenge. ...do we suppose there aren't those in our daily lives who wouldn't like to see us weakened in faith for their own subjective advantage? ...do we think that "once saved" we are immediately and forever encased in God's protective armor? ...or that it's God's responsibility from that point on to ensure we arrive safely and well rested at the finish line? ...neither our daily lives nor even our churches are free from satan's influence. ....every brick of the Bible that is abandoned by our churches is a victory for satan and cause for concern as to what is and isn't being presented there. ...a pointed example is the growing prevalence of abortion or gay lifestyle or "mature subject matter" in books and film. ...as we become aware that someone close to us is willingly acquainted with those issues then we don't want to hear them mentioned in our churches nor be made aware of what the Bible says about them. ...that isn't the "perfect love" of God ...it's covering our ears and eyes or putting our heads in the sand.

...how selectively tolerant and accepting do we want to become in bypassing God's word? ...as God's laws fall ...can man's laws be far behind? ...where will it end?

...it seems that when we're blessed with relative peace within our own shores, we self destruct morally. ...will we again question "how could God let this happen?"

...there's a disturbing song (from the 60s or 70s) called "Tin Soldier" about a people, with self-limited light, destroying the source of light in their frustration to have more of it. ...that we tolerate limited corruption, even in our officials, doesn't bode well for our future. ...to knowingly and silently tolerate or condone what we know to be against God's will, is probably sin ....even though it may appear to bring us peace ...whether in the home, the church or community. .....and to be unaware of God's will is of our own choosing.(Matt. 7: 21) …the Bible says "Not every one that saith, Lord, Lord, shall enter into the Kingdom of Heaven but rather those who doeth the will of God.

(verse 20) "wherefore by their fruits (witness) ye shall know them.

…mankind's greatest barrier to salvation is probably pride ….and pride is probably satan's greatest leverage. …maybe it's better for us to not be blessed by God ….rather than to be blessed and take any pride in it.

(1 Peter 5: 5) …the Bible says "….for God resisteth the proud and giveth grace to the humble." …I'd be real careful about forging God's signature on my salvation diploma in advance of the end of he exams.

…especially in light of our knowing that God's thoughts are not our thoughts.

(Isa. 55: 8) …neither are our ways His ways.

…the other night, my friend suggested (stated) "we all sin!" …as though she had resigned herself to that fact …which seems paramount to condoning sin.

…I don't agree that "we all sin" although I believe we all have sinned

…yet I do believe that we all make mistakes. …to make a mistake isn't a sin.

(James 4: 17) …..but "to know to do good, yet don't do it" is sin …and to not strive to know what is good according to scripture, is sin. (at least that's how I see it.)

(Psa. 1: 2) …the Bible says "to meditate on God's law (word) day and night." ….and …

(2 Cor. 10: 5) "Bring into captivity (submission) every thought to the obedience of Christ." …that, for sure, is a tall order

…and no one alive can do that in their own strength. …but that's no reason to dismiss making the effort! …but if we (like the hymn says) "turn our eyes upon Jesus" …then all things are possible. …only if we trust Christ to be our navigator can we steer our shop amongst the perilous reefs that lie just beneath the surface.

…actually, there's not a whole lot of people, even at church, whom I particularly trust …there may be some whom I don't know well who are continuing to work out their own salvation but it appears that most think the race is already finished!

...better for me to consider that "what is of me" is junk ....and that only "what is of Christ" is life. ...personally ....I like junk. ....I work part time at a thrift store ....so it's a huge effort for me to be discerning ....yet I know I have to be highly selective. ...God graciously met my hour of need, in supplying a tiny apartment ...else I'd spend my entire earnings at the store and have none left for rent or food!

...I'm continually learning that the more I entrust to Him then the less I have to assume control for. ...it's like the difference between night and day. ...am I "out of the woods" as far as satan is concerned? ...not a chance ...but as I spend more and more time in God's word, I expect satan will veer off in search of an easier target. ...(whoever might be reading this ...don't let it be you ...and neither think you're above it being you.) ...I suppose that if I felt assured right now that my eternity was irrevocably secured then I would no longer need to give thought to whether I was pleasing God. ...but I do feel assured that vainglory is a resting place of satan's seed and I'm cautious of those who boast advanced salvation. ...I don't think the Bible speaks of "greater" or "lesser" sin. ...sin is sin ...period and it encompasses everything we do that is not of faith.

(Rom. 14: 23)

...and it doesn't appear that any amount of rationalizing can change that. ...if there are only two teams (and the Bible says there are only two) and if, from the age of being able to reason, we have to choose which team we'll be on (and the Bible says we do) and we can't flutter back and forth at will (and the Bible says we can't). ...for the Holy Spirit to be with me, I have to be dead to sin. ...the purity of Christ will not abide where there is sin!

...if I'm dead to self yet alive in Christ then sin can bring me no pleasure ...I would in fact detest it in my allegiance to Christ who is "life itself" to me.

(Rom. 6: 2) ...the Bible says "How shall we, that are dead to sin, live any longer therein?" ...that's a very good question ...and it closes every loophole. ...I either have the Spirit and don't sin or I sin and don't have the Spirit. ...to have the Holy Spirit doesn't make us instantly holy nor mistake free. ...but it makes us wiggle like stink at even the temptation of sin …plus …it's only through the Spirit that we desire to grow in faith and in our understanding and enjoying God's word.

…as we eat-up that good food …God puts more on our plate but you never get so full that you don't always want more. …I imagine that we all would like to be and feel more complete or more content within ourselves …and I believe only Christ's Spirit (which He has promised if we seek Him) can provide for that completeness. ….otherwise we can be like a lost child at Disneyland, where, despite being surrounded by fun and excitement we are despondent because our parent (security) is missing from us. …but once re-united with our source of security we can be joyous …even without the fun and excitement. …and what a shame to have never experienced being lost …that we might gain the "finding". …as with children, we can easily take the love and provision of our Heavenly Father for granted until faced with the absence of it. …hell is probably a bit like that …except imagine the torment of that lost child were he or she to become separated from the parent then find themselves not in fun and friendly Disneyland but rather a burning desolate land infested with snakes and spiders. …then being told your parents are dead to you and what was once available to you of their comfort has ceased and further, that this shock, torment and anguish you feel is yours forever and ever …not further hope …only sickening regret. …if a child knew all that ahead of time …they'd probably be less head-strong in how far they wanted to wander from their parent ….even at Disneyland, where the attractions and distractions are a great temptation …we've been repeatedly warned in the Bible that a fate beyond our worst imaginings awaits those, young or old, who die without Christ's Comforter in them.

…I respect God, and I'm in awe of God but above all …because I believe His word …I fear God (including trembling). …yet through nothing of myself, I find that I'm at rest with that fear. …I'm not "saved" but I have the hope of salvation. …and I don't know anyone who's saved but I know a lot of over-anxious people.

…if someone is talking to me …then they're still here! …if they're still here, they haven't written the final exam! …so when people tell me they're "saved" …then I hope they don't mind if I don't believe them. ...their ascribing salvation to themselves, actually causes me more concern for them ...rather than comfort about their eventual eternity. ...whatever our emotions or best intent ...it must never contravene scripture.

(Matt. 16: 19) ...the Bible says ...of Christ speaking to His friend Peter ..."I will give unto thee the keys of the kingdom of Heaven". ...then only four verses later, through Peter's trying to comfort Christ, in spite of what Christ has told him, must be, something not "of faith" must have been the source of Peter's attempt to give comfort ...because Christ then further said (verse 23) to Peter

"Get thee behind me satan: thou art an offence unto me: ....."

...after just having been told (and encouraged) of his getting the key of Heaven, ...I can only guess at Peter's being dumb –struck at satan's presence in him!

...and it ought to give us reason to pause, before signing off on our own salvation in advance. ...I don't think we can be "assured" ...without being "overly assured". ...we would think that someone, somewhere could safely have confidence in their salvation. ...surely the Pope ...right? ...or Mother Teresa or Bill Graham? ...what about Bill Gates or Queen Elizabeth? ....could all of these, potentially, be destined for hell? ...surely, someone, must have spine over we mere peons??

...our nature, of course, is ...that if we ever do think of hell ...we immediately and conclusively think that neither us nor those we love can possibly go there (be going there by any means).... and so we invent and adopt a fool-proof plan: A. .....don't think about or talk about hell ....and B. ...if there is such a place we have the capacity to interpret our faith to the extent that we (and our own) are exempt. (with or without the Bible's concurrence.) ...we don't have to compromise God in our hearts ...we can just compromise the English language.

(John 3: 16) God loves the world ...even gave His son to die for some bad stuff that was happening back then, so that we can now enjoy the good ! ...right?

...that's not hard to believe if that's all it takes to get into Heaven ....right?

…"why can't churches just stick with the basics, and leave the doom and gloom to those who, for some unknown reason, want to bit into that apple??

…"I said I believe ….so I'm saved! ….right? …the Bible says we will each see a hard road …and an easy road. …when was the last time we heard someone say "given the choice, I think I'll take the hard road."

…in Bible times they put those people in jail …today we put them in asylums. …the Bible tells us to "deny self" …and so we "tithe" ..sometimes …the Bible also says that things are seldom as we believe. …the world doesn't teach us that if we give up (surrender) something then we'll be better off. …the Bible tells us "surrender" is mandatory. …which do we want to "believe"? …lucky us …we do get to choose.

…Bill Gates or Queen Elizabeth could surrender every penny they have or will ever have to worthy charities …yet find themselves in tormented hell unless they

repent and humbly ask Christ to fill their lives with only His Spirit and His comfort. …"Knighthood" has absolutely nothing to do with "sainthood".

…It doesn't seem possible that a loving God would ask us to surrender "everything" we've created for ourselves …and yet without the fear of hell, I don't think we'll surrender much of anything. …it's not like we can get fired if we don't produce for God! …except that the Bible says we can absolutely get fired yet be too thick to know it!…saved vs. unsaved ….Heaven vs. hell …it's not our call.

…the Bible is full of "just about" people ….right from Adam and Eve.

(Luke 8: 5) ….the parable of the sower and the seed …well illustrates man's dilemma in faith. …it's not that we don't want to please God …it's just that we want other things more ….and those "other things" unfortunately, please satan. …go figure!

…in our eyes ….it's a "catch 22 situation" ……if God gave us more of what we want ….then we wouldn't have to look elsewhere for it!

…yet the Bible says (Psa. 37: 4) …if we patiently trust in God …then He will give us our hearts desire"! …so …is our impatience our greatest barrier to salvation? …has God failed us, once again, by creating us with insufficient patience? ….perhaps were we born at age 50, we could more easily dispense with our immaturity.

...delivering papers this a.m. I thought on the blessing of a Christian upbringing. ("to whom much is given" etc. etc.)

...without Christian nurturing in our youth, we can easily ...or must! ...I suppose ...get locked into (habit) life solutions that are void of faith in Christ and what a monumental task it must be to dismantle that house of cards which can only collapse us into hell at the end. ...we don't have to believe in hell for it to be our final destination ....just ignoring it, is sufficient....there's a verse in the Bible that's long puzzled me, and it's Christ, speaking in the book of Revelation. (Rev. 3: 15) "I know the works, that thou art neither cold nor hot: I would thou wert cold or hot (verse 16) So because thou art lukewarm, and neither cold nor hot, I will spue thee out of my mouth:.

...I have concern for those who have been given God's word yet adopt casual faith and further ...have no problem with casual faith. ....even through their "works" (treasures) promote lukewarmness! ...am I a Christian ...who retains a bit of vainglory for myself? ....rather than emptying for the glory of God?

....don't ask me what's with me and Disneyland these days ...I've never been there so hardly know what I'm talking about ...but I imagined a church family returning form Disneyland and on the following Sunday morning a church brother asks the father of that family "did the Holy Spirit enjoy Disneyland? ....and the family father says "The Holy Spirit didn't go! " ...and the church brother asks "Oh? ...did He stay at home?"

...for the "other than" lukewarm Christian, the Holy Spirit is, at every moment, exactly where we are ...from waking up ...to the breakfast table ...to our drive to work ...to helping us at our work (attitude) ....the drive home ....the dinner table, our evenings and weekends ...and our thoughts before sleep ...not to mention our rest . ...there's no place ...at anytime ...we can drop Him off someplace.

...He's with us ...or He's not. ...period! ...if He's with us ...then what we do ...He does...period. ...He watches what we watch ...He listens to what we listen to ...He goes everywhere we go. ...and what please Him ...pleases us ....right? ...because the

Bible confirms it …right? …and that is why "all is well with our souls."…right? …somebody say "right!" …"everywhere we go" ….I'm off to church in an hour. …church is not "out of bounds" for satan …so I'm going to be looking out for him in someone there.

…how can we be certain he's not going to church in ourselves?

…how much "world" have we taken in (of a Sunday morning) in our preparation for worship? "church" (the assembling of ourselves together) ought to pretty much "mirror image" our state of mind apart from church.

…fellowship (a mutual sharing) under Christ, is to uphold what is of Christ

…so that His church (body) might be strengthened in relative unity.

…if we are stewing at home over our own personal agendas, then that is just what we bring into His church. …unless substantial "in scripture" our own agenda are of a source other than unity under Christ. (Rom. 14: 23) ….."of faith or of sin."

…how can we be Christian (followers of Christ) and yet bring sin to the table which is for feeding His body? (Rev. 3: 15) "I would thou wert cold or hot"

…better to not come to the "table" at all if we have only a "cold dish" to bring …presented by obstinate hands. …loving "exhortation" in church is to prevent cold dishes from compromising Christ's body. …of the people who surround us in church ….which can we deem as absolutely not of satan or worldliness?

…is it just those who know to be nice people? ….just those who help out in the church? …surely, those in the choir who make such a nice worship noise unto God, would never bring worldliness into the house of the Lord!

…it perhaps sounds negative to suggest satan enters our churches disguised as Christians …so do we prefer to accept that it could never happen? …it certainly appears to have happened in the ? early churches, to whom Christ speaks to in Revelations …how is it that we have, somehow, escaped lukewarmness in our churches today?

…what's the big deal if we are a little tolerant of being lukewarmly devoted to God's word or God's will?

(Matt. 12: 30) …Christ said "He that is not with me is against me, and he that gathereth not with me scattereth abroad."

…seems a might rigid for like in the 21st century …so maybe we could somehow just tone that down a little …right? …after all …we do have scholars of high esteem …right? ….and we are, of course, human …right? …so those scholars should be lobbied a little on our behalf to soften a few of these rigid implications …right? …"it's already happened!???"

…well then, maybe just a little more is needed! …otherwise I may have to consider attending a different church! …and it would be a mistake to underestimate my influence on others to do likewise!

…best to just give us what we want …it's not like we're asking for the sun and the moon! …God is accepting and tolerant …so shouldn't the church reflect God?

…it's often the expectations of church Christians, that they expect from the church, that which only Christ can give them, with or without the church.

…I, personally, don't appear to have a problem with chipping away, from the church, anything that isn't Bible based …and am open to discussing any errors I make (if scripture is offered to challenge my understanding or views.)

…I'm just learning, that any time I spend away from God's word …is usually time wasted in temptation to have my own way.

…the church of God's kingdom on earth will be totally subservient to Him. ….it will be built and maintained by those who have His interest (His will) covering their hearts.

…there is no need of new and improved slant (or interpretation) of either His Spirit, or His word. (Psa 119: 105) …the Bible says "Thy word in a lamp unto my feet and a light unto my path." (verse 104) "Through Thy precepts (directions) I get understanding: therefore I hate every false way."

…God has provided a lamp and a light …it's for us, to make it "the only lamp" and "the only light" to guide every area of our lives.

…anything we think or do, which departs from His word, is fodder for satan to work through us by imposing "self" above God. …the more "self", then the more doubt, indecision and wasted time away from God's Kingdom on earth.

(James 4: 2) …the Bible says "ye have not because ye ask not."

…we ask not of God's providence but rather look to ourselves and our fellowman to provide what we and they can never provide for.

…we can be good people ….never hurt a fly …labor selflessly in volunteer work …yet if we decline the Spirit of Christ in our lives, so do we also forsake God who made us "and lightly esteem the rock of our salvation. (Deut. 32: 15)

(verse 20) " …for they are a very forward (willful) generation, children in whom is no faith."

…the Bible says that our claims of being "Christian" is of no significance to God, who sees our hearts and the deceit of our hearts. (Jer. 17: 9)

(Rom. 8: 9) …without Christ's Spirit in us, we are not Christian …nor of His flock.

…I can, perhaps, display the fruits of a good person, but without Christ's Spirit there will always be rats in my cellar, gnawing away at the rock of my salvation ….and when unexpectedly tested, those rats will be exposed as sources of pride, short temper, haughtiness, gossip, anger, anxiety, fear, etc. …..none of which are of Christ …and all of which Christ, living also in my cellar, can quell.

…no seed of discontent is of Christ save for those which push us closer to Him, for our own good, through Him. …I have many weaknesses and through some semblance of humility I hesitate to call myself "Christian" …and although maybe just a little right now, by and by, I'm determined to display more and more of what Christ shares with me, as, and only if I reach out to Him, for help.

…I recall a song from the late 60s …"to Love Somebody" by the Bee Gees

…a line in that song says "There's a light …a certain kind of light that never shone on me." …I doubt that song was ever meant to have religious overtones (or undertones) …but that line well expresses my spiritual walk over the past ten years.

…(courtesy of my son Richard and my upbringing, which led me to take him to church regularly) …taking Richard to church started out being all about him.

…when my parents died, about five years ago …I was severed from my theory of "salvation through association." …what a "loss" to Christ's ministry ….yet an "uneasy blessing" to me, personally. …"comfort" in "sadness" sounds like an "oxymoron" …and may I leave that oxymoron with Richard, in my eventual passing from this world to the next. (actually …may Christ leave that oxymoron with Richard.) …what greater gift to leave those we care about …than "unconcern" for our hereafter? "O what peace we often forfeit …Oh, what needless pain we bear." …I think we (including myself) too often underestimate the importance of being in prayer. ….I don't mean the orthodox (hands together, eyes closed) type of prayer ….but rather the (hands apart, eyes wide open) type of constant "the Lord is my Shepherd" prayer …as we go about our daily routines and adventures in life. …my own experience is …that as I wander about, day to day, humming, whistling, singing or listening to secular tunes (even golden oldies) doesn't charge my Spiritual battery …while, of course, it's lawful …it's just not spiritually edifying, …whereas …if I catch myself and slide into a favorite hymn …then God can share with me through what is of Him, as my heart and mind are turned towards my walk in faith. (1 Cor. 6: 12) …secular songs evoke words and also memories that are far from walking in "faith believing" …so even down to my memories, I have a choice to walk with the Lord in the light of His word ..or not. (…"yeh, …but ya gotta love those oldies!") …"get behind me satan, …I know thee not." …Christ was tempted by satan …Christ went a month and ten days without food, yet refused satan's bidding …which was to turn stones into bread (sustenance).

(I happen to be from a generations that turned the Rolling Stones into some form of weak sustenance… (joke)

…in due time, I expect satan himself will know what it's like to be in a bread oven ….as will those who follow after what he provides. …I think every temptation is of satan ….and Christ's response will be our response also …if we are of Christ.

(Matt. 4: 4) …"It is written, man shall not live by bread alone but by every word that proceedeth out of the mouth of God."

…we have the Bible….and we have the Spirit of Christ …and that's enough to clear away every thin web of deceit …whether out of church or in church.

…a "tolerant" people are a "just let it go" people in a downward sliding society, provided they are not "personally" impacted to any great extent.

…we want whatever it is we want and if we overstep the boundaries of safety then hopefully others can be compelled to share the burden of any costs that might arise.

…youth wants more freedom, parents want less responsibility, elderly want more assistance …the louder squeak get the grease.

…what destroys families is tolerated and our foundational faith is ousted to allow it.

…whether it's freedom or equality or relief from something …we're naturally inclined towards serving "self" interest over the greater good. …how can that mindset not leech into our churches? …it seems evident that the vast majority in this world don't want Christ's message. …even the vast majority in our churches don't really want Christ's message (or if they do, they wish it was different) …I wish I we're wrong but I don't think I am.

…I regularly attend three different churches and have friends in each …yet surprisingly, I have a non-Christian friend (cold?) who most frequently encourages me to "hold fast" to the Bibles teachings. …maybe he sees I'm a more positive or happy person for doing so …or maybe because he carries no guilt of "lukewarm- ness" he can objectively discuss beliefs. …he's my friend (on my part) because I see him as honest …and I don't often see that in church friends. …I pray that my friend separates from whatever is holding him back from faith so that he can find life "anew". ….I pray that for everyone ….even me! (and I won't pretend there aren't things holding me back from a closer walk with God …things I'm still unwilling to surrender).

…I ask …are these churches I attend, growing in Christ's strength? ….or are they slowly giving grown (on Bible teaching)? …and I, honestly, see them slowly giving ground. …what is that? ….does it just "happen"? ….do we ….or the church ….just "give ground" to nothing? …or nobody? ….do we give ground to "our nature"? ….certainly, no church would give ground to satan, ….would they?

…supposing that were possible ….how would that maybe happen?

…would satan enter our churches growling loudly and emitting a foul smell? …or would he likely enter even as an "angel of light"?   (2 Cor. 11: 14)

…(verse 15) "Therefore it is no great thing if his ministers also be transformed as the minister of righteousness ….." …if the alternative is to be duped into hell ….then I guess I don't mind so much being labeled as "negative" ….(although I prefer "overly discerning ") …if based on His word, then I doubt God will fault me on the "overly" aspect of discernment.

(Rev. 3: 16) ….I have no intention of being "spued out" ….whatever it takes!

…I'm not saying "to heck with everybody else" …..only that "it's imperative" that I be selfish on this one point of not straying from the life more abundant here nor in the hereafter through Christ. ….if I accept and promote a diminished life. (courtesy of this world) then I'm failing myself and more yet those close to me. …and I can imagine no worse thing on my conscience.

…how diluted or how weak can a church become before it essentially loses it's "church" status? …does orthodoxy (approval, conventional) even hold any merit if it exceeds the envelope of Christ's teachings? …every Christian should probably enter his or her church, not relaxed …but rather, on guard. …what's to keep us from being deceived by apparent "angels of light"?

(2 Thes. 2: 3) ….the Bible says there will come "a falling away" ….and I expect there's but a brief step between "lukewarm" and "falling away." (verse 10) "…because they received not the love of the truth, that they might be saved." …it appears, from this Bible chapter, that satan's deception is but a prelude ….because God Himself will further separate the goats from His sheep through testing us.

(verse 11) …"And for this cause God shall send them strong delusion that they should believe a lie:."

…in school I used to do the "last minute" cramming to pass tests …these, present and coming, tests aren't going to be "cram able". …we'll never "make the cut" in our own strength nor in the apparent strength of our denomination or church facility.

(James 4: 8)   "Draw near to God and He will draw near to you."   …do we assume the second without performing the first? …I'm reminded of the extent to which corporate (and I therefore presume personal) prayer is ever imploring God to do everything on our behalf. …is His Spirit insufficient?

…is it perhaps more convenient for us to bypass our need of the Holy Spirit? …maybe just figure getting by on our expectations of God? …He can see that we're good people with or without the Holy Spirit …right?   (I'd better, "watch-it")

…the Bible doesn't say we get to understand everything, should we choose to turn to Christ and I probably have appropriate "rest" in those things I don't understand. …generally, the further we are from God the more at fault everyone else is for our not being happy or fulfilled.

…we rarely praise others for our successes, so why criticize them for our faults?

…have we signed our lives over to their control? …..their choices?…even our spouses …to whom we have vowed love until death …are not accountable for our being fulfilled or complete. …only God, through His Spirit, has promised and is able to suffice for our completeness.

…our greatest fault is in our looking elsewhere (locally) for "meaning to life". …nothing is more sufficient, important or local, than His Spirit in us.

…every single little thing that isn't of Him is an obstruction or barrier to our finding completeness …money, status, romance, expectations, etc ….are, in the end, all of "self." …the anxieties and concerns of life will never, ever dim …except we turn our eyes upon Jesus …fully. …Adam and Eve separated us from God …for a time ….the Bible tells us God is just and He is merciful …through sending His love for mankind, in the form of His son Christ, we are no longer separated from God unless we choose it. …either way, the Bible shares and also warns of His just reward or wrath at our choosing.…the fight is not between us and God …it's between God and satan. …we are but willful and willing participants (accomplices) …the stakes are beyond our comprehension, though satan would have us believe otherwise.

(Isa. 53: 8) …the Bible says to us "Your thoughts are not my thoughts; neither are my ways your ways." (Prov. 3: 5) …."Lean not to your own understanding:.

(James 4: 2) …."Ye have not because ye ask not" (.….of God …with a contrite and humble heart.) …Christ wants us either for only faith in God ….or against faith.

(Rev. 3: 15) …."I wert that thou were cold or hot"

…seems interesting, that while the "church" majority don't seem "hot" for Christ yet none seem confident in "speaking out against His teachings.

…are we just cowardly? …or simply disinterested? (Rev. 3: 13) …"he that hath an ear, let him hear". (John 8: 47) …"he that is of God hears God's words."

(John 9: 31) …"God heareth not sinners: but if any be worshipers of God and doeth His will, them He heareth."

…I suppose it's no surprise that people claim premature confidence in "always saved" …does it not offer us some license to control the Spirit? …while it's true that surrender to Christ will alleviate fears ….and the Bible says that (1 John 4: 18) "perfect love casteth out fear" …..there is considerable criteria of "surrender" …and none of us has yet attained "perfect love". …so why, amidst our stumbling, do we get to take a giant step over the finish line??? (Matt. 11: 28) …have we labored for God? ….and so become heavy laden??? ….then maybe we are granted some rest from struggle through His Spirit …but the Bible doesn't say we can also snatch the prize for which we are suppose to continue endeavoring to earn. …best to not puff up in victory while others around us are slipping away. …I think the Bible fairly states that it's obedience and our seeing to the needs of others in lieu of ourselves that constitutes our reward (prize) at the end of the race. …and for those "whoso have an ear" to hear, the Bible likewise warns of the dire consequences of going to the world or another faith… for that which is available only through Christ's Spirit in us.

(Matt. 7: 13)   "….for wide is the gate, and broad is the way, that leadeth to destruction and many there be that enter there at".   (Matt. 7: 19) "Every tree that bringeth not forth good fruit is hewn down and cast into the fire."

…no "church" will enter Heaven as an assembly (unit) ….nor is "church" to be our treasure. …our church is not His church ….but hopefully (prayerfully) our church is leading us to and encouraging us towards His church being personally established in our own lives. …it might be good to write down what we want in life …and what we hope for …then look to the Bible to find what (of our desires) are of the Spirit of Christ …or what (of our desires) are perhaps of "other". …personally …I've tried that and I didn't like it but I can't see where it would pose a problem for those who are assured of their salvation. …it would, actually, confirm their assurance!

…I'm certain my folks prayed continually for the salvation of their every child and for all others also ….but they never mentioned the meter stopping the moment I finally and humbly acknowledged my need of and my accepting of Christ to direct all my ways. (Jer. 17: 9) ….when the Bible says "my heart is deceitful above all things" how can I trust it? …yet, for those who know beyond any doubt of their salvation …they must overcome that Bible claim ….or else bypass it.

…maybe a clear conscience permits a guilt-free life ….and some perceive that as "always saved"??? …yet even non-Christians have clear consciences that may …at the end of the race …be the death of them.

…so, I suppose, church affiliation really has nothing to do with eternal salvation except if "holds fast" to "every" word of God.

…a "club" reflects it's members interests but that's not the purpose of a "church".

…how many hundreds of years of childhood does a church need before it begins to mature into a responsible ministry of "every word that comes out of the mouth of God."   …preaching hell, fire and damnation is preaching the Bible also. …it will bother only those who have the "need" to be bothered by it. …the sobering influence of "damnation" is required ministry, to impress the dire gravity of the lukewarm spiritual walk or no spirit at all. …our "individual" strength in Spirit is what sustains us and is also the only thing of value in what we contribute to any assembly of Christ (church) …without which, we should contribute nothing but rather humbly draw and learn from the church what is (scriptural) of Christ.

…our church's discernment isn't necessarily the Holy Spirit's discernment but the Bible will validate what is and what isn't the Spirit's leading.

…I think churches which depart the Bible, pretty much qualify as "cults" …or at best "clubs". …it's interesting how even "prayer" (which used to be private or public) has graduated to private or corporate. (shared by all members of a unified group).   (…I wonder when that change happened???)   …have churches outgrown their purpose? ….has it gotten a bit heavy on the business end? …President (pastor) …Board of directors …regularly constituted General Business meetings …elections …treasurers …assistant treasurers …clerks …secretaries …auditors …chairpersons and committee upon committee (maybe one for each letter in the alphabet.) …each hoping to proudly announce something positive.   …is it possible that God's will "might escape us through" the business of churching"???   …some churches appear to do very well! ….would it be inappropriate to sell shares to the public? …the word "dividend" isn't in the Bible (KJV) …but what it is …is "a gift of something extra …or bonus" (Webster).

…the word "gift" is in the Bible at least a couple dozen times!

…imagine the church growth if a religious organization could offer a membership bonus above and beyond salvation!!! …a perceived, good cause …and the potential to invest in it doesn't sound out of keeping, …right?

…how big a step is it from tax receipts for tithing …to T4 slips for investing?

…a church is to have a deep concern to draw the lost to Christ …right?

…can't the means justify the end? …makes one wonder if perhaps some churches aren't indirectly (under the table) already listed on the stock exchange.   …what of stewardship???   …although we may consider tithing (10%) as of "our giving" …the Bible infers that our 10% is already God's.   …it's the portion we gladly and humbly return to God to further His will.   (Luke 12: 48) …..yet "to whom much is given, much is expected". ...do Christians protest against investing due to the gamble involved? .....do Christians refrain from any form of investing? ...do they doggedly give to the poor all that is beyond their needs ...fully trusting God to provide? ...does not the "parable of the talents" (10, 5, 1) give some credence to the opening of a "business door"?

...many churches have an "associated business door" already ....be it Thrift store ...or theme park. ...is there potential harm in the Business Church? ...I know many church members profit from their church associates in their private lines of business ...and most churches have "member" business directories. ...so what are the "reasonable limits" in supporting (investing in) like-mindedness? ..."buy nationally", "support your province or state", "support you local community", "support your local union (assembly)", "support your family". ...we are actually admonished and exhorted in scripture to support our own in compliance with God's instruction.

(1 Tim. 5: 8) ..."But if any provide not for his own and especially for those of his own house, he has denied the faith and is worse than an infidel."

...that one verse, by itself, could prompt an interesting Bible study!

...do we give second thought as to whether the monies we are blessed with (a part from tithes) might be supportive of causes or efforts which, if known, are actually counter to God's wishes? ...does it suffice to say "jeess ....we had no idea!!!"

...some faiths overcome the "convenience factor" and do actually support "their own" exclusively where possible.

...objectively is difficult given our prideful natures yet, in all honesty, we know there to be faiths or denominations or even some whom we may consider as cults ....who perhaps shame us through their discipline and adherence to portions of God's instruction. ...are they" holding fast" in areas where (for whatever reasons and excuses) we have perhaps compromised? ...it should be of little comfort if we, alternatively, "hold fast" in other areas. ...faith isn't "a competition" ...but rather ...are we obedient to every word of God? ...convenient ...or otherwise? ...far from our own rationalizing, Christ's spirit ...and only Christ's Spirit will lead us in the paths of righteousness for His name's sake. ...I see nothing in the Bible to suggest that God loves the Baptist ...any more than He loves the Mormon or Catholic.

(Rom. 8: 38, 39) ...nothing, of our choice, can separate us from His impartial love.

...though we may hate God ...He loves us still ...even as the defiant teen may hate his or her parent ...the loving parent, though grieved, cannot "turn off" the flow of love.

...we can, however, deny the presence of His Spirit through which is revealed to us the greatness of His love above all things.

(1 Cor. 13: 12) ....what we are "unaware of" ...we are "in darkness to" ("see through a glass darkly") ...too often, when satan says that ...we sit up and pay attention ...but when God says that, we dull our ears.

...our pathetic (and insulting) whining of "not being loved" is of "ingratitude". ...our turning a blind eye to the great love of God ...who sacrificed His son that we might know of His love. ...without our making ourselves aware of His love, we are left to our own devices to manufacture every emotion and attraction that suits us in our attempts to escape our self-enforced isolation. ...conversely, we're less shy about making ourselves aware of every attraction and distraction from God. ...it's as though the "world" (satan) has a ring through our nose and we are defenseless against being dragged (are even willingly dragged) away from all that is wholesome or of good report. ...the Bible says it's our nature to sin, so we simply follow our nature. ...the majority, in the world, are not Christian and so discount any ill effects created by Adam and Eve. ...I think even would-be Christians discount that effort is required to repel sin. ...we repel obvious wrong doing as best we can in our own strength ...then concede that we all sin and always will ...so why fight it .....right? ..."our strength" isn't much in the Spiritual realm ...and without Christ's Spirit, upholding and directing us, we will be in a constant state of defeat while alive here and endure hell for eternity after ...unless the Bible is wrong. ...and without Christ's Spirit the Bible will be wrong for us because everything else will sound better. ...I believe only His Spirit can see through the wrapping on sin ...the wrappings we see as "probably harmless"

...the wrappings we see as civil freedoms. ...the foremost authorities on "pandemics" (illness causing millions of deaths) make front page of the newspaper today (lesser portion) with the warning of clear and present danger. ...we have been made aware (wrappings are off) of a coming catastrophe yet we probably won't ("put our house in order") prepare until it comes directly to our door. ...except for aids and some cancers, science has been good to us here in the west and we put our trust in science even though we know it to be fallible.

...not many Christians want to die but if we have made what God treasures our own treasure also, then our sure hope of Heaven takes away the fear of death in this life. ...it's an intangible comfort and frees us to concern ourselves with the souls of those close to us and those near to our hearts. ....our love of others is of Christ and it's in His name that we care for others.

(Psa. 23) "......though I walk through the valley of the shadow of death, I will fear no evil." ...His omnipotent supervision comforts us.

...Christ's miracles, amongst those in need, draw people to Him to hear His message of healing and life everlasting (salvation) ....the well off, the arrogant and the proud, largely ignored His words ...in fact, largely belittled His message.

...even 911 ...(a reaping of what we've sown at Hiroshima?) has, over time, made us even more resolute in our defiance to obeying God.

(1 Cor. 2: 6)   ...the Bible says satan is the prince of this world (ruler).

(John 14: 30) ...satan will separate us from God and impress in us that we (with him) can overcome any malady that comes our way ....and that we don't need God to do it! rist says faith is essential ...and we choose ...we are either with Christ (and He with us) or we are against Christ (with this world and satan). (Matt. 12: 30)

...there may be much that appears "of good" ...but without Christ, is shrouded in layers of weakness and deceit (wrappings) which when exposed to the light of truth will show itself to be based in darkness. ..."good" which crumbles under load is not trustworthy....both the Bible and the Koran (Islam) say it's honorable to die for the faith rather than betray it. ...the early, "professedly" Christian church, mistakenly, also killed for the faith. …that is not of Christ and is why we need surrender our ways to Christ's Spirit. …only His Spirit, in us, is to be trusted for good. …only His word is without the "wrappings" of deceit. …of the many gifts we receive from God and the many gifts we purchase for ourselves and others …what standard determines our "needs"? …as opposed to our "wants"? …and so, what determines our wants?

…for the sincere (discerning) Christian, the "wrappings" are what Christ's Spirit helps us to see. …and without His spirit we have no hope of seeing ….nor even desire to see.

…the greater blessing for the Christian is the greater hardship for the worldly. …to be separated from "what is not of faith" is the desire of the unfettered Christian …as it makes us dependant on Christ's Spirit.

…years ago (before loonies or toonies) I had a brass planter full of spare change from years of collecting …to me it was a bit of a nuisance …but some visiting nieces and nephews saw it …and their young eyes lit up! …I told them they were welcome to as much as their small hands could scoop-up in one try …after which, none of them were seen for hours as they departed to count and recount their booty. …those kids have all grown now …have children of their own and I'm sure have forgotten that "moment in the sun" …but it's a reminder for me of worldly offerings and how we can acquire the habit of grabbing all we can. …more money, bigger house, newer car, finer cloths, etc. are not the "life more abundant" through Christ. (John 10: 10)….Christ said "…I am come that ye might have life and that ye might have it more abundantly. (verse 12) …what is of faith in Christ, gathereth …and what is not, scattereth. (James 4: 2) …."we have not (life more abundant) because we ask not " of Christ. …as children, we want and ask for everything our eyes see …through being immature and not discerning the harm in the possessing of everything. …most children, given the freedom, would eat candy until their teeth fall out (then convert to coke or pepsi) …as adults, we imbue ourselves with every trinket, treasure or tawdry bauble available from the world until our souls begin to rot (wrought) then complain at the scarcity of peace and joy that God is suppose to provide for us. (James 4: 8)

"…and He will draw near to you." follows "Draw near to God"   …don'cha think we're a kind-of-a-lazy-bunch-of-mutts?

(Rom. 8: 9) …the Bible says, that if we're Christians then the Holy Spirit abides in us ….yet so many of our hymns and prayers are pleadings for what we are already suppose to have! …and be thankful for! …we pray and sing "Jesus keep me near the cross" ….or "Be Thou my vision". …emotional grandeur is a blight of faith if we continually expect God to do for us what our surrender to Him is suppose to have already accomplished! …should we not be praying and singing "Jesus, thank you that I am near the cross

…and "Thank you, Lord, for providing for me Your vision of Your will"?

…we might (should) well doubt the Spirit's presence and influence in our lives if we need continually seek evidence of It! (a pastor recently admonished (reprimanded) me on use of "It" when referring to the Holy Spirit. …yet …until the Spirit leads me otherwise …I'll maintain that "gender" (re: the Spirit)…could be more "faith derisive" than otherwise …the Father, the Son, the Holy Spirit …..right?) …is the Holy Spirit not of the trinity with God and Christ? ….and therefore avails us of all that God and Christ offer us? …the trinity cannot be separated to suit ourselves. ….we cannot believe in God but not Christ …nor in a gentle Christ without also believing there is a hell for those who choose not to believe in God and trust Him that there is a reason for hell.

…to be a grand parent isn't possible except that what we are given bears fruit. …and to be Christian is like that also. …God gave us Christ to light our way …Christ gives us the Spirit to reveal His light to ourselves …and to others. …only through the Spirit can we be of God's flock …and if we're of God's flock through His Spirit in us

…then why is it we continue to plead for God to "let the Spirit of Jesus be seen in us"???

…are we just pretending? ….or do we really believe and trust God's every word?

…a highly publicized shooting just occurred in a southern state, in which four innocent people were killed. …we don't have forever to determine where our forever will be spent. …some only have right now.

…the Bible says those four people's lives haven't ended but have rather come to a fork on their road at which there is a courthouse far different from the one in Atlanta.

(Micah 6: 8) …the Bible says "…and what doth the Lord require of thee but to do justly and to love mercy and to walk humbly with thy God."

(Ex. 20: 5) …and in the midst of the ten commandments, God said ":… for I the Lord thy God am a jealous God, visiting the iniquity (injustice) of the fathers upon the children unto the third and fourth generations of them that hate me."

…Apartheid in Africa and racism aren't dead …they're just no longer advocated.

(Luke 11: 4) ….the Bible says "forgive us our trespasses as we forgive those who trespass against us."

…in Christian faith …it's required that we do justly, love mercy and walk humbly before God …and it will take much humility and appetite for eating crow to sustain our visitation back five generations

…in God's eyes (impartial) the rape of people of color by our ancestors, or us, is of no credence whatsoever. …pride of color has been and still is a huge burden (only one of many) that will drag us straight to hell if we don't make amends.

…the Bible doesn't say we are to "forget" …only "forgive" …and I think we need "forgiveness" far more than we need "forgive" others.

….especially, when we're talking generations! …parents (1), grandparents (2), great grandparents (3), great-great grandparents (4) …if none of them knowingly sinned (and myself also) then I shouldn't have to pay the toll …..right?

(Ex. 20: 4) "….visiting the iniquity of the "fathers" …is more "gender" specific than I'd like but that's what God's word says. …somehow, I think a "gender neutral" Bible wouldn't alter that part! (Richard …don't ever repeat that I said that !)

(private father-son joke) …if people of color ever visit upon whites what we have sown, then the seams of civility would surely burst.

(Gal. 6: 7) …the Bible says "Be not deceived, God is not mocked: for whatsoever a man soweth, that shall he also reap." …and his offspring also, if God's justice prevails??? …we are, all of us, the fruit of a tree, as the Bible says …both good fruit …or bad fruit …from good and bad trees. (Matt. 12: 33)   "Either make the tree good and his fruit good or else make the tree corrupt and the fruit corrupt: for the tree is know by his fruit."   (and the fruit by his tree???)

…I don't know any of those people shot at that Atlanta courthouse and I don't know the fella who shot them …but the young woman, who encouraged him to surrender, used the word "hurt" rather than the word "killed" in reference to what that man had done. …the Bible says that we cannot be killed but rather that we will continue to live on forever, elsewhere.   (…"to kill" has many meanings, in my dictionary)

…the Bible says, don't kill …and non Christians ignore it while perhaps Christians in authority or high places justify it and use the word "execute".

…pro choice uses the word ("terminate".)

…"where" we continue on, is of our own choices.

…I think the Bible says that our "choices" terminate at our earthly death.

…untimely deaths, by many means, ends our options to choose for "what does the Lord require of thee"   (Micah 6: 8)   …the "line that God draws" is not vague or :flexible according to our own wants" …but is clear and decisive according to He who created us.

…those four who died last week (and thousands besides) …their trials and joys of this life are over ….and they knew there was no guarantee of long life (however hopeful). …their responsibility, if they were Christian …was to leave their loved ones with "evidence" of their going to a better place. …I don't think "any other intention" is greater than that sure hope, for those left behind. …so …in the end, it isn't that we have "zero tolerance" for killing people …rather only that it be justified …i.e. war, self-defense, punishment, etc…and for crimes and injustice from even years and years ago. …which killings are of "faith" (God) and which are of "sin" (unjust) or self-deceit?

(1 Thes. 4: 14)   "For if we believe that Jesus died and rose again, even so them also which sleep in Jesus will God bring with Him." …therefore, this life and it's treasures and it's shallowness, all pales compared to what is offered through Christ's Spirit.

…the time we spend reflecting on ourselves as to appearance or image or status is probably counter-productive spiritually.

…I have a Christian friend who claims nothing will separate her from her make-up stuff. …she says God wants us to look as good as possible. I think she's still looking for the Bible verse that says that or is waiting for a new translation that supports that.

(2 Cor. 6: 16) …she may be looking to "for ye are the temple of the living God. ….."

…but couldn't the harlot, as well as the Christian, claim that scripture???

…personally, given my diet and expanding waist, I take comfort in …"there is nothing from without a man, that entering into him can defile him: " (Mark 7: 15)

…and also, "For bodily exercise profiteth little: ….." (1 Tim. 4: 8)

…and so we see that the Bible is stringent …yet kind …right?

…is it so boring ….to err on the side of caution, with our eternity at stake?

…can we be indwelt by the Holy Spirit yet find ourselves without commission (gift) to purposefully bring glory to God? …if we are of God then we have purpose.

…the Spirit will direct us to purposefully please God (per scripture) in every area of our thinking and our actions. (2 Cor. 10: 5) …the Bible calls us to "bring every thought into captivity as to obedience to Christ."…as Christian, we are to submit. …that's very difficult if we're always fighting against what the Bible says or else looking for loop-holes and wiggle-room. …we know for certain that this sort of monkey business is not "of the Spirit nor of faith."

…newspapers and television are growingly full of instances and issues that wrench our hearts…life and death issues that tear at the foundations of stability.

(Micah 6: 8) …to "do justly, love mercy and walk humbly with God" and to "lean not to our own understanding" …(Prov. 3: 5) …has probably never (in my generation) been so greatly tested. …numbing or distracting ourselves may defer our going insane but only Christ can quell the storms that rage about us. …evil has been evident since

Cain killed Abel …yet we continue to choose to walk in darkness …ignoring the light in God's word. …it may be that, if not now, we'll never get the chance to repent or say to God we're sorry for ignoring Him. …I think that only through repentance and believing (trust) every word of God through the Spirit can the sting of death be removed by Him.

…dying is not the tragedy …not trying to secure God's favor (please Him) and thus be without hope of life more abundant and eternal is the tragedy for us and those we leave behind. …to not taste God is by far, far, far, the greater death in the here and in the hereafter more so.

…from our young teen years, we haven't long to determine (choose) whether we will pursue faith in Christ or otherwise. …the "otherwise" comes quite naturally and …as my dear mother once responded …unless we are faced with some crisis beyond our own capacity to remedy …then it's unlikely we will, in that broken state, humbly ask God to intercede. …should we attain the age of reason in pride or with exposure to God's word ….then political leaders, teachers and finally parents are to blame and they will, in the end, be accountable to God for their failure.

(…."better for them that they be drowned" is how the Bible puts it.) …we may think, that to avoid doing intentional wrong, is sufficient …but the Bible says that if you know to do good yet do it not …then for you, it is sin. (James 4: 17)

…a friend phoned me last night from an intermission at a Neil Diamond concert to say she wished I was there. …even as she spoke, I was thanking God that I wasn't. …I doubt he sang a single hymn, let alone a hymn that I might have liked! ….besides …I thought Neil Diamond was Jewish! ….if so, what would he have to do with Christ? …in all honesty …when she phoned, I was TV channel hopping, which also had little to do with Christ …but her call prompted me to stop even that …and go to bed.

…a pastor's wife recently told me, "we can't spend our whole day with our faces in the Bible!" (…I think I'd prefer not to hear …if she was at that concert also).

(Heb. 8: 10) ...according to the Bible ...we're to "write God's words on our hearts" that they be ever with us.

...what God has made available to His chosen people, is available to all who seek after His truth through Christ's Spirit.

...despite the importance we place on our own lives ...or the adulation we bestow on others for whatever reasons ...we are all expendable. ...that's why we provide for Godparents, in the event of our "unexpected" demise. ...we, ourselves, cannot put our minds and hearts at ease with grave issues nor shocking occurrences.

(Matt. 28: 20) ...in the Bible, following the disciples desperation (....with Christ's crucifixion-and burial) Christ, again, appeared and spoke to them saying "....and lo, I am with you always, even unto the end of the world". ...it wasn't for no good reason that Christ died and arose again ...but rather that now, through His Spirit, can we be comforted throughout emotional trauma beyond our capacity to rest.

...if we have made our spouse or child or friend to be our God (source of deliverance) then we'll be inconsolable should they be, forever, taken from us. ....but to walk with the Lord, in the light of His word. ...there need not be great weeping or gnashing of teeth, neither here nor hereafter.

...that's not to say we'll join the cast of "Happy Days (old TV show) ...but it rather eliminates the need for closure, if we humbly turn over to Him, in supplication, our grievous concerns and wrenching disappointments. ...His indwelling Spirit will quiet our hearts to the cause of His will ...except we experience the presence of His Spirit in this life ...we'll live on to regret it in the next life ...big time! ...it has been said ..."The clock of this life is wound but once and no man has the power to tell just when the hands will stop ...be it late or early hour. ...now is the only time you have ....live, love, toil with a will ...place no faith in tomorrow

...for the clock may then be still." (sobering message from a book I read years ago..." Apples of Gold".) ...I don't see the word "closure" anywhere in the Bible ....not to do with grief, not to do with anything. ...those without faith may require closure (a finish, end or conclusion) but it's my experience that those without Christ's Spirit (comforter) spend much idle time in complaining and grieving, with or without much valid reason, anyway. ...in faith, even the death of a loved one is temporal ...not finished ...not ended ...and not concluded. ...there is and always will be ..."what comes next?"

...if the Christian is to adopt the character of Christ, they must do so objectively (every word ...every character ...and not selectively, as they may wish.) ...Christ emphasized the family of God, over the paternal family, when He said   (Luke 8: 21) "My mother and my brethren are these which hear the word of God, and do it." ...of such, the sting of death and anguish of conclusion is comforted by our hope of eternal life for others and ourselves also. ...we are not to neglect our paternal family to favor our Christian family but we are to exhort them and encourage them towards what is "of faith" ...else they will remain "of sin". ...and, for sure, woe are they who depart this world in that state. ...to "not exhort" (warn) is to "not care so much" (should their last breath be imminent) for the whereabouts of their eternity. ...how could ambivalence to another's eternity be of other than a casual or lukewarm caring? ...do most simply not believe in there even being an eternity for themselves or for others after they die? ...that would be sort-of like believing there is no law ...moral or otherwise ....except for tangible evidence to the contrary through just retribution.

...I think, were the truth known, that many Christians live amongst the worldly not so much for to share Christ's word or His ways ...but rather to enjoy the things (attributes) of the world. (I hear my mom "but Paul ...that isn't for us to judge.")

...the "who are of God" is not for us to judge ...but the "what is of God" is absolutely required for us to, individually, determine. ...the Bible will lead us to Christ's Spirit, wherein, only Christ's Spirit will lead us to (reveal) the truth in God's word. ...it may not qualify as "fun" ...or even "pleasant" but conviction is what the humble heart will desire, rather than be affronted by it. ..."faith" has never been about feeling good about ourselves ...that's the desire of those who choose the "world."

...I imagine millions of Atheists and Agnostics feel good about themselves and will continue to feel good, right up to death and judgment. ...ambivalence is not without it's own comfort. ...I suppose the "goal" of the Christian is to feel bad, then invite feeling worse, until God's love and God's grief, honestly becomes our love and our grief.

...the Bible says there can't be any of "the world" in that pursuit. ...there can be no compromise or blending or adding to or taking away ...except it be an abomination to God. (Rev. 22: 18) ...the Bible says "...if any man shall add unto these things, God shall add unto him the plagues that are written in this book: and words of the book of this prophesy, God shall take away his part out of the book of life ...."

...how easy it is for us to judge (determine) that if God is going to ordain (allow) ...911 ...or the abuse and murder of an innocent child ....or the painful death of millions through a virus, etc. etc. ...then we are surely allowed to seek some solace or comfort apart from Him. ...I have no doubt that today ...somewhere ....someone is re-writing the Bible to expand on what we are allowed. ...I fear for my son's exposure to these new translations ....and for his son's, more so.

...I wonder if there aren't moderate Christians or professed Christians who, even now, wouldn't take some comfort were the King James or more strict translations to quietly disappear ...so that the more "user friendly" translations could take root.

...would a "world Bible" that accommodates some measure of every religion not be a force for a world unity?

...I was at a "packed house" church service this past Sunday evening where the pastor explained that communion would be presented every other Sunday, in an effort to maintain the relevance of partaking of communion ...then he invited all who believe in the precepts of that church to come and receive communion. ...never a mention or warning or even a brief quiet time to consider the implications of possible unworthiness. (1 Cor. 11: 29) ...the Bible says, "For he that eateth and drinketh unworthily, eateth and drinketh damnation to himself, not discerning the Lord's body.

...probably 95% of those in attendance (maybe 450 people) immediately arose to line up at six stations. ...I suppose that should maybe hearten me ...instead, it concerned me as I was near trampled at the response. ..is "communion" between us and whatever "church" we attend? ...or is it personal?

(1 Cor. 11: 30) ...suggests we are to honestly discern whether we are so living as to be dead to self and are disciples of Christ, else we, through the act of taking communion, invite damnation unto ourselves. ...any spurious trust towards pretence of faith without first honestly assessing (discerning) our treasure as being Christ and only Christ will merit us nothing but ill. (1 Cor. 11: 30) "For this cause many are weak and sickly among you."

...(verse 28) "But let a man examine himself ......"

...under man's law, we are to presume innocence until proven guilty ...but under God's we are ever to presume ourselves guilty yet continue striving towards greater and greater surrender of our own natures to Christ's likeness, unto our earthly death.

(1 Cor. 10: 31) "Whatever ye eat, drink or do ...do all to the glory of God.

...not "much" ...nor "most" ...but "all" ....that's a very large envelope! ...but it's the envelope that pleases God. ...I suppose it's up to each believer to discern if a lesser envelope is safe for the partaking of communion. ...personally, sometimes I take communion and sometimes not. ....except I'm near tears, at both my thankfulness and also my wretchedness before Christ ...then I'm better to pass.

(...even as "an old geezer" (my son's analogy). ...I rarely feel sick or weakly.) ...that's somewhat of a miracle in itself! ...and it's, for sure, no glory to me.

...today is Wednesday and "Good Friday" is two days off and I'm already hoping it's going to be overcast and raining. ....it just seems appropriate.

...I guess I'm greedy ...today we have the Bible and Christ's Spirit to reveal it's truth and light ...yet, for a few short years, some of our ancestors had the physical presence of Christ to see and to listen to! ...imagine ...being in the physical presence of perfect love! ...it boggles the mind! ...there's a hymn or song of faith called "I can only Imagine"

...a lady sang it at church (this past Sunday morning!) ...good stuff! ...yet even in Christ's day, "perfect love" is not what people were looking for. ....they were looking for revenge on all who had mistreated them ...and also for anyone who would give them what they, themselves, wanted.

...and so, like a pack of hungry dogs, they turned on the loving hand that came to feed them. ...even atheists and evolutionists must agree that we also are descendants of that pack and we continue to divest or get rid of that which interferes with our base "wants".

...what we lack in Spirit we compensate for through ceremony and pomp.

...I'm reminded that even Peter (of Christ's own flock) must have weakened in Spirit, that Christ saw satan in him, so that Christ said to Peter,

(Matt. 16: 23)   "Get thee behind me, satan: thou art an offense unto me.

...that Bible passage is a good example of how quickly we can get caught up in ourselves ...yet be deceived that we are of Christ.

...my folks left this world in Aug. 1999 and made it known they desired no mechanical means of life support and that, upon their passing, their bodies be made available to the furtherance of medical study.

...as Christians, this world was never their home. ...their life was from God.

...their blessings and trials were appointed of God ...and they have returned to Him.

...as Christians, if we are beyond bringing glory to God then what is there for us here?

...the Apostle Paul said that years ago and I heard Billy Graham say as much on television, just maybe a year ago. ...multi-media can be a real eye-opener ...right?

...did you ever read an author or hear a piece of music and be enamored ...and then find their "public persona" repugnant (distasteful)?

...high emotion in newscasts seem to expose the true color of professed Christians who feel the need to interject their own views, over what the Bible says.

...it's disconcerting how when tested, the news of the professed Christian quickly aligns with the views of the non-Christian, over important issues of life and death.

...does righteousness and unrighteousness at times resemble one another?

(2 Cor. 6:14)   ….the Bible says "be ye not unequally yoked (joined together) with unbelievers for what fellowship hath righteousness with unrighteousness?"

…I think pastors, priests and popular Christian singers (past and present) might best simply share God's word, (the Bible) objectively, with all who choose to "have an ear" …and seek forgiveness through Christ, should they misconstrue His truth and light or become sanctimonious. …the unbeliever may in desperation also cite the Bible

…but it will likely be subjective and only to support their own ends and viewpoint, rather than truth. …as we become increasingly ensconced in what this world supplies and provides for through medicine, science, technology, etc. …so then do we also fail to see and appreciate blessings from God and so look to ourselves to attain the joy or peace we deem ourselves deserving of.   …in essence …we lean to our own understanding …which the Bible warns us against …unless we first consider, then base our ways on, Christ's ways…if we go to God's word only as a last resort then our determinations will be of darkness (apart from God's light). …without hope of eternal life through Christ, then this life becomes our "be all/end all" …high emotion dominates our choices …which leads to wrong doing of passion …even crimes of passion.

…for most, the defense (plea) of insanity is merely the work of the devil which we allow ourselves to be a tool of, if only through our neglecting the word of God.

…whatever is not of faith advances what is of wrong doing ….even be it indirectly.

…there is nothing of Christ which can beget wrong doing, except we twist it to our own purpose.

…Easter Sunday today and I expect churches will fill in celebration of the risen Christ. …while delivering newspapers, in the quiet early hours this morning, I was pondering how ceremony and celebration implies elements of "greater and lesser" occasion …which brings to mind "Christian of occasion (Sunday Christians) which I suppose is a characteristic of us all. …how have we interpreted the command of God to "Remember the Sabbath to keep it Holy"? …is it a "more frequented" Christmas and Easter

…that offers us some license or leniency of faith in the remaining fifty weekends …or the remaining six days in the week? …can we live on day of the week unto God and the remaining six not unto God and still be pleasing in God's sight? …I don't think so.

…it seems a highly negative ratio.

(Ex. 20: 9) "Six days shalt thou labor and do all thy work:" …who would ever suggest that means "apart from God"??   …whatever is done in those six days …if it is "apart from God" then it will be apart from His light (truth or faith).

(Rom. 14: 23) …the Bible says " :for whatsoever is not (apart) from faith is sin."

…the surface elements of wrong doing and sin are often blurry or illusive ….but one thing is certain …and that is that they won't be of faith or of Christ's Spirit.

…how often have our best intentions which we perceived as "good" (although not "of faith") crumbled into remorse or worse, despite our good intent?

…in pride …we might claim to have done everything we could …but we can't claim to have done as the Bible directed us to.

…it's been said "a little knowledge is a dangerous thing" ….and the Bible says

(Isa. 55: 9)   "so are my ways higher than your ways"

…whatsoever "good" we do that isn't of faith or doesn't bring glory to God, should be suspect. (2 Cor. 11: 14) …"and no wonder …for satan himself is transformed into an angel of light." …how can we not be discerning of "good" yet a good that is apart from God's instruction. (Micah 6: 8) …the Bible says to do justly, be merciful and to walk humbly under His guidance …it says that is a "requirement".   …the New Testament confirms that requirement …especially in the new covenant and in (Phil. 4) …our surrender of our self-will to His will is not dependant upon the actions or beliefs of others but rather our becoming born again of Christ's Spirit …only through which His will can be accomplished here on earth.

…there's an interesting aspect in the Bible that clarifies (for me) the abiding essence of Christ's love …in that we are to love our spouse as ourselves …and also likewise love our neighbor (brothers and sisters in faith) as ourselves.

…through His Spirit, we are to be self-less and to embrace those who are growing in Him as our family also …all the while saying and doing nothing to create doubt, even in non-believers. …what a rewarding challenge! …it's a good (and Godly) thing to have our feet held to the fire of potential hell.

(1 John 4: 18)   …while the Bible says "perfect love casteth out fear" (worldly fear) …the Bible also says "Fear of the Lord is the beginning of knowledge" (required Spiritual knowledge) …worldly knowledge and trust will cause us to miss the boat …and thus consign us to navigate in an unstable canoe through storms of life …then, eventually, perish to be swallowed by a fate far worse than death.

…and with satan prowling about like a hungry lion …I'm good abiding in the fear if it propels me to greater and greater faith in God.

…I live in a comparatively affluent part of the world (sometimes embarrassingly affluent). …with clean drinking water, I could probably maintain good health with one nutritious meal a day. ….given the circumstances in other countries.

…I expect God would like me to smarten-up. …is it for nothing that the Bible says (Luke 12: 48)   "to whom much is given, much shall be required:?

…I suppose we can easy think our easier road is somehow of our own deserving or perhaps that we are set apart to not need endure the burdens that others carry.

…that's the mindset of the proud and is absolutely "anti" Christ's teaching.

…to be "better off" and protective of it, is really to be "worse off" in the eyes of God.

…the beatitudes, found in (Matt. 5: 3-11) and every "blessed are ye….." Bible verse will define our Spiritual walk as regards "better off". …no Christian is beyond the need to be constantly reminded as to "what is of faith" …and what isn't. …and too bad if it's a pain.

(Prov. 3: 3) …the Bible says to write God's word on our hearts. …our so doing will bring joy to Christ's Spirit in us …while our not doing will bring grief.

…an unwell Christian friend shared with me last night, over the phone, that a certain amount of human physical contact brings her a measure of relief from physical pain …yet her boyfriend (also Christian) has physical needs which don't pertain to any chronic discomfort or medical need. ...lusts of the flesh are oft spoken of in the Bible ...but apart from "in marriage" these lusts are never pleasing to the Spirit

...and only "through the Spirit can they be tamed. ...I don't think any society can be overly moral ...nor can the immoral elements sustain any reasonable status quo. ...immorality will always advance it's own precepts through justification of one kind or another. ...the non-believer may claim "it's only natural" ...or "we're only human" ...but the Christian cannot. ...where the non-Christian may recognize their own conscience ...the Christian recognizes Christ's Spirit in them.

...general social mores may be the benchmark of the secular world ...whereas the Bible is the standard for Christian conduct. ...there can be little or no rest (peace) in serving our own appetites except our appetites be those of Christ. ...even our church may condone a little leniency but it won't be a Bible speaking church ...church ... twice on Sunday and Bible studies every evening of the week may help keep us from worldly mischief ...but nowhere in the Bible does it say our church accounts for even 1% of our salvation. ...while the Bible calls us to "not forsake the assembly of ourselves together."

(Heb. 10: 25) ...every "cult" in the world could raise that flag in attracting the easily deceived or the weak ...and so the Bible calls us to be continually discerning as to what is of faith and what if of sin. ...I don't think it's our time spent in church ...but rather our time spent in "solitude" that defines our walk with God. ...if we even profess to have one. ...it's much like a "tour bus" vs. "the car rental" ...the "collective" vs. the "personal". ..."salvation" is in no way collective.

...the "Christian" advice from any church should be that we develop a discerning mind according to the truth and light in God's word.

...my wish is that my son Richard ever hold my feet to the fire in God's word and that he care enough for myself and others to see past the petty sensitivities which are of satan

and this world.

...compared to anything which might subtly cause loss of salvation ...a few hurt feelings is a drop in the bucket.

...I have full confidence in Christ's Spirit which is in me but I know there is also a sinful nature which tempts me. ...I know I can't trust "church" minded people but rather only "Christ" minded people ...yes, there are some of them in the churches I go to ...but I keep looking for more. ...it's only as I am right with Christ that I'm of any good to my son or anyone else. ...just as we put screens on our windows or doors to protect us from flies or mosquitoes ...so also do we need the screening of the Bible to protect us from interesting, yet harmful, external temptation which is not "of faith"...the "world" may tell us to trust everyone until we have reason not to ...the Bible doesn't.

(Rom. 15: 5) the Bible says "Now the God of patience and consolation grant you to be likeminded one toward another according to Christ Jesus". ...except we prioritize the "according" part ...we are a "net negative" to His church and the Christian faith, whether the church we attend be of 5 or of 5000.

...I pray my son never become "likeminded" with a "lukewarm" church.

...may any association he have with a "lukewarm" church (....or Christian) be a reminder to him, what not to be like! ..."lukewarm" may be a pleasant or comfy church and faith ...but the Bible calls it "a form of Godliness but denying the power thereof".

(2 Tim. 3: 5)   (2 Tim. 3: 7)   "Ever learning and never able to come to the knowledge of the truth.   (verse 16) "all scripture is given by inspiration of God and is profitable for doctrine, for reproof, for our correction and instruction in righteousness."

...good stuff! .....right? ...I guess I'm about in the "autumn" of my life (which I like to push towards "summer") and I heard yesterday of a school hood acquaintance, who died.

...my first response was "was he Christian?" ...regretfully, I wasn't relieved of that "sting" for another. ...I suppose it's the lot of every middle age person to be increasingly visited with either sting or comfort in the passing of one we have known. …our lives are a compilation of people and experiences together …a series of adding unto and taking away …as we are to others also. …it's sort-a like we're gardens …where plants spring up …then fade away to be replaced by other plants …until we ourselves fade away.

…we don't mind so much when dandelions or weeds fade away but we're very aware of roses and orchids and those plants we have earnestly nurtured. …maybe it's our garden of "good and evil" …and without our attention to good, it will soon be overtaken by evil…though evil also may produce it's deceptive flower and attractions.

…the Bible says every good and perfect gift from God above, and without that firm belief we will unavoidably nurture something other than His good.

…and while our hands may appear of having failed to "hold fast" to the good which remains. (1 Thes. 5: 21)

…I don't know that fella, who died, very well …I only know he married my good friend's sister and I hope he added some truth and light to his family and those around him. …I guess because otherwise, he didn't

…and where we don't, weeds of darkness grow and who wants that cloud over their head. ….here and in the hereafter? …whether there's long term "love" (per se`) in a relationship (or marriage) …or not …we nevertheless grow accustomed to a certain level of stability or routine by which the death of a loved one or partner causes a void and our personal stability is shaken. …I believe there is but one "solid rock" from which to conduct all our affairs whether in life or in death.

…in Christ, there is a passing from this life …but it's by no means "death" but is rather unto greater life! ….if we so live that our treasure is laid up in preparation for what is yet to come after our earthly life ends.

…it's not that faith keeps us from being shaken in loss or tragedy …but rather that faith is an intangible but secure hand to help carry the burden of loss.

…my past and present experience has proven time after time the vast difference in my reaction to loss and unexpected turns in events …all depending on my Spiritual walk.

…for me …the Bible is trustworthy and sure, provided I accept it's truth and seek to own all of that truth.

(2 Chr. 15: 2) …..the Bible says "if ye forsake Him, He will forsake you".

(Heb. 13: 5) …and again …"…and be content with such things as ye have: for He hath said, I will never leave thee, nor forsake thee." (those in whom He abides).

…when I hear, so often, of years of pain and suffering over divorce …or the death of a loved one, then I wonder where our treasure is. …to encourage another to "take it to the Lord in prayer" is probably of little comfort to those who walk apart from Him …yet that is His truth and light and if there is sufficient continual encouragement to seek His ready comfort …then perhaps another will eventually turn to God and seek His ways. …any alternative remedy will be against God …and history shows the dismal end for those who defy God. …are we vain enough to think we can be the exception?

…a Christian friend shared with me yesterday that she doesn't always act in accordance to God's word. …even the "awareness" is a blessing and a warning to turn away from those things which she knows to be displeasing to God. …if we choose to be a child of God, we need invite whatever "spankings" He sees fit to impart …that we be protected from satan's grasp. …if we know or even experienced a taste of "hell"

…we'd probably invite the harshest reprimand, not seven times but rather seventy times seven! …that we might avoid eternity there.

…the story of Job is perhaps the greatest encouragement for the Christian heart to draw sustenance from, as regards endurance of suffering.

…don't wonder "have you erred" …but rather wonder "am I of any good use to God's purposes, here on earth?" …as a child of His …without that wonder …we have actually forsaken Him. …isn't "to forsake" as "to betray a trust?"

…we may justifiably get pretty indignant at being betrayed …whereas I think God just hurts (grieves) at our disregard for all He has given us. …the Bible says a day will come when He will remove His goodness from us after returning the faithful to

Himself. …I've sometimes wondered what this world would be like with no churches and no people of faith and no Bible. …what does our true character look like, void of the faith our ancestors and past generations? …will we not descend to our lower natures of self-pleasure?? gratification?? self-dependency?? …without faith …where is our hope?

…the Bible says that …through Christ we have hope.

…without faith there is no Christ for us. (Rom. 14: 23) "therefore whatever is not of faith, is sin." …whatever is not of faith, adds to our hopelessness.

…the newscasts today (increasingly) are filled with the fruits of hopelessness. …even a positive attitude can't inevitable succumb to a certain despair. …good men dying in Iraq, little children raped then murdered, the Atlanta courthouse killings, Terri Schiavo's journey from life to death, a Pope's passing …even for the Christian, we find prayer after prayer seemingly unanswered. …if only God would be our servant …like Aladdin's genie in a bottle. …I guess we're too busy to read the Bible and uphold what God asks of us …much like the young person, stricken with aids, ignores their parent's plea to be careful of their associations. …good people …even great people …have died heinous deaths through, just once, letting their guard down.

…baseball is fun and entertaining …but it's bad if we come to think that we get three strikes in every circumstance or that we're due some measure of extra warning, simply because we haven't paid attention.

…we're free to think this is our world …but it's not …it's God's world.

…our view of consistency isn't really of much interest to God …nor will He change …ever! …I'm thankful for that but it means I have to learn of His ways.

…and only His Spirit will show me His ways. …the words in the Bible are true but only the Spirit will reveal their intent. …my own understanding will tell me that the Bible is saying what I want it to …and I always have to question my initial interpretation and defer to supportive scripture a elsewhere in God's word to validate His meaning.

(Psa. 1: 2) ...the Bible says to meditate on God's word day and night. ...and further to (1 Tim. 4: 16) "take heed unto thyself and unto the doctrine; continue in them, for in doing this thou shalt both save thyself and them that hear thee." ...the message at church this morning was from (John 16).

(John 16: 13) "....when the Spirit of truth, is come (after Christ's physical departing), He will guide you into all truth ......" ...good stuff!!!

...the pastor shared how difficult it is, even for us, to know one another though we distinctly see, hear and even touch one another. ...so how more so to perceive God's truth? ....except the Spirit abide in us. ...not everything is distinctly black and white to me personally and I for sure don't know the "whys" of many developments in this world

...but I have no doubts that God knows why and it's thanks only to Him that I have any peace in these grim worldly events. ...I'm sure the Bible tells us much about why there is "bad" among us, if we but open ourselves to what it says. ...it's a constant comfort to consider the "news of the day" under the light of what the Bible says and there's been much talk and conjecture regarding the death of the Pope, over this past weekend ...i.e. accomplishments or failures, his focus, his intellect, his writings, his salvation, his replacement, etc., etc.

...being raised Protestant (Salvation Army) I've long been quietly puzzled by other faiths ... i.e. Catholic, Mormon, Jehovah Witness, etc.

...I know people in each of those who appear to show a heart for God yet also appear to defy the last admonishment in the Bible ...(Rev. 22: 18) "If any man shall add unto these things, God shall add unto him the plagues that are written in this book."

...that sounds pretty straightforward. ...so under what conditions can we defy God and yet escape God's plagues? ...I don't expect there are any such conditions.

(Rom. 14: 22) ...the Bible says "Hast thou faith? Have it to thyself before God." ...whether or not the Pope is in Heaven, isn't for me to judge or be concerned about ...will those I love find themselves in Heaven, is my concern ...and am I an encouragement or a detriment to their abiding within the confines of His word?

..."one in the Spirit" doesn't just mean in the Spirit of any ol' thing. ...there's very little merit being "one in the Spirit of "defiance" or "lukewarm ness". ...in the church pews yesterday, just before the service started, I overheard a lady on my right say what a saintly man the Pope was ...while on my left, a man said the Pope supported idolatry by encouraging the praying to Mary or to the saints. ...I don't think the Bible says that God has special love for special people. ...David was a King ...my dad was a preacher. John Paul was a Pope ...I expect they all pleased God and displeased God ...yet due to their greater influence, the Bible says they will be called to a higher accounting and if errant, shall receive the greater condemnation. (James 3: 1) ...this world is God's estate

...and God is not a lackadaisical nor flippant Master ...but is rather austere and vigilant and exacting ...the Bible, throughout, tells us He is demanding

...especially so of those with influence over others! ...I believe there is more than sufficient instruction in the Bible to enable us to humbly receive Christ's Spirit

...yet there is great enticement to ease compliance by deleting or diluting difficult requirements of surrender ...or alternately, adding to the Bible favorable additions which alter Bible doctrine. ...can deletions and additions be of the leading by Christ's Spirit? ...when the Bible says they can't? ...what greater encouragement to cultism or lukewarm churches? ...I would expect that once any prominent church adopts some spiritual license, then that door is open to all churches wherein churches become "of the people" (majority), rather than "of Christ" (devout). (1 Tim. 2: 5) ...the Bible says "For there is one God and one mediator between "God and men, the man Christ Jesus."

...I think we err greatly to glory in any church or any church leader. ...the church that doesn't lead us to surrender to Christ's Spirit personally but rather confines it's adherents to follow that "church" above following Christ is probably a greater detriment to salvation than it is a tool of salvation. (Micah 6: 8) ..."do justly, love mercy, walk humbly with your God". ...no person of esteem can do that except they defer all glory to God and minimize their own office. ...even Christ, though perfect and equal with God, He nevertheless continually deferred honor to the Father and away from Himself.

…it's probably a challenge for most …to shy away from vainglory and further discourage it as a humble Spirit would have us …and so I expect I'll always be suspicious of pomp and ceremony and lavish institutions which ascribe to be of the Spirit of Christ.

…to grow in the Spirit of Christ is a wonderful experience and the Bible is not remiss in speaking to the blessings of that growth. …I know that I need to be careful about my own "adding to" ("must also be", "probably is", is perhaps" etc.) what is a blessing, as opposed to, what is not of God. …only a healthy and honest habit of vigilance will help me hold fast to what is "of faith" vs. what is "of other" than faith.

…although those in high places don't appear to have descended to debauchery …that doesn't mean they haven't been tempted …what we look at …and listen to, as Christians …the Holy Spirit in us also watches and listens to.

…have we manufactured a "part-time" Holy Spirit for ourselves?

…in all faiths, some activities by professed Christians are perhaps questionable

…other activities are, for sure, heinous. …the Holy Spirit is absolutely not in those who succumb to heinous activity.

…I understand there is now a "push" to allow priests to marry …as though God is no longer sufficient to meet the wants of the devout. …personally, I don't think either pastors nor priests should marry. (1 Cor. 7: 22) "For he that is called in the Lord, being a servant, is the Lord's freeman... he that is called…is Christ's servant."

(1 Co. 7: 32) "…he that is unmarried careth for the things that belong to the Lord, how he may please the Lord: But he that is married careth for the things that are of the world, how he may please his wife. …the unmarried woman also likewise.

…only in the power of Christ's Spirit can we overcome greater temptations.

…I believe the Apostle Paul offers great clarity …to state "it is good for man not to touch a woman." (Mat. 19: 11) "But Christ said unto them …"All men cannot receive this saying, save they to whom it is given."

...of course, the Bible says it's imperative to salvation that man never touch another man or animal, also! ...at least the King James Version still states that ...other versions may have a more tolerant bent ....(more easy to read and more secular oriented.)

...I suppose by the time my son, Richard, is my age ...the King James version will be paramount to the Dead Sea Scrolls.) ...I'm not altogether certain as to how many are or are not leaders of the Spirit. ...I think I know only one or two whom I'm absolutely certain ...and myself isn't one of them. ...so I usually look pretty closely (with suspicion) at those who profess to have surrendered their worldliness to Christ. (John 13: 16)

...the Bible says (Christ said) "when the Spirit comes, He will guide you into all truth" ...not "give" ...but rather "guide" ...and hence will the course of our lives be directed by the vigilant desire to seek His will ...through the stern (not liberal) confirmation in His word. ...His Spirit will encourage us towards nothing that is not backed up by the Bible ....though we may wish it otherwise. ...sounds kind of boring by today's standards but the Bible says the temporal pleasures of this world fade quietly, leaving us once again comparatively empty and with no hope of inner contentment nor hope of eternal life.

...there's little security (especially in turbulent times) to be living in a house built on sand

and controlled by shifting wisdom. ...in the world is perpetual darkness ...but in Christ's Spirit is perpetual truth and light. ...even darkness has it's seemingly innocent attractions, yet, through no merit of our own, may we (I) be granted sufficient truth and light to pierce the "seeming" part and press onwards and upwards in faith believing. ...to allow good (Godliness) to die, through neglect or through simply preferring alternate treasures, is to invite eventual pandemonium in which "regret" will be our grim legacy. ..."man cannot serve both God and manna." (money) see (1 Cor. 7: 32) ...perhaps even the "façade" of a Bible teaching church warrants "some support, despite our ease to be critical or cynical. ...else any number of "monkey business" churches might erupt to offer a "form" of Godliness to those who realize their emptiness within.

...whether or not this past Pope is in Heaven ...or will get to Heaven ...is thought worthy of our objective consideration as regards our own Spiritual journeys.

...the Bible says that if the Pope added anything to "It" or deleted anything from "It" ...then he's going to at least endure the plagues mentioned in the Bible ...same with Joseph Smith of the Mormons or any other religious leader.

...the Bible says God's love and mercy are impartial. ...God doesn't love the Pope any more than He loves you or I. ...for every "good" we do in faith we probably either do or in silence allow something bad. (not of faith). ...only Christ, was and is, the son of God ...and by comparison, the Pope, you and I and all mankind are "bags of dirt"

(as filthy rags) ...and to venerate ourselves or each other to some lofty position is to detract from the holiness of Christ. ...we are to admire and emulate only what is "of Christ" in each other, whether priest or pastor or whatever.

...all is to be to God's glory and nothing to our own glory. (who would glorify filthy rags???) ...even youth don't seem to respect their elders as we were once told to do ...and I'm glad today's youth don't. ...I hope today's youth can be "considerate" of the very old or infirmed (scattered marbles) ...but I hope they can also disregard my generation's penchant for accumulating unnecessary wealth or status ...and rather "respect" only those things which are objectively noble and edifying for all.

...the Bible says "every good and perfect gift is from God" ...so the Bible is the place to look as regards what we are to respect and what we are not to respect.

...so much of our lives hinge on what others think ....the average person is constantly asked to conform to the world ...our jobs, our kids, our peers and neighbors quietly call us to be on the leading edge (with it!) ....to make a good impression (appearance) becomes a requirement to advance in the world ...or even to just maintain the status quo ...but concern for wealth or appearance can soon become a prison of our own making. ...a little self pride can impede, rather than impart, freedom.

…it's good to admire skill or talent or beauty, if we attach it to God and not ourselves …even our appreciation of these things is a blessing of God. …whatever we treasure (respect) that we don't attribute to God's goodness will be indirectly gathered unto satan to somehow fester and become pride or arrogance or even ambivalence …which is like death by a thousand cuts.

(Rom. 14: 23) ….."of faith or of sin". …the Bible speaks to how those without faith often appear to prosper …but it also says self-interest is it's own reward and how great is the loss for those who pursue self-interest. …I'm certain I'm not without fault in the demise of my recently ended marriage of twenty-three years …but I'm without guilt that my need of faith exceeded my need of marriage. …I'm convinced that without faith in Christ we can never know what "love" is. …I read somewhere, that love never dies …it can only grow if it's truly love. …romance and hormones can do all kinds of things but they can't manufacture love. …it can provide temporal satisfaction or gratification which leads to general frustration …but will never fill the void that only Christ's Spirit can fill. …nor can money or what money can provide …nor praise of our fellow man.

…until we honestly and fervently seek Christ, we're like cars running on partially fowled spark plugs …no amount of tinkering will remedy what only new plugs will provide. …and so …unwilling to surrender what's required …we limp along in a semi-life-like state …right??? …maybe I don't know very many church couples but I'd like to see a marriage (love) that I sort of envy …but I suppose we're all a bit beyond the simplicity of that potential "giving" unless we prepare ourselves to give as the Spirit gives to us.

(1 Cor. 2: 14) "But the natural man receiveth not the things of the Spirit of God for they are foolishness unto him – neither can he know them because they are Spiritually discerned." …when we begin to settle for "getting along" …..we cease to strive for the love of Christ and so ambivalence takes root.

…I was thinking yesterday about taking drugs …or rather "the taking of drugs" ….and how sincere faith in Christ should produce a noticeable (but positive) change in us but the source would not be apparent because the change is internal.

…a euphoria or buzz that is personally pleasing yet hard to explain to those who close their eyes, ears and hearts to it. …maybe like dope or booze, only those who are in a similar internal condition are able to relate to it. …the difference being that the side effects produced by humbly seeking Christ will never, ever, promote suicide or tragedy or harm or hatred or even disharmony or burden …but rather peace on earth and goodwill to all …and "so what" if it's at some cost to us! …unlike drugs …faith in Christ is free …with the exception of sacrificing things which aren't good for us anyways! …do we really want our pride? …our over-sensitivity? …our gluttony? …our dependency on others to establish our own self-worth? …better (a blessing) to be poor …and abandoned by the worldly, than be praised for a thing of no virtue.

(1 Tim. 6: 7) "For we brought nothing into this world and it is certain we can carry nothing out" …(although I understand a few things accompanied the Pope's body)??? …(verse 8) And having food and raiment (covering), let us therewith be content. (verse 9) But they that will be rich fall into temptation and a snare (deceit) and into many foolish and hurtful lusts which drown men in destruction and perdition."

…good stuff! ….right?

…on papers this morning, I was thinking (once again) about prayer …and of "hearts" (people) I wish for Christ to soften. …how often do we suppose our will must be God's will? …it doesn't bother me much, how bummed-out I get when I hear prayer after prayer of "God do this and God do that". …my greater gall arises when in church, I hear "Lord, send your Spirit upon us." …He has already sent His Spirit!!! …so what's keeping us from taking off dark glassed and opening our eyes and ears to Him!?!

…rather than step forth boldly in His strength …we rather choose to cower in our own "baby's milk" faith. …"weak faith" is highly contagious and we're soon led to ask "where was God when I needed Him? …when we ought be considering" where were we, when God needed us?" ...there's an old hymn that asks "Were you there, when they crucified my Lord?" ...the Christian is ever there ...in that, he is discerning ...else he is defying what God asks. ...it's our nature to look out for number one first but that nature is not of Christ's Spirit ...nor can it support His will. ...even in our providing for our families, we're good to be far thinking as to where that "provision" might possibly lead to in future years. ...are there areas outside of scripture that are safe?

...or are we providing the seeds of further darkness? ...what if we are indeed finite vessels, incapable of housing faith except we shed whatever is not of faith ...or likewise housing what is not of faith except we shed faith? ...the Bible says it's impossible for us to be proficient jugglers and yet remain spiritually minded. ...some "Bibles" say, whatever is not of faith, is of sin ...while others suggest that if you're not uncomfortable with something, then it's fine. ...lucky us ...we get to choose! (or is it "unlucky us"???) ...the stakes are pretty high ...especially long term ...to play fast and loose with God's word. ...some live in a world (state) where God has drawn near to them but the Bible says the prerequisite is that they draw near to God first with the sincere motive of continually seeking His will through the Spirit of Christ within them. (James 4: 8)

...to invite Christ's Spirit to direct our lives, in an effective manner, involves a huge "stepping back" from our worldly treasures (paramount to invasive major surgery).

...a new tenant in the apartment building here has taken on the task of landscaping the grounds shrubs and trees which have long since been neglected. ...his efforts are shocking! ...so much so, that I fear for his being tarred and feathered by an angry mob of fellow tenants! ...as I watch this man apply his aggressive talent, I'm reminded of Christ's words in the Bible as regards the pruning away of what is unproductive or "dead" to righteousness. ...areas of long neglect in our lives may well require excruciating and severe pruning before our conduct conforms to what, the Bible says, is pleasing to God.

…I still enjoy watching golf, especially if Tiger Woods is in contention in the final round of a major tournament ….and actually pray during my viewing …that Tiger Woods will somehow come to faith in Christ and be a witness through the talent given him.

…yet I doubt my enjoyment of watching golf is pleasing to God …especially, as my watching the final round of the Master's Tournament, this past Sunday, kept me out of church. ….4th green jacket for Tiger, or not!

…I'm still learning that what's important to me isn't important to God. …the fellow who's doing the pruning here …his name is Thomas and unlike the Thomas in the Bible …this Thomas appears to be the only one without doubts. …and after his cutting, trees and shrubs are but a mere semblance of their previous grandeur …not unlike ourselves …should we determine to cut away our pride and self image so that new growth can be produced from our roots in Christ so that we can become a child of God.

…there's a 4 lane stretch, of Shelbourne Street north, in Victoria …where the lamp posts are right at the curb …and as I needed to get gas at 4:30 am before delivering papers, I drove that stretch but immediately went to the center lane. …there's evidence that a number of side mirrors have fallen prey to those lamp posts. …and I'd prefer to avoid that concern. …it's a busy stretch, so the outside lane is frequently used throughout the day. …if it were a continual concrete wall (as opposed to separate lamp posts) probably no one would go near it! …if I had the "ears to hear" what hell is going to be like and applied that to my daily life, I would contemporaneously avoid Shelbourne Street entirely! …you tell me …what happens when a bloke veers left to save his mirror from one of those posts, with me in the safe lane next to him?

…sporadic vigilance in faith is lukewarm faith …which is a faith Christ says He will "spue from His mouth." (Rev. 3: 16) …I guess the reason the Bible says to "come out from the worldly and be separated" is so that we can avoid being impacted by or implicated in the risks that non-believers or lukewarm believers choose to expose themselves to (…like the outside lane drivers on that stretch of Shelbourne Street.)

…only through vigilance and protecting Christ's church on every battlefront can we manage to (1 Thes. 5: 21) "hold fast to that good which remains."

…not our own good, which is subject to deceit and decay …but rather Christ's good will, which gives eternal life. …the line between "be not equally yoked" and our (by necessity) being "somewhat" yoked …that line can grow very thin as relates to our companions and associates. …I guess whatever, in the world, we partake of …we become a part of. …personally, that causes me considerable concern …for myself and also for companions and associates …and more importantly, our children.

…if we "are" what we partake of and the Bible commands that children honor their parents …then children are to honor (uphold) what their parents partake of.

(…"do as I say …not as I do???) …I doubt there is a more engrossing or adventurous journey than a newfound journey in faith. …my own continually leaves me wondering "what's going on here!??!" …what used to make me feel good, makes me feel bad. …and what I used to not like much is now intriguing and interesting! ….go figure!

…as far back as "Ghost Riders in the Sky" …I've always liked listening to music

…but lately, I don't listen to music at all …not even gospel music, which for years has been meaningful and comforting. …now I feel like I might miss something, if I'm distracted by even hymns! …what's going on here? …surely "music" can't be "of sin"!

…my mother used to listen to Christian music, near continually!

(…although, I suppose the alternative was listening to my dad.)

…I recall speaking with a pastor, Leigh Robinson, (now back in S. Africa) who shared with me that there were good hymns and also not so good hymns …and I find myself more and more discerning of what enters my ears or exits my mouth, as regards music (and Bible teachings) …I'm sure all hymns are fine as instrumentals. …if played with glory to God in mind.

…God is not "hiding" from us. …..there's a mellow-dramatic hymn that says "Open my eyes Lord, I want to see Jesus" …and I'm not saying that line is exactly pathetic …but doesn't the Bible repeatedly tell us that it's ourselves that have to open our own eyes? …and ears? …and hearts to His Spirit? …aren't we waiting for a train that already is in the station? …or is this a train that we simply don't want to get on? …perhaps it doesn't hold sufficient amenities for our civilized tastes?

…we sometimes need to shelve prior faith precepts that we're comfortable with before we can open ourselves to growth …but it's well worth it. …there's nothing in the Bible to suggest we have already arrived nor that we are to stagnate our efforts towards Spiritual growth, leading to salvation. …nothing about relaxing our vigilance or our pursuit of greater truth, through Christ. …of course, sin is usually fun and that's satan's great hook …but fun without vigilance in faith is like the aids virus without a cure, in that both come to a grim conclusion.

…popular singer Billy Joel once wrote that "he'd rather laugh with the sinners than cry with the saints and sinners have much more fun …and only the good die young". …when, in fact, it's only the sinners that die – period!

…the saints, having the Spirit of Christ, can never die …our finite understanding of "life", through Christ, will be expanded …not ended!

…I was encouraged yesterday by a Christian friend and mentor, who said he was excited over the progress in faith he's seen in me over the past couple of years.

(…I must have been in grim shape two years ago!) (James 4: 8) …I reckon it's true that …if we draw near to God sufficiently then He will draw near to us. …that same admired friend and mentor used to bug me regularly by often asking me where I was at in my faith journey. …yet I now see that question was the best impetus to move me onwards and upwards. …I now, gratefully, hear that question at the mere sight or thought of my good friend Dave Benson …and I pray his pesky exhortation be emulated throughout the family of God.

…singer/song writer, Stan Rogers (now dead) once wrote "Now, for one last time, I will seek the Northwest Passage to find …etc. …my son Richard knows that song (unfortunately, he knows a whole lot of other songs as well.)

…I hope he applies that inferred determination in his "tasting of God and his seeing that God is good." (Psa. 34: 8)

...I might be a poor mentor ...but I hope one day to say to my son and friend, Richard, what Dave Benson said to me ...and may his secular everything always be bound by his Spiritual everything.

..."Christian" is not synonymous with "no fun" ...it's just different from secular fun!

...everything (fun included) given us through Christ's Spirit is not only harmless but is beneficial to all and leads to life more abundant ....forever!

...if there's any good thing in the Bible that we are not claiming as our own "experience" ...we can be certain that the fault lies within us and our meager efforts at grasping what is available to us through faith and trust.

...God only withholds what we are unprepared to accept of Him.

(Deut. 2: 31) "I have begun to give ...begin to possess!" ...what God gives us, is of course for us ....but it's more importantly for others. ...God doesn't comfort us to make us comfortable but rather to make us comforters. (Dr. Jowett) (Isa. 40: 1)

...good stuff! ......right? ...nothing will diffuse our own problems more quickly than to help carry another's burden. ...keeping in mind, to be circumspect (vigilant) as regards another's differences or gender or existing relationships ...lest one become embroiled in burdens beyond our capacity to help. ...the wisdom found in the Bible avails the best remedy for every dilemma in life ...whether for us or for others ...and straying from the Bible's wisdom, despite good intent, will surely compound problems and bleed them into other areas of our lives.   ...without the Bible's light (enlightenment) it's often difficult to discern between a blessing and a potential curse. ...temptations abounds and what may at first seem sweet can turn sour before we even know it. ...the tasting of the sweet comes easily ...but the purging of the sour can take years. (nothing at all like the sweet and sour found in Chinese chicken or pork.) ...the sweet and sour of the secular world can never be trusted to supply for the peace or joy we long for. ...I'm sure the majority of every generation and every civilization has longed for freedoms which, if granted, they have no idea how to control. ...they only know they're discontent with what they have.

..."food and raiment" isn't near enough. ..."in control" is the minimum now.

...actually, it applies to me too but I hope to control my wander lust towards all that is beyond the protective armor of God.   (Eph. 6: 11) ...it'll never happen without His help, nor can I enjoy that "expectation" of His help except His Spirit be in me, and His will be my will also.

(Eph. 4: 14)   "That we henceforth no more be children tossed to and fro and carried about with every wind of doctrine by the sleight of men and cunning craftiness, whereby they lie in wait to deceive." ...I think we need to be careful (vigilant) not to qualify deceit as "greater" or "lesser" deceit. ...isn't one always of the other? ...but rather always work to expose deceit wherever we find it.   ...whether at home, at work or in church. ...deceit can often be useful to us but it's never "of the Spirit" and (along with it's friend "delusion") will always come between us and Spiritual growth.

...I was thinking this morning about divorce and re-marriage and the Bible.

...is there anything in scripture to suggest that re-marriage after divorce pleases God? ...and is there anything to suggest it displeases God and is therefore "in defiance" of God's will? ...it's a great opportunity to delude ourselves and we can readily search out a church and pastor who can see clear to bend God's word to accommodate us. ...tolerant and accepting ...right? ...how come God's always, bugging us?

...why doesn't He just say that everything we want, is fine? ...right!?! ...unfortunately ...most of what we "want" isn't "fine" in the end. ...probably is even harmful to another and ourselves also. ...and alternately, much of the disaster, illness and grief that we bear is probably what we need to finally turn to Jesus in utter submission. ...perhaps we adopt a tolerance for how far we can safely venture into "out of bounds" worldly life areas??? ...like the moth and the flame.

...the pastor at church this morning alluded to secret rooms of sin in our hearts, that we may not even be aware of ...yet which are real obstacles to a realistic hope of salvation and bar peace of mind while yet in this life. ...we don't have to wander about being suspicious of everyone and everything ...but we'd be wise to ...at least until we give them strong consideration in the light of God's word and support only what's pleasing to Him....else we please "other" than Him.

...I understand that caffeine is a addictive (controlling) substance ...as is nicotine, alcohol, etc. etc. ...yet most faiths (maybe not Mormon) adopt a tolerance for coffee, tea, chocolate, etc. ...even serve it in God's house after the Sunday morning worship. ....maybe even a little white sugar, if requested ...and yet maintain, per scripture, that our body is the temple of Christ. ...once our resolve is broken by our modest craving, then a thin veil is erected and we can begin to rationalize a "little" departure from our "stated" belief. ...I think "moderation" is what we prefer to call it ...otherwise we begin to appear as "zealots" ...which of course, is what the Bible calls us to be.

(Rev. 3: 16) "So then because thou art lukewarm and neither cold nor hot (in faith) I will spue thee out of my mouth."...(verse 19) As many as I love, I rebuke and chasten: be zealous therefore, and repent." ...(verse 21) To him that overcometh will I grant to sit with me in my throne, ..."   ...overcome what? ...sin? ...temptation? ...moderation?

...if we overcome our treasured moderation, what will people think?

(Phil. 4: 5)   "Let your moderation be known unto all men," doesn't mean "moderation in all things" as per "license to taste everything." ...the context suggests rather "temperance and restraint before all" through prayer and supplication (humble petition) in every thing. ...nothing to do with "sampling" a little of this or that outside of the envelope of "what is of faith"

...imagine the popularity of any church that endorses the sampling of worldly pleasures! ...even with the vague promise that we keep our sampling under control! ...can we drink moderately, then abuse moderately? ...who gets to decide "moderate" ...the husband? ...whom the Bible says the wife is to submit to? ...I hope not! ...all "submission" ought be to the glory of God ...whether in the household or otherwise. ...how can the Christian woman encourage her non Christian husband to faith through honoring worldly ways? ...or visa versa?! ...humble modesty and restraint ...not moderation or lukewarm ness of faith ...lest both be lost.

…there's "something" in the innocent coffee, tea, and chocolate that is addictive.

…what if Starbucks or Tim Horton's were to add just a pinch of cocaine to their special blends?

…even then could we exercise restraint? …or would we become "further" moderates? …I suppose the government would first need moderate it's license (law) then we might righteously moderate ours. …right? …whenever we enjoy anything which we know to be bad for us, we secretly or publicly, become advocates for that thing and stem our capacity to speak out against bad.

…it's rightfully unusual for us to encourage our children towards coffee and tea, over hot chocolate, though it be our beverage of choice …and "well done" to those faiths that don't. …right? …how do we rightfully keep that same self tolerance from all areas of our lives? …."talking the talk" becomes second nature to (against) us.

…a couple of cigarettes a day (moderation) probably isn't so bad for us…right? …even maybe three??? …same with our driving and speeding just a little. ….right? …except that is actually breaking the law …but we're usually moderately justified ….right?

(James 1: 17) …if every good and perfect gift is from God and if the Christian is partaking only of God's good gifts, then why the hesitation to proudly espouse our every thought, word, deed, book, movie, beverage, desire, characteristic, etc. as pleasing to God? …to our children and to our fellow man?

…will the truth and light of God's word not validate it to be so? …and if not …then why not? …is it to avoid separation from the world? …isn't that the very "separation" that the Bible calls the Christian to expect so that he might attain salvation? …else we remain lost?

(Heb. 12: 11) "Now no chastening for the present seemeth to be joyous but grievous nevertheless afterward it yeildeth the peaceable fruit of righteousness unto them which are exercised thereby." …"everything in moderation" is far removed from Christ's character and is a recipe for lukewarm faith and deceit.

...it's the seed that will stifle the "exhortation of one another" towards Spiritual growth and rather promote anti-Christ doctrine.

...anyway ...that's my story and I'm sticking to it!

...is our surrender to Christ's Spirit and His direction, moderate? ...is that then, also pleasing to God? ..."moderate surrender" reduces any rightful expectation of inner peace that is offered through faith. ...it often takes the most difficult or wrenching events to topple our established ego and self pride. ...the more we "full-out" take the big and the small to the Lord in prayer ...the more we can appreciate His presence in our every facet of daily life ...and the more we know God's word, the more eager we are to share what "the Bible says" in light of problems and blessings in daily conversations.

...no amount of tithing or charitable works can replace the benefits found in God's truth, through His word and Spirit.

...what we give and do, encourages ...but what God gives and does "enables".

...I once disputed my need for God's immediate influence in even the smaller, less important, areas of my life ...with God being just out there, somewhere on the side-lines. (...I think the Bible calls that "feeding still on the mother's milk")

...I didn't find that a bad place to be but it's pretty shaky and it limits the armor God makes available to all. ...better to plug all the weak spots in our resisting temptation ...and we'll never do it except through His constant continual help.

...without Him we'll always delude and justify our actions to our own wisdom and ego. ...a sobering reminder of our wisdom vs. God's plan, is our proclivity to abortion and divorce ...man doesn't honor God ....so women don't honor men. ...so each new generation of children has less and less to honor in either mother or father. ...hence "honor" has become passé` or redundant. ...it's merely the fruit of the seed we've sown and what will be the seed they sow? ...rather than pray for future generations, we merely cross our fingers. ...because of the extent of our egos, children ought to be shamed to not have Christian parents and parents ought to be shamed to have failed to raise Christian children. ...instead ...both take pride in the other's "worldly treasures".

...when we read the Bible, do we think there wasn't fun and laughter and good natured ness and freedom in the Roman coliseums or in their orgies? ...of course there was fun but that extremity of worldly fun always caused someone, somewhere, to endure suffering or emotional discomfort ...and it was self perpetuating (took on a life of it's own making) ...freedom or "what's free" ...doesn't mean "without cost".

...today (2005) our children can turn on the television and have an "of age" buddy call toll free to order a "fun and laughter" video called "Girls Gone Wild" ...which is like "Candid Camera" gone haywire. ...it's a far-cry from piano lessons or junior choir practice. ...television (and I suppose even computers) has become much like having a loaded gun in our homes while we hope our children don't get hurt by it

...yet we know that even that "hope" is based on self delusion and deceit.

...some studies now claim that children (God's great gift of life) are a detriment to marriages. ...that for sure isn't of God's doing, it's us!

...my point is ...that for all these wonderful freedoms that the western world embraces and lobbies for ...there is a day of reckoning approaching and if we carry the product (fruit) of democratic freedom to the world at large (and for sure we're made (allowed) television the primary medium) ...then at least let's not pretend that we haven't become "Romanesque" in our supplying entertainment to the masses according to their wants ...nor judge too harshly countries who oppose our liberal democratic values for their own future generations (children).

...are we really so wonderful ...while others are archaic to the point where they need to be conformed to our likeness? ...is our being labeled "infidel" really that outlandish??? ...a people of faith must display their faith as opposed to merely claim to be of a given faith ...and "liberal" isn't a faith ...it's an easy lifestyle and perhaps the easiest.

...what's the ratio between peoples who have demanded discipline vs. peoples who have demanded freedoms? ...discipline, towards upholding and maintaining Bible values, is like the hex-nut once put on snugly years ago but has suffered continual attempts to turn it the wrong way with an oversized wrench. ...the once clearly defined corners have been worn off to the point where any upgrading is futile. ...in a God's minute we'll come to regret what we have silently permitted, through our neglect of discipline. ...if we're not in faith contributing to God's good purposes then we're not doing our part

...which in turn renders us to be, essentially, "weeds" in His garden and our only rightful value being potential compost material to nourish what He wants grown.

...it's a humbling prospect.

...I've just heard the new Pope has now been selected ...and how much of the church is disappointed that he's unlikely to be nay more favorable re birth control, abortion, marriage of priests, etc. etc. ...do Catholics really want a leader who is more in keeping with the more liberal will of it's people? ...our only hope of attaining Heaven is through Christ's Spirit in us, and the test of having Christ's Spirit, is in our wanting what the Bible, and only the Bible confirms as His will.

...if it doesn't immediately look and taste like candy or chocolate cake then better to mistrust our eyes and tastes, rather than mistrust God. ...candy and chocolate cake can turn sour over time but nothing "of God" will ever sour ...but rather sweetens over time. (Rom. 12: 2) ...we are not to conform God's word to our wants" ...rather, our wants to "God's word" ...even our own thinking! (verse 10: 5) "bring every thought into captivity of Christ. ...it's good to know the Bible ...but not much good ...unless you experience the contents! ...not unlike having been given a present with pleasant wrappings ...yet not opening the package. ...knowing the Bible cover to cover won't avail you anything except you apply what it says and make it your personal experience. ...the whole of the Bible says "stop living for yourselves" ...the rest is up to us. ...what's the sense of getting a good McDonald's chocolate milk shake and then grasping the straw and putting our mouth over the end ...but not drawing up the contents? ...anticipation but no experience! ...without the "way" there is no going ...without the "truth" there is no knowing ...without the "life" there is no living.

(John 4: 8) …the Bible says "draw near to God …that's the "what" of what we are to do …but the "how, why, when and where" is the challenge in the "continuing to work out our salvation". (Phil. 2: 12)

…I spoke with my sister Sharon today on the phone (great conversation on faith!) …and she spoke of her assurance of being saved and the comfort it brought her.

…whereas I continue to seem to experience the "sure hope" of salvation yet find myself reveling (sometimes almost privately giddy) in that hope …and don't give a second's thought to any "assurance". …that may or may not be a gender thing …but I find assurances and security, in many areas, are frequently and predominantly …and historically a need or concern for the fairer gender, more so than for us grumpy old men.

(Jer. 17: 9) …."our hearts are deceitful above all things …and so, do we have good cause to doubt our own …and the Spirit hasn't yet encouraged me to excuse myself from the Bible claim that "all my righteousness is as filthy rags." (Isa. 64: 6) …even all 12 verses in chapter 64 are a relevant and sobering reminder of how far we have allowed our self pride to carry us away from God's ways and the fear that is due Him.

…I hope I never lose my fear of what awaits me should I not maintain (to death) the continual "working out" of my hope for salvation.

…the Bible says my sister's calling is to encourage her husband James to greater faith …and glory in her husband's doing so …whereas a man's calling is to glory in God, with or without a wife's glorying in himself. (1 Cor. 11: 3)

…what's the merit of the cart in front of the horse? …it's void of symmetry and it also voids the horse's great value. …so in life, if the husband follows after the wife …is it not in defiance of God's plan and His word? …do we perceive we have outsmarted God's plan with our own devices? …"Hey God …look at this! …we're pretty good, eh? …funny You didn't think of this!?! …have we presumed that, being made in His image …that we are like Him and He like us? …or do we just, pretty much, discount God altogether? …it's obvious, we can live (or exist) without faith in God through Christ. …millions do it every day! …and we see our freedoms as being hard fought for (wars, protests, lobbying etc.) and therefore may feel obliged to exercise (maximize) our use of freedoms …but exercising every lawful freedom may (for sure …will) create a death of it's own, if it causes a further separation from God. (John 10: 10) ….if there's life more abundant in Christ, can there be anything but life more redundant apart from Christ? …I would say no! …the Bible tells us that what is apart from Christ, is sin …and that sin is death! …it doesn't really matter (except in a positive light) that we might be challenged or even offended by that Bible claim …to be uncomfortable is to be in a place of potential Spiritual growth …no matter or age or status. …brief interludes of "treading water" may be fine …provided we not look to the nearest shore ….but rather keep our eyes on the prize for which we are striving.

…I don't think anyone, save Christ's Spirit, can give us the "hope" of salvation. …not pastor …nor church …nor loving friend: …no do I believe any of us is qualified to sign our own salvation papers. …is someone sufficiently holy that they can substitute or fill in for God's omnipotent and final judgment over their life? …then, if so, they ought be trusted to pronounce their children and friends saved also because of their having attained God's stature.

…the hopeful Christian would give everything they have ….for that "God-like" person to give them assurance …just like in cults. …even the most obedient sheep can never become the shepherd nor ascribe to determinations which the shepherd and only shepherd can judge. …the most obedient of sheep can, at best, be a good example to other sheep …and encourage the others to listen more closely to the Master …no sheep can be "assistant manager".

…I was reminded in the quiet of delivering papers early this morning, of what I believe to be my salvation (hope of) experience. …I envision a multi-hundred foot extension cord stretched out with both ends disappearing around corners (unseen) …in the center somewhere …that's me …if I focus on one little ¼ inch piece in the center somewhere …that's me …to all appearances "useless" …except being a small part (conduit) between a power source and a power need somewhere else. …the source is constant but my little " ¼ inch life" is stagnant, except the need be applied at the other end and then! ..my little section knows "life more abundant!

…we're "not knowing" much life if we're not used by the source (God).

…spinning our tires might be sporadic fun but "burnt out tires" takes a lot of money …and much of our "time" in the earning of that pastime of replacing old spinnings! …with new and improved spinnings (pastimes).

…God is always available to us …are we seldom available to Him (His service)???

…the seeking Christian knows, from the Bible, the exacting cost for those who choose (allow themselves) to be distracted from involvement in God's good purposes.

…our "resulting unrest "demands time and money away from God …which put s us squarely in satan's camp.

…the Bible repeatedly tells us God is never ambivalent in how He sees us. …we either please Him or we displease Him …and to displease Him is to grieve Him. …..very risky business, that! …the Bible calls us to set our sights on "things above" (not worldly). …how readily we can defend a waywardness with the dismissive claim "the Bible says a lot of things!" …as to suggest we can't be expected to abide by the extensive callings of God. …may as well insult God by saying He's built a faulty product.

…God's expectations of us in faith, is maybe like our expectations of our children in school …to the extent our children apply themselves (make effort)

…so our expectations can understandably be realized. …the child who is looking for distraction from the task at hand will easily find it …as will the man who takes his mind off the things of God. …both the child ….and the man can find "short term" relief ….yet gain nothing of substance from it.

(Mark 8: 36) ….the Bible says "For what shall it profit a man, if he shall gain the whole world and lose his own soul?" (his salvation). …our life (more abundant) and our eternity …hinges on our "unworldly" determination to, in fact, not be distracted from God's light (truth) no matter how temptingly satan presents it! …irregardless of our "natural" tendencies to seek comforts where they are most easily found! …the

Bible repeatedly says to "fear God and give glory to Him" …it just doesn't blatantly say it on every page! …maybe, by now, we're about thick enough that we need a Bible with that reminder on every page.

…"fear" isn't negative, if it's enroute to greater faith.

…from my apartment I can easily view the parking lot and the comings and goings.

…my landlady, Teresa Job (now hurting from the recent death of her husband) left in her car a while ago and I wondered was she maybe heading for church somewhere??

…actually ….she may be "the church" going somewhere."

…if we have surrendered our worldliness to accommodate Christ's Spirit in us …then how could it be otherwise? …if His Spirit is truly "in us" then we are "of Him" …and thus represent Him whether we go to a religiously dominated building or to a grocery store. …the "gathering together" isn't what established His church here on earth (that only establishes our churches here on earth). …whether or not we claim to be Christian or choir member or elder or priest or pastor etc. doesn't have one iota of bearing on His church, except His Spirit be present in those people who "profess" faith.

…there's a seldom referred to warning in the Bible, as relates to the unworthy taking of communion. (1 Cor. 11: 30) ….the Bible says "For this cause (reason?) many are weak and sickly among you ….."….(verse 29) "But let a man examine himself…."

…I think every seeking Christian knows his weakness and sickness and Spiritual void …except he be delivered (relieved) of those things, through Christ Jesus.

…our strength and hope is of grace from above and without that we are indeed weak and sickly (if not essentially dead) …communion or without communion. …in fairness to that proposition, the Bible also repeatedly states that evil doers appear to prosper while the faithful appear to suffer loss. …"prosperity" can be a strong enticement away from a vigilant walk in faith and I don't believe there is "anyone" not tempted to moderate their faith to accommodate a bit of prosperity. …I don't know that we, as Christians, can honestly call prosperity "stewardship" …I suppose, like some Bible translations suggest …if our wealth doesn't bug us then it's okay …but then is it the same thing with a little lust …a little deceit …a little neglect or carelessness etc. etc.

…is that how we want to accept and live with our sin? …by simply adjusting our conscience? …if we can claim "assurance" of salvation before our judgment by God, then we can surely also intercede for God in dealing ourselves a little of His mercy …and we can, perhaps, ease up a little on His asking that we do all to His glory.

…we could never intercede for God unless we have become righteous like Him

… right? …so couldn't just a little of the glory, due Him, come to us who are like Him? …even if just a small proportional amount??? …jees …if we can appoint ourselves saved thus avoiding the ultimate judgment by God …well then we must be pretty special!

…maybe we're even righteous! …and as righteousness precedes salvation, we may as well appoint ourselves righteous in the mix! (I'm starting to feel a whole lot better about myself as I ponder these options opening up to my discretion !) …there's an old spy movie, called "In like Flint" …those are the words that are ringing our here!

(Rom. 3: 10) …and where the Bible says, "As it is written, there is none righteous, no, not one:" …that must only apply to non-Christians ….right? …if we are saved by God's grace …according to our righteousness, then to have assurance of salvation we must also have righteousness "in the bag" already. …I wonder why those who proudly proclaim their "already saved" status don't also proclaim their "already righteous" status??? …must be because of their "already humble" status.

(Rom. 10: 2) …the Bible says "For I bear them record that they have a zeal for God but not according to knowledge. (verse 10: 3) …For their being ignorant of God's righteousness and going about to establish their own righteousness, have not submitted themselves unto the righteousness of God.

(Rom. 11: 20) "….be not high minded but fear:" (God)

…the familiar 23rd Psalm says "He leads us in the paths of righteousness for His name's sake." …if we have already attained salvation, do we suppose the purpose for His leading has already been accomplished?

…can a priest or pastor or church establish minimum requirements for salvation?

…it may well be that where the Spirit gives another "assurance of salvation" the same Spirit gives me "only the hope" of salvation. …but I perceive a danger, for me and mine, lest we appoint ourselves a status for which the Bible warns us not to. …I frequently heard one pastor named Cowan, state that "none of us have arrived"

…yet some Calvinists and the like appear to be persuaded differently …and I hope their conviction (being convinced) is truly "Spirit led" and not just "denomination led". (Rom. 8: 9) …no Spirit …no Christian. …that's a "tough love" passage and don't I wish Paul could have put these verses a different way …but I believe he said what the Spirit gave him to say. …the same Spirit whom directs our own speech and conduct …right?

…the "same" who is "pleased" by every show we watch, book we read, conversation we have, purchase we make and humble attitude we express through our Spirit's representing Christ ….right? …the same Spirit who leads us to boldly defend our differences by honestly citing God's word.

…I was wondering this morning how it is that we exclude God's word from so many areas of our daily lives …even our marriages …then invoke selected Bible verse to somehow justify our wants and our actions. …the domineering husband and father quite readily cites "wives submit" …or "children obey" to validate his worldliness, his need to control, his selfishness, his sin. …have I done that? …do I do that? ….attach myself to any elevated wisdom in support of my own thinking and actions, while disregarding the "whole"? ….and then expect God to honor my feeble and deceitful blasphemy?

…if so, may I always receive God's scorn and accept that scorn as a blessing that I may look inward and ward off anything good or bad that, in the end, separates me from the truth and light found only through His Spirit.

…in the 60s, a popular Welsh singer, Tom Jones has a hit song …I think it was called "Shadow of your love" …I'm sure it wasn't Christian motivated but the first line said "I …I who have nothing and I …I who am no one " …anyway …that wants to be us (me) except through Christ's presence in my life. …Tom Jones or "keep-up-with-the-Jones" or John Doe or anyone ….can gain the whole world through whatever means …yet lose his soul. …most of us probably know we're lost …some, more lost than others

…but we're not yet aware of how desperately lost we are! …nor the extent of our doom. …because I've been granted enough days to even think about it …is a huge blessing …but what if my son Richard, even through no fault of his own, isn't? …he wants to come to that realization real soon. …I'm sure there are many young men just like him …who have squandered opportunity after opportunity to know "life more abundant" and had their available time to do so cut short by an unforeseen simple twist of fate. …regardless of how much I wish it were otherwise, the Bible says those people will live an eternity somewhere of regret, torment and gnashing of teeth without relief.

…because one chooses not to believe that, doesn't mean "hell" won't be so for them.

…its God's wish that all come to Him …but just as a loving father would never twist the arm of his children …so God won't twist your arm nor my arm though the day come when we would cut off an arm that He might favor us once again.

…every day a hundred thousand "eligible voters for Christ" die …probably.

(please give me a little dramatic license here) …people who have had opportunity to elect to be saved yet choose to focus on other treasures than pursuing greater faith.

…up and gone to hell because no viable source (in their eyes) warned them.

…I must say …I was blessed with a dad who continuously warned his children, despite deaf ears, against ignoring or neglecting our spiritual walk. …a practice he continued to the finish of his race. …while my mom was the example of peace and goodwill to all, in Christ …ever removing herself from disturbings.

(Phil. 2: 13) "For it is God which worketh in you both to will (pursue) and to do of His good pleasure. (verse 14) Do all things without murmurings and disputings."

…it's good for us to wonder on how much of our "doing" is "of His good pleasure ??? …God is not a "babysitter" to pamper our own self serving lifestyles.

…what the immature teen does, behind the parent's back, is what we do out of the presence of Christ's Spirit. …the difference being that the teen can "expect" the parent's intercession for their chosen errors …whereas if we choose to go against God, we become the enemy of God.   (James 4: 4) …the Bible says "…whosoever therefore will be a friend of the world is the enemy of God." …we needn't wonder much at our ill lot when we even choose a church wedding (bells and whistles) then depart God's word of instruction to back it up …only to find marriages and families in tatters on the ground. …isn't it a microcosm of whole societies? …God cares for us …it's we who don't care for God. …God helps those of His flock ….if we choose to be of the world's flock, then look to it for solace and help. …why waste your time looking to Him who you've chosen to ignore? …if pleasure apart from God has sustained you then at least be honest enough to claim it and leave God out of the mix. …unless we're beaten up sufficiently to humbly repent, change our ways, apply for grace and begin life anew through Christ.

…we see deceit when it is sufficiently established ….whereas God see our deceit even as the seed is planted. …we can't fool God any of the time!   …just accept that if we're not for Christ then we're against Christ.   (Matt. 12: 30)

…the Bible says, over and over, that the worldly are doomed.

…I don't imagine that Noah didn't spread that same message …yet none chose to listen …else there'd have been more than one ark.   (Matt. 24: 40-41) …I think the Bible says that in the next "destruction" the faithful will be taken up out of harms way …whereas the pious, the proud and the defiant …left behind. (I'll know real fear the day the fella next to me on the bus suddenly disappears.) …it's interesting how we look to the church (religion) for respectability …as in our marriage ceremony …yet shy away from the doctrine in our maintaining our conduct of daily life or even doctrine on divorce.

…I wonder how many (if any) of my childhood heroes ever made it to Heaven …or are now in eternal torment through their neglect and carelessness.

…Roy Rogers? …Mister Rogers? …Elliot Ness? …JFK? …Christopher Reeves (Superman)? …great sports figures etc. etc.

(Micah 6: 8) ….did they "do justly, lover mercy and walk humbly with God? …doing all things to His glory? …or was all that just too much trouble for them …inconvenient …maybe they granted themselves assurance on account of their righteousness or charity. …some may claim, to assure me, they're a "shoe-in" for Heaven ….but if not, there'll be no time to back-peddle if left behind. (…it will, of course, be God's error, as they run to their Bible to find the exact isolated verse on which they had hung their assurance.)

…the cups from which we drink in life, are the cups we choose. …not all blessings make us more comfortable nor ease our pain …but the Bible promises that, through faith in Christ, He will sustain us under even the heaviest load …even the death of a loved one …not only the shadow of death but our own death also

…but He can do that only if we put our trust "completely" in His capable hands. …all other trusts (doctors, lawyers, scientists, etc.) are fallible …no matter the blackness that hangs over us, He will carry us when we can no longer walk or even stand.

…as these bodies of our age (matures) words like "tests", "blood work", "treatment", "prescription", "therapy" etc., increasingly become part of our daily vocabulary.

…if we choose to make this world our home (final home) then these words become the language of our demise. …only if we pursue and walk in God's ways …will we know His relief from concern, be it for ourselves or for those we love. …in Christ …that's suppose to be everyone …even those we may not like.

…to be non-discriminating or non-preferential is impossible yet through Christ we can avoid all unkindly thoughts towards those we dislike for whatever reasons.

(Rom. 12: 14) …the Bible says for us to "bless (attempt to comfort) them whish persecute you: bless and curse not". (verse 18) "if it be possible, as much as lieth in you, live peaceably with all." …to hold on to negative disputings or feelings probably impacts ourselves more than any other person.

…we can learn from disagreement, without tying ourselves to it's bondage. …love the sinner …hate the sin. …through our hatred of sin and exposing every source of it is what frees us to "live" rather than exist. …doesn't every wrong …every abuse …every malice or murder stem from the neglect in our holding fast to that which is good?

(Rev. 3: 2) …the Bible says "Be watchful (vigilant) and strengthen the things which remain, that are ready to die:" …except we be aware of our neglect in "strengthening" good then good will be overtaken by evil. …and evil flourishes in many ways both overt and covert. …why is it that we turn a blind eye or retreat from what we know to be wrong? …it's the stuff that feeds our living death which in turn secures our eternal death. …unless we ardently pursue what is of faith (Christ) we will ingest the bait which is of sin. …it isn't "just by accident" that we are human and weak in Spirit …it's by what we have allowed to take root by our being worldly distracted. …when given the choice of "Christ" vs. "other" …we have chosen "other" …and so reap the results in our empty lives. …what is "anti-Bible" …is "anti-Christ" and once we accommodate defiance of one verse, so then do all verses arrive on the same table for our subjective discretion.

…what was once "unheard of" by the past generation is now "proudly paraded".

…will child abuse also follow suit? …will it become so common place that we will simply shrug and tsk? …is every commandment given to Moses and to others …up for grabs?

…if our solo hero isn't Christ or those of Christ then how strongly are we prepared to identify (sympathize) with them? …will we follow where they lead? …regardless?

…or how about adjust our beliefs to align with theirs? …for me …if Tiger Woods said I should make some changes in order to grow in some areas …I'd probably give it a try! …what of other past and present heroes? …Rock Hudson, James Dean, Jimmy Swaggart, Elton John etc.? …how pervasive is their influence on the average person? …as we attach "hero status" to media hype persons then so are our values dictated by those persons. …even church pastors & priests are fallible and can succumb to personal, rather than Godly, desires. …the "highly esteemed of the world" are never to be the

benchmark of acceptable Christian conduct …rather only God's word, revealed through Christ's Spirit.

…some of these new-fan-dangled translations are maybe okay for beginners or for light reading …bit of a reach to call them Bibles though. …some might even be blasphemous. …the King James version hasn't gotten harder over the years …we've gotten lazier or more distracted. …and we're getting worse! …sure it's nice to curl up in the fetal position and have someone sing us a lullaby …but "life more abundant" in faith means getting off the mattress …or setting down the remote control …then moving onwards and upwards in looking for "more abundance". (Psa. 34: 8) ….the Bible says "O taste and see that the Lord is good: …." …to decline that invitation is "sure loss" for any hope of all that is available for us to receive.

…not many are prepared to surrender our many man-made treasures …things the lukewarm Christian desperately attempts, in vain, to tie to faith in any remote manner of delusion. …we'll never taste and further, thirst for His bountiful meal if our eyes are ever on the pastry tray which is "not of Him".

…if we had more time, I suppose, we could each devise our own "personal" Bible translation that suits us alone. …maybe we already have.

…is it possible to be His salt and light …and yet appear as sand???

(Psa. 15: 4) ….the Bible tells us to honor and respect them that fear the Lord.

…why would the Christian honor or respect any other???

…those who have authority over us, we are to obey only ….and not cast our pearls (honor) before swine, to be trampled. (we can and should be considerate (civil) to all …even those we may not respect …it's self-defeating to repay rudeness with rudeness.)

…it's best to display neither support nor spitefulness but rather cite God's word to discourage wrongdoings and encourage good.

…it occurred to me this a.m. that when "every good and perfect gift is from God" …and we are to share all that God gives us, then hence, nothing we have is ours and whoever's it is, it's to be to God's glory. …(i.e.) when we give something and are thanked …just add "don't thank me …rather, thank God".

…everything is His and we are but tools to move a thing from A to B as we see another's need.

…once we replace the subjective "my" or "mine" with the objective "the, then we can, hopefully, breakdown our self-centeredness and possessiveness …be it in material goods or (more importantly) in relationships. …genuine kindness stems from good conduct (deeds) …I don't know that I've ever done a good deed that I didn't tell everybody about …even people I didn't know! (it's always sad to see the blank and troubled look on their faces) …the poor souls have no understanding of modesty, good deeds …or even good taste! …the "heathen" (unchurched) are such interesting case studies …right? …I should have been an anthropologist …there are a lot of sick and demented people out there whom those of us, with the gift of "vision", could probably help …right? (Acts 2: 17) …the Bible says "…and your young men shall see visions and your old men shall dream dreams" …so despite gray hair …I must still be young!

(I don't dream much, just yet.) …it's only thanks to God, that each is given something

(a gift) to impart to others. …the "having" is of limited purpose, unless we give it away.

…I expect thousands of pan-handlers and street people would gladly "vote in" that platform. …nevertheless, despite it's potential for being taken advantage of …it's still a good principle when we consider the antithesis or the hoarding of what we are given. …if we keep God's gifts to ourselves then as with "surplus manna" …it will rot.

…God repeatedly shows us that we are to trust, not our own ideas of preservation …but to trust only Him to provide. …I don't' think He wants our help (or even our prayers) regarding our own well being but rather He wants us to discern and then fulfill His will for others, "on this earth, as it is in Heaven." …for us to fail the "discerning", then the "undertaking", will for sure impact any "hope" of salvation.

(2 Cor. 10: 5) …has our every thought been brought into captivity (submission) to Christ? …or have we surrendered (compromised) only many thoughts? …and of the ones we've refused to surrender to Christ …"where" exactly are they??? …have we given those thoughts over to harmless or relatively harmless? …we're lucky God gave us the brains to decide those things which, though "not of faith" …are, nevertheless, "surely" harmless …right? …harmless to everyone? …or just me? …harmless to children? …or just us mature adults?

…does the Holy Spirit in us control those things that are "not exactly of faith"?

…or do we excuse Him while we indulge ourselves just a little?

…what if we're "spiritually allergic" to those things that are "not of faith but harmless"? …or what if our spouse or children are allergic?

…my friend Dave says he has a Spiritual allergy (bad reaction) to sports …any sport.

…he says if it's on television, he watches it …everything else takes second place.

…most of us aren't blessed with that awareness.

…for me, it's only one sport where a bunch of grown men chase a little white ball around a park …and that's how they make a living and provide for their families.

…so Dave doesn't have a television in the house anymore …most people probably think he wastes too much time reading and meditating on God's word day and night.

…I've read somewhere that we're suppose to do that …but no one really takes that seriously anymore. …where's the fun in that? …..right?

…it's kind of a shame …'cause guys like Dave could be a real asset in promoting sports and television revenues ….he might even become a sports broadcaster. …promoting the Christian view! …he might even branch out to soap operas or reality survival shows! …maybe even his own syndicated program …like "Super Dave!" …how are we going to impact the world for Christ if we don't get out and mix with the worldly? …or be adopted by the worldly? …instead, poor ol' Dave puts an ad in the newspaper that says "if you are struggling with a problem, please let me try to help you." ...then he prays to God for a response. ...doesn't he know that it doesn't pay to care for others? ...that it actually costs? (Matt. 5: 3-11) ...Dave will probably die with a bunch of those "old beatitudes" on his tombstone ...and maybe some young sports ruffians will graffiti it or knock it face down ...than laugh and later brag at their actions with n'er a thought for who is watching ...but there will come "a day" when they'll be reminded that "sport" was their infernal weakness also ...and how "harmless sport" contributed greatly to their fall from God's grace. ...macho or aggressive competition and the interest in such doesn't appear to be a characteristic of faith ....nor is it cited as a fruit of the Spirit. ...can the Christian simply dismiss sport as a "benign" pastime?

...can anything we do, either publicly or privately, be dismissed as benign (of no consequence)? ...we know we can't eat junk food without it impacting our physical health ....despite it's convenience and often moderate expense it eventually will exact it's toll on even the soundest body. ...so ...for the professed Christian who indulges himself in what is "other than of faith" won't there also be a price paid for what we consume? ...what we take in "of the world" cannot but subtract from the available space within us for "of the Spirit." ...church last night, was the beginning of a series on the book of Colossians. ...good stuff! ...the pastor spoke to "the feeding of our Spiritual roots." ...adults ...as well as children soak in everything they're exposed to in our seeking of greater life. ...for tree roots around a house seeking moisture ...sewer tiles may be most convenient to draw from ...but it's not the best for the tree. ...if it's a fruit tree, we might question the end fruit. ...for the Christian, the world surrounding us is pretty much a sewer tile and we are well to be suspicious, always, as to what we are drawing (taking in) from it: ...not to mention our giving consideration as to what we are supporting of "benign pastimes that have nothing to do with faith".

...there's no mention in any of Christ's parables that any of his flock are looking over the fence of His fold. ...we are free to choose to enter His fold but we are not to bring in what is not of Him. ...rather we are to shed those worldly things beforehand ...and then defend our born-again life from such temptations as would soil us or ours. ...I don't deny "evolution", except where it contradicts "creation by God".

...what we protect (that isn't in scriptures) is what we ought reap or endure ...be it women's rights, pro choice, environment ....whatever. ...what is "of God" assumes a life of it's own ...as does what is "of other".

...where I live, the supposedly stately bald eagle has been protected and is now flourishing ...yet it seems the bald eagle has "evolved" from the family of falcon or hawk ...into (primarily) a scavenger ...more like the family of seagull, crow or turkey buzzard! ...it's now impacting the blue heron population by robbing the young heron of it's nest to feed itself and it's own young. ...is the eagle evolving?

...I'm still that thick that I still enjoy the sight of that eagle soaring overhead in majestic grace ...but my enjoyment is more brief than it once was. ..."exposed truth" may make us uncomfortable but it far surpasses "delusion". ...if we wish to evolve towards "life more abundant" whether in Spirit ...or in nature. ...we impose our wishes and desires in faith and nature ...then figure it's up to God if He wants to catch up or not.

...it's a proud people who suggests if God doesn't "get with the program" then He'll be sorry and miss out on the pleasure of all we have done. "if God was smart ...He's see how sufficient we are and want to be more like us ....right? ...someone asked last night ..."why didn't God just make everything easy? ...He did ...once ...but we weren't happy with that, either. ...I suppose bugs and worms have it easy! ...we can doubt God and question His motives six ways from Sunday but our doubt and reservation only serve to separate us from Him. ...we are not earnestly separating from the world nor displaying the fruit of His Spirit nor seeking His counsel when we are double-minded in our trust of the Spirit's leading ...rather we become as a rudderless ship tossed hither and fro.

... non-Christian co-worker asked me today if I believed in life after death.

…I answered "yes, if I live according to the Bible." …in truth, there is no death for anyone, save the absence of "life" in the here and now. …emptiness, without hope, is a sort-of-death here on earth …but that all changes for both the righteous and the unrighteous on the drawing of our last breath.

…both are then rewarded according to our faith and obedience. …even now, we know gladness or sorrow …but after this life lies our eternities through our just rewards from He who gave us even this life to establish our eternities. …in this life, my dad chose well …as did my mom …friction and all. …my ex-wife and I chose not as well …different criteria … possibly "protest criteria" against our individual upbringings.

…(both of church but radically different churches.)

…today, even different Bibles will cause breaches in relationships within the home.

…differences in faith are not of Christ's Spirit but rather of our abstinence to Christ's Spirit. …we may find ourselves looking in the same general direction as another yet knowing we are on different roads (different pages.)

…the Bible says there is but one truth, one way and but one through whom His Spirit can give us life. …that "life" can be "abundant" or it can be "peanuts" depending on the degree of surrender. …I don't think God holds any blessing or truth back from the heart that is seeking to bring every thought into captivity of Christ.

…if a portion of my heart (treasure) is still for the world then I expect no amount of begging or prayer will or should induce God to grant petitions to the semi-receptive believer. …do I suppose I can mock God? …especially when He's already told me that my heart is deceitful above all things? (….better to pray He cripple every distraction that I allow to come between myself and His free offering of truth and light (His "life")

…I hear church prayers that continue to plead God to do everything.

…little tiny children plead likewise of their parents …but there comes a time when the parent yells (if necessary, "stop it!…I've told you how …and I've shown you how …stop whining for me to do everything while you just play with toys! …now that you're 16, I'm not tying your shoes anymore." (….or something like that.) …there's no "Velcro" cure for lazy faith …as there is for shoe laces.

(Matt. 16: 24) "Jesus said "If any man will come after me, let him deny himself and take up his cross and follow after me." …I wonder …do we even know what "our cross" is? …is "our cross" not "His will"? …where do we find the time to learn that? …or do we suppose it might just land at our doorstep and then we will, perhaps, opt to consider doing it? …we don't all have our whole lives (3 score and ten years) to plod along. …Cameron Simon died this past Sunday morning around 3:30 am in a car accident ….a mere 16 years into his life. …if that had been me at 16, I know from the Bible, that I'd have been dead to this life …and gone to hell for eternity. …maybe that's why we choose to not put too much stock in the Bible …not enough loopholes for our likings ….right? …I may be somewhat of a "lukewarm" Christian just now (which means I was probably a "lukewarm" Christian a few years back)? …it used to be, if I couldn't find a loophole …then I would simply strike that Bible verse from memory …or else appease myself with a softer translation. …interestingly …those verses, I most withdrew from, have now become the rock of my faith in God's word.

…when someone close to us dies, the very fact that they're close to us is a blessing. (we can avoid "sure pain" by never getting close to anyone and some folks exist that way.) …but the very fact that we've established "closeness" means we've had opportunity to share something of "lasting good" with another person.

…if we fail in that then emotional remorse will probably flood our souls.

…maybe "emotional remorse" is what we want "closure" from, when someone close dies. …we've advanced to perceive that natural, peaceful death at a ripe old age is ideal, even though I think we know that few find that ideal end. …many, worldwide, die extremely young and probably in extreme pain …be it from hunger or disease or accident (unforeseen event without fault). …we tend to push unpleasant reality away until it actually comes to our door but it's there nonetheless.

…I would say my son, Richard, is pretty choked about that young fella dying last Sunday. …they were friends. …by all accounts, Cameron Simon was a real nice fella, and my heart goes out to his parents …especially his mother …and to all who took him into their hearts. …it's especially grim if we concede (believe) that he has no further life (which I don't believe). …the Bible says we reap what we have sown, so even in untimely death, we can have the hope that one has sown what is of God and hopefully his parents encouraged that seed and find comfort in their doing so.

…even in general, the Bible says to put the concerns of others ahead of our own

…so there's a huge onus to consider our children in that light (truth).

…my mother was a Christian woman long before I knew her and long before my younger brother, Glen, was killed on a Michigan road at age 24 …but being Christian didn't stop her hair from turning white in her grief. …yet, because of her faith, there was no bitterness but rather a heart breaking quiet resignation that this was allowed to happen. …joy and praise and thankfulness …isn't always at the fingertips of the Christian but God promises we'll not be burdened beyond our capacity if we trust in Him. …I often feel inadequate (stupid) when asked why God allows something bad to happen. …maybe the question itself, is a test of faith. …we readily accept that we're worthy of "good happenings" …yet protest our being deserving of "bad happenings."

(1 Cor. 1: 27) …"trust in God" quiets the "whys?" …(and also the Godly "wise") …but without trust in God, we are confounded continually. …the Christian can cite comforting scripture to a bereaved Christian friend …whereas to the non believer it may be an affront to do so.

…my own life, before faith, was a series of general escapes (fun) with occasional need for "knock-out pills" when the going got rough. (…maybe if I'd had more money, those years would be more memorable …although there was little of lasting sustenance there. (…"lawful …but not edifying) …today, far more entertainment and escapes and distractions are lawful …still few are edifying. …this morning on papers I was pleasantly and softly singing an old hymn "Turn you eyes upon Jesus" …when something made me look up …then I tried adapting that old hymn to a more contemporary mind set …but "Turn you satellite dish towards Jesus" was a short lived adaptation. ...a new friend suggested recently that I should see a movie called "Bruce Almighty". ...I don't like the name ...and though he's a very effective actor ..I'm not partial to the "star" of that movie. ...I don't think I "hate" fun ...but I think I can find more of it in an hour or so elsewhere.

...we can't focus time "somewhere" without missing our "somewhere else". ..."doing" and "missing" are like our two hands ...irrevocably connected to each other by our choices. ..."church" is a "choice" also. ...I admire that Billy Graham encourages us to go to church on Sunday ...and I accept there's a greater likelihood of our hearts being affected by Christ through the word of God in church. ...but our church may not be Christ's church ...especially if our church grows lukewarm. ...it's probably not too difficult to attract people to church by presenting a "form of Godliness but denying the power thereof" ...the Bible continues "from such turn away." (2 Tim. 3: 5)

...as with moderate Bible translations, God can use any medium to plant His seed of salvation but are we to support that which the Bible repeatedly speaks out against? ...seems a dangerous precedent ...by which every and any Bible admonishment might be challenged. ...I wonder what happens when we become accustomed to leniency in faith ...or leniency in morals ...or right and wrong. ...where does it end?

...is it sufficient to say "try not to break the law unless it's too inconvenient?

...my early morning's analogy, between the King James version and the more easy to read or paraphrased version, is that the King James says "two plus two equals four" ...whereas the more moderate translations say "two plus two equals somewhere between three and five." (that would be the "more strict" liberal translations.) ...as I recall, my siblings and I weren't allowed to watch television on Sunday! ...to legalistic ...you figure? ...as for my son ....I drew the line at movies or malls ...and I wonder, will Richard draw any lines? ...we're an ever evolving people ....right? ...I wonder what it will cost us in the end? ...and what it's costing our children? ...and their children yet to appear? ...just how much "fun" can the world potentially provide for us in generations to come? ...I don't think even television had been invented fifty years ago. ...AM radio was the marvel of modern science back then! ....Foster Hewitt as the Tom Cruise of my youth ...and no one even knew what he looked like! ...years ago, faith and discipline were far more prominent in daily life ...what was politically correct was covered by what the Bible said about it. ...how much tolerance and acceptance is too much and can we ever turn back a clock effectively?

(1 Thes. 5: 21) ...the Bible says to "hold fast to that which is good and abstain from all appearance of evil. ...not just "good" by our reasoning but rather "good" by Bible standards which express to us exactly which "good" is pleasing to God.

...a good book or good movie or good friend, that doesn't bring glory to God, is probably not pleasing to God but is rather displeasing.

(Rev. 22: 14) ...the Bible says "Blessed are they that do His commandments, that they may have right to the tree of life ..."

(Matt. 5: 45) ...while God's rain may fall on "both the just and the unjust" only to the seeking Christian is it a blessing from God and of His glory ...though it be of His grace, the non believer or lukewarm believer, will see it as "lucky" or "self deserving".

...if we're not steadily growing in His Spirit and His light then we are straying

...and any and all "straying" is to satan's pleasure.

(Rom. 14: 23)   "...whatsoever is not of faith is sin."

...we're well not to be too kind to ourselves.   ...if we are indeed dead to self and slaves to God through Christ, then as slaves we are important to our Master according to the extent we are of service to Him. ....the slave who advances the cause of any other master or of none at all is of little use or concern. ...they pretty much ignore the Master's wishes right up until they find themselves in desperate need, yet ....

(Luke 16: 25)   because of their deceitfulness, they find the Master is unavailable for solace, except to His faithful servants.   (Matt. 7: 21)

(Matt. 12: 30) ...we are either for Christ ....or else we are against Christ.

...I don't know what "sort of for Christ" gains us other than what the Bible suggests.

(Rev. 3: 16)   (something to do with "getting spued out", as I recall).

...a friend said, this morning, how she didn't want to have to "fear" God.

....to translate "fear" to mean "be in awe" is a common response …but that negates (actually "mutes") (Phil. 2: 12) the "fear and trembling" of Apostle Paul wrote to even the "saints in Jesus Christ" at Philippi. (Phil. 1: 1)

…I reckon it takes a fair amount of work and self deprivation to consider oneself a "saint" in the Biblical sense. (Vines Expository Dictionary (Greek))

…to my thinking, a saint ought be reasonably confident in their salvation …so why the admonishment to "continue working out"? …I fear satan tempts even saints away from faithful obedience …else professed Christians (having assumed saintly status) could wander about at their leisure having conviction that they are beyond satan's grasp

(i.e. a "shoe in") …I think the humble and the vigilant know better.

(Matt. 9: 13) Christ said "…for I am not come to call the righteous but sinners to repentance …so I suppose we need only consider ourselves among the righteous.

…then we can exclude ourselves from "those others" to whom the Bible admonishes. …lucky us! …right? …are we really "the crème de la crème" in God's eyes that we are in our own eyes? …it's not for us to judge if another is a Christian or saint but it is for us to discern their conduct and attitude before we accept them as one adhering to God's word or one likeminded to ourselves. …attending church or Bible study and calling ourselves Christian, doesn't mean it's so.

…it's by our "fruit" that the source (tree) is made know and accredited (glorified). …good deeds may abound but only those which bring glory to God are of any account for the Christian. …all other "good" is self-claimed and glorifies only man (or woman) …which, in turn, is against scripture and against God …and only becomes a barrier to greater faith. …we can easy come to enjoy "praise" in establishing our own self-worth …be it at home, school, work, play or church …as Christian, we know Christ never fell into that trap …nor are we to. …scripture is often quoted in the secular world to validate what we want but it's limited scripture and very isolated …with God and Christ being left out entirely. …spouses expect honor and submission from each other and their children …but it's with themselves as the "end" glory. ...whatever (whoever) is unseen is of little or no consequence to the secular world. ...it's interesting how revered scripture comes in so handy in it's defense of our objectives and wants, though our "wants" be so very "subjective". ...God never intended His truth, enlightenment and knowledge to be only for scholars of Greek or Aramaic ...but rather for all mankind.

...a respected mentor told me yesterday ...that in the Vines Greek Expository Dictionary there are fourteen meanings for the word "fear"

...my "Webster's Deluxe Color Edition New World" lists only four ...the mildest being "fear that it might rain (which to my simple thinking is as to "wonder if it might rain") ..."respectful dread" is my own personal preference, of the four, when it come to my pursuing greater faith ....and even that may border on ambivalence in God's eyes.

...is it better that our salvation err on the side of leniency? ...or on the side of caution (vigilance)? ...for me ...it's important I be over aware that the players are not just me and God but rather "me and God and satan".

...if satan thought he'd try his luck at tempting Christ! ...then he must be rubbing his hand when he see me. ...I'm a goner, hands down, in my own strengths.

(Rom. 14: 23) ....the Bible says "...therefore whatsoever is not of faith is sin"

...if I'm "essentially without" except what is provided me ...then all I have is either of God ...or "of satan" ....right?

...my health, my family, my job, my car, my television, stereo, clothes, food, freedoms and choices etc. are all tools. ...I suppose even successes and failures are tools.

...I wondered, a few years ago ...if there were (are) things that were neither of faith ...nor of sin. ...there's a popular saying of "don't ask, if you don't want to know the answer." ...for the Christian, that's the route to Spiritual death.

(Luke 11: 9) ....Ask ...Seek ...Knock! ...there's no good thing that God wants to withhold from anyone who sincerely pursues His truth. ...but if our treasures are of this world then why would He lay His pearls at our feet to be trampled??? ...right?

…Christ's church and Christ's truth are not fragile …it's we who are the weak link in our own stamina …and are rarely to be trusted with His truth and His light.

…every teen will scream, 'till they're blue, that they can be trusted with the keys to the new Rolls Royce …though their past history and present attitude show otherwise. ….and just like they don't get it ….so in faith we (I) don't get it.(Eph. 4: 7) …we are each given (grace) as by God's "measure" through Christ. …it's probably hardly anything to do with what our "mouths say" in prayer but rather the attitude of our hearts prior to opening our mouths.

…the Bible says God knows our hearts and whether they be truly of Him and of what pleases Him. …I hear it said that "God wants us to be happy" …do we focus on the "being happy" and by doing so ignore what God's prescription for it is???

…"He wants to be the sole source of that happiness (joy plus guiltless rest)

…and what He doesn't want is our turning to the world or our own devices to attain our happiness (….which actually bars our capacity to "receive" from Him). …sort-a-like us wanting our kids to learn piano …but they prefer watching television …the one impedes the other. …we also like television …even though little of it encourages faith and even though the Bible tells us God wants us to meditate on His word day and night.

…Christ's Spirit in us wants to and hence we have a good yardstick to measure the presence of His Spirit. …we have thy freewill to partake of anything "not of faith" but to appease our Christian conscience we have to, in essence, "put the cat out" in order to do it. …we may not think it kills us to "put the cat out" …but it slowly does …as we "conform our faith" to "our desires". …cat's don't always return when we open the door in the morning and we soon adjust to that as well.

(Rom. 8: 39) …while it's true that "nothing shall (can) separate us from "God's love through Christ" …it's "our" loves (treasures) that hold the potential to place us in harm's way. (Jer. 17: 5) "Thus saith the Lord, Cursed be the man that trusteth in man and maketh flesh his arm and whose heart departeth from the Lord."

…I think it was in a movie called "Dirty Harry" …where Clint Eastwood points a 44 magnum handgun at someone who strayed from the "law" and said "Go ahead …make my day". …satan says the same thing …only he holds out a piece of cheesecake. …how long before it hits us that we've "put the cat out" once too often …and have maybe become addicted to cheesecake? …is it a lucky thing that we won't suffer what our children (the next generation) will suffer? …the Bible says it's a deadly gamble …

(Matt. 16: 6) "…..it were better for him that a millstone were hanged about his neck and that he were drowned in the depth of the sea." …whatever our ideas of "love" …God's love is a "tough love" ….it's pretty demanding of us but the rewards outweigh the sacrifice required. …doesn't His love require that we lovingly and prayerfully smile

(His smile) at every child we see? …that we might be "His" tool on earth?

…if we know certain children to behave as brats, we have to bite our tongues to smile …but that's good practice for when we confront adult brats.

…it would have been so helpful, had Christ encouraged us to just ignore weirdoes …but the Apostle Paul says to indulge them (us) as much as possible.

…smokers, drinkers, egotists, braggarts, liars, offenders, the self-righteous, the sinners etc. …indulge them as much as is within you …but don't be dissuaded from our focus on Christ and His word.

…it doesn't mean we're to be tolerant of sin nor adopt sin's habits but rather be patient in our steadfastness and hopeful for humble change in others. …not looking for "agreement with ourselves" but rather, "alignment with the Bible".

(2 Cor. 10: 5) …"every thought into captivity to Christ"

…even in the secular world, whether in school or in our jobs, we accept to commit ourselves to an undertaking in return (hopefully) for an agreed upon reward.

…it's better to resign (terminate) our job (position) rather than to knowingly, or through laziness, squelch on our commitment. …many are quick to claim having attended university or college but decline to confess that they baled out prior to graduation. …even the lowly newspaper carrier agrees to provide a stipulated service whether or not he likes all the conditions. …what I agree to is what is rightfully expected of me. …"semantics", are both boring and interesting …..even most austere mentors claims the

words "Christian" and "Saint" are interchangeable.

…I'm not "sold" on that but I'm up for giving it strong thought. …I'd never considered that there are greater and lesser "Saints" …whereas I see evidence of greater and lesser Christians. …it's probably a failing in me that I need attend to. …if we're "holy" then we're Spiritually perfect or pure …right?

…and unless we're that …we're not Saints ….right? …my dictionary's #2 definition of "Christian" is "a decent, respectable person." …who would have thought that 95% of people in the world were just like Christ? ….boggles the mind!

…is it for the sake of "unity" that we incline to relegate Christ's rigid doctrine to a more compatible doctrine? …that it be more encompassing? …is our faith the bold, searching, pursuing passion? …or maybe just the vague, community, back-draft faith that is commensurate with our Christian friends?

…"community churches" seem to be somewhat of the rage just now.

…each church calls out "Are you with us!?! " …and in the hype we respond with "Yes!!" …before even finding out, "with what?" …if we don't have an aversion to clubs

…then "the club" of church is maybe acceptable …provided there's nothing too "flaky" involved …right? …any respectable church should leave those who attend with at least some respectable (decent) amount of self-respect …..right? …if we wanted to feel beaten up or abused …we may as well stay home and watch the news or read the morning paper on a Sunday …right? …the "community church" ought reflect the community's desire for relief from anxiety and guilt.

…that, of course, was the great failing in the churches of our parents and grandparents. …they failed to appreciate what we want from a church. …are we finally bringing the church out of the dark ages obeying scripture?

...not long ago a pastor of a Bible study I went to ...drew a triangle with God as the top point and us as the bottom line. ...he suggested that our Christian walk was approximately midway, given that we're now into the 21st century. (I don't know that a single invention is even mentioned in the Bible!???) ...is the industrial revolution or television or computer, etc. of no account to faith? ...although the Bible doesn't exactly say so, God must want us (His creation) to advance as a society ....right? ...else, why do we sing "Onward Christian Soldiers"??? ....right?

...if we content ourselves with a "midway walk" in faith then I think we'd better adjust our expectations accordingly as regards expected blessings and eternity.

...I saw a program (television) recently about a fella who is studying wolves

...and he lives with them in a somewhat controlled environment and attempts to behave as wolves do. ....otherwise .....he won't be accepted as one of them.

...am I "studying" my secular world and community in a likewise manner? ...is my conduct and demeanor as wholly unto Christ? ...or partially unto having no desire to be considered "weird" by my neighbors: ...(which, of itself, falls far short of the "persecution" which the Bible says I'm to expect.) ...the Bible says (and I believe it) ...that we cannot be both of the world and of Christ.

(1 John 2: 15) ...the Bible says "Love not the world, neither the things that are of the world. If any man love the world, the love of the Father is not in him."

(1 John 3: 17) ..."But whoso has this world's good and seeth his brother have need and shutteth up his bowels (selfishly) of compassion from him, how dwelleth the love of God in him?"

(1 John 3: 24) "...And hereby we know that He abideth in us by the Spirit which He hath given us. ...is a "moderate faith" sufficient? ...we know moderate faith is generally tolerated by the world, provided it not interfere, ...is "moderate worldliness" tolerable to God? ...or does it grieve Him?

...can we love and honor even a parent or spouse, or friend and yet practice causing them grief? ...then how much less so can the Christian honor God by letting go His hand and turning away to eat of the world? ...are we all to "let our conscience be our guide?" …if we truly, as Christians, surrender to Christ's Spirit then our conscience goes to Him as well. (2 Cor. 10: 5) …by which our "every thought is brought into captivity (submission) to Christ and Christ's will." …right?

….as we find ourselves not resisting the temptations to be entertained by the world, so ought we find (and expect) diminished blessing.

(Rom. 14: 23) "…..wherefore whatsoever is not of faith is sin." …the Bible tells us throughout ….that if we attempt to resist worldly temptations in our own strength, then we are lost. …only when we have a firm grip on God's hand ….welded to Him …can we resist satan's deceptive pull.

…a Christian lady told me, after one Bible study …that, after her day's work she needs at least an hour or so of television in order to relax. …I never asked her if that was of the Spirit's leading …and she perhaps found she needed somewhat more than an hour or so because I don't see her at church anymore. (maybe she's at another church …I hope so.) …that lady was very busy in community services and would be an asset to any church. …I just now remember her name …it's May …as in a busy "May'bee".

…speaking of "conscience" …I know for myself …that "television" is a great conviction for me. …I'm thankful for that. …I used to really enjoy "bestseller" novels

…that's gone ….and "good" movies …that's gone …and reading the newspaper cover to cover – even doing the daily crossword puzzle …all gone …I enjoyed having a house and toys and making improvement all over the place …gone. …I guess I thought I had good taste and vision …I wonder where all that stuff went??? …I thought it was pretty good stuff! …until recently, I was always listening to Christian music! ….that's gotta be alright! …right? …gone. …what's wrong with me !?! …(I bet Billy Graham gets to listen to Christian music….right?) …what's with that? …some do …and some don't???

…I was encouraged by my brother-in-law's sharing, (via telephone) this morning, of unexplainable worldly interest loss, also.

...I'm convinced that these changes we experience, that encourage us away from "the worldly" and towards "faith", are not of ourselves but rather of One who is far greater than us. ...I noticed yesterday, that in the beginning of 1 John 4 ...we're warned to not believe every spirit ...but rather to try the spirits ...whether they be of God.

...only that which encourages us to confess "Christ" as the reality of salvation is "of God." ...all else (is of the anti-Christ ..."even now already in the world". ....heavy stuff!! ...it takes some serious "discerning" to pass on the "cheesecake" of the world ...even if it's "free" or near free. ......our nature is to "take" what we're given so long as it's free but we're slow to blame it all on ourselves when our moral health fails us or our children.

...what is "truly" of God won't fail us on any front (battle) and I think every seeking Christian can remove their rose colored glasses and alert themselves to activity and attitudes which are not of faith.

...the Bible speaks to the magnified impact of small things on larger things.
(James 3: 3-6) ...the bit on the horse ....the rudder on the ship.

...I was thinking this morning on the example of a small thing (person) at the control (wielding) of a car and the tremendous impact on others that sometimes even the slightest of errors can cause. ...in faith and in driving we have an awesome responsibility to be sober and vigilant. ....our minor failures can wreak havoc on our children and on whole societies whether it be by our intentions or even by slight negligence.

...we can easy acquire habits of ease that will dominate the next generation.

...I was surprised last week speaking with my sister on the phone ...she said she didn't hear "Christ's joy and peace" in my conversations with her.

...that's funny ...because I feel it immensely! ...pretty much always! ...but maybe "others" don't see it or hear it in me either??? ...and now that I think about it ...I don't think I've been invited out to dinner for months. ...I wonder if I'm not much fun??? (...I'm probably just old)

...I'll probably start having those dreams the Bible speaks of, any day now.

…right now, my joy and peace comes from earnestly seeking a truth and light I've only recently found. …it's not fluffy or light (whimsical) or vague …and I'm good with that.

…it doesn't have to make anyone else happy …though I'm told, by a few, that I'm encouraging them. …like in the movie, I occasionally hear God say to me, "that's good enough, pig" …for me, that's loving and humbling. …I pretty much "hear" that at the end of each day …if my head hits the pillow at an early hour.

(…I've spent (wasted) too many years trying to find rest in my our self.)

…"symmetry in faith, is it's own reward. (…somebody should write that down! …maybe my son Richard will.)

…our "interests" are also their own reward. …the Bible speaks to that where it says (Matt. 6: 21) …"For where your treasure is, there will your heart be also"

(Matt. 6: 19) ….and also "Lay not up for yourself treasures upon earth, where moth and rust doth corrupt" (verse 20) "But lay up for yourselves treasures in Heaven…"

…personally, I don't think my "conscience" (inner thoughts or feelings) really gives, nor has ever given, me much peace (relief from guilt) …except my conscience be surrendered (as in, dead to self) along with everything else, to Christ's Spirit.

…when my will is surrendered, all is surrendered. …the Bible says if I am in the Father, then (only then) is the Father in me.

…for right now, I absolutely have the God given freedom to muck about (experiment) with every (deceptive) ratio of surrender …I just don't know for how long

… personally, I've gotten a lot more freedom at 56 …than did my son's friend Cameron at 16. …I hope he was smarter at that age than I was.

…I see today is Friday the 13th and I expect more than a few people will tread carefully today …best to tread carefully everyday and forget superstitions

…rather considering that every day may be our last opportunity to choose for Christ.

…everyday may be our child's or our spouse's or our friend's …last opportunity to separate from satan's eternal snare, which the Bible says, "even now already is in the world. (1 John 4: 3)

…it may not now be construed as a "fun process" …but every other alternative will kill the life that's in us …probably sudden …or through anxiety, fear, remorse, sickness, lost hope, etc. etc.

…I was thinking this morning while on papers, how best to answer the question of what happened to my marriage to Maureen? …and the answer is probably the same for every broken marriage or broken friendship …and it's well described in a line from a Tom Waits song "House where nobody lived" …the line says "If you find someone to have and to hold …don't throw it away …don't let it grow cold."

…that "throwing away and letting grow cold" …applies to our Spiritual walk and our dependence on God also.

…are we able to cozy up to the world, even a long-time Christians, without alienating our "first love"? …isn't "temptation" a test of conscience?

…do we live on the outer limit of our conscience and yet maintain (profess) that our love for God is steadfast and constant?

(1 John 3: 22) …the Bible says we receive (are able to receive) from God "…because we keep His commandments, and do those things that are pleasing in His sight."

…do we have to stop before every bite of the apple and consider "is this pleasing in God's sight?" ….I would say "you bet!" …at least until pleasing God becomes the habit of us through His Spirit in us. …and then never let that habit grow cold.

…I cut my own hair …have for years and don't recall the last time I saw a barber.

…I'm probably not good at it but at least people on the street don't scatter at the sight of me. …as I sit and write, I often lean back and my hand goes to the back of my head as I stretch a bit. …when I cut my hair, the mirror is of limited use for the back part

…and so my hand has adopted the habit of seeking out minute discrepancies during these stretching and my stomach is well exercised in my lurching forward to withdraw my handy scissors from a nearby drawer to remedy these irregularities.

...so, in my Spiritual walk, I would like to identify every little thing that might displease God ....many of which are not readily visible and though I may think them minute

(my-neut) nevertheless, snip them from my day to day life.

...it may sound intensive but I never find it too intensive ...nor without the effort's own rewards. ...that's no thank to me and all thanks to God. ...there's no remote control to experience what God has to offer, unlike for the televisions offerings.

...to go to the Bible is a start but it's not enough to just look at the pictures and turn the pages ...we have to read and test it. ...with technology, often little effort is required to get by in this 21st century.

...gardening may be the last stronghold for manual effort for many in suburbia and it's probably a blessing if we can't afford to rent somebody to do it for us

...and it's a blessing that so many of Christ's parables relate to the land ...i.e. tares, (weeds) vines, branches, fruit, wheat, stubble.

...despite all my personal views and complaints of what's right and not right ...or just and unjust ...God's truth in   (Gal. 6: 7)   "Be not deceived, God is not mocked for whatsoever a man soweth, that shall he also reap.   (verse 8) For, he that soweth to his flesh (world) shall of the flesh reap corruption but he that soweth to the Spirit shall of the Spirit reap life everlasting." ...good stuff !!

(verse 9) "...in due season we shall reap, if we faint not." ...unless we experience the presence of His Spirit ...we cannot be led (encouraged) by His Spirit to turn away from the world's distractions and rather focus on God's gifts, which are more precious than the greatest treasures the world has to offer.

...the Bible tells us what to do to phase God and when we do something "either" then, for us, it's sin ...and I think the Bible tells us that if we continue to sin everyday ...then Christ's Spirit is not in us ...but possibly, rather some other Spirit is in us. (Rom. 14: 23) ...maybe we're content to just have "a" spirit in us??? ...how many spirits are there, anyways!? ...the Bible says "Beloved, believe not every spirit but try (test) the spirits whether they are of God"

…many false premises (prophets) are gone out into the world …and anybody of the world, finds them acceptable. …is Christ really at Disneyland??? ….or Canada's Wonderland??? …is He there sometimes??? …maybe during the daylight? …but not so much as darkness falls??? …if the Holy Spirit is in the Christian (Saint) then where the Christian goes, the Holy Spirit goes also …right?

….or does the Holy Spirit maybe stay at home and guard the Bible in the study? (Matt. 20: 16) …the Bible says " …for many be called but few chosen."

…when we go to entertaining places, is it with the express purpose to share Christ?

…or the express purpose to evade Christ??? …when we pray with our lips that God watch over family and loved ones, do we pray that He does it through us?

…or rather in our absence, as we busy ourselves elsewhere?

…I "choose" to work "part-time" …it seems to be sufficient for my needs:

…is my Spiritual walk like that also? …a "combination walk" of sufficient and insufficient " dependant on the degree of crisis in my personal life.?

…can I stray as far from His fold as my conscience (confidence) allows?

…does "assurance of salvation" give us God's eyes, to know every wolf (spirit) in sheep's clothing? …we know the Holy Spirit in us is inseparably shackled (tied) to God, in holiness …right? …that's why we want to do God's will ….right?

…it's what makes us eager to know more and more about how best we can please God, through our meditating on His word day and night, so that His Spirit can reveal His truth to us ….right? …so where does that leave secular amusement and entertainment? …whatever is of us, we bring into His fold ….right? …do I split hairs over what pleases God vs. what is tolerable to God? …(to my advantage?) …if I'm a professed Christian …then where I go, Christ's Spirit goes. …the music I listen to …the Holy Spirit listens to …I make the Holy Spirit (holy!) watch the television programs that I watch …if I complain or gossip, I make the Holy spirit a part of that …if I see rape or abuse or injustice or poverty or anything that flies in the face of God's truth and yet turn a blind eye and do nothing …then I make God's Spirit a part of that also. …is it unfair that the secular person doesn't share this dilemma? …ask

Job or better yet …ask Christ …who, though sinless, endured the cross. …if I'm just a little careful of the circle of people I confide in …I can probably "pull off" claiming to be Christian …but that "claim" doesn't really have much to with "faith reality". …in many respects, non Christian folk are closer to true faith than are many "professed Christians" who live in denial of worldliness. …"pretense" is an ugly thing and never more ugly than when disguised a righteousness. …it's a blessing to know those outside our circle of faith who comment on Christians "walking the walk" …or just "talking the talk".

…it's "worse than useless" to simply "talk the talk" to appease family and church friends. …without "honest" introspection, "faith" is an empty corridor or space …void of hope …and worse yet, it encourages others to a similar emptiness.

…lukewarm faith is a wide, wide road and so widely used so as it continually erodes that good which remains. (1 Thes. 5: 21)

(Rev. 3: 2) …Christ exhorts us to "…be watchful and strengthen the things (of God) which remain, that are ready to die ……"

…probably for every inch of Spiritual gain our casual efforts produce …six inches are lost by our silent compliance with about every distraction the world offers.

…while we perhaps fathom "some" loss to society …it's our children who will inherit (reap) the fruit of our neglect. …I wonder what "tormented regret" is going to taste like as a steady diet for our retirement years, as we sit and watch broadcast after broadcast of atrocities and woeful circumstances …..probably televised viewings (not suitable for the faint of heart) of people eating dead, burnt bodies …fangs in their teeth! …craving blood and gore and guts! (thanks a lot Arlo) …like the NHL without rules.

…seriously …we may reconsider pursuing longevity, in light of what we have produced. …long life will probably be more disappointing than we now think.

…I'm reminded of that bible verse that speaks of things not to cherish, though they be acceptable to the world. (1 Cor. 10: 23) "….all things are lawful for me but all things edify not." …not me …not my son …nor friends …nor co-workers.

…is my faith such that I need "apart from faith" also, to establish my own self-worth and meaning? …woe is me…and woe is my credibility as Christian.

…what freedom do we have, if we don't become a life long prisoner to Christ?

…do we put our faith in "PARK" at times …then get out and wander about the world in spiritual comfort until the storm draws us back to the car? …if so, then storms are a blessing. …any Christian experiencing pain or anxiety …yet says "I'm too busy" …or "I'm good where I'm at" might come to realize that their "attitude" is the recipe for pain and anxiety. …the Bible repeatedly says God wants us totally dependant on Him to supply for our needs. …it's not His job to keep us from wandering …it's our job!

…and it's to become our "desire" to not wander. …God can't nourish (feed) us if we're off considering what some other shepherd has to offer.

…it's only natural that the non believer ask …."what does God have to offer in exchange for my relinquishing my worldly treasures?" …and our words of response will be empty, except our attitudes support them. …will we answer that we can keep our worldly treasures (in moderation) and in our own strength, expand our consciousness to accommodate a little trust in God for when we need it? …I think that possibility would be acceptable to many non-believers …but is it Bible based?

…I'm certain the casual approach is acceptable to satan. …"everything in moderation (no excesses)" is sufficient for satan's purposes. …"don't make waves" is at the root of satan's determinations. …do we suppose satan could never use God's word out of context to advance his cause? (2 Cor. 13: 15) …it's true the Bible says "live in peace" (1 Tim. 2: 2) ……or "…we may live a quiet and peaceable life".
(Mark 9: 50) …..or "have peace one with another".

…we're lucky to have so many churches, to flock to, that promote peaceful, easy feelings …and avoid conviction and repentance …whereby we barely have to lift a finger …and "bingo!" ….we're saved! …at the church I went to last, the pastor said we were all holy and to come and have some communion supper.

…his message had been from Colossians 1 and our struggle towards holiness.

(Col. 1: 10) "that ye might walk worthy of the Lord unto all pleasing, being fruitful in every good work and increasing in the knowledge of God. (verse 11) Strengthened with all might according to His glorious power, unto all patience and longsuffering with joyfulness." …I believe what the Bible says is true …in that it's in the struggle and in the defeat over temptation that we find His rest and His worth …which opens the door to His joy within us. …all else is interference.

…I have one friend with whom I most often speak …and our conversations revolve totally around scripture …and our conversations are always lengthy, which inevitably make one of late for something. …there's a weird pleasure in being late, yet not feeling the least bit guilty.

…what's important in our lives, will honestly be represented in where we go …who we see …what we listen to, etc. etc. …is my heart for "whatsoever is of faith"?

(Luke 12: 34) "where your treasure is, there will your heart be also." …is another of the Bible's Sobering truths …and like "love" we can't hide it where it is nor feign it where it is not. …whatever is of faith, the Christian will revel in and encourage.

…how can he do otherwise? …love never dies …it can only grow …if it's truly love.

…God is love and only what is of God is truly of love.

…there may be multiple sources of romance …or passion …or fun …or interest, etc.

…but without God they will have an underlying root of deception.

…the Bible speaks of the man who builds his house on sand …and what happens to his house when the rain come.

…what will my legacy be, as regards the materials and foundation I'm leaving my son, Richard, to build his house on? …not only Richard but Richard's friends and their friends? …the world has a storehouse of nicely packaged goodies (cheesecake) for him to choose from …even more than I myself had at his age.

…will he follow the same wayward paths that I followed? …is there anyone who doesn't seek a life more abundant. …is there any depth to which satan won't descend to mislead us? …"decent and respectable" doesn't mean much if satan is pulling strings, be we Christian or otherwise.

…I'm eagerly awaiting a visit, in the next day or so, from a longtime friend whom I haven't seen in years. …I'm pleasantly curious about what he might be bringing with him …not in his suitcase but rather in his heart and mind …we've had good faith conversations via letters and phone calls but for too long, not face to face.

(…I'm trying to think of the group who said "Life is a Carnival" ("two bits a shot") ….might have been "The Band"???) …(not Salvation Army))

…the pastor, Sunday night, talked a bit about awaking every morning being "pumped" about how God might use us this day! …to somehow share Him in our families, our communities …cities, countries etc. etc. …good stuff!!

…I remember days past, of awaking and wishing I hadn't. (…probably not indicative of a very fulfilling life.) …I guess we awake with the fruits of what we've gone to sleep with. …lots of carnivals also have a "house of horrors". …best to choose a carnival (wagon) that is discerning of that sort of thing.

…I admire that Americans make "faith" such a dominant part of their political forums. …today is election day for our community leaders (MPs) …(major participants)

…I don't think the Bible is on the table here in this election for fear of offending some group (…."jack of all trades …master of none")

…I guess politicians are like preachers …either offend everyone …and fade away …or else offend no one and be popular. …long ago, men of conviction (disciples) spent a lot of time in prison because of their convictions (both ways) …but "lukewarm faith" really constitutes little threat to power here in Canada. …we've attained many of the freedoms we protested for in the 60s and I'm wondering what we've gained vs. what we've lost. …we weren't big on the institution of marriage and today's divorce rate reflects that. …I guess that's "one of us!" ….except when we protested legal marriage …we didn't have kids …like legally married people did (whoops!) …that's a bit of a miracle we were largely unaware of

(at least …I was unaware of!) …"miracles, unawares" is heavy stuff!

..."childbirth" may be "all in the cards" for the ladies ...but this new "father participation thing" is an eye-opener for most guys!   (...."new" as in the past 30 years .) ...for me, it took everything I knew as fact ...and threw it all out the window.

...it's not at all like coming home to find you have a giant French lop rabbit as a house pet! ...although that was interesting.

...getting excited about breathing and pushing is much like our surrendering to Christ ...you don't know what it's all about ...but you just do it! ...and never mind the "why?"

...our ways aren't God's ways.

(..."it's written in the wind ...it's everywhere I go ...you gave my promise to me and I gave mine to you" (Troggs)

...what a ride!!!" (Romancing the Stone ...Michael Douglas line)

...loving parents know what it's like to be separated from their treasure (children) which is a part of them ...does the Christian not experience the same loss when separated from things of faith when we turn to the world for comforts and pleasures?

...is my faith on of "out of sight ...out of mind"?   ...how small a distraction does it take to turn off God's word and turn up the volume?

...I've long had a general meaning of the word "steadfast", ...and the concordance says it's used about a dozen times in the Bible to describe God's will, as regards our walk with Him. ...the dictionary defines "steadfast" as (1) firm, fixed, settled or established. (2) not changing, fickle or wavering; constant. ...that's a little more rigid than I'd prefer.

...not much wiggle room. ...I probably need a different dictionary.

...at least it doesn't say "as poured in concrete" ...right?

...my eyes also slipped down to the word "steady" ...which is also a good read.

...why would our lives change if Christ were "physically" with us at all times?

...does that suggest we're not walking steadfastly by His Spirit leading?

...over the past 30 years we've gained some freedoms ...right?

...and if we want to walk "lukewarmly" rather than steadfastly"

….nobody can stop us …..right?

…as Christian, we have every right to righteous indignation! …right?

…I'm slowly learning to question all activity and thought as to those which push me towards God ….vs. those which come between myself and God.

(Matt. 11: 24) "If any man will come after me, let him deny himself and take up his cross (Christ's cause) and follow me".

…to deny ourselves, in pursuit of Christ, is to desire conviction (feeling bad) about every aspect of our demeanor that is void of faith.

…to be placid (undisturbed) in our faith walk, is to be "without".

…"content" has no place in "growing in Christ".   …as it pertains to "faith"
…"content" is probably the recipe for "anxiety and pain".

…the phrase "I don't mind" …isn't necessarily the route of spiritual contentment and more probably a holding cell which holds us back from growth.

…a few years ago I was painting the exterior of a house. …I was doing a section by standing on the attached garage roof …and looking up at the job at hand (as I was suppose to) …but I ignored another "suppose to" …and consequently stepped off the roof and fell about 12 feet onto a prickly bush. …shocked and scraped …but otherwise apparently (and gratefully) unscathed …I carried on …but I'm forever reminded to look upward and onward …but look also to the road I'm on …lest I stumble.

…faith requires we be ever vigilant on all fronts, else satan will trip us up.

…the many things in our daily lives that (we may think) have no bearing on our faith can, through Christ's Spirit, be brought into submission (captivity) of faith if it's our desire to put forth the effort to bring that about.

…there's nothing the Bible asks of us that isn't within the Spirit's power to effect.
…what is required of us to tap that power, is our surrender of self will. …and then to guard against it's re-emergence. …the Christian is called by scripture to guard against giving in to temptation ….how or why would we receive rewards for our failing in diligence through carelessness or neglect?

…our cross to bear is Christ's burden to bring every man, woman and child to the Father. …His burden is to be our treasure if we indeed love Him above the world.

(Mark 8: 34) "whosoever will come after me" (join me) let him take up his cross (his caring for lost souls) through self-denial and carry on the work that Christ began.

…the cause for which He gave his life, out of His love for us.

…Christ cared enough that His message upset worldly authority to the point where they chose to publicly execute Him.

…"fear" of losing power (authority) does and has done great ill. …men especially

…I wonder why that is ??? …I appreciate that the Bible supports the authority of man …but that authority applies only to men who respect and fear God …and who abide by His word. …otherwise there can only be some other spirit steering the ship of man's will. …scary thought! …to suggest it may simply be the spirit of human nature is probably being overly kind to ourselves. …human nature …is to plug the guy next door and take all that he has …it's "might over right".

…and it's the antithesis of everything Christ shared with this world. …so then it needn't come as great surprise that, through our ignoring the word of God, we find ourselves burdened with the fears and baggage we carry around by our own choosing.

…how badly need we burn ourselves to learn to keep our fingers out of the flame?

…I was just thinking on this recent visit by my friend Dave. …great visit and good symmetry in that he was a good influence on those he met and I think he was well influenced by those he met. …he got mildly involved in some landscape reconstruction happening about the building how it's going to beautify the place over the coming years …and even if I were to move away or die (same thing) …he'd probably visit here to see the completion (fruits) of what he had seen begun.

…a week ago I was anticipating seeing the fruits (growth) of his own Spiritual walk.

…(I wasn't disappointed.) …it's a good thing for Christians to continually look for in each other. …"no change" may be better than "negative change" …but it's not "our hope" …"no change" is stagnation …and how can "stagnation" encourage us upwards?   ...I heard a Bible message recently about "Spiritual diagnosis" ...and guarding our Spiritual walk against worldly influence.   ......good stuff!

...Pastor Ian Goligher shared how, if we're not feeding on God's word day and night, we can starve ourselves "to death" ...and that "death" is an eternity of torment (gnashing of teeth) and regret ...who wants that !?! ....what am I willing (stupid enough) to risk?

...if God says "life" is in the gruel" then what am I doing looking over the desert tray?

...do I just want to separate from God and take my chances elsewhere?

...who am I to question God? ...when God says something through His light (the Bible) ...we immediately go into defense mode and claim "surely, God can't mean what this says!" ...."it must mean something more to my liking ...especially as I've already professed myself as "Christian". ...I seem to recall, when I carelessly stepped off that roof ...a similar defense for a few seconds ..."there must be some mistake!"

...Christians can become so focused on "receiving" ...that we forget the "giving" of attention to serious matters of obeying and trusting the source of "every good and perfect gift."

...we can "envision" ourselves as becoming the pillars of the temple! ...or preacher of the year! ...Christian actor or author of renown! ...but if it's not solely to His glory then our "capacity to receive" of Him is foiled.

...I'm just back from papers, and was thinking on what Pastor Goliher said about guarding our Spiritual walk ...and he specifically cited "guarding the Sabbath" as a priority. ...I've heard many pastors "water down" that commandment ...so much so, that where I was once shocked to hear that from a pulpit ...I now am no longer surprised. ...isn't to open that door also the opening of every door to the demands of a changing world? ...Heaven forbid we be persecuted for taking a stand against "world required lukewarm faith!"

(Luke 11: 2-4) ...Christ told us how we ought pray, yet the Christian's world has now brought everything from soup to nuts into "how we ought pray" ...then claim the Holy Spirit's direction as their defense for so doing.

i.e. ...."Lord, please give us traveling mercies and sunny weather on our trip to Disneyland. (and we regret the circumstances of our brothers and sisters in Christ in other countries who, being in jail, are unable to join us.) ...and Lord, just because I've failed to engender my disciplined Christian walk upon my children and close friends doesn't mean I don't want You to do it by some means other than me. ....thank you for doing what You can, amen. ...Okay! ...is everyone packed?!?"

...is the Sabbath merely symbolic? ...is it of little import, when we set time aside for God, just so long as we do it? ...is it that dastardly legalism, once again, rearing it's ugly head? ...the communion I observe, uses bread (wafer) and wine (juice) ...why not alter that to pepperoni and beer, if that's what the people want? (...I personally think it should be a piece of gravel and vinegar and trust God as to whether it kills us – or not.) ...as Christian, we don't fear death ...right? ...Christ didn't simply die (like, calmly in His sleep) so that we can have stuff and be happy.

...like my son Richard used to yell out when he was a little fella and couldn't make himself heard ..."Hey people!!!" ...he did that, when necessary, because it worked in getting our undivided attention! ...what a blessing to hear that little voice yell out.

...Christ said it quietly ..." (Matt. 11: 15) "He that hath ears to hear, let him hear."

...quietly ...but repeatedly ... (Mark 4: 9, 23, Mark 7: 16, Luke 8: 8, 13: 35, Rev. 2: 11, 17, 29, Rev. 3: 6, 9, 13, 22) ...how many times is enough???

...Christ was persecuted, abused, beaten to a pulp, then nailed to a stake (cross) and publicly humiliated unto death ...never, so that we could have stuff and be happy

...but rather that we might be rejoined to our creator ...wallow in His peace ...know His joy in ourselves ...and have eternal life through (and only through) loving Him with all our heart, soul and strength ...and trusting His Spirit to suffice for it all.

...the "whole ball of wax" (whatever that means?) isn't a few hymns and a Bible talk ...it's our lives!! (...where's Richard when I need him ...)

..."Hey People!!! ....don't be deceived! ....taste ....and see that God is good!"

...the "time" to taste God and see" probably isn't going to land on our doorstep ...unlike with temptation, distraction and satan's cheesecake. .....even our initial tasting will require that we turn away from something we presently enjoy.

...our days and hours are numbered and we can't add, even minutes, to that ...but we can re-evaluate a portion of the time we now have, in order to favor "whatsoever is of faith", so as to taste and then "see". ...would it kill us to do that!?!

...I think the Bible says there's death (unseen) if we don't.

...if we allow God to work through us then we become healthier and happier in Him.

...if we don't want to help ...we can at least get out of His way and not encourage things we know are not pleasing Him ....right?

...we know that whatever is not pleasing to God can never bring pleasure or peace to our own souls ...right? .....so why do we allow those thing to be established in us or become habit? ...we don't give our children candy after candy after candy

...yet we don't mind them watching us eat cheesecake after cheesecake. ...what's with that?? ...where will it end? ...history shows that we have the past generation's (our parent's) treasures, plus tons to boot! ...aren't we able to bridle anything!?!

...is this our legacy ...our carelessness, plus theirs to boot??? ...and us ever clamoring for more and more goodies.

(1 Thes. 5: 18) ...the Bible says, "In everything give thanks" (verse 21) "Prove all things hold fast that which is good."

(Rev.d 3: 2) "Be watchful, and strengthen the things which remain, that are ready to die......" ...are we watchful? (...maybe "wishful" is close enough ...right?)

(...I wonder where we go, after we die if it's not??? ...probably not Heaven)

...is "wishful" close enough for those we are close to ...profess to care about?

...in Christ, getting ourselves "bridled" (under His control) is the "first but smaller" reward ...through Him we're to put "others" ahead of ourselves, wherein is the "greater reward." ...if we can't show "His light" without forgoing the crap of the world, then non-believers are right to perceive us as jokes to any "faith of substance."

…if I'm a person of little or no religious belief, then I have no problem being labeled "infidel" …or "heathen" …"the proof is in the pudding" …I am, to you, just what you see. …any religion worth it's salt …is worth sharing!

…we're a communicative people and eager to speak to others about our treasures

…be they our children, our friends, houses, cars, books, movies, pastimes etc.

…all that I see and that brings me pleasure, is mine. ….my experience…it's not legally mine …but it doesn't have to be. …the Bible says "every good and perfect gift is from above" (God) and all that is from God is everyone's

…through obeying Him, we can claim to ourselves all that He offers.

…amassing material possessions for our own purposes and the fear of losing them derails our obedience to God and comes between us and God.

…we buy insurance from the world to protect the world's offerings (treasures).

…is there anything "of God" for which we can buy insurance? …or even need insurance? …I don't think there's anything from God that we're meant to keep for ourselves ….rather, we're to guard against keeping it for ourselves.

…maybe that's the test for what is of faith vs. what is sin???

(…do we need to be "un-insured" to be Christian???)

(Matt. 6: 19) …if our treasures, laid up on earth, require "insurance" from the world against moth or rust or theft …then what have these treasures to do with trust in God?

…don't they, rather have to do "without" trust in God to provide for His own flock?

…(verse 24) "No man can serve two masters"

…(verse 21) "For where your treasure is, there will your heart be also."

…(verse 22) "….if thine eye be single, thy whole body shall be full of light."

…if we place both our hands in God's hands …then we must have a third (invisible) hand with which we embrace the world …right?

…it sure is a blessing to not be fickle …am I sufficiently thankful for that blessing???

…(watch-it!) ….I hear ya, mom.)   …'sarcasm" is probably "not of God" …right?

...Eskimos ....seem to have "owned" nothing except tools necessary to basic survival ...yet all they saw (which of course wasn't much) ...was theirs.

...it appears "possessiveness" wasn't their way ...even to the point of sharing their source of warmth (perhaps even their wives) with visitors, that their visitor be complicated caring (love) makes hi-brows look bad ....right?

...I just had one of best friends visit and shared a 4 x 6 room for him to sleep in (no door) ...that's the best I could offer from a bachelor apartment. ...our "adopted" way of life determines our perception ...and hopefully our short-fallings.

...as "supposed" grown-ups, our inherited values hold little thanks or blame as regards our blessings and baggage. ...I suppose we're born equal ...and die equal ...and in God's eyes are judged according to what we do to His glory, with what were able to contribute without lame excuse. ...am I sharing what I'm blessed with?...or am I hoarding a bit of it??? ...and if I'm hoarding a bit ...why am I doing that? ...do I want to do it? ...or ...does my spouse or family want me to? ...in the "end"....when asked ...am I going to say, "jees God, I wished You'd been more explicit! ...please don't blame this on me!" ...when we see what we're wrought for our families and friends, we'll be "defensive" big time! ...whether humbly or otherwise ...I know I'm not the sharpest tool in the shed ...yet even I grow tired of the same empty excuses time after time.

...much of what we do and many of our pastimes are indefensible through scripture ...yet we scramble shamedly to pull some verse or part of a verse out of context to somehow support errant Christian lifestyle.

...if we like competition and sports, we can claim (1Timothy 4: 8) where indeed it says, "For bodily exercise profiteth"

...unfortunately though ...it says "For bodily exercise profiteth little: But Godliness is profitable unto all things, having promise of the life that now is and of that which is to come." ...for sure, it doesn't say "profiteth nothing" ...but for the Christian to defend a "worldly want" with Bible scripture, seems a bit desperate!

…how can we encourage any good thing for ourselves or our children with that sort of "weak tea and white bread"? …most every parent knows the sunken feeling of when a child first attempts to deceive them. …their wide-eyed innocence departs, even briefly, as that cloud of doubt forms. …it's like, out of our sight, they've been to the tree of knowledge (garden of Eden) and had a taste of it's fruit. …their having reached the age of reasoning is a sobering reality for the parent. …God sees our hearts …regardless that our lips and ears and hands be allowed to deceive.

…maybe "bodily exercise profiteth …." …but better to be pear shaped and honest as regards what is and what isn't of faith. (1 Cor. 3: 16) …yes, the Bible says we are to be the temple of God and we ought maintain ourselves as such, as the Spirit of God dwells in us. …but to be out of shape has no bearing (or little) on the passage's concern with defilement of His temple.

…the Bible says "God see our hearts"…I don't think it says He sees our physical fitness …nor our I.Q. tests or university degrees.

…the world says "apply yourself" …God says apply yourself in all things to His glory alone. …our applications "otherwise" must be against Him …and therefore, sin. …when we choose thoughts or activities we wouldn't share with Christ (were He physically present) then we, as Christians, shame ourselves and shame the honor due Him. …the Bible tells us throughout what is pleasing to God, Christ and the Holy Spirit (comforter) …have we been given authority to expand on those things to include things that are socially edifying or acceptable?

…is the Christian and non Christian now to obey random conscience rather than only those things scripturally verified?

(Rev. 3: 16) ….what is the "source" of "lukewarm" faith that's admonished against in the Bible? …to be lukewarm is to taste of God but then turn away and choose what of the world to supply and nourish for our needs and the needs of our family and friends. …as Christ was in the world yet not of the world …are we not to be likewise challenged?

...since God spoke to Adam in the Bible, there must be hundreds of times or ways we've been told not to conform to this world but rather ...

(Rom. 12: 2) be "transformed" by His Spirit ...yet, as did Eve ...we hear what we want to hear ...though we have ears to hear Him.

...it wasn't that long ago that I was excited and pumped about golf. ...I tracked the world rankings and posted them on the fridge ...dragged my poor son Richard to the course though he be kicking and screaming (he only did that when it was pouring rain ...but no lightning.) ...if his friends didn't golf ...I'm sorry ...but they couldn't be his friends. ...I bought him Tiger Woods biographies to read (if he's old enough to watch cartoons, he should be able to read biographies ....right?)

...anyways ...I'm not suggesting I was obsessed with golf but I did find it mildly interesting (one can get excited and pumped about "mildly interesting ....right?)

...the beauty of "faith in Christ" ...over "golf" ...is the bar graph.

...in "gold" there's a huge range of peaks and valleys ("pumped" vs. "deflation") ...in "Christ" we are supported (carried) through the valleys by His Spirit (comforter) even through the valleys of the death of a loved one or our own impending departure from this world.

(1 Cor. 15: 55) "O death, where is thy sting? O grave, where is thy victory?"

...until recently, I never knew there was life without fear ...and I never knew fear was unnecessary! ...there's probably about a million "fears" that satan holds in his left hand, as alternatives to the "cheesecake" he holds in his right hand

...but he doesn't tell us the cheesecake he holds is made from all the fears.

...whereas the Bible tells us that over and over and over. ...how many times is enough? ...eventually, we'll say "Enough! ...I'm not taking this garbage anymore!!!"

...it's no blessing to be complacent

...Christ's blessing is in our discontentment to accept an empty life of being jerked around by every wind of change. ...maybe a generation not at war, establishes war on itself. ...I guess social freedoms within can perhaps generate equal, or even greater, destruction than an outside enemy. …how does a society recover from moral destruction" ….does the majority even want to?

…Christ died a heinous death, so that we might choose life more abundant here on earth …and life eternal afterwards …but our parents, our children, our friends have died heinous deaths or perhaps have been heinously maimed …so that we can have the freedoms to choose whatsoever we want, as a democratic (majority rule) society.

…the spilled blood of Christ, calls out to the Christian…but doesn't even the spilled blood of our own, call out to the secular world to not take lightly the price that has been paid so that those who remain and those who follow …will uphold values and decency?

…"morose" isn't the only alternative to fun or lightheartedness …the Bible calls us to sobriety and vigilance and to "hold fast to the good that remains, which is ready to die." (Rom. 3: 2) …are we ready to gamble with "good"? …"what if we don't gain anything? …we're a proud people ….are we too proud??? …and is it at the sacrifice of others? …if we err …who will lead us back? …Billy Graham?? …the Pope?? …the U.S. President?? …United Nations?? …how do you lead a people who don't want to be led? …who actually want freedom from being led? …the Bible gives great example of the aimless wanderings of such people …and when hunger or emptiness develops …we exclaim "what an unfortunate twist of fate! …woe is us, upon whom this has been visited!" …it has not been "visited upon us" …it's the reaping of what we've sown. …life jackets aren't for sissies …they're for and carried by people who "care" …and there's no guarantee our choice of lifejacket will save us but in our selection is our hope. …and in our sharing is our love for another. …in our love, is life, …without which is banality.

…I listened to a fella speak on his faith for about an hour last night …slept soundly …and this morning, on reflection …realize I have no idea what he was talking about. …maybe I was too tired …maybe the Spirit in me was protecting me

…I only know that he and I, last night, were not "one in the Spirit" and I'm not drawn to where he's at. …I don't have a problem with that and I'm not in any way offended.

...it was simply an eye-opener for me. ...another might well garner some substance from that conversation

...but I was wondering on papers this morning about "why" we converse with others? ...is it to stave off loneliness? ...maybe to validate ourselves?? ...to share some good thing which will be for all people?? ...training?? ...we were trained to speak and so we found it was good to do it??? ...some people speak ...and even think, in several different languages! ...I imagine those people can have amazing conversations with themselves! (...Jack, speak with Jacque!) ...the possibilities boggle the mind! ...I imagine that would be a big asset for those who like to speak a lot ...less likely to get bored with ourselves.

...anyway ....it's interesting that although we claim to be "one in the Spirit"

...yet we prefer one pastor's presentation over another's of the same word of God (truth and light)

...at church on Sunday night (Coll. 2:) the pastor spoke to the importance of being rooted and built up in Christ ...and avoid false teachings which come of men and not of Christ. ...he cited a Star Wars character who spoke maybe 90% truth ...but, knowingly, embraced even 10% evil or untruth.

...that's a scary scenario and for sure a predicament for many who aspire to growth in faith. ...what's the prognosis for our churches that settle (knowingly) for 90% truth? ...and the churches for our children? ...is 90% more likely to go to 95%? ...or more likely 85 and falling??? ...I think we know by now that we're not going to recover from (restore) the "good" that we allow to slide into the abyss ...so how do we stem the flow? ...as my dear mom used to say to me ..."watch-it!"

...or ...as the Bible says "be discerning" (Rev. 3: 16) "Be watchful and strengthen the things which remain, that are ready to die: ...." suggests we have already "lost" some things ...and that, as Christ used the word "strengthen", suggests that to merely "protect" is inadequate.

…God's love and God's Kingdom will endure forever (all eternity) but with the ever increasing worldly distractions and increased freedoms, the task of His church here (us) requires that we not become lukewarm in our sharing of our treasure (faith).

…with fellow believers, we can enthusiastically converse and share …but with others it's maybe better to "listen" more and offer an occasional scripture verse that applies to each conversation. …we're not called to "preach at" …but rather to "share with" others

…so that through God's workings they might slowly turn from the world's (satan's) enticements and seek a gradual walk in faith believing.

…"Only love (God's love) can break a heart ….only love (God's love) can mend-it again." (sort-of Gene Pitney …60s stuff)

(2 Cor. 10: 5) ("bring every thought into captivity") ….right?

…the secular world supplies for so many of our need, that it's easy to quickly adopt it's ways and provisions …but in doing so we're tempted to forgo some of the more firm admonitions in God's word and we soon begin picking out our likes and our dislikes. …same with churches, do we seek a church that holds fast to God's word? …or another more suitable to our private wants? …maybe we seek a balance between our convictions and our spouse's convictions? …that's probably the most democratic ….right? …so then, do we attain a moderated faith?

(Rom. 8: 9) …the Bible says if any have not the Spirit of Christ, they are none of His. …the Spirit is one Spirit and His leading is a singular direction towards revealing God's greater truth …so why moderation in focus? …do we, as Christians, differ primarily in the extent of lukewarm ness we're each trying to justify…irrespective of what the Bible says??? …I don't' suppose that would be a home or a church that encourages one another to "be watchful and strengthen the things which remain, that are ready to die" ….right? …we prefer to not think of ourselves as deceitful …but maybe we are, just a little??? …a church, I attend, is starting a new Branch in a distant (10 miles away?) neighborhood …as are some other "friend" churches also. …these are probably based on projected growth and will supply a venue for up-and-coming pastors without pulpits ...of different denominations.

...we're called in the Bible to be busy about the Lord's work (His will) and we pray that new church starts be Spirit driven rather than market-share driven, yet why several "friend" churches in a growing community?

...why the confusion and friction in existing congregations?

(1 Cor. 14: 33)   "For God is not the author of confusion but of peace, as in all the churches of the saints". ...so what's the source of this friction and confusion, and what spirit is it the role of? (1 Peter 5: 8) ....the Bible tells us "Be sober, be vigilant because your adversary the devil, as a roaring lion, walketh about seeking whom he may devour." ...I like to relax after a hard day ...and put my feet up, maybe even doze off for a few minutes. (Eccl. 4: 9-12) ...that's why "two are better than one" ...somebody needs to man-the-watch, else we're soon overtaken. ...for sure, God could have made it easier for us ...but He could also have made us robots! ...He's given us the perfect balance to strive for ...and attain His end reward! ...there's no failure ...except we rebuff Him (decline His advice and His Spirit). ...no ...we can't hedge nor take little bites or samples. ...we cannot conform to a little of "what is against Him" (the world)

...but we can choose! ...for one or the other and take our licks depending on our choice.

...not everything in the Bible makes sense to me right now ...but when I was a child not everything my parents told me to do, made sense either. ...some children never do surrender their own self will to their parents advice and wisdom. ...some stay head down, teeth set and hell bent ...some say "okay" but they don't and some children are obedient, yet happy nonetheless and greatly please their parents. ...loving parents don't wash their hands of defiant or disobedient children, though the parent receives little or no honor or respect. ...though grieved, the parent's love brings to bear every means possible to break a defiant or deceptive will ...hard love is not a lesser love ...it's a more bumpy and not preferred application ...but never complacent. ...to love, is to continually look for ways to please with no thought for what I'll get in return.

…I guess "love" is it's own reward. …so, to be a child of God (of His flock) we (I) ought seek to push down and away all that is not "of faith" or not pleasing to what God asks through His word and Spirit.

I guess it's good debate as to what is "of faith" and what isn't …and then …if not of faith ….what is it of??? …are all people spiritual beings???…or are we without spirits until we choose one?

…the Bible says we're born into a sinful world, and with a sinful nature.

…dead towards righteousness but alive to selfishness. …in that state, even our good deeds and charitable works hold an expectation (though we can suppress it) of self serving return. …only Christ's Spirit will motivate us to conduct our affairs from a state of His pure love, without ulterior motive now or in the future.

…there's probably no greater self deception than should we feel betrayed after investing in a friendship, relationship or charitable cause.

…betrayal and perhaps even disappointment are perhaps the proofs of having failed to "love without expectation of commensurate return."

…I don't think we often see or come across "humble love" but when we do, it's good and wise to look for it's source in that person's life …and if possible, to tap into the source ourselves. …it's always possible, if we want it. …the Bible says "taste and see that God is good". …when we see "selflessness" in another, we see the primary characteristic of Christ. …it's beauty is not unlike the beauty of a sunrise or a sunset (or that of a newborn fawn, which I happened to see this morning on the paper route, as it galloped unsteadily behind it's mother)

…some things compel us to smile inside and wish all others could experience our present inner ecstasy. ….it's a blessing, through Christ, that can't be bottled or sold but rather, as with all grace, is another unwarranted gift from a loving Father.

…we can attempt to speak of it and attempt to share it but unless another experiences it, all description fall short.

…the "experience" can be truly shared with another who has experienced it.

…the only time I ever seriously traveled, was about 10 years ago to South Africa.

…I didn't want to go, even though money wasn't really an issue then …but was, in the end, persuaded to go. …a day or so in London …a few weeks in Pretoria, Kruger Park and Capetown ….I loved every minute

…on returning, I talked about South Africa, bought books on South Africa …watched film on South Africa …interrupted other's conversations …."it" changed me …despite all my resistance prior to the experience …Hey People!!! ….you don't know what you're missing!!! …my South Africa "experience" was my down home "faith experience"

…it changed everything! …and continues to change everything!

…people often wonder how another, seemingly intelligent person, could get (allow themselves to get) addicted to something …yet I now see how someone could get addicted to travel or vacations etc. …(substance addiction is probably more serious)

…everything is relative to our source of reference. …i.e. I've never gambled, so I don't relate well to those who share that addiction.

…I personally think television and entertainment is an acceptable but serious addiction for most people. …the best defense for any addiction is to get the majority of people on board. …wrongdoing and sin follows the same pattern. …first we tolerate it

("don't judge") then we accept it and maybe even take an occasional taste ourselves.

…and while the Bible says the sins of the father will be visited upon their children unto the 3rd and 4tgh generations, the "reaping what we sow" part makes some sense for those "other people" who, unlike ourselves, don't lead good clean lives ……right?

…should our own children go astray, we can say, "tsk (for shame) after everything we did for them!" …self esteem really has no part in faith nor in bringing any glory to God for His goodness to us. …it's actually pro satan (anti-Christ) and if our families, communities, cities, province or state etc. (oikos) is doing well, we're inclined to credit ourselves and our choices. ….if there's credit left over, then God can have any surplus. ....if our choices fail the respectability test ...we can immediately point straight to God and say to each other "How could He??? ...after all we've done!?!"

...like the hymn says "O what peace we often forfeit ...O what needless pain we bear." ...better to figure that "glory" and "prayers" go to the same source.

(1 Cor. 10: 31) ....if we "do all to the glory of God" ...then to please Him, our prayers will be "effectual and fervent ....and availeth much"   (James 5: 16)

...otherwise, forget it! ...right? (Luke 6: 46)   "why call me Lord, yet not do what I say?"

...God is not a toy ...the Bible says ...(Gal 6: 7)   "Be not deceived, God is not mocked, for whatsoever a man soweth, that shall he also reap"

(verse 9) "....in due season we shall reap, if we faint not." ....Good stuff!

...best to surrender (put in God's hands) our self esteem, along with everything else, ...that it be only to His glory. ...every alternative invites eventual expectation and disappointment down the road. ...we're each important equally, to God. ...apart from Him, we always see ourselves as more important than anyone else see us.

...we may question whether "what goes around, comes around" (....or "what goes to God is returned from God) ...but (slow though it may be in coming) patience (in due season) is a fruit (characteristic) of Christ's Spirit and of faith. ...what we give, in glory to God, may be returned to us in any number of unexpected forms.

...better to trust God's measure than to entertain our own limited calculations.

(Luke 6: 20-26) ...in the Bible, there are a series of basic blessings and woes which we can apply to our Christian walk to help us understand our joys and our plights.

..."faithfulness" is a demanding adventure but the rewards are great (in due season) ...the alternative is like quicksand and very unstable.

....good message at church this morning from (John 3: 1-21)

...the pastor geared this passage to the "inclusiveness" of Christ's invitation that all (every race, every faith, every age) be transformed by the Holy Spirit and attain everlasting life. ...though other faith may seem more sensible to us, the Bible says (and Christ's Spirit of truth and light confirms) they are of darkness.

...it's more peaceful to accept that "all roads lead to everlasting life "but we must denounce the Bible to accept that. ...it's more peaceful to accept that sin and wrongdoings are better adjusted to ...rather than spoken against but we know that's against what scripture tells us. ...to be "accepting and tolerant" is the antithesis of "hold fast to the good which remains that is ready to die."

...there's a certain respectability to church and I bet thousands more would flock to a church if churches would just ease up on what's okay and what isn't okay ...people would just conform a little more to the 21st century world.

...there's probably lots of stuff we "could" be doing that we "shouldn't have" to feel bad about ...right? ...but we need a church leader to give us the "nod" ....right? ...there's lots of Christians ...so ...I, myself, probably just have to "hold quickly (fast) to just "some" of the good which remains" ....right? ...it's not my nature to hold fast to too much. ...I'm not an octopus.

...a good message at church tonight ...on Colossians 3: 1-17 ...and a good guest speaker to deliver it. ...dead to self ...born in Christ ...keep seeking Spiritual growth as we're fed by His Spirit in us ...separate from things of this world ...don't weaken! ......good stuff!

...through Christ's death and resurrection, every man and woman, young and old, every race, etc. etc. has a personal ticket to life more abundant here and a home in Heaven later, if we surrender our "fight tooth and nail" lives here and trust ourselves to God's grace through the Spirit of Christ.

...do we really think our 40-60 hour a week treasures are bringing us peace or joy or contentment? ....or is it merely staving off our fear of the unknown?

...every family member and friend on this earth could disown you ...yet in Christ you'll never walk or be alone. ...and while you don't invite trouble or sickness etc. etc. ...you don't have to fear it ...any more than though you were a little child in a loving home. ...you need not even fear death! ...there's no potential breakthrough in science or medicine that's going to alleviate that natural fear for survival ...Christ can.

…is there any drug or panacea to which you can pleasantly go to bed (and wake up) saying "thank you" to, night after night and day after day continually?

…"every good and perfect gift is from above" though there is much available to us that is not from God nor is it "of faith".

…it's not a case of "God vs. us" …the Bible tells us it's always "God vs. satan"

…as to our affections. …the test is our unwavering love and our obedience to either one or the other and there can never be a peaceful truce between the two.

…everything from God is of love and truth and simple trust …and what's of satan is discontentment, guilt and ever wanting more …more freedom, more money, more respect …more confusion.

…children see something then want it. …they don't see the hidden attachments. …toys are discarded, puppies ignored, bikes not maintained, friendships discarded, spouses ignored, honor not maintained, etc. etc.

…God offers precious gifts …while we pine for greener grass elsewhere.

…yet He never withdraws His offer.

…if, out of love and caring, our spouse said we could do whatever we want …with whoever we want …it would probably close every door to every wanderlust and cause us to realize the wondrous treasure of that spouse. …to be so loved, would compel us to cherish, above all else, our being blessed with such a relationship …and to risk losing it would be utmost indolence and transgression.

…"lukewarmness" in faith or marriage or friendship carries the seed of apathy and death …but worse yet …it carries and nourishes the seed of self-will and self-gratification. …I've long thought, that "depression" comes from self-absorption.

…to conclude that there's no way out of a grim situation that's within our grasp, is just what the Bible repeatedly tells us. …we were never created to operate on our own understanding or reasoning …because it's of darkness.

…God's ways are of light and peace. …we each apply ourselves to light or to darkness and the scales tip accordingly.

…we can entertain and honor all the empty treasures of this world, or not

...but we've been told there is life far more abundant, by denouncing those treasures.

..."he that hath an ear to hear, let him hear."

...it might help, if we assume that every temptation and every leading is of either God or of satan. ...no in betweens or gray areas. ...any Christian can justify any gray area his or her conscience allows ...for whatever reason ...but if it contravenes scripture, they've cut themselves off from a large (or small) measure of God's light.

(James 1: 18) "A double minded man is unstable in all his ways."

..(verse 5) "if any of you lack wisdom, let him ask of God, that giveth to all men liberally ..." ...best we let His wisdom and His council determine faith vs. sin.

...we use the word "civilized" to denote an advanced culture or decorum ...and while the Christian is to be considerate of all others, he or she is not to "fit in" ...but rather be seen as different or apart ...and not caught up in the sway of civilization.

...I sometimes wish I wasn't cynical, critical, sarcastic, etc. etc. ...except for that it seems to encourage my discernment regarding my own thoughts and conduct (not all of which I'm content with) ...I have a good friend who displays similar characteristics and he can sometimes sound pretty negative, yet he's been a blessing to my growth in faith because of that. ...I'm "sometimes" a bit zealous about getting more of God's truth ...but he's "always" zealous! ...and I'm glad he is. ...as with any good thing ...the more we get ...the more we want ...just like addictions! ...the determining factor being our definition of "good". ...there's an element that greatly alters our perspective of "good" ...and perhaps softens "evil" or "bad" to the point of "resembling" good.

...that element is a tough one to face down and is determined to fracture our resolve to "hold fast" to that good which remains that is ready to die." ...that little element ...is our subjectivity and it's control is, largely, our family members and friends.

...while "blood is thicker than water" ...is it to be thicker than "living water" ???

...do we, as Christian, pray that every barrier between us and God be dismantled

...but then add "except for those people and things that mean the most"?

(Matt. 16: 24) ...."If any will come after me, let him deny himself ...." ...the Bible doesn't say to deny a "reasonable part" of our self.

(Mark 3: 33-35) ...when Christ's mother and brother sought to approach Him above His followers, He denounced any preferred status for blood ties. (33) "who is my mother or my bretheren?" (verse 35) For whosoever shall do the will of God, the same is my brother and my sister and mother." ...emotional ties (beyond honoring parents) can be a major source of our separation from God and from faith. ...how many evils will we accommodate rather than denounce because they are "too close to home"?

...some time ago a friend and I were discussing faith vs. plastic (flexible) Christianity. ...it was an encouraging (faith strengthening) talk until I mentioned I was pro life and not pro choice . ...he said he was pro life, until his sister had an abortion.

...although he didn't know why she did that, it changed his views on the issue – so that it's maybe not so bad. ...I suppose an evolutionist (survival of the fittest) would suggest that if tests show a fetus is unlikely to be normal, then it's better to stifle that life, in favor of something more promising ...but they have to walk away from God to do it and thus forfeit their own "life" as well "...Thy Kingdom come on earth ...." is only as strong as we (His tools) make it. ...if every Christian compromises God's word (light) through our personal family ties, ...then "darkness" will prevail. ...no amount of "artificial" light will compensate for the loss of "His" light. ...what sin cannot be, somehow, rationalized??? ...what rationalization or compromise is our personal faith safe from???

(James 4: 7) "Submit yourselves therefore to God. Resist the devil, and he will flee from you." ...though it makes us desolate and lonely, it's a valley we must traverse (make one's way through) before we ascend the other side through His power and light. (verse 10) Humble yourselves in the sight of the Lord, and He shall lift you up."

(Rom. 14: 23) ".....for whatever is not of faith is sin."

...weak faith will never empower us to resist temptations of the devil.

(1 Cor. 11: 14)   "And no marvel; for satan himself is transformed into an angel of light."   ….and his cancerous bile looks, smells …even tastes like sweet cheesecake ….but when his fruit has been ingested ….it takes root and grows within us ….devouring our resistance. …satan, …or a cult leader may say "I've had a vision!" …or "I've had a rhema (personal) prophesy!" …"God has changed His mind! …and now wishes us to eat from the "tree of life!" …I bet every Christian would like to hear those words …from a civilized and reputable man of God. …maybe many Christians have heard that already. …so then what do we do??? …to "not judge" isn't "to not share God's word."

…an author I read some time ago …suggesting that "sin" was "missing the mark." …I took comfort in agreeing with that definition when I was on "the mother's milk" of faith …but "sin" is more than that.…so have I now become a Bible Thumper??? …I sort-of hope so …only in that I hope that nothing I ever say carries any conviction to anyone but rather that I might be some encouragement for another to go, themselves, to God's word and His truth …and if they so wish, they can dispute what the Bible says.

…that there is dysfunction in both professed Christian and non Christian families, is evidence that there is much that's "not of faith" at work in both. …those of us weak in faith are prime targets for satan and most prone to self deception or double-mindedness. (1 Peter 5: 8) "Be sober, be vigilant because your adversary the devil, as a roaring lion, walketh about seeking whom he may devour".

(2 Cor. 11: 14) …a "devouring lion" that takes on the appearance of an "angel of light" is a formidable foe to even detect …let alone overcome!

…it's not our nature to look for problems or foes, until we're visibly bitten.

…but like the mosquito or flea, sin often bites us while we sleep (unawares) …and while we may spew out self-convincing excuses …we're usually bitten because we neglected to mount the screen (armor of God, or vigilance) needed to protect us and our household. …the Bible tells us God loves all …saint and sinner alike …and all were (are) created for His pleasure and His will ….not our own.

…we are all broken (handicapped) people yet, through Christ, can contribute to the glory of our creator, in some fashion.

…if we determine to be our own god and seek our own glory then the Bible and it's truth will be little more than an empty and negative focus for complaint and babbling because it detracts from our own glory. …without God …we (man) are of certain importance …whereas when compared against God, we become very small. …the Bible says satan chose the "without God route" and was consequently "turfed".

…I consider that we are to God, as insects are to us …those that are useful, we encourage …those that cause us grief …we swat or step on. …so with us …we either make our own way …or we seek God's way (will) and conduct ourselves accordingly.

…the Bible says God prunes off (separates away from Him) every branch that fails to produce (encourage) His fruit. …what useful purpose has a dead branch to the tree or vine? …or even the weak (lukewarm) branch?

…we've largely departed the fields and orchards and vineyards …except we still want the fruits of them …we're smart enough to leave the efforts and labour to lesser (less important) peons.

…most of us have advanced to the worlds of dubious commerce and speculation and entertainment. …the Bible says "these will be our end reward" but that the final tally will be "horrendous" in God's accounting. (gnashing of teeth)

…the Bible says every Christian's focus is to bear more fruit of the vine …and "to fear" he not be pruned away as being of little use (weak).

…by this measure every Christian can readily choose their companions and their good friends …as can non Christians.

…without the vine, the branch is indeed dead. …even the weak branch, once severed, has no future …except to be burned along with the dead.

…the healthy, producing branch has the hope of being grafted back into the tree or vine because of it's usefulness and perhaps live forever! …amen!

…the dictionary I use, was copy written in 1988 …"Webster's New World Dictionary" …it carries the (in some circles, objectionable) word "shit" with an extensive foray of uses. ..."worthless" is perhaps the more scriptural connotation of a branch that produces little or no fruit. (I apologize, if any offence is taken.)

...there's a man living in this building, who does the landscaping ...I won't mention his name (June /05, 1550 Arrow Rd., Victoria BC Canada, V8N 1C6) whose language is deplorable, in any civilized country! ...he seems as far from "Christian" as possible ...yet, if anyone, friend or foe asked him to do something for them, he would, without hesitation, lay down his tools and go. (...short of anything illegal) ...no questions, no explanations .....just "what are we waiting for!?!" ...his wife lives here too ...in a separate apartment and no wonder ...who could find "settlement" with a man so giving?

...I try to be a Christian but this man shames me by "the fruit of love" he shares.

...what comes from one's mouth, isn't always indicative of what's in one's heart.

...I sometimes think that if we Christians didn't "say" we were Christians (fruit producing branches) then few might ever know we were (are).

...it seems we've learned to blend well with the world ...I just hope we don't thank or praise God, that we've managed to do it. ...our many blessings aren't supposed to be for us ...right?

...if our material goods and our health are of God and for His glory, then why do we allow things to cling to us or why our health, except to serve His will, be His tool, carry His burden for the lost???

...back to family ties: ...the family (flock) of God bears little or no resemblance to our earthy family. ...family reunions draw everyone from soup to nuts, under an umbrella to physically connect. ...it makes no difference that we display (or not) values or characteristics of our parents ...nor even that we may not like one another.

...they're essentially "surname picnics"

...whereas the "family of God" is just the opposite ...neither surname nor given name hold any effect whatsoever. ...it doesn't matter if our lineage is from Billy Graham or Attila the Hun ...it only matters "have we chosen to seek Christ's Spirit to direct our every thought and deed"

(Rom. 8: 9) ….the Bible says "…Now if any man have not the Spirit of Christ, he is none of His." …not of His family …and can have no part of His family reunion.

…for many, this life has abundant struggles and pain

…whether Christian or not. …and we need draw strength regularly from our source of belief. …I believe all and every struggle or pain is appointed (allowed) by God for His own purposes, as the story of Job supports. …what's fair and not fair is for God to determine …not us. …(I'm personally relieved that it's not up to me!)

…some …even Christians invite death, whether as "a means to escape" pain or as "a looking forward" to our hopeful reward. …death is neither escape nor end

…it's only the reaching of a mandatory and irreversible "fork" on our road.

…for those "of God's flock (family) that have been faithful, it's "O death, where is thy sting?" (1 Cor. 15: 55) …but for those who have chosen otherwise

(Luke 13: 25) …it's the futile pleading "Lord, Lord, open unto us."

…and His response, "I know you not whence ye are:"…our "choices" and "personal options" cease at, or even before, death.

(Isa. 55: 6) …"Seek ye the Lord while He may be found, call ye upon Him while He is near."

…it's fine and well to "think positive" …but not "so positive" that we lose sight of our dependency on God and our allegiance to ever bear fruit for His cause.

…I don't know how the Christian can take a holiday from that without becoming a traitor to God which foils even our "hope" of salvation unless we deceive ourselves.

(Jer. 17: 9) …the Bible says "the heart is deceitful above all things and desperately wicked,: who can know it?" (verse 10) "I the Lord, searcheth the heart, I try

(test, judge) the reins (direction) even to give every man according to his ways and according the fruits of his doings. according to the fruit of his doings."

…it would seem to require an almost constant struggle, to maintain "clean hands and pure heart"

(Psa. 24) …who could ever remotely hope to do it, except it be through the power and grace of Christ's Spirit in them?

...for the professed Christian, there is only the Spirit ...or else deceit.

...the non Christian or those no longer pursuing greater faith through Christ, may have qualms but I guess they must seek remedy elsewhere.

...I think the Bible says that only Christ's Spirit can reveal His truth and light.

...if we discard everything solid, we're left standing on shifting sand ...but it's mostly by our hands ...our own choices.

...we may not have the time or the pain required to even scramble for pebbles, let alone rock, to re-establish our footing. ..."it's not fair, that we reap what we sow!!" will be a hollow cry when the end comes.

(Rev. 3: 13) ...."he that hath an ear to hear, let him hear what the Lord saith"

...if I'm not at rest in Christ, then what or who, have I been listening to???

...this "adult"? apartment building I've moved into is a "doozie"! ...while it has a real community feel ...I think I already know everyone as well as I want to.

...I consider myself fairly sociable ...but I'm beginning to appreciate all the recluses here, who one rarely ever sees. ...it's for sure an interesting range of personalities all under one roof! ...soup to nuts. ...some folks have been here for over 20 years! ...maybe 30! (those one's aren't young ...like me)

...I'm learning to never sit and talk (listen) with just one person....if I find myself sitting out front with just one, I soon start silently praying for someone, anyone, ...to come home and then I watch for my "friends" mouth to open in greeting ....then I mumble, anything, and run inside to my humble cell (room) ...where I sit and languish in gratitude. ...I wonder if I appear to others as a bit of a nut-case myself!?

(....jees,....I hope they don't think I'm one of "them")

...they're probably thinking the same thing about me. ...Richard ...if you're reading this, look up an old television series called the Life of Riley and listen to his closing line of every show. ...it'll come in handy, time after time.

...I think some folk here think I'm a good listener ...but I'm not. ...I'm happy to move a piece of furniture or a roll of carpet if I can ...but I'm best to steer clear of personal advice. ...I haven't the training and I'm not qualified ...but I'm happy to cite

Bible verses, if I can recall one in context …but apart from that, I suggest they maybe get a book or see a doctor. …I don't really want to be responsible for how someone responds to what I say. …as I would advise my son, Richard …don't eat crap …and don't serve it to others either. …best to just direct them to what the Bible says on any given issue that is of concern to them. …in sharing advice …what we say and intend, is not always what another hears. …we often hear what we want to hear and bend another's words to conform to that. …the word of God is quotable …and unchangeable …and trustworthy. …nothing "of us" can add to His word or His council.

…we may "speak" volumes but it's never a patch on one single line of His.

…yet we continue to ramble on and on, as though we are the great instrument of God's enlightenment. …(…that's probably what I'm doing right now!) …that's why it's important to continue to earnestly seek His intent (will) and openly place all, He gives us, at His disposal so that His will might, indeed, "be done on earth as it is in Heaven."

…when we're "less old" …we see the many benefits of "who" we know and the potential therein. …my son Richard …now that he can read …has long figured (as would I, at his age) that, if available, a free sample newspaper might be graciously delivered to him, as I deliver the papers on his street.

…months ago, I even gave him the money to "subscribe" for at least a few month. …we haven't talked about it …but I recently got a "new start" under his (Richard's) name and his address! …I was shocked and pleased. …but now I'm concerned about the "junk" that I supply my son with, daily. (….I rarely read a newspaper for that reason.)

…there's a peculiar irony in that my dad delivered the word of God …yet I deliver the word of the world! and I view that exercise as "devotional" time! …go figure!?!

…there's a laundry/billiard room next to my cell here and I had a few games with my landscaper friend last night.

...I think I've mentioned before that I admire and encourage "passion" as a footstool to "sincere faith" (provided it be a lawful passion) ...and how easy it is to be casual (sort-of) in so many things. ...my dad once liked that landscaping stuff and I can see there's a certain artistry involved, even though I don't get it.

...how often do we offer something that we're "unprepared to supply?

...my apartment, being so close, I offered my friend fresh coffee last night ...but when it was made, remembered I was out of milk ...so I "substituted" a couple of dollops of ice cream and took our coffees back to present his, with my apologies. ...I've substituted milk with ice cream before ...but I guess he never has.

...it's funny how sheltered some people's lives have been ...anyway, he looked at his coffee, then at me, then at his coffee again ...then, after a few moments, said he'd better not have it. ...I was thinking about his reaction, this morning on papers ...as regards my spiritual walk ...and how often I say, "God ...You are my treasure and I surrender my all to You!" ...but I've forgotten to be prepared for what I've offered. ...so I substitute (rationalize) my offering, assuming (from my own source of reference) that my neglect will be acceptable to Him also.

...time was short last night ...no time for my friend to go all the way over to his "cell" for milk, especially given that I'd already ruined "what could have been." ...Richard ...don't' forget. (I'm thinking ...if I hadn't had ice cream ...I probably would have tried substituting cheesecake.) ...I drank my coffee last night ...it wasn't that great, but I accepted what was readily available. ...no "friend" will encourage you to do that.

...the Bible says that whatever we do, whoever we're with ...conduct ourselves as we would were it God beside us in person. (1 Cor. 10: 31) (Coll. 3: 17)

...the obedient child doesn't swipe a candy with his left hand ...while his right is in the hand of his austere father.

...so how can the Christian not consider the Father's wishes in their daily walk?

(Luke 16: 13) "No servant can serve two masters. ...". ...Richard ....please don't forget this. ...don't ever offer what you don't have to give nor surrender what you're unprepared to sacrifice ...be it a shot of milk or anything greater.

...in the bigger picture, what I or your mother leave you is nothing by comparison to what is freely given by God, if you only overcome temptations to substitute ice cream (or cheesecake) in place of the "required" or the "mandatory".

(John 12: 35) "...walk while ye have the light, lest darkness come upon you: for he that walketh in darkness knoweth not whither he goeth." (verse 44) "Him that believeth on me, believeth not on me, but on Him that sent me." ...if, in His perfection, Christ can defer all glory to God ...then what is our problem??? ...is it merely that we're selfish, greedy and egotistical???

...how difficult can that be to overcome? ...."piece of cake!" .....right? ...is it satan's "cheesecake" that deceives us into "believing that we are attempting" to overcome those elements which continue to cloud our capacity to be filled by Christ's Spirit?

...I just made coffee, only it's a lesser brand than my usual choice ....acceptable but not the best ...we can, through our choices, content ourselves with a "form" of faith" which is also "acceptable" ...but lacking in flavor or power.

(Mark 4: 19) "...and the cares of this world and the deceitfulness of riches, the lusts of other things entering in, choke the word and it becometh unfruitful" (branch).

(Heb. 12: 1) ...."...let us lay aside every weight and the sin which doth so easily beset us and let us run, with patience, the race that is set before us.

...not every affliction or conviction is of the adversary (satan).

(Heb. 12: 6) "For whom the Lord loveth He chasteneth and scourageth (causes to suffer) every son whom He receiveth."

...from birth (...even before) we have been exposed to pollution and undesirable elements and hence must endure the process of "refining" in order that we become sufficiently pure (Holy) and returned, through salvation, to He who created us.

…God's ways are puzzling and humbling. …Job …who appears to not even have done anything wrong …is a most interesting example of how deep our trust in God is to run.

…yet, then there's Rahab, a harlot, who appears to have been plucked from sure doom, by her heart being softened towards faith in God and her service to His cause (will). …maybe I can learn to remember Job and Rahab whenever I pridefully think I've got some things figured out or when I think something makes no sense to me.

…it's going to take a potent trust for me to accept what God allows or appoints.

…I have Christian friends who live in variable states of chronic physical pain, which, though they describe the pain, I am unable to experience nor appreciate their suffering. …it must be grim for them.

…I can only be supportive and make myself available for their needs.

(Heb. 3: 3) …the Bible says "Remember them that are in bonds (persecuted) as bound with them and them which suffer adversity, as being yourselves also in the body

(of Christ's cause)" (interestingly …marriage is mentioned immediately in the next verse!)

…anyways ….my Aunt Ethel (what a gift to this world) remained a devoted warrior for Christ, through (what appeared to be) a Spiritually fractious marriage …then crippling arthritis after Uncle Tim passed on. …her walk "in faith trusting" had to be an inspiration to all who crossed her path. …doubled over in pain, she would continue to sing God's praises with the clear voice of a songbird.

…back then,I wasn't a Christian, yet I couldn't resist smiling in wonder at this woman's fortitude in spite of her obvious burden. …because of her suffering, she, for sure, was a shepherd to me. …I'm blessed and thankful that my road to faith was made easy

(despite my stubbornness) by the family I was born into.

(if I don't watch out …I'll tear up here.) (real men don't eat quiche, either …right?)

...there's a hymn or song that says "let me be as Christ to you ...'til we see this journey through." ...good stuff.

...best not to discount everything that doesn't make sense to us. ...my friend Dave has serious diabetes. ...he had to have a couple of toes removed after which healing was first questionable ...then eventually slow, extremely painful and throbbing. ...this, for a devout quiet man of God.

...in quiet agony he heard (felt) God speak (ask) "why don't you praise me for your pain?" ...naturally baffled ...but obedient...he prayed, not his own will ...but rather God's will be done (....just like the Bible says) ...and was granted some relief. ...it all sounds unreasonable but I believe it because I believe the Bible and the Bible speaks of devout Christians singing praise to God, even while being burned at the stake.

...we can "pooh-pooh" the unreasonable attributes of faith ...but what does that avail us ...other than greater despair? ...for sure, there are dollars to be made in advancing anti-Bible sentiments ...we may even gain a chunk or piece of this world ...if that's to be our treasure ...it may even afford us a few extra days of existence on this earth. ...I suppose enough money might enable science to keep our eyes and mind functioning sufficiently to be cognoscente of the arrival of a great-great-great grandchild, though the balance of our body be dead and useless for months or years in the waiting.

...and providing it didn't cost millions, it could even be construed as noble ...or at the least, acceptable! .....right?

...the Bible speaks somewhere to our potential to "gain the whole world".

...is that what we're striving for? ...to get our share? ...to keep up an "average" living and life style? ...to compare ourselves and our lot against that of our neighbor???

...and for "that" we turn from God??? ...stray from trust in His providence??

...I heard yesterday of a "new believer" who "came to faith" because scientific evidence supported that there, indeed, may have been a flood in the approximate time of Noah. ...and I think the lady who shared that tid-bit wishes she hadn't.

...that's not "faith" ...that's hedging your bets! ...is there scientific evidence that Christ died and arose again?

...I've known a few desperate times in my 56 years and despite my attempts ...I'm so thankful that God never seemed to respond to my pleas for relief.

...if I heard God say anything to me, it was, "Go away, I never knew you."

...I know my self deceit can manufacture mountains out of molehills

...and I know my pleadings were self serving. ...I may be far from humble but I'm not so far as I once was.

...I don't think I had any definitive Spiritual "experience" until my prayer was that God help someone else whom I, in my own strength, was unable to help much.

...that request to God wasn't made on my knees in church ...it was made at about 5:30 am one morning, between my house and the next, while delivering the morning newspaper ...and at that moment, for once in my life, I felt like a nobody ...sort-of like a piece of conduit ...of no good use except I contribute somehow (maybe as a bit of stream bed) between a source of living water and a distant dying plant.

...the "seed" of faith was planted by my parents ...and nourished by them.

...the "nourishment" just wasn't "accepted" by me. ...over the years I maybe pleased some people. ...I certainly pleased myself! ...I was an idiot. (probably still am.) ...but I'm learning there's more to "life" than waking up ...doing mundane stuff ...then going to bed.

...I read a book years ago called "Alive in Christ" ...I don't recall the content of that book ...only the "title".

...I guess my son, Richard, will (like myself) try every door in life that's easy to open ....my hope and prayer, for him, is that he not pass-by the door that's labeled ...
"Alive in Christ" ...though it not have the glitter and sparkle of the other doors.

...I hope my contribution in his growth hasn't been towards glitter and sparkle but rather in things more trustworthy.

...it was an unexpected treat to exit church last night and find "himself" standing there with friends! (...it's a little embarrassing to hug your son when your head comes to his mid-chest ....but I can handle a little embarrassment ...as I recall ...I'm suppose to be "dead to self"

...so what's this "embarrassment" nonsense? ...am I "dead to self" ...or not!?!

...because embarrassment is all about "self" .....right?

(1 Peter 4: 16) ..."Yet if any man suffer as a Christian, let him not be ashamed ..."

...I don't think embarrassment comes from "whatsoever is of faith" ...nor from whatsoever He has asked of us...rather it's based on what "we make" of something.

...are the frequently embarrassed not the "frequently full of themselves"?

...we may perceive it as shy ...or cute ...or demure ...but I don't think it's the same as "humble" before God.

...is everything and every choice we make, as Christians ....to be edifying or expedient??? .....and if not, then why the admonishment in (1 Cor. 10: 23)?

...can a "worldly" heart "change channels" on a given day or moment to partake of Christ's shed body or blood (life)? ...maybe, as a devout disciple, it can be so

...but "what" if in one less so disposed? ....deceit???

...the Sunday evening pastor ...to the 500 or so seated, continues to impress on us that, as Christians, we are now all "Holy" and thus invited to partake of "communion" and "the life more abundant" ...and how, that although we continue to sin, we are nevertheless "Holy". ...as I think I've mentioned ...this "holy-sinner" business is, for me, where Christianity gets sketchy and things start to fly apart according to what I know of the Bible.

...as I understand it ..."to sin" ...is to "knowingly" depart from what the Bible and Holy Spirit tells us is pleasing to God ...in favor of pleasing ourselves ...in which case, we're not "dead to self" as holiness requires ...but pretend that we are ...right? ....yet, somehow that practice isn't deceit ....right?

(1 Cor. 10: 21) ...the Bible says "we cannot be partakers of the Lord's table and also of the world's (satan's) ...I know then ...there must be something I'm missing here. ...what's my problem with my being a Holy-sinner? ...according to the Bible, there's no preferential status ...whether one be a preacher or lowly helper.

...if of Christ's body, neither will knowingly neglect reverence to the whole body of Christ. ...does "dead to self" simply mean "somewhat dead to self"?

...if "dead" can be translated to mean "deadened" ...well then, maybe we can indeed be "Holy-sinners" ...and thus indeed be lukewarm Christians and yet free from self-deceit.

(2 Cor. 5: 17) ...(some) old things are passed away and (some) all things are become new??? ...Hey people!!! ....(this may be an Epiphany!!)

...a Bible verse that's oft puzzled me, regarding our discernment and our judging of matters, is in the writings of Paul to the Romans. (Rom. 14: 22)

"Hast thou faith? Have it to thyself before God ....." ...I, personally, like plain English and have long assumed that if we have faith, then we are not "to keep it to ourselves" but rather share it! (...if we're going to keep it to ourselves, we may as well not have it!) ...the Bible wasn't written "in plain English" ....in the Greek or Aramaic, many words have many meanings, depending on their context.

...in English we perhaps prefer generalities ...lest we wander into (nit-picky) semantics and confusion.

(Rom. 6: 24) "....that we being dead to sins, should live unto righteousness by whose stripes (sufferings) ye were healed." ...so ...the Christian, though dead to sin (having now the Spirit of Christ abiding within) can yet occasionally sin? ...like maybe every day!?! ...if so, perhaps "dead" doesn't mean "dead" as I understand it but rather dead means "less inclined" .....right?

(1 John 3: 9) ...the Bible says "whatsoever is born of God doth not commit sin" for God's seed is in him and he cannot sin because he is born of God.

...whatever our common sense tells us, as we trundle along towards the 22nd century ...the knowledge God avails to us, of itself, neither increases nor diminishes nor changes. ...our appetites may change ...God doesn't'. ...I don't think the explosion of worldly distractions over the years hold any sway over what pleases God and what brings glory to Him. ...my friend and mentor, Dave suggested this morning that the Christian can be tempted to sin and succumb to sin and the Holy Spirit will yet abide in us…but said he didn't know for how long. …it seems somewhat inviting to "lukewarm faith" to promote that premise …yet there's nothing from God's word that we should avoid promoting. ……having received Christ we are now without our old sinful nature but satan will tempt us, until death, away from following Christ's Spirit …and we can't resist temptation in our strength.

…I suppose that being "dead to self" ultimately implies that it is not ourselves who experience happiness or joy or peace …but rather His Spirit in us, that is either pleased or troubled or worse yet …"grieved".

(Heb. 6: 4) …though God present us plate upon plate of nourishment from His word, do we continue to look away at some distant desert tray, ignoring what is presently before us? …is there a popular movie or sport on television tonight to which I'll succumb? …preferring "it" to seeking a greater understanding of what God has for me?…probably won't grieve the Spirit all that much ….right?

…there'll be time for the other, after the show …..right?

…don't understand all this talk about struggle and perseverance and holding fast

…I've got all that down pat, so now it's a piece of cake! …speaking of cake

…I probably shouldn't …but a piece of cheesecake (after the movie sounds pretty good …..so long as I don't get caught.)

…I wonder how many times I have to say that Christ's Spirit is in me, before it comes true??? …I guess then I'll continually seek righteousness over distractions. …He better do it soon …'cause I'm not waiting around forever!

…I know "patience" is a fruit of the Spirit …and if I had some of that fruit I could maybe wait a bit longer.)

…just an aside ….it would be encouraging to see more folk with seeking minds for understanding God's truth and His means of revealing it.

…we pray for remedies …most of which God has already shared through His word.

…I recall year after year of praying (at church on Sundays) that God please make me a sincere Christian in addition to the life I presently had of fun family and fun friends …even though the Bible already told me it wasn't possible.

...I guess I thought maybe I was special and could have it all and when the Bible says, old things are to pass away before I have life anew...I figured, what with me being an okay guy, it must only apply to sinners and murderers and vampires.

...I recall a telephone conversation a few years ago with a dear elderly lady whom I often sat beside in church, over the past ten years or so ...she had moved to a nearby town.

...when I shared with via this conversation...that I had just recently experienced a change in my life through Christ, she incredulously exclaimed "What!!" ...all those years you weren't saved !?! ...I sort of felt like a piece of poop when she said that ...although I know I had never claimed salvation, I still felt like a traitor. ...I guess I knew the lingo or jargon and she had just assumed I was a brother in Christ. ...I guess it might be like me having a friend named Richard, only to find years later that he was really Rochelle.

(as I suggested might be the case, when my son got an earring.) ...as for my attempts to discourage him from "tawdry baubles"! ...and despite his recollection, I never, except in jest, would have verbally suggested he might be a pervert.

...every child and teen digests what they choose to, of what they're given and apply that to their journey ...it becomes their "source of reference" for future choices.

...some go to drugs, some to less harmful distractions and entertainment ...some to the Bible. ...adults do that also. ...a certain amount of "empty" material is given us and we either reject it or we adopt it "into our source of reference" and thereby become restless and anxious to fill that void. ...others may have a roadmap ...but Christians, for sure, have a roadmap. ...while we speak of "the walk of faith" ...the Bible calls it "the race to the finish" (1 Cor. 9: 24) ...it may even become "boring" if the walk should become habit ...and so the distractions become more and more attractive.

...we may rest here for a hot-dog or there for French-fries, then turn our minds to cheesecake or desert ...the astute may even, eventually say "Hey ...where's the beef!?!" …I think God holds "all" the beef and gives it generously to all who decline the hot-dogs, French fries and cheesecakes.

(Matt. 7: 6)   ("pearls before swine")   (Matt. 13: 47) ….we choose what we take into ourselves and that dictates what (of substance) is in us to give to others.

…I don't think God withholds any good thing …even be it test or trial from those whose "hearts" (not lips) are for His good will. …Hollywood feeds thousands and satan also feeds thousands more …what room in us is left for God to feed?

…the hungry trout will take the bait until it is, itself, consumed.

(…somebody should write that down!!!) (James 1: 3) …if we are double minded we have hearts that are uncommitted and hearts that are unstable.…I don't think God is so desperate to have need of such. …are even we so desperate to have need of such???

…the Bible says "……………….." and we either comply or decline.

(…this isn't rocket science …but rather childlike obedience.

…whether or not we "like" demanding portions of the Bible, probably hinges on our depth of faith and our trust in God …and also on our desire to be more and more accepting of what He allows or appoints in our daily lives.

…if we're slaves to "self" and in bondage to "self" …then I don't think there's very much that "we're positioned" to receive from God.

…is our treasure in thing above?   (Luke 12: 31) …are we "seeking first the Kingdom of God, that all these things (goodness) might be added to us"?

…are we "keeping our minds stayed on God, that we might be kept in perfect peace"?

…are we qualifying to receive the blessings available in the beatitudes?

…I know I can pretty much do what I want, either away from Spiritual growth or towards Spiritual growth. (…I was going to add "having reached the age of majority" …but I guess I'm now well beyond the age of the majority.)

…anyways …I guess everything we do and think has it's eventual consequences in drawing us in one direction or another, as does it influence our children and others.

…maybe in the secular world we can follow the wind wherever it blows …but the Christian has a "predetermined" route if they hope to attain joy, peace and love

...as accorded by following every word of God.

...all things contribute to ...or detract from the characteristics of Christ presented by us ...if there's an escape or loophole, I never found it in the years I earnestly looked for one. (Rom. 14: 23) ..."either of faith or of sin" wreaks havoc on the many "gray areas" of our walk (race) in faith ...yet to not address those areas and put them to rest in God's light, is to invite prolonged darkness or even a "form" of faith, yet lacking in the Spirit's power ...essentially without any real, applicable value. ...I don't think there's anything that's from God which is superfluous to our needs and well being or that of our families.

...we need to be continually growing in His Spirit else we negate the receiving of His righteousness and further negate the fervency and effectiveness of prayer.

(James 5: 16) ...the Bible tells us to pray in faith receiving ....do we suppose greater or lesser faith is of no bearing? ...can we have a form of Christian faith that is self serving? ...I fear we can ...worse ...I fear I can and so I need to be ever vigilant ...and still I probably deceive myself.......what then of my prayers? ...is it sufficient that we pray our brothers and sisters and selves be used by God whenever and wherever ...be it even hospital bed or prison cell ...to advance God's message and that the Christian, being His church, be an implement of His will done on Earth? ...are we a sharp implement? ...or a dull implement? ...passionate and zealous? ...or lukewarm and uncertain? ...as much as I seem to knock lukewarm faith and lukewarm churches ....I yet believe in their potential to plant seed for His harvest. ...were God to smite every lukewarm body then I think, for sure, His cause would be hindered.

...I don't suppose any Christian likes to see hypocrisy or self delusion or deceit in any part of Christ's body on Earth, nevertheless ....if it be that a whole congregation perish ...yet one attain salvation, then such is the price paid for that "one" ...even though God would that all overcome satan's pull towards tainting Holiness. (aside) ...for the first time in many years, I'm experiencing a degree of balance and control over my like and attribute it all to God's grace and so am respectful (I hope!) of His goodness. …and I'm also, somewhat, protective of what I perceive to be His blessings. …because of "His rest" within me, I believe I'm "suppose" to be where I am …for reasons I don't presently understand. …I'm experiencing something I'm unfamiliar with here for to in my 57 years. …in my son's vernacular (…."I'm chill" …if this world lasts another hundred years, it'll be called something different.) …anyways …it's probably great error for us to unworthily consider ourselves (or each other) to be a part of God's flock (or His church) yet remain tied to this (sinful) world via any means or string whatsoever. …to my knowledge, the Bible has left no stone unturned under which we can hide from His loving wrath ..(not an oxymoron in the light of our love for our children and our wrath towards any who would harm them). …there's nothing vague in Christ's claim… (Matt. 12: 30) "He that is not with me is against me and he that gathereth not with me scattereth abroad."

(Rom. 14: 23) "…..for whatsoever is not of faith is sin."

(Rom. 8: 9) "…Now if any man have not the Spirit of Christ, he is none of His."

…in our teens, my brother thought he could expand the rules of my dad in order to accommodate his own wants …my dad would have none of that and my brother was willful and so was expelled. (…it's many years passed since I've recalled that event and yet another thought I've brought into captivity) (2 Cor. 10: 8)

…even with the "seed" of Christ's Spirit, we can remain willful (self focused) and it's no small struggle to seek the relevance of God's word and apply it to every area of our lives ….but in the seeking is "life".

…like children, we continue to ask "why this?" and "what that?" …why 911?

…why war? …why rape or why innocent children abused, even killed? …why disease?

…why aids? …why my son or my daughter killed in a needless, senseless accident?

…why drugs and alcohol and the havoc they reap on others?

…a kind and quiet man in a wheelchair who casually entered my world about a year ago, was buried today at age 59. …we never discussed faith, but I read now, that he was a faithful Bahai. …I'm glad I met Tom but I try not to think of his present whereabouts.

...the Bible spells out that we don't "die" but rather we go to "only one" of two places and it spells out the "sole" glory our fruit (conduct in this life) is to be towards. ...lukewarm faith is the domain of satan. ...in the book of Revelations, Christ says He will "spue" the "lukewarm" from His mouth.   (Rev. 3: 16) ....(nothing) vague there either!)   ...I conferred with my friend and mentor early this morning, whether there might be any merit (per the Bible's teachings) of "lukewarm faith" over, say, Hinduism or Islam or Bahai , etc. etc. ...it appears the non believer has the greater hope for eternal life than has one who has received of God then tainted His doctrine towards the worldly. ..no wonder every Christian claims they're in "no way" lukewarm! ...maybe there's a "moderate lukewarm ness" that Christ's Spirit will abide (put up with) so as we could "sin a little" yet slip back into God's good grace before curfew??? (...drat! ...I just remembered Christ's parable of the brides and the bridegroom and the lamps and the oil.) ...the wisdom in the Bible is such that not only is no stone left unturned but no little pebble either!

...as regards having received enlightenment through the presence of Christ's Spirit abiding in us and then growing lukewarm and falling away, the Bible says it is impossible to renew them again to repentance and salvation.   (Heb. 6: 4–6)

...so I guess that if our faith is lukewarm we had better hope we've never "known" the Holy Spirit in our lives ...right? ..."lukewarm" is to be avoided at all cost.

...the Bible says we're born with a sinful (self focused) nature and despite all the seemingly decent people I know, I'm learning to actually trust only those who have a seeking heart for understanding God's word and abiding by it.

...and I see a slight shadow cross the demeanor of even the nicest non Christians if even slightly challenged. ...it's like a warning bell being sounded somewhere inside me.

...we can't dispel our sinful nature in our own power no matter how pleasant we are nor through a plathenta of good deeds ...no more than our cuddly domesticated house cat can shed it's nature to pounce on a little bird or bunny or mouse. ...it's born with that nature and will fulfill that nature's will even if it never ever saw another cat to mimic.

…most folk are adept at restraining the antisocial actions of their sinful natures ('cause we're domesticated or civilized).

…but even our good deeds and our righteousness is nevertheless "rooted" in our sinful nature, as evidenced in our occasional inclination to gossip or be prideful or to attain power or social status. …the tree rooted in sinful nature will produce fruit that is the product of that nature.

…the Bible says (and I believe it) that only by humbly acknowledging our nature and sincerely regretting that we've overlooked or ignored the reality of our sinful nature and ask Christ to replace it with His Spirit of righteousness

…only then can we hope to effect any lasting good thing and forthwith produce fruit of righteousness. …the Bible says …and we're wise to accept, that "our righteousness is as filthy rags." (Isa. 64: 6)

…I think some "faiths" suggest that we can, ourselves, develop righteousness by avoiding doing bad things or having bad thoughts.

…that's contrary to the Bible. ….there is no cosmic ("each to their own") God …rather there is one God and only one mediator between God and man….that being Jesus Christ …not Buddha …not Mohammad….not Krishna …not Billy Graham nor the Pope. …except we receive Christ's Spirit …we are lost. (it's not my intent to offend anyone but because I like (care for) them …doesn't mean they have to like me or my views but I hope they like the Bible …else nothing else really matters much.)

…although I personally differ with those other faiths, I'm still encouraged by their apparent need for faith and more so for the discipline and passion they display …provided it not harm or disadvantage another. …it's been of interest to me for awhile that the Bible says "Pure religion and undefiled before God and the Father is this …to visit the fatherless and widows in their affliction and to keep himself unspotted from the world." (James 1: 27) …I suppose any religion that contains itself within that envelope …is a religion with merit and though it might well hold attraction for some, without the Spirit of Christ, they can never hold the power over satan nor power over our sinful natures. …if we limit ourselves to our own individual fortitude or stamina, we can generally be "pretty good" men and women …or if we down play those portions of the Bible that warn us that "whatsoever is not of faith is sin" (Rom. 14: 23)

….or that anyone (spirit) not claiming Christ as Lord and savior is not of God but rather of the anti-Christ now already in the world.   (1 John 4: 3)

(1 John 5)   …those not loyal solely to Christ are "of the world" and their present and eternal hope is limited to what the world offers.

(1 John 4: 6) "Hereby know me, the Spirit or truth and the spirit of error."

(1 John 7)   "…..for love is of "God and every one that loveth is born of God and knoweth God." …many religions could claim possession of 1 John 4: 7 in their doctrines …but without the context of the entire Bible, it's empty of God's righteousness through Christ and thus any cult could some how "appear" to tie their horse to the wagon of Christianity.

(2 Tim. 3: 5) "Having a form of godliness but denying the power thereof from such turn away. …what's to be our excuse come our final judgment …be it today or some other day? …is it that we're a bit busy and have been waiting for adequate quiet time? …forget our "life and death" decisions …this is about "life more abundant vs. eternal (forever gnashing of teeth) torment" decisions for us and those we profess to love!

…I was thinking on papers this morning of a soundtrack for when Christ returns to take His faithful flock home to glory …and the theme from "Jaws" came to mind …blaring from the four corners of the Earth …unexpectedly …maybe in the middle of the night …and we may be camping in a thin tent away from all our treasures and security. …some will cover their ears and scream out and yell in terror at their not understanding.

…yet Christ's faithful probably won't even hear this chaos …I think the Bible says they'll already have been removed to safety, while others are scrambling for flashlights and Coleman lanterns and looking for their children (...who have already, also been spared).

...I sort of wish I hadn't seen that movie "Jaws" and I'm sort of glad that I did.

...those that chose not to hearken to the warnings were consumed by fear and dread. ...our choices either make us blessed or they make us victims. ...it's not "up to" (contingent upon) God to save us ...our "present" and our "forever without end" is up to each of us choosing and accepting our treasure and what our treasure has to offer.

...our younger children are safe but our youth and teens are the fruit of our choices ...and "woe" are we who fail to "hold fast" to what is of "God's only begotten".

...do we know where our children are? ...I can squander whatever I want ...as could my folks and their folks before them ...but my "distractions" better not lead me to squander my son's "eternal birthright" ...or I'm a drowned man with a "millstone about my neck".

...we read and hear of more and more people packing it in early (suicide) through their succumbing to satan's distractions from Christ and the love of Christ ...deceived into thinking there's a final escape. ...the Bible says there is neither escape nor is there death to regret and pain. ...our only hope is change ...from worldliness to Christ's righteousness by His Spirit.

...I think it's a bit late to be trying every alternate recipe according to our personal tastes. ..."what we like" has no real relevance in the Bible, unless we'd like to "forget" what "we" like. ...for any who choose to be of His flock there is no hiding anymore ...we may as well wear bright fluorescent red clothing or targets ...because we are henceforth "marked" men and women ...and like it or not ...are blessed to be so. ..."carefree" (as we've know it) is left in the wake of "careful". ...pretty much all through my life I was carefree (footloose) while my dad and mom were careful ...and no doubt paid a big "worldly" price in their being so. ...both were "individually" raised to pay that price ...as was I. ...it should be far easier for me than for those less blessed ....yet stupid me ...I still resist.

...through Christ we are each called to be mother, father, brother or sister to those less fortunate regarding their "source of reference" (upbringing)!

...a Christian home and heritage is a huge, huge blessing and I only now realize the grief caused by we children who squander the "treasure" our parents have tried to share. ...my parents had six children and were consistent in faith ...yet I'm certain a new immediacy (probably a word) arose when my younger brother, Glen, was taken, as regards any "laying off" of reminders to pursue God's truth and His will for the rest of us. ...despite appeasing rhetoric, on my part ....they (my folks) were sound in faith ...while I (see now that I) was dysfunctional and busy about my own "worldly" pursuits (in retrospect, frequently referred to as "being a dummy")and paying attention only to the "small picture".

...had I not had a son, I might still be "enjoying" my "birth nature" (sin) ...and perhaps even still "sort-of" be happily married with the house in the "burbs"!...first, with Richard ...then with the Bible and my upbringing ...I got to wondering how heavy a "millstone" might be ...and how much time I'd have to spend at a gym to get strong enough to counter a millstone. (....the research and calculation led to a fair amount of surrender.)

...to lead a young person astray can happen in an instant and it might even be with harmless or good intentions.

...for the Christian it can merely be the introducing, to our children, any one of a hundred products or material found in nearly every household ...like uncensored television or computers ...or questionable music or books or clothes. ...I suppose even junk food establishes a precedent that is difficult to contain.

...if the world has entered our homes...is God using it to our benefit? ...or is satan using it to our Spiritual detriment? ...if something is not "of faith" ...how assured can we be that it's not "of sin" nor will lead to (encourage) sin?

…I guess we all want variety …is the Bible vague about how much variety is a safe amount? …if my pursuit of variety exceeds that of my dad's …why should my son's pursuit not exceed that of his dad's? …I think my carelessness and neglect would also qualify as my "leading a young person astray, thus once again finding unrest with that "millstone/drowning" thing.   (Matt. 18: 6)

…am I "holding fast to that good which remains, which is ready to die"???

…am I "protecting" that good even??? …or has the treasure lost it's luster for me as I allow layer upon layer of dust to settle over it? …like a diamond, Christ's own church will never ever be smeared nor loose it's crystalline perfection. …the only weakness is ourselves, if we fail to adequately value it's life-giving nourishment ….by tinkering with it or turning from it in preference to something artificial.

…if Christ is our "treasure without limit" why does our conversation so quickly turn to events and entertainments of the world? …did we hear that satan has now put a cap (limit) on his distractions away from the knowledge of God?

…is our dependency on God so strong now that we trust Him to not allow anything "untoward" reach us or our families …while we relax our vigilance and enjoy a little freedom from the heavy armor He's made available?…exactly what is it we do with our freedom from vigilance and personal struggle? …is it that within our race for the prize we look back and perceive ourselves as far enough ahead of the pack …that we allow ourselves a breather to enjoy the man-made scenery that surrounds us? …are we allowed off the narrow road to investigate a little?   (Wow!! …some of the wares are pretty interesting! …you say it's free!?!

…well …I'm suppose to be in that race over there but I suppose I could taste maybe just a little sample …hey …this feels pretty good! …maybe just one or two more …hey! …wha-dya-mean …there's a "cost" just because I'm one the racers!?! …there's a special discount for non-racers!?! ….Oh …well then …I'm not really that big on "racing" ya know …and what's with this stuff tasting so good …and me being so tired …and that discount you mentioned …I guess I'll pass on the race after all and hang out here for awhile …and maybe I can bring the prize home for my kids and another day ....rigtht? ...by the way sir ...um ...exactly how small is a millstone? ...you say about the size of a gallstone!?! ...hey! ...no problem.)

...temptation is everywhere and one seldom falls prey but what they draw (encourage) others along with them ...especially the young or impressionable.

...to sin is a bit like "to litter" ...to walk past a noticeable piece of litter yet not pick it up when we know we should, makes us a part of the problem.

...to pick it up out of curiosity then immediately discard it again is worse and leaves our personal finger print on that piece of junk and we hence can never delude even ourselves that "we're sorry that we didn't notice that litter, else we'd have done something about it"

(James 4: 17) ....the Bible says "Therefore to him that knoweth to do good and doeth it not, to him it is sin." ...it's not enough to "not intentionally sin" ...we have to mind (discourage) sin where we see it ...else our neglect becomes our sin.

...the Christian need fear neither death nor God's judgment if he has both encouraged what is "of faith" and also "discouraged" that which is not of faith ...isn't it both what we do and also what we don't do? ...it's one think if we let our guard down and get suckered by satan ...but far worse is to not face it (own it) nor warn others of imminent danger. ...otherwise do we not become tools of satan?

...it's no encouragement to continually walk with those who either litter or ignore litter. ...Christ walked amongst sinners but never made them His companions except if they changed their ways and became disciples to His cause ...whether they be strangers or family. ...in Christ we never walk alone, whereas without Christ we can never have enough friends and family.

...I've learned (only to well) that there are those whose physical beauty takes my breath away, yet to comply with their wishes would literally take my breath away to the point of eternal death. ...it's not for me to say if they're "satan's angels of light" ...I only know they don't proclaim Christ as Savior   (2 Cor. 11: 14) ...and that's sufficient to turn me away (in deed ...if not entirely in thought ...but I'm working on the thought part). ...one needs to be extremely cautious wherein they take their comforts. (I sometimes look at an "apple" long and hard before I take a bite.)

...our nature may, at best, produce societies of "law and order" ...whereas Christ's Spirit produces societies of "love and order".

...a "semi" is a big truck that hauls a big load ...they're on every highway and we seldom know what they're carrying. ...am I like them? ...semi-Christian and semi-worldly? ...semi-social and semi-not? ...semi-passionate but semi-casual? ...what am I carrying to others? ...double minded ness is a real dilemma for me ...but I'm glad it is, else I could succumb to being semi-alive!

...this world can put a pleasing face on sin ...I saw a movie a few years ago ..."Silence of the Lambs" ...it sounded sort of Christian ...but it wasn't. ...not everyone finds time to analyze every ingredient in every choice of every meal we take in ...but the penalties of overlooking possibilities can be steeper than we can imagine. ...there is nothing of this world that is to come between us and God no matter how highly revered.

(...of course, not money or status) ...not even paternal family ties. (Mark 10: 29)

....what Christ offers through His Spirit exceeds every Earthly treasure.

...we can have both ...but only in that Christ comes first, else double minded ness and instability.

...I suppose a non believer doesn't really concern themselves much with having, at some point, to answer for their choices made each day.

...the Bible says we will have to ...and some recent deaths of both young and old friends and acquaintances leaves me pondering as to "are my affairs in order"?

...the Bible says and so the Christian knows, that to avoid "eternal torment" we won't be able to talk ourselves out of our just reward with loquacious pontification.

...it maybe, in god's eyes, that each "day" is as a life time of it's own! ...in which case we've been granted ample opportunity to receive of His truth and light ...and did we squander these precious lives (days) preferring those things "not of Him"?

...if we are not pleasing our Creator according to His will (word) then of what purpose are we to Him? ...would we not be to God, as weeds in our gardens are to us? ...discarded as being detrimental to our will (desire)? ...what we plant, either is nourished and lives to please us or may be allowed to die, to also please us.

...in our lawns, to maintain health, we both "weed-out" and we "feed".

...a weed, if given the option and the capacity to do so, would ask for help to change itself into something that pleases us, having been told that to remain a weed, means ending up on the burn-pile. ...weeds encourage and produce weeds ...but worse, they interfere (hinder) with the growth of flowers and beauty (love).

...weeds can't change ...we can ...but we can't in our own strength.

...our sinful natures are too weak. ...but only through Christ, God has and does, graciously offer to help us become a thing pleasing to His eyes and purposes, wherein our purpose (reason for living) reflects His intent.

...I would say my dad's life as a minister of the gospel, was a fruitful life ...yet it wasn't until his passing from this world that the seed he had sown, took root in me. ...the Bible says that the sower will not always reap the harvest but every Christian will sow regardless, else how could the Spirit of Christ be in him? ...and the Bible warns against any false teachings or "forms of Godliness" that have no power.

(1 Thes. 5: 5) "We are not of the night nor of darkness: (verse 6) Therefore let us not sleep as do others but let us watch and be sober". (verse 21) "Prove all things, hold fast that which is good (verse 22) abstain from all appearance of evil (wrongdoing)."

...to "watch and be sober" are the same requirements for operating (controlling) a vehicle ...so that we not bring death or dismemberment to ourselves or others.

...in our daily lives, the Christian is not to feed on (take in) anything that we would not offer our children or loved ones ...(it's a "millstone" thing)

...the ladies at the store, where I work three days a week, have made it known (without outright asking) that they would enjoy the daily newspaper if I had extras (which I always do) …and there's probably only five to ten reasons why I don't offer. …I don't read the paper because I think it's mostly junk.

(I need a little money and God seems to see clear to speak to me, though my hand be on junk) …I don't always shy away from readily available "junk" and that's for me to pay any consequence …but there's many an "unknown consequence" to my feeding it to others. …it's sort-of like advice …I'd prefer to offer God's word and then leave it with others to have ears to hear. …I have in the past bitten off more than my conscience can chew and found great unrest there.

…best to steer clear of (what my Papa Gifford would call) "monkey business".

…to be "watchful and sober" doesn't mean everything has to be "life and death" (…though I, personally, think everything is "attached" to one or the other by and by in the spiritual sense) …but rather everything perhaps be given a little more consideration regarding where things lead. …someone once wrote "the bird with the broken pinion never again soared so high but it's song was sweeter." …to have our wings clipped isn't the worst thing to happen …ask the duck that flew to close to the jet turbine.

…"what if" everything changes everything!?! …would we not then be without any solid footing? …is that what we want? …if we eat something and it makes us kind of sick …why would we then offer it to others except it be in malice or negligence??

…maybe our defending negligence is the seed of malice???

(Micah 6: 8) …the Bible says, do justly, love mercy and "walk humbly with thy God." …and if we do that in trust and faith then God will reward us in His own way, in His own season. …and we can choose to believe it or not …or anywhere in between.

…"maybe" is probably "fine" with satan (sin) but the Bible says "maybe" is not "fine" with God.

…I just remembered a lady at work defending that she need not go to church to find faith …and I agreed …provided we humbly spend time in God's word (and truth) wherever we are. (…a "lukewarm church is a questionable enterprise at best.)

...a church I often attend Sunday mornings has "refreshments" and a social time after the service (probably not uncommon to many churches)

...tea and coffee (although caffeine is addictive) are fine ...but it would probably take "hot dogs" to break my own resolve to not partake of junk after being "refreshed" by God's word. ...and I'm certain I could refrain from bolting from the pew to be fist in line. ...my son, Richard, probably doesn't have that "maturity in faith" just yet but I think I do. ...after all ...I'm almost 60!

...how long does "maturity in faith" take!?!...an old song from the 60s just came to mind ..."My world is empty without you babe" (...Supremes ...I think) ...those old songs get better when we take out the "secular" and introduce "faith" in their place ...just like in real life!

..."My world is empty without you Lord."

...it's come to my attention that my (somewhat) free-wheeling mouth has perhaps offended someone. (I, myself, am somewhat offended at that!)

...it's a good reminder, for me to consider, that those "not of fiath" are also those "not likeminded." ...if one has surrendered "nothing" of themselves to receive even the seed of Christ's Spirit ...then what is their substance (character) other than "self" (ego)? ..."ego" is very demanding and often very sensitive to being slighted.

...that doesn't excuse my being overly open (or free) in my report with others

...but rather is an encouragement to seek "life more abundant" with those who are "likewise minded" lest I forget and step on unprotected toes ....right?

...humble surrender to Christ can't help but dismantle our self pride which is the cause of much unnecessary hurt. ..."O what peace we often forfeit".

...the Christian knows that the "true friend" is the one who continually encourages us onward and upwards in faith ...no turning back. ...that "friend" is invaluable (rare) ...but those who continually show little or no interest in faith are (I suppose) dispensable, as what they bring to friendship will not be of Christ's Spirit but of some other spirit which, though it may look like fun, (or cheesecake) will spoil quickly in either direct sun or rain. ...there is no stable environment in which it is safe.

…believers and non believers are given ears to hear what the Lord says and the Christian is to unburden both their own pain and heartache as well as the pain and heartache of all others, by taking all burdens to the Lord in prayer and leaving them there in the sure trust that God is capable of rendering any and all relief He deems appropriate.

…without faith in Christ, the non believer renders himself solely to the comfort and peace of those treasures he has cultivated …maybe money, maybe spouse or family or friends …but except for "fervent prayer" (James 5: 16) by those who have cultivated righteousness, I don't see that our wish lists will avail us much. …God gives continually but unless we surrender our will, we close "the door of our receiving" His fullness. …except through surrender, we remain outside His fold and His countenance (favor). …no pastor or priest or parent or friend can help us if we, ourselves, fail to come to God ourselves in submission.

…we are all broken people and fallen …even though we may allow our ego and pride to deceive us otherwise ….exercise can help physical fitness and health …surgery can tighten wrinkles …churches and social clubs can provide a feeling of belonging

…only Christ can make our worldly wish list seem almost laughable if we in truth want relief.…the challenge and struggle of surrendering potential "fun" never looks attractive to our natural instincts, so it's always good to be suspect of our natures …but we soon begin to see the wisdom of resisting our natural

tendencies which the Bible affirms are not in our best interest nor can lasting good come through impulsive reactions to our desires or wishes.

…to have "life more abundant" there's probably a "faith element" to every choice we make, be it positive or negative. …old habits are to fall away as we grow in Christ. …for us older people, that adds up to a lot of habits and initially makes for a difficult row to hoe. (Richard. …a "hoe" is a garden tool) …(as in "work around the house" …an area you're largely unfamiliar with)

(I used to see more of Richard before I got booted from the house and he would often respond to my snipes with a kindly "very funny, Dad" (no smile)

…anyway …I hope he doesn't go all worldly and over sensitive on me)

…today's front page of the paper, I deliver, carried a large color picture of a teary eyed man carrying a child in his arms …with the headline "Bandits kill Island boy".

…I didn't "read all about it!!" …and don't want to …but neither am I like the ostrich that foolishly deceives itself

…I believe, from the Bible, that the boy is now in Heaven …but for the parent, it may be their only truly loving treasure has been taken from them and I ache at the devastation that has now visited those who loved that boy.

…somewhere in the past we've failed to be watchful and sober and protect that good which remains and is ready to die. …my momentary glance at a front page story today has changed me (everything affects everything) and I can never be the same.

…if I wasn't much "fun" before …I'll be even less fun now …the volume on vigilance (self vigilance) has just been turned up.

…whether 3rd world starvation, the senseless murder of a child, killed in the line of duty, rapes, muggings, etc. etc. …man's inhumanity to those hurting is a blaring testament to our sinful nature and it's largely fed by the democracy of the civilized western world and the multitude of freedoms afforded us.

…I'm not like the foolish ostrich but I know I lean heavily towards the "out of sight – out of mind" mentality. …I'm also of the "I want – I want – I want mentality

…I want no guilt for anyone …I want no pain for anyone …I want no conflict or bad feelings for anyone …and I want God to do it all and not ask me to get involved.

…it's not much to ask ….provided I not be Christian or read the Bible much.

(James 4: 8) …doesn't the Bible say " He will draw nigh to me" !?! …right?

…or what about "God is suppose to keep me in "perfect peace"!?! (Isa. 26: 3)

…"what's coming off here!?! …have we come to the point where even God can't be trusted!?! ….do we have to take things into our own hands?

…if we didn't hide … or deceive ourselves from the majority of that which we support …then maybe we'd get an inkling of how great God's love is and see that it's ourselves who are throwing His love away.

…Adam and Eve traded God's garden for satan's garden and found death.

…are we now but chips off that old block??? …it was from that point that our (sinful) nature was established, whereby, apart from God, even our noblest efforts by our own wisdom must falter though we praise our cleverness.

…when I say this stuff, I know it! ….except I forget it …because I'm not used to appreciating (realizing) that without God I'm just a second rate parent …or spouse …or worker …or whatever. …I need to continue working on making God's word and instruction "my habit" …to help "bring every thought into captivity" (submission) to Christ's will. (2 Cor. 10: 5) …maybe by and by I'll become sufficiently righteous that my "fervent and effectual prayers" have a chance of availing something. …Webster's says "fervent" is "passionate or intense" …and "effective" is "active and not merely potential or theoretical". …sounds like "prayer" is to be somewhat more than wishing and hoping, to our "good friend" Jesus. …if I'm not here "for Him" then what expectation (prospect) have I that He would be there "for me or my prayers"?

…if we're in a fold "apart" from His fold, will He accept collect long distance calls? …the Bible says every need (call) of His obedient sheep, has been prepaid through Christ's death and resurrection but if we refuse His call or not be stayed on Him, then what hope have we?

…does the Christian noticeably refrain from self glory and more than those of no faith whatsoever? …in some other faiths, man is to be the glory of God and wives are to be the glory of the Godly husband and thus to veil or hide their glory (beauty) from all, save their God and their husband. …we consider that practice archaic and we've advanced, whether non Christian or Christian alike, to support what's probably a multi-billion dollar industry of external glory enhancement for male and female alike.

…the Christian may claim that if our bodies are indeed the temple of Christ's church then we should look as good as possible …but I'm certain that premise is highly sketchy to non Christians and those of other faiths. …I've seen many pastor's wives, who, just a single generation ago, would easily be mistaken for harlots.

...I guess per (Romans 14: 23) if it's of faith ...then it's not sin

...or as the Living Bible translates ...if a Christian feels it's okay ...then it's right to do it. (para-paraphrased) ...and that's fine ...except then if the Christian claims their sinful nature is dead in Christ, why do we continue to sin everyday in support of our old nature? ...why do I maintain the interest in golf even though I'm quite certain there's nothing of faith in it? ...do I perceive God patting me gently on the back and whispering "that's okay for you Paul because your mind is stayed on me"??? ...I don't seem to "pray" a whole lot and it may be because I'm suspicious of what comes out of my mouth. ...I easily forget that God doesn't support our causes but rather He uses us (if we're available) to support His causes.

...except maybe during sleep, I don't think God ever stops talking to us or sharing His will, through His "word" and His "Spirit" ...and He never wonders if I'm listening ...rather, He absolutely knows I'm not if I'm distracted by a "secular" hero like Tiger Woods ...or the NHL ...or NBA ....or Donald Trump's rising star ...or Tom Cruise's cruise from wife to wife. (no offense)

(Matt. 12: 30) ...in all my ways, I'm either "gathering to Him ...or I'm scattering abroad. ...do I wish it was otherwise? ...of course! ...but nothing I can do to "make" it otherwise. ...for sure I can juggle the numbers and listen to my friends who commiserate ...it doesn't change God's truth or my deception.

...and under those rules the best I can hope for is my "three score and ten" (approximate) ...then an eternity without end of teeth gnashing torment and regret.

...I expect that young couple who lost their boy to "bandits" is regretfully experiencing a taste of "hell" ...not unlike all who decline Christ will one day come to know.

...do we "suppose" satan is at work in this world? ....where do we think he's at work? ....is he out in the woods converting the deer and raccoons? ....or maybe in third world countries, starving people? ...what about here in the civilized western world? ...maybe in the porn shops or seedy bars? ...do we think he wouldn't have the nerve to enter a five star hotel or restaurant? ...or popular malls? ...or Abercrombie &

Finch? …how about Wal-mart? …or McDonalds? or McChurch? (McBaptist? or McCatholic? or McMormon? .or McSalvation Army? or McSeventh Day? or McUnited?)

…lucky is the "true Christian" who is above the fray ….right? (not me, just yet …but) some Christians have attained "cruise control" option available on many models. (although I haven't tested it, my new car has that option (12 years old))

…I wonder if it still works?

…the story of Job suggests that God even invites satan to test those of stalwart faith, making our own particular church the primary battleground. …I wonder how many ways satan would dare use in our churches to chip away at the demanding surrender required of the sincere seeking Christian? (Matt. 7: 13) …the Bible says "because straight is the gate, and narrow is the way, which leadeth unto life and few there be that find it." (verse 21) .."Not everyone that saith unto me, Lord, Lord, shall enter into the Kingdom of Heaven but he that doeth the will of my Father which is in Heaven." …so how "narrow" do we suppose that "way" is? …can it be "moderately narrow"? …or is it to be "very narrow" according to what the Bible says? …I guess if God doesn't put enough of the Holy Spirit in us to sustain us, well then, we must be free to also look elsewhere for the stuff we need to be comfortable. (without guilt).

…my son Richared spent a few hours with me today (Father's day) …he asked if I was happy …I said yes …he asked what I do for fun, I said mostly read the Bible and maybe write a bit …he said that's interesting but that he didn't "get it".

…I'm concerned that over the years "I've given" him too many pairs of "dark glasses" and he maybe uses them too often. …I pray any damage I've done isn't irreparable

…I, myself, didn't "get it" until after my own Dad's passing even though his whole life was the "passing on" of God's light and truth.

…it's okay for things to not always be "just fine" else why would we ever change or grow? …Richard still like to "party" …and maybe that's a step towards learning that there's not much "life" in living from one "fun" to the next "fun" …laughs can grow pretty hollow and they don't hold up when considering our eternities …nor when tragedy can strike us at a moments notice. ...the body's immune system is complex and remarkable but it's of little, if any, help in mending the ills of making bad choices to gain worldly reward.

...the pondering mind might grasp that Christ can supply some things that the world can't ...but I think that only experiencing Christ's presence in us will confirm that our "personal world" will remain empty without Him. ...anything the world can do ...Christ can do better here and now ...but more importantly, "this world offers worse than death" in the end ...whereas Christ offers joy beyond our dreams in the end. ...with our dark glasses (glass of darkness) we don't see our brokenness ...but it's right here below the surface.

...on papers this morning I was thinking how we're like wounded children who crawl to loving parent to receive healing and to mend in a loving and caring safe environment. ...knowing the love of His Heavenly Father, Christ said "I am the way, the truth and the life; no man cometh unto the Father but by me. (John 14: 6) ...the cheating heart can dissect that verse from now 'til doomsday and I don't suppose God is even concerned because the cheating heart is of satan's flock and though has ears to hear, chooses not to. ...cheating hearts are always sons or daughters or brothers or sisters or moms or dads ...and it's our nature to give them special status and special allowances, if of our own paternal family. ...don't do it...."special" is like the tentacles of an octopus and will drag us down to the depths of darkness to slowly devour us unseen.

...we ought invite the exhortation or warning of Christian family and friends. ...I have a true friend and Bible mentor who used to bug me all the time, when I didn't want to be bugged ...and now I'm sure it bugs him that I'm always thanking him for that. (serves him right – eousness.) ...I somehow think he revels in my struggle with (what I see as) "Christian worldliness". (lukewarm faith)

...it's hardly anything I can get self-righteous or snotty about on account of I smoke and drink and have lustful thoughts and selfish interests ...only to name a few of my failings ...but I do believe that God knows my heart, in spite of my failings and I'm thankful of every conviction He brings to my evasive attention. …He knows my "ratio average" between Him and the world and my efforts to separate from the worldly."

…for others, a great mind (high I.Q.) must be a huge challenge to overcome in any quest towards elevating faith in Christ above all we see about us every day.

…it's of particular concern to me that Richard may have such a mind ….which is cause for me to try to be more and more watchful for him. …in every vigilance I entertain on my son's behalf is great benefit to myself also. …how can another mentor me …except he or she be sound (established) in Christ themselves? …can one be "established" except they surround themselves with those who are "holding fast"?

…that we "have fun" looking pretty much where the secular world looks for their fun, is no testament to faith in Christ …but rather the opposite! …and our children and peers see that …and it's good they do.

…if I don't remember the Sabbath, to keep it Holy …then why should Richard or any other put stock in my self-deceptive encouragement that they look to the Bible for a guidance to "life more abundant?" …"fickle" is even "more fickle" when espoused from the lips of the "professed Christian". …"objective and selective Christianity is a woeful thing. …"self disgust" isn't a "fruit of the Spirit" …and it's a good thing! …else those who are "indwelt" by the Holy Spirit might have a problem. …can the Holy Spirit be of such (little) significance, in one's life, that they might be mistaken as being non Christian? ….does one take some comfort if that should be the case? ….or bliss?

…do we have a "battle of treasures" where there should clearly be none?

…I know I do …and it's of great concern to me (well, at least of "some" concern to me) (I trust God to suffice for me …I just don't trust myself to be attentive.) …there's some relief from anxiety in being a dummy …but it's no help if I deny that I am one. …there's a book about "Venus and Mars" (women and men) which (as I recall it's content) could apply to our spiritual efforts as well.

....if we don't put aside our own agenda (our own sinful nature) then how can we grow in faith ....or "continue to work out our salvation" which the Bible calls us to do (even in "fear and trembling)?   (Phil. 2: 12)

...I often have trouble just getting past my humble "please! ...anybody ...just give me what I want!" ...do I have enough days left to discipline myself (mature) to receive blessings reserved by God for only those with servant's hearts?

...the secular world proudly upholds the attitude of "You've come a long way, Baby!"

...satan whispers that premise continually to us in many many different ways

...yet it's the antithesis of humility, due respect and fear of the One from whom all blessing fall. ...a proud attitude is, in essence, our opportunity to step back a couple of thousand years and join others who spat on Christ while He carried our burden of sin. (...all of which means nothing to those who choose to decline faith in Christ alone nor means much to any who embrace lukewarm faith.)   ...lukewarm ...is double minded ...which in turn is "unstable" (not to be trusted)....I pray Richard develops a "discernment" in faith to protect him from false teachings, whether it comes from me or a professed "loved one or a professed pastor or priest or guru or employer, etc. etc. (James 4: 2) ...the Bible says "ye have not, because ye ask not."   (Rom. 8: 39) ...nothing can separate us from God's love, through Christ ...and though He loves us completely ...yet "we can separate ourselves" from His protection and His armor against the ever present deceit that surrounds us, which is from satan.   (Eph. 6: 11) ...nobody wants to feel bad about the things they do ...

(Heb. 12: 11) ...the Bible says "Now no chastening (refining) for the present seemeth to be joyous but grievous: nevertheless afterward it yieldeth the peaceable fruit of righteousness unto them which are exercised (inclined) thereby."

...no child of man or of God "likes to be told "no ....you can't do that ...or can't have that."   ...yet all come to know chastening is necessary.

...even Christ, the Prince of Peace on Earth, reminds us in His words that "His peace" is to be counted on only by those of His own flock and that entrance to His fold is arduous.   (Luke 12: 51) ..."Suppose ye that I am come to give peace on

Earth?   I tell you, nay, but rather division."   …while "His peace" is available to all …how can one find peace while pushing it away in exchange for "some other" form of rest following "some other" form of joy?   (Gal. 6: 7) …"Be not deceived; God is not mocked: for whatsoever a man soweth, that shall he also reap".   …as we look away from Christ to fulfill our hearts desires, so do we cement our separation from Him …though we may on occasion (snag, or) have a blessing from Him land on us …it will likewise be a form of blessing and largely void of thankfulness or love.

…from this world, the greatest love we can know or realize is one of reason and compromise and emotion …there's a far greater love that we've forgotten; of safe unreasonable dependency …and unfathomable wonder.

…satan would have all of us denied of that love and that comfort …and in our own strength and reasoning we must fall to satan's will.

…while, in this life, it may not all be anxiety and torment …this life is but a short page leading to our eternity.   …if we are cultivating a taste for the things of this world that are not of faith …then this short page of time we have will be of poison.   …I think there are some poisons that even smell and taste pretty good …but they carry an inherent diminishing capacity to sustain life.   …if these poisons don't kill us outright then they bleed us slowly of any hope we might have to recover from our ills, whereby we simply self-destruct.   …with "this world" as our treasure, so we become desperate for someone or something "of this world" to mend or heal our broken families or our sick children or our barrenness (emptiness).   …where we have sown, is where we anticipate reaping.   …it's like we dig ourselves a huge hole, then find we have to live "in it".   …and though doctors or counselors can call down to us with suggestions …they can never come into our hole to see "our" darkness.   …they may bring light bulbs and extension cords to help us see our wretched environment but it's probably of little or no comfort.   …the Bible says thee is only one who will reach down to us …but not if we're angry or vengeful or unrepentant.   (which, of course, is what we mostly want to be when we feel we've been unfairly treated)   (…probably the same tools we used to dig the hole we're in!)

...Christ will reveal, scoop by scoop, what we need to slowly repair our brokenness and it'll likely always require our asking forgiveness from someone we don't like.

...as in every step of faith, Christ says "do this" ...and we have to choose if we want to please Him over pleasing ourselves. ...Christ can be trusted to reveal truth to us ...while satan will provide every distraction and deceit to keep us from the "light" of honest faith. ...the devil doesn't "make me do it" my "nature," without Christ, encourages unrighteousness ...and it's that unrighteousness which I allow that takes away the hope of salvation.

...in the world there is added worldly value to "name brand clothing" to suggest we have good taste and money and status.

(James 4: 4) ....the Bible says "...friendship of the world is enmity with God....."

...I don't think our having a "clear conscience" has anything to do with one's assurance of salvation. ...satan can probably supply a clear conscience for us. ...are we seeking God's will continually, through His word, in spite of the world's offerings?

...the Bible cites many instances of people just like me, who had very logical reasons (even good reasons) to linger momentarily with distractions of this world, yet Christ closed every door to that. ...we may choose to open doors that Christ has closed, it's just that we have to "depart God's word and His will" in order to open them.

...the Bible doesn't have to "name" every single conduct or toy or thought as being an abomination to righteousness and holiness ...Christ said (John 15: 26) "But when the Comforter is come, whom I will send unto you from the Father, even the Spirit of truth ...also" (John 14: 16) "I will pray the Father and He shall give you another Comforter, that He may abide with you forever (verse 17) Even the Spirit of truth, whom the world cannot receive because it seeth Him not, neither knoweth Him: but ye know Him, for He dwelleth with you, and shall be in you."

...I have an uneasy admiration for those Christians who claim "assurance of salvation" or "once saved always saved" ...they can (and should) have the boldness, in their conviction, to walk up to anyone and share their status as a "holy person" then share the gospel message of salvation available to "all who will forsake houses or brethren or sister or father or mother or wife or children or lands for Christ's name's sake, shall receive a hundredfold and shall inherit everlasting life." (Matt. 19: 29)

…I hope one day I have that confidence that other's have already. …it can't be easy to surrender that much worldliness for the cause and will of Christ.

…I'm blessed that my dad was pretty much that way. …if I said to my dad "the weather has been good lately" …my dad would say "speaking of "the" …."the" Bible says …etc. etc.. …it's not that he wasn't interested in the weather …he was just more interested in sharing God's word.

…it got to where the only "safe" greeting was to smile and nod, then look away quick! ….there was always the slim chance that might "stymie" him.

…it's pretty rare to see that joy and purpose in the Lord, anymore.

…and don't I wish I could call him on the phone today and run a few things past him??? (….but he moved on sometime ago.)

…it seems to getting harder to see God's will in what's suppose to be "His" church.

….it could be that I need to look harder …by why is that? …to be without "need"

…is to be without "focus" and in such a state we can easily wander about aimlessly

…and are thus prime targets for "all" that is the "enemy" of greater faith in Christ.

(James 1: 2) ….the says "My brethren, count it all joy when ye fall into diverse (various) temptations (verse 3) …knowing this, that the trying of your faith worketh patience." …to fall "into sin" is defeat and victory for satan …but to "defeat temptation" is strength for Christ's cause and can be listed under "Victory in Jesus (good hymn!)

…to be "diverted" from continually seeking more and more of the Bible's truth and light is for the sincere Christian a certain dimming of "life more abundant" …I know I can choose diversion but I also know the price I pay, which is also compounded, should I influence others as well …by my mind not being "stayed on thee" (Isa. 26: 3) …there's much in the Bible that doesn't necessarily generate pleasant thought …yet is required compliance for the "perfect peace" that results from our mind being stayed on things of God.

...I hear professed non believer after non believer claim they're "going to Heaven" because they're "good people" and I can only share (though unpopular) that the Bible says otherwise. (Isa. 64: 6) ...the Bible says that our own righteousness is like filthy rags. ...it may be of value for our own self worth but it's of no value as regards our faith or salvation. ...its like a "hoax righteousness" and is a portion of satan's arsenal which, because of it's ease, we readily accept as "of good" ...if righteousness (or goodness) is "of faith" then we know it's not ours but rather is God's ...from Him and all glory is to Him. ...any praise or glory we hold to ourselves is merely evidence of our foolishness. (Eph. 5: 6) "Let no man deceive you with vain words ...."

(1 Cor. 3: 18) "Let no man deceive himself, if any among you seemeth to be wise in this world, let him become a fool, that he may be wise.

(1 Cor. 3: 19) For the wisdom of the world is foolishness with God....."

...wherever our eyes turn, we need ask, "Is God in it?" ...if God isn't in it, then whatsoever it is, it's not of faith ...so then if not of sin ...then what's it of? ...can it be of something that's "maybe not too bad" in God's eyes? ...the Bible doesn't proffer that option. ...but satan always proffers that option!

...whatever ...bestseller book or academy award winning movie ...makes no difference! ...as a Christian, if God isn't in it, then what am I doing in it???

...if it's_apart from God, then those who touch it (partake) are apart from God. ...doesn't matter if it's your loving spouse or parent ...or if it's some degenerate repulsive individual. ...if we sow casual deceit, the Bible says we are removed from God's flock. (John 7: 7) "If anyone wants to do His (God's) will he shall know concerning the doctrine (Bible) whether it is from God."

...the whole Bible, might possibly be summed up in a single sentence:

(I don't know what that sentence might be ...perhaps "the new covenant"???) yet we cannot "exempt" any words from that sentence else we invite on ourselves exemption from salvation and thus an eternity of torment. (Rev. 22: 19)

...unpleasant as it is ...I have no reason to believe that many, many people I have known aren't already now in a state of "gnashing of teeth" torment, from which there is not now, nor ever will be, relief.

...many had only day after day to choose their fate ....most had year after year ...yet chose not to hear what the Lord saith.

...had I been born and raised in some remote jungle, then might I have cause to escape eternal hell ...otherwise, no.

...."pity parties" aren't mentioned in the Bible, though we may have them our whole lives through.

(John 9: 31)   "Now we know that God heareth not sinners: but if any be a worshipper of God and doeth His will, him He heareth."

...I don't think it's given for us to know who will be saved from hell and who won't be ...but I think it's given to us to discern "deceit" in others and in ourselves also (the Bible encourages us to exhort one another to put off anything that impedes growth in Christ). ...discernment in itself can be a puzzling challenge in faith.

...we can have brothers or sisters in faith whose conduct may be highly influenced by non Christians or by lukewarm Christians ...often even their spouse ...which in turn creates burdens for ourselves of frustration.

(1 Cor. 14: 33) ....the Bible says it's not God who is the author of our confusion.

...it's probably not our continual Bible thumping but rather our constant peace and harmony in our being separate from the world that might encourage a non believer to consider the merit of a personal relationship with Christ.

...for some, the greatest mistake they can make is to "first" form a relationship with a church (because of some worldly discontentment)

...no denomination or gathering can do what, the Bible says, only Christ can do.

...as Christian, we can do little to lighten the burden of non believers if, though they have ears, they refuse to listen to what the Lord says.

...I recall a time many years ago, when as a young man, the world I had created for myself suddenly "caved in". ...that was the day of my longest drive (90 miles non stop except gas and coffee) to touch base with my church, which at that time was also my folks …I was hopeful they could pray and my burden would be lifted. …I think my dad said it was impossible for them to pray more fervently or effectually than how they prayed for me (and others) everyday since I was born. …they shared my obvious pain and turmoil but they basically said they couldn't be my church or my rock because, even though ministers of a church, they weren't qualified above being "helpers."

…they had always given me "road maps" and I had always not looked at them!

…I'm a slow learner and I'm thankful I was granted many years (as opposed to the "few" that some are granted) for my eyes and ears to be opened. …I'll have to remember never again to say "ignorance is bliss" …I can't imagine it's a blissful experience when a large bird stuffs it's face into the dirt.

…do we really not want to know what causes us injury and death? …if so, we have not the "hope" of preventing it. …I can't force my son or relative or neighbor or co-worker to see or hear what they don't "want" to. …the days we have are only gifts from above

…if we use them to stray from God, our remaining days will be of increasing emptiness and increasing conflict …even beyond any doctor's or any pastor's help.

…the "crusher" comes when we realize that we, each, largely have ourselves to blame as we obstinately decline "the peace of God, which passeth all understanding". (Phil. 4: 7)

… I turned on the television briefly last night (clicker in hand) and within about 15 minutes was briefed on a missing teen girl in Aruba …a prominent Christian Science/actor suggesting psychology and its medications are near useless …and a program on the prevalence of college suicides and how we're to look for unstable behavior in others. (…and I don't think I slept well) …it could have been the Bible speaking to worldly lusts, inner emptiness and slow but eventual death through lack of desire for life.

(I forgot to mention: yesterday was the worst day since world war II for American service women killed in action …that, from the action in Iraq.…here in Victoria, B.C. there is newsworthy unrest about the line-ups to view a dozen or so "Tall Ships" presently in the harbor here.

…do we need to organize to protest against the protesters!?!

("…and I think to myself …what a wonderful world" …Louis Armstrong)

(James 1: 17) …"every good and perfect gift is from above" …and each gift is "really saying, I love you". …that's God's message to us throughout the Bible …but there's an enemy of that message who, as long ago with Eve, says to us "But there's way more that I can give you! …so just relax, lay back (chill) and enjoy the goodies." …and it's our nature to do just that. …things seem to go easier …parenting seems easier …school or work seems easier …relationships seem easier …to take our paddle out of the water and drift and not be challenged seems easier …to just do what comes natural seems easier but the effort to regain the ground we lose …seems impossible. …and rightly so

…as it is impossible in our own strength.

…I can "disclaim" that my own nature is "anti-Christ" even though the Bible says that can't be so. …likewise, I can claim to be "neutral" or ambivalent …but the Bible says that can't be so either. …there is no neutral. (Luke 11: 23)

…Christ says "He that is not with me is against me and he that gathereth not with me, scattereth." …to not be Christian simply means that our lives will be in hell

…the Bible says …"for He (God) maketh His son to rise on the evil and the good and sendeth rain on the just and the unjust." …to not be Christian simply means that we we perceive ourselves to be self-made or perceive Christ as of lesser importance.

…the Bible says our "hell" (not our trivial despondencies or heartache or traumas) our reality of "gnashing of teeth hell" won't be realized until after we die …and after our having squandered our opportunity to turn from our worldly (sinful) natures.

…as the Christian exercises vigilance on behalf of his treasure (Christ) …so the natural man exercises vigilance on behalf of all that is not of Christ (faith).

…I once placed human (worldly) relationship (marriage) above my Spiritual relationship (Christ) and for many, many years provided for (supported) a buffer against fragilities and marital conflict …wherefore I did build my house on sand.

…I may well be deluded …but I believe now, that "length page" was turned not by me (but for me) …and in "due season" at that.

…the Bible quote in Luke 11: 23 does not exclude marriage …#1 seek "God and #2 don't marry anyone who doesn't encourage #1. (are we listening, Richard?)

……personally, when I find myself with someone with whom I need to mince or temper God's truth or His word …then do I know my faith is weak and that I'm with someone I shouldn't be with. …God is love …if I'm not sharing something of God, then I must be sharing something ungodly. …every trusted friend (spouse or otherwise) is a part of us and like an electric current, whatsoever is "of God" desires to flow to every part of us …to create or allow resistance to that flow is to knowingly squander opportunity to be a part of "life more abundant in Christ" for both us and others.

…the wishes and the conduct of others can tempt us to toy with the flow of Christ in us but we are each responsible for our holding fast and not give in to that temptation.

…when my son asked me a week ago, what I did for fun if I don't party or socialize much …it occurred to me that I'm not so tempted anymore to pursue worldly fun.

…although I'm still tempted some, there's something in me that more and more says "I'd better not" …and I never seem to regret obeying that advice.

…talking with people is fun and being apart from people is fun (although I maybe laugh less when I'm apart) ….helping a good cause is fun and being helped is fun.

…maybe the better question is "what do I do that isn't fun?" (causes anxiety or confusion for myself or others) …and why would I continue to do those things?

(Micah 6: 8) …inevitably those negative things are apart from "doing justly, loving mercy or walking humbly with God "whether through my own doings …or the doings of others with whom I'm confronted. …to see wrongdoing, then be ambivalent or do nothing, isn't fun. …to build my life on shifting sand isn't fun.

(Rom. 14: 22) the Bible says "…happy is he that condemneth not himself in that which he alloweth". …that line on it's own would make a good Bible study …but I don't think it quite means "do whatever you want until you feel too bad to keep doing it." …the preceding verse says that whatever we do, we are to consider the potential impact on others. …does our conduct encourage what is "of faith"? …or encourage what is "apart from faith"?

…church last night began a series on "fruits of the Spirit" (Gal. 5: 22) ….the pastor's Bible appears to have replaced "suffering" with the more palatable "patience" …and also "gentleness" with "kindness". …is there any recognized religion that doesn't promote patience and kindness? (Matt. 16: 24) Christ said "If any will come after me, let him deny himself and take up his cross and follow me." …is the "long suffering" in the King James, unattractive to the new believer? …is a Styrofoam replica cross, then some idle waiting, really the burden of Christ's church? …wasn't Christ's a life of struggle for the lost and suffering horrendously that we might be saved from hell? …to me "patience" hardly resembles "long suffering" …yet there it was on the pulpit's big screen. …maybe I'm wrong and maybe we're all worthy of the communion of Christ's body and Christ's blood that was shed.

…maybe if I "don't go looking" for sinful things to do, then I'm holy! …so why do I still feel a bit "vacant" of Christ's Spirit in me??? …it wasn't very long ago that if I gave thought to "faith" vs. "other than" that I would conclude that "faith" was overrated.

…I'm certain my son and maybe others think I'm "missing out" …whereas to me …I'm just beginning to "not miss out!" …and much of what I enjoy (fun) comes from not doing things I used to want to do. …faith has given me a softer perception of "slavery" …provided it's voluntary slavery.

…in Christ we can be defiant slaves to our faith or we can choose to break down the walls and become thankful, subservient slaves to a trusting faith in the only One through whom we can be saved from present darkness and eventual hell.

...every "life" is a wondrous thing ...even ones that appear (to our eyes) to be deformed and different from us.

...my body, in the eyes of the world, is no great thing of beauty ...but there are some, even in this building I live in, who struggle to walk even one single block (through no failure of their own) yet their countenance is a blessing to me ...yet there are beautiful, healthy people here who leave me cold. ...to my own nature, that doesn't make sense ...but I know my own nature is defective and dirty (soiled).

...right now I probably only have a little part of Christ's nature in me but even that little part is enough for me to see some of my failings and that little part of Christ in me is removing the darker film from the glass through which I look.

(1 Cor. 13: 12) "For now we see through a glass, darkly...."

...I saw a war movie, years ago, called "The Great Escape" (Steve McQueen) ...the name of that movie speaks volumes to the war between faith and sin. ...our lives are a journeys of changing bondage and escapes. ...I recall that I, also, once saw "religion" as escape from "life". ...religiosity ...maybe just that ...but religiosity has nothing to do with "experience ...and except we "experience" the changing power of He who created everything good ...then religion is empty of goodness and righteousness and so is, for sure, just another "escape" ...religion without experiencing ...can be lumped in with fun or booze or drugs or entertainment or sports or any escape we choose to name.

...unless we can "define where God is in it" even our most important relationships are merely an "escape" from our own loneliness.

...we won't know the full meaning of "wanting to escape" until after these lives of ours here are ended and all venues of "escape" are gone.

(Luke 13: 25) ...the Bible says there is no way to breach the chasm between Heaven and hell, beyond our choices here and now. ...for many of us, tomorrow will never come ...we'll die unexpectedly tonight ...our fate sealed in choices of yesterday.

…was I, yesterday, carrying the burden of a Christian friend? …or was I at Disneyland or the ball game or at the movies …or missing church (God) by watching the final round of the US Open with Tiger challenging the leaders?

…am I still available to God's voice in the midst of all the excitement and fun that He's, somehow, provided for us? …I imagine I would hear God, though I was watching some favorite television show (of an edifying sort …maybe like PBS) provided He raised His voice a little ….right? …that's reasonable! ….right?

…it's not exactly like I have to be in the "front lines" of God's arm all the time….right? …what about my R & R time? …I only agreed to full-time service on the "condition" that others serve full-time also! …just because I'm saved in Christ doesn't mean I have to be a dummy! …right? …if other Christians get goodies …then I do too! …right? …so …now that God and I understand each other and as I've chewed on this tough meat He's given me …well then …it's time I got a bit of the gravy! ….right?

…(this is where my imaginary audience of hundreds …maybe thousands!) rise in unison …fists raised and yell out …"RIGHT!!!")

(…the unified response need not be a resounding "RIGHT" …it could also be an "amen!" …or "Hail!" …or "halleluiah!"

…I guess I wonder about "church unity for unity's sake" over personal unity in our "individual" relationship with our personal savior.

…it's tempting to align (membership) with one of the churches I attend …and one fella told me he's a member of several churches! (…I suppose that gives him voting privileges to register support or otherwise.)

…I see, by today's newspaper headline, that Canada now supports same sex marriage in law. …once again "God's word" takes a back seat to popular opinion.

…"we've come a long way!" …the unthinkable becomes tolerable, then allowable, then acceptable, then supported …I guess for the sake of unity.

…even in our churches if enough members (congregation) find they have a friend or family member involved in gay or lesbian activity and relationships …then they don't want it to be a bad thing or a condemning thing …so, subjectively …it's maybe better to embrace this life style that God has said is forbidden.

(Lev. 18: 24) …the Bible says "Defile not ye yourselves in any of these things …"

…"abominations" is an old word, yet even Webster's says it means "very bad"

…what's our prognosis in faith, when we accommodate "very bad???

…when confronted with "abomination" (cancer) in our church or in our life

…do we claim it and cut it away? …or do we conceal and rationalize it?

(2 Cor. 6: 17) …if we don't "come out from amongst them and be separate …then how will we ever (2 Cor. 10: 5) "bring every though into captivity to Christ's will"?

…every web of deception has some starting point and better to define it early on lest we succumb to temptation to conform ourselves to conduct which God has clearly stated is abominable.   (Lev. 18: 30)   …whatever Godly love that abides in us can never be a part of accommodating what God has spoken against.

(Rom. !2: 2)   "And be not conformed to this world: but be transformed by the renewing of your mind, that ye may prove what is that good and acceptable and perfect will of God."   (verse 9) "…abhor that which is evil; cleave to that which is good". …to "cleave" is to adhere and be faithful …to "abhor" is to hate and detest. …to be "double minded" is death …though it may be gradual and even reasonable or justifiable in our own eyes. …to "allow" ourselves to "be conformed to this world" may appear peaceable just as a few little cancer cells may at first "appear peaceable" …I'm sure there are people, in poor countries, who live amidst the stench of abject squalor, where I would probably starve for not being able to hold food down against that stench; whereas they have gotten use to it and can abide it. …maybe incense helps to deny their reality.

…the Bible says that its not what goes into our mouth (or noses) that defiles us (makes us unclean or corrupt) but rather it's what we knowingly allow or advocate despite our having God's word and God's warnings.

…I understand the "leader" of this country, Paul Martin …had defiled himself in the eyes of his church by his knowingly conducting himself "against" his "professed" faith. ...he's probably a busy man ...perhaps too busy. ...worse yet for him if he encouraged others against God. ...I hope he remembers that leaders are called to a higher judgment on departing this life. ...if Paul Martin was Christian ...I wonder what wore down his steadfastness in faith? ...is he one who has slowly gained the whole world ...yet lost his soul??

(Mark 8: 36)   (...probably seems to many, who think they know him, like an average Christian...whereas he's maybe just an average man.)

(2 Tim. 3: 5) ...the Bible says there's a big "power loss" through settling on just "a form of Godliness:. ...I don't know how any of us, having been given ample opportunity to read God's word, can defy what it says and then continue to expect His blessing or answer to prayer, having knowingly compromised righteousness.

...for whatever reason, when we have to set aside "what God says is right" in order to do "what we think is right" (under any circumstance) then no "good" thing will come from it. ...God closed the door to same sex relationships and to sexual relationships with close family members and sexual relationships with animals

...as He closed the door to murder, idolatry, adultery, etc. etc.

...Webster's defines "alright" as satisfactory or safe or correct.

(Isa. 64: 6) ...the Bible defines our own ideas of alright (righteousness) not merely as "rags" ...but as "filthy rags" (there must be a more kindly way for us to word that ....right?) ...I wonder what heinous atrocity ...or how many of them it would take to unveil the presence of satan being at work in the world right now.

...I bet even many Christians give little thought to the seeds of evil being sown all around them ...preferring to believe satan will appear easily identifiable

...like King Kong or Godzilla.

(2 Cor. 11: 14) ...the Bible says he will appear more as an angel of light (enlightenment) ...maybe as the short term giver of peace or prosperity.

...in the mid 1940s, do we suppose the German people wanted concentration camps and exterminations? ...they wanted peace ...and if possible, prosperity.

...and there arose a leader, whose name (Adolph) means "noble wolf"

…so I suppose the "majority" chorused a tenuous "alright" …provided they not have to load the freight trains with people, nor personally turn the gas valves to end their lives.

…the Bible repeatedly speaks of our sinful "natures" but who wants to dwell on that? ….better to leave that undecided until it roars at our own doors….right? …I think the greater portion (display) of our "sinful nature" lies not so much in what we actually restrain ourselves from personally doing …but rather in what we silently allow. …for any professed Christian …"politically correct" if it be against God's will is a weak tree to lean against, being infested with vermin and rot …and it's highly contagious.

…it's not for us to judge others …yet, by our reading God's word and listening to the Spirit's revealing it's truth …so also do we find relief through trust in God's omnipotence over all that is His.

…with my own failings and weaknesses, I hesitate to profess "Christianity" as my treasure and faith above all else …but thanks to some people I know, who actually pursue God's will …according to His word …so do I have the hope of continuing to work out my salvation…. (Phil. 2: 12)

…but I know it'll never be my own nature but rather Christ's nature in those I surround myself with and in "what" I surround myself with. …that, only, will encourage my route to any lasting goodness or any hope to the "righteousness" I need daily to have any hope of peace now or Heaven later.

…I don't think the Bible says anywhere that the Prime Minister …or any minister has a "special" nature that grants them special kudos, should they align their daily choices with whatsoever is against God's word. …I think their own nature to be drawn to darkness, is the same nature as everyone's, including mine.

(Psa. 19: 105) ….the Bible says "Thy word is a lamp unto my feet and a light unto my path" …how can anyone, professing Christianity, turn from God's word and yet not enter into darkness. …"worldly" good works or appeasements are of our sinful natures and so are contrary to God's doctrine.

(Richard ….you're a good guy …and probably think you don't have the sinful nature that the Bible says you have …I'm sure I have on occasion (like today, being your birthday) …told you that you were special. ….you are to me …and you are to God. …you are, somewhat "of me (whether you like it or not) …but foremost, you are a gift to me from God (…as was I, to my folks). …and of all the tangible blessings I'll ever know on this "ol' ball" everything else pales next to you.

…each of us is special to God, although I wonder if or how that changes should we join His enemy. …the Bible says there are some (many?) who will, in the end, come to Him espousing all their good deeds …yet Christ will say "I never knew you".

…so …punk! …if it comes to "your dad" saying "you're special" ….vs. God saying "you're not "overly" special ….I suggest you trust God.

…in everything …no matter what you "want to hear" …drop it all …and trust God's word …through His Spirit …by comparison "our own wisdom really is as foolishness" as the Bible says.

(Matt. 6: 20) …to "lay up treasure in things above" is getting ever harder to do as we see even our leaders trample underfoot any of God's word which interferes with their own rise in popularity and power.

…it may be hopeful or comforting to think that "maybe these occasional violations won't be so bad."…I, personally, had thought that legalizing marijuana was the next moral issue to discern …yet that issue, to my mind, pales next to same sex marriage.

…I don't think potentially addictive substances "defiles man" in God's eyes

(Mark 7: 15) …..but to be silent, or worse, "support" whatsoever God's word states to be abomination …how can that conduct and mindset not defile us?

…does chocolate or caffeine or nicotine or beer or wine or marijuana defile our hearts? …what about pork fat …or chicken skin?

…it's our "choices for" what the Bible says is of "God and faith" …or our choices "otherwise" that determines whether or not we be of His flock …and our choices are determined by our hearts and minds being stayed on God or else, otherwise disposed.

…for the Christian …if same sex marriage is okay…then what isn't okay? …where does the Bible stand on sex-change or computers or Disneyland or trips to the space station or the moon? ...can Christians entertain these pursuits whether or not they be "of faith"???

...just off the phone to #1 mentor ...Dave says, yes ...provided they "not be aware" should these things be "not of faith" ...which to me is an encouragement to avoiding God's word. ..if we, somehow, make it a point to not be aware of what God says ...then it's not a sin?? ...maybe not even wrong! ...without God's word nor His Spirit ...do we not conduct ourselves according to our natures? ...and further seek entertainment that is pleasing to our own natures? ...what other option is there??? ...the Bible says we can't have both God's nature and our own nature also, except we deceive ourselves.

...can we, ourselves, make our own natures righteous, unless we deny our own natures in exchange for Christ's Spirit? ...for the Christian, any blend of God's light with our own natures (darkness) doesn't seem possible.

(2 Cor. 6: 14) "...what communion hath light with darkness?"

...do we suppose it matters to God that we like (have strong attraction to) certain people or things, who and which are of the world? ...and are unrighteous in His eyes? ...having prepared strong meat for us to eat, do we suppose that when we turn our heads away that He will immediately go and begin warming the bottle for the baby's milk that we are more keen on? ...I'm surprised more churches don't elevate a "mother" figure to appease and succor us in our less mature wants ...which may not exactly coincide with the Bible's exhortation

(2 Cor. 6: 17) to "touch not the unclean (forbidden, or unrighteous) thing."

...there are "degrees" of "unclean" ....right? ...golf is pretty "clean" ...and it promotes honor too! ....right? ...maybe not righteousness ...according to the Bible but honor is a "Christian thing" ...right? ...and "tennis" is pretty clean also! (not football, rugby or soccer though)

...I seem to have been gifted with a good grasp of what's acceptable unto righteousness and what isn't ...I probably could have been handy to Christ's cause, a couple thousand years ago! (I'm trying to imagine these "more noble" sports as might be 2000 years ago ….Titus Woods???) …truth is ….there's probably not much "Godly righteousness" in any sport …period! …or in any movie, best selling novel, popular television series or computer program, etc. etc.

…and I may be in a bit of trouble, both now and down the road, if my "reward" is based on those hours I spend being watchful and sober and holding fast and not distracted. (2 Cor. 13: 5) …the Bible says "Examine yourselves, whether ye be in the faith, prove your own selves, how that Jesus Christ is in you ….."

…else I'll be disapproved, condemned, rejected and lost ….like "reprobate".

…maybe Christians without the gift of having children will have a lesser accountability come judgment …if so, I won't qualify under the "lesser" status.

(Luke 12: 48)   "to whom much is given, much is required" …not all that we personally own, are gifts from God nor blessings. …probably not health nor house nor car nor 2nd car nor cottage nor vacation etc. etc. except we use them to fulfill God's will.

…I imagine satan can also shower us with his own form of gifts and goodies for which we may be thanking God   …when God may, in fact, abhor our thanks for them.

(2 Tim. 6: 8)   "And having food and raiment (clothes) let us be therewith content.

…that verse in (2 Cor. 13: 5) about "Examine yourselves …" is probably a paramount element in the "working out (effort) your own salvation. (Phil.2:12)

…I don't know that "anything" which appears as "gain" to our own natures can likewise appear as "gain" to a Godly (Christian) nature. …the Bible says my own nature is sinful (darkness) whereas God's nature is of righteousness (light). …I suppose this is of "no concern" (guilt) to the non believer …and of maybe "moderate" (limited) concern to the lukewarm Christian …neither of which appear to have any real concern as regards "hellfire and damnation" …but these opposing natures must present a dilemma of conviction for people, like my folks, who having accepted Christ's "light" must henceforth walk in that light, though it be at odds with the world around them.

...it strikes me that the Bible calls Christians to be "salt and light" ...while wearing sack cloth and a crown of thorns in humble deference to carrying Christ's burden ...that's no small understanding!

...plus, we're to be continually growing in faith and in Christ's Spirit.

...a common defense for lukewarm faith is that fallible men (sinners themselves) wrote the Bible ...and therefore we ought trust our hearts to discern what is truth.

...and so, are we to individually, dismiss those parts with which we're uncomfortable? ...where does that differ from non-believers who dismiss all of it?

...I used to loosely suggest that I was Christian, based on my attending church regularly (at a regular church) and helping people out here and there and my feeling that my heart was in the right place ...plus, other Christians said I was Christian ...and that's what I wanted to hear. ...my enjoyment was in fellowship (Christian and otherwise also) but also in regular sampling (moderate) of much that's not specifically spoken "against" in the Bible. ...I may have even thought (assumed) that these "worldly" samplings on my part, gave me a base to share my "devout" faith.

(and God help any who might suggest that my motives could possibly be otherwise!)

(1 Cor. 9: 22) ...in the Bible, the Apostle Paul supports becoming "all things to all men, that he might by all means, save some." ...save for – the truly righteous ...that verse can come in mighty handy in our accommodating "all things".

...lucky me, I get to choose to enjoy the worldly, yet claim it as potential to share Christ with others! ...and the more worldly elements I familiarize myself ...then the deeper my capacity to share Christ ...right? ...there's probably Christian novelists or movie stars or sports figures...even porn stars! ...who, through their interests are able to share with others the real, abiding treasure of their hearts. ...I'm weak ...and don't have that inner discipline. ...maybe there's some knack or truck to it that I just haven't caught onto, just yet. ...maybe it's a particular gift of the Spirit ...and falls to some but not all???

…an acquaintance recently shared that their teenage boys find some comfort at having Bibles in their own rooms. …maybe that's like having a crucifix on a wall …or an elastic around a finger …or a vitamin in a bottle …it's of no effect, except we apply it's merit.

…the Bible, like the church is but printed word and possibility. …it's perhaps comforting to know there is "healing" in a container …even salvation …but it's only of merit to those who "avail" themselves "of it". …to ignore it is to "deny yourself" what it has to offer you. …no book nor building nor vial nor belief nor inoculation can be of any merit except we avail ourselves "of" that merit. …we can take a ¼ dose or ½ dose or the full shot and have a "proportional" hope for what ails us.

…other faiths may entertain proportional (gradient) reward or merit …but not Christianity. …without Christ's Spirit in us ….we are "far worse" than dead. …to have a "form" of Godliness …or a "form" of faith through Christ(Rev. 3: 16) …is to be spewed from eternal salvation, no matter what we ourselves may ascertain as to our having avoided forbidden fruit like adultery, theft, murder, etc. etc. …is it evidence of His Spirit being in us, if 50 or 75% of what we do "is pleasing" to God? …and 50 or 25% "maybe not so pleasing"???

(2 Tim. 3: 16) …the Bible says "All scripture is given by inspiration of God and is profitable for doctrine, for reproof, for correction ("our" correction…not it's correction!) for instruction in righteousness." …and the Bible also speaks to our relating to those who wander from the Bible's doctrine knowingly …or don't care.

(Rom. 16: 17) "Now I beseech you, brethren, mark them which cause divisions and offence "contrary" to the doctrine which ye have learned and avoid them." (Rom. 16: 18) For they, that are such, serve not our Lord Jesus Christ but their own belly (hearts and desires) and by good words and fair speeches deceive the hearts of the simple."

…many churches, being "democratic" are probably inclined towards other than "holding fast" to the doctrine and have moved to the "center" in hopes of both "holding" the devout …while also "attracting" the more liberal people so as to maintain sufficiency in numbers and intake (money).

...although I can't recall the message, I nevertheless made it to church yesterday morning ...actually, the message I recall getting "wasn't positive ...it was rather in some hymns we sang, that once again pleaded God to do this and that for us, as though He somehow wasn't maybe trying hard enough at present.

...I guess God hasn't realized yet that we're busy people and while His efforts may have been sufficient for previous generations to bring them to salvation, this 21st century is very demanding and so we ask or pray that He expand His contribution on our behalf.

...this, despite the Bible's teachings that it's we who must surrender busyness in order to avail ourselves of any expectation (hope) of the blessings (rewards) available to obedient numbers who deny themselves in order that we might be counted among His flock.

...I think the Bible pretty well clarifies that God has no interest in being our "last resort" when our ride (journey) is in a nosedive.(Gal. 6: 7) "Be not deceived, God is not mocked for whatsoever a man soweth, that shall he also reap. ..."sowing" is the result of a lengthy process of preparation and nurturing. ...there's no parable to advance (promote) the premise of "fast food harvesting"

(2 Cor. 3: 5) ...rather, the continual examining of ourselves in vigilance of the light of God's word. ...there's nothing in the Bible to suggest that God is going to direct His blessings on someone just for the heck of it!

...if it's "adequate trials" that will break one's resolve against holding onto pride and worldliness ...then pray those trials be intensified ...even for our most loved ones ...that they might come to the hope of salvation. ...in the Bible, miracles came to broken people ...so pray for brokenness rather than miracles!

...I can be as proud or pious as I want but except I be righteous (and humbly so) then I don't expect my prayers to avail much of anything, for anyone!

(James 5: 16) ...except my prayers are accompanied by "tears" of angst and caring ...then I don't expect them to avail much. ...am I smarter than the Bible? ....or am I more special than all those to whom the Bible speaks?

…maybe to Santa Claus or the birthday cake "candle fairy", I can blurt out some things I want and chuckle if I perchance get them.

…that type of wishful thinking, along with that type of attitude has absolutely no place in even the remotest Christian prayer life, according to the Bible.

…my guess is, that even our most fervent and the most effectual prayers will be rarely answered according to our expectations.

…even my foremost mentor suggests our prayer frequently are akin to throwing out a multitude of fishing lines and hoping for something like a bite on at least a couple of the …is it "our will" …or "His will" we are praying for???

…if we are indwelt by His Spirit and being directed by His Spirit and obeying His Spirit …then "His will" is our will …..right? …and therefore "our will" is His will …right? ….and it's precisely because of that, that we can, in faith believing, "trust God" for the outcome, knowing full well that despite our devoutness, His thoughts are not our thoughts, neither are our ways His ways. (Isa. 55: 8) …where I stumble and where my faith falters …is in those things which I do or listen to or watch (though they seem harmless) yet I fail to see clearly how they are of service to His Kingdom on Earth.

…do I allow "God to lead me" in all things? …or do I just suppose God can't mind them too much because I know He loves me and therefore won't punish me …just now? …is Christ-likeness really what I want? …or is it rather just a "form thereof" what I really want? …is it really the Holy Spirit of God that prompts one to find enjoyment in secular music or movies or television? …what about "that other" spirit and force which the Bible says "is even now already in the world"? (1 John 4: 3)

…am I immune because I profess to be Christian? …what about Christians who, somehow, find themselves watching violence or pornography, football, soap operas, golf, etc.?

…are they immune also??? …isn't it our own personal assessment or discernment that determines "possibly of faith vs. "possibly of sin"? (Rom. 14: 23)

…which of the "fruits of the Spirit" am I nourishing in my more secular hours?

...or is it the fruits of a spirit other than Christ's?...how often do I forget that Christ isn't like me? ...if a "Christ-like" person were my neighbor, he'd probably make me somewhat uncomfortable. ...how could I best share with him or her those things which interest me ...knowing, from the Bible, those things which interest them? ...I'd probably sadly shake my head and give up trying ...figuring they would probably never understand anyway. ....go figure ...having ears to hear and eyes to see ..."they" yet refuse to get with the program. ...so sad ....their loss ...right?

...this mornings newspaper headline blazed the final release (12 year sentence) of a notorious Canadian convicted criminal and I thought "if they did the things they were convicted of ...then I'm probably not such a bad person, myself.

...it's an interesting weakness I have ...of comparing myself to others ...rather than to

God's word. ...if I can magnify another's sin ...or evil ...or wrongdoing, then I automatically minimize my own failings as a "professed Christian" ...and I just have to let my Bible collect a bit of dust, to do that! ...I wonder what it is that prompts me to escape niggling conviction? ...I expect there are "holier than thou" Christians ...but those people who are, don't seem to know it! ...nor even care that another might praise them for their plodding faithfulness.

...the gradient range for "holiness" probably runs from "zero" to "devout" and probably not many holidays or recreational interests are about reaching the "devout" status.

...it's very nice that pastors bestow holiness status on those who sit before them ...but puzzling that no hands go up when the request for "volunteers for the Lord's work: is proffered.

...I'm aware that "my" faith is fickle at times and because of that, I hesitate to profess myself as Christian ...which I guess means a saint, which I guess means righteous, which I guess means holy. ...maybe I'm merely a pilgrim.

...i.e. (Webster's) "a person who travels to a shrine or a holy place as a religious act" being one definition and I suppose "a church" could qualify as a shrine (any site or structure used in worship or devotion.) ...maybe I'm more of a "shriner" than a Christian! ...if so ...I should probably smarten up (besides ...I thought a shriner was either a small fish or else a rich fella with a tall red hat who does good things!} ...(I must be the "small fish" variety)...I would have thought that "holy people" would be only concerned with things of "holiness" or things "of" God. ...that must be where God's grace to His faithful comes in. ...we can do pretty much what we want, then at night, say "forgive me for doing the same things I did last week and please, You, God, make me different than what I want to be ...and I hope You can improve on Your most recent efforts because not much seems to be changing in me ...amen."

(James 5: 16) ...the Bible says "the fervent effectual prayer of a righteous man availeth much" ...I don't know that it says "anything" about wordy casual prayer, other than it better not be repetitious ...sometimes I think I must just like asking for things. ...but I suppose I ought know and consider God's will before spewing out personal requests. (James 4: 3) ...the Bible says "Ye ask and receive not, because ye ask amiss ....."
...it's not that I haven't been "told" what to pray for ...it's just that I don't want to "hear" what to pray for. (John 14: 13) ...the Bible says "and whatsoever ye shall ask in my name(my will?) that will I do ...." ...through Christ, our every prayer should probably first be prefaced with "If it might bring glory to the Father, then ....."
...realistically, how can "prayer" be otherwise? ...I shudder to think of the volume of things prayed for, that are actually of sin! ...for the professed Christian, how can there be forces at work apart from "of faith" or else "of sin"?
...do we suppose there's maybe some vague "force" of "socially acceptable"?
...no way! ...I think there comes a day (maybe about age 12) from whence we taste of the "tree of sin" and at that point we choose to tie our horse to either the wagon of "faith" (Christ) or the wagon of "other than" (sin). (age 12 appears to be the age at which Christ is reported to have chosen to place God ahead of all other considerations ...though "my own nature" would prefer it to be age 30 ...or 50!)

...the Bible says there is no "Mister In between" wagon ...it's Christ's wagon or else it's the anti-Christ's wagon ...and to "not choose" is as to have our horse (choice) automatically ties to satan's deceptive entourage ...no matter if we do what appears a hundred good deeds every day ...the fluff of the world is what will eventually bury us and close the door to "hope".

...some have great talents or great gifts of aptitude but what is it those gifts promote? ...when the same hands that mend bodies following an accident, can, the next day, terminate the life of a fetus?

(James 1: 17) ...the Bible says "Every good and perfect gift is from above and cometh down from the Father...." ...what comes naturally (of ourselves) are not those "good and perfect" gifts of God ...but rather only what brings glory to Him, is of Him.

...all else, we ourselves, own outright and have ourselves to account for why things aren't going right in our lives. ...it's like we ourselves have designed and assembles a 1000 piece jigsaw puzzle ....but we've had to separate from God in order to do it ....but now find the pieces never actually fitted well and the picture is all distorted ...but after all our effort over the years, we don't want to take it apart and we find we're addicted to making the puzzle even bigger ...maybe up to 10,000 pieces!!

...Boy! ...one day ...it's maybe going to really be something big! ...maybe bigger than the "wonders of the world" or the Tower of Babel! (whoops ...forget the last one) ...our past transgressions can be forgiven us but not if we are determined to carry on as before. (2 Cor. 5: 17) ..."old things are passed away"

...only if we want all things to become new. ...we're pretty clever people ...but we can't make God's light, blend with the darkness that repels light, then darkness has us in it's grasp of lukewarmness.

...while Christ is the Prince of Peace, nevertheless, the route to the peace He offers is often arduous. ...our struggle and trials are not departures from the straight and narrow road but rather just seemingly slow lanes of refinement.

(Luke 12: 51) "Suppose ye that I am come to give peace on earth? I tell you, Nay, but rather division"

…it's sad and disappointing when we ourselves are unable to mend and comfort those we love …but we can constantly encourage (as best we can) our loved ones to seek the comfort only Christ can provide, if they will honestly humble themselves and seek Him. …our word is our honor and our bond …until we don't want it to be …and as God sees our hearts, so He knows our nature to barter when our need is great …only to ease up in the more smooth sailings.

…when we get back to feeling fine we're inclined to neglect "prescribed medicine" that doesn't taste good …that's our nature.

…we can deny it with our lips and we can believe whatever our lips or another's lips say …but to my son Richard or any other …best to trust only the fruit or proof …and let all the lip service slide …in ourselves and others.

…many reflect on their great …even charitable deeds …but if all glory isn't deferred to God, then be wary. …in general …Christian doesn't mean Christian anymore …or rather it does but only to the extent and definition we want it to.…my once good friend Tissa said he was Christian but I later found he was also Muslim and Buddhist (probably not Jewish) …he was probably Bahai also, though maybe didn't know it.

…like my our brother, Glen, also now gone from this world. I don't like to think on their present whereabouts. …both Glen and Tissa were well liked by probably all who met them …that's small reward, should their eternity be away from Heaven. …so …where is my treasure??

(Matt. 5: 11) …the Bible counters "Blessed are ye, when men shall revile you and persecute you and shall say all manner of evil against you falsely, for my sake.

…where are those guys who those things are happening to?? …it sure isn't me! …so where are they? …was the Pope reviled or persecuted? ..or Billy Graham? …do they get the blessing regardless: …or do they "pass" on that one?

…maybe "reviled" doesn't mean reviled, anymore?? …maybe it just means "not overly praised" at least here in the civilized western world.

…there are parts of the world where faithfully serving Christ brings stripes, imprisonment and even death. (2 Cor. 6: 5) …thankfully, I guess, we're above and beyond that …but probably also don't hold quite so fast to that good which remains which is ready to die. (Rev. 3: 2)

…the western world provides well for the Christians here and great is our reward ….right? …one of Webster's definitions for "bless" is "to favor or endow with"

…we may be favored or endowed with any number of "no good things" (2 Cor. 11: 14) …"and no marvel; for satan himself is transformed into an angel of light." …but only the "good and perfect gifts from above" will return glory to the Father …and it's kind-a too bad that we're uncertain of as to where the glory and thanks is directed concerning goodies that probably aren't "from above" (like "cheesecake" for instance) …worldly "cheesecake" is every "temptation to be overcome"

…and it's probably nowhere more prevalent than here in the "land of plenty".

…"our consciences" may not be up to "Bible standards" …and there's the rub …..do we raise our standards? …or lower the Bible's???

…have we disciplined ourselves sufficiently to deny our own nature's?? …or do we, by professing Christianity, just assume that our nature is now Christ's nature also??

(Jer. 17: 9) …the Bible says our hearts are deceitful above all things …but it doesn't say at what point (shy of death) our hearts are released from deceit as we progress in our born again walk …I guess "not ever" …lest we falter and succumb to pride or piety …none of which has any part in faith but is rather of satan.

(1 John 2: 16) …the Bible says "For all that is in the world, the lust of the flesh and the lust of the eyes and the pride of life is not of the Father but is of the world."

…it's probably so, that for every "thing of the world" that we choose to embrace, there is an equal and opposite blessing of which we deprive ourselves …and there's probably a compounding (expanding) element to both.

…I may think that a little "piddling" relaxation in vigilance or discernment probably doesn't make much difference …but even "baby steps" add up over the course of years, whereby I may find myself far from God's faithful flock …and His available countenance. …and the way back to God's grace, even more daunting and perilous to my nature, than I imagine at worst. …impossible in fact …except I humbly plead help through Christ.

("grace" is for sure, an interesting short read in any sizeable dictionary!)

…can the sincere and seeking Christian grow in God's good grace, without losing the favor (grace) of those family and friends who purposefully decline nor have the desire to separate from the worldly attraction ever present and available?

…what purpose for life is there if we don't support the desires of our hearts and perpetuate those interests?

…whatever we perceive as "adding" to our daily lives, is what we will encourage.

…the Bible calls it "the fruit" of whatever tree we have chosen to become

…every interest is nourished, or not, by mankind (us) and we determine what thrives, lingers, or perishes …accordingly.

…does sin support holiness? …or visa versa? …it can't be! …at lest it can't be for any who sincerely cite the Bible as their guide. …as the Bible consistently speaks against such a premise and says those who choose to live that way cannot be of God's flock.

…while it's not for us to judge or criticize lukewarm ness in faith, we can nevertheless exhort one another as to what is and what isn't supported by scripture.

…now that my son, Richard, has grown to manhood, there's no one I want to "tell" about how they "should" live their lives …I don't want the burden or responsibility of accounting to God, someday (maybe soon) should I encourage some agenda which might lead another away from a closer walk with God. …but neither do I want to account for why I didn't share God's word when I had opportunity to do so. …in some ways, one might rightfully say that I'm an "escape artist" …I actually do "fear" God. …beyond "awe" …and beyond "respect" …(I have those things also for Billy

Graham or Mother Theresa …even Bill Gates or Donald Trump or the guy who carved Mount Rushmore! ….but I don't "fear" those people.

…I fear God because I believe the Bible and I "believe" my eternity (forever) could very easily be one of "gnashing of teeth torment" unless I continue to "work out my own salvation with fear and trembling"

(Phil. 2: 12) …and attempt daily to "Cast down imaginations and every high thing that exalteth itself "against" the knowledge of God

(2 Cor. 10: 5) "and bring into captivity (submission) every thought to the obedience of Christ…" …I'm a long, long, long way from "that" …but where I once thought that verse must be a joke …I now believe it means just what it says …and to try to "soften" it's truth, is to risk "all hope" of salvation. (Rom. 14: 23) …for the Christian …"of faith or of sin" is the reality …and whatever I choose to ignore or downplay, of what is in God's word, will always be to my own detriment spiritually. …I'm much improved from back when I was a "plastic Christian" …to where, now, I'm just an "ostrich Christian" and growing weary of spitting sand.

…I don't see how there can be much Spiritual life or growth if we remain ambivalent to the truth and light in God's word …and though I may say "I'm Christian" a gazillion times, it doesn't make one bit of difference.

…Christ's Spirit, if in me, will compel me to depart the "worldly" against my own nature …and in exchange, draw me to seek out only what is of greater faith in Christ. …again …the Bible will confirm if I am being deceived by some spirit other than Christ's. …sporadic inner contentment can easily be supplied by my own nature …or even satan's spirit, "even now already in the world". (1 John 4: 3)

…it's not my nature to want to doubt or even discern my every move or every thought ….to be "nit-picky" never endears others to us.

…in the past, when I've had domestic pets (not "pet" peeves)…it used to bug me when it was "me" who discovered "ticks" or "fur-mites" on them …I would sternly confront the family members as to how it was that it was never "them" who made this repugnant discovery! …am I the only one with suspicious feelings in their fingers?!?!

…must be an age thing …where only the oldest in the group has that particular "gift". …my dad also had that particular gift.

…before a remedy for "wrong" can be applied "someone" needs to determine (discern) that something is "not right" (not as it should be).

…the person to determine that …should probably not be the weakest link in the chain …else that link becomes the common denominator.

…has the "tolerant, appeasing link" become the common denominator in our churches? …maybe "a lifetime" wasn't sufficient time for Calvin or Wesley or any other to identify their errors??? …no church and no group …will pass away from this world having attained "pure" holiness …only Christ left this world having arrived at holiness. …all mortals will have fallen short …and no humble servant of Christ was nor will be unaware of it. …an interesting perspective was recently shared with me, being that "life is God's gift to us …and what we do is our gift to God."

…there's something in that which makes me uneasy. ….as though there might be a "form of commerce" involved.

…when we finally land that job we've long hoped for, we don't turn around to negotiate what we will or won't do. …likewise, the probation period for "salvation" isn't three months or three years or even thirty years! …it's until we leave this company (in a pine box) …even when we're too weary or too old to proudly raise our heads …we're still in a good position to pray that God's will be done on earth. …I expect "God's will" will be known to the Christian because they will have sought to learn God's will and the Spirit will have shared (revealed) what is and what isn't "of" God's will.…I suppose that "what we do that pleases God might be loosely perceived as our gift "to" Him

…but everything "good" that we have or do is already from Him, so it's a bit sketchy to suggest that anything of "our own" sinful nature might be construed as a "gift" to God. …in the parable of the talents (Matt. 13: 30) the master demanded back not only what he had give but also the fruit (interest) on what he had originally given. …God's blessings come to Christian and non Christian alike; but only the Christian will utilize that blessing to bear fruit pleasing to God and thus secure the further blessing of giving back to God with a joyful heart.

(Rom. 14: 23) …what isn't of faith, is against faith.

…normally …for us to give a card or gift, yet not receive likewise, is nothing or perhaps a little disappointment but how about if the price for our not returning a gift …was the teeth gnashing torment of having our fingernails pulled out (either slowly or one by one …or maybe all at once …just whatever produces "gnashing of teeth") (Luke 13: 28) …it doesn't seem remotely possible that a loving God would allow such a thing …so there must be several mistakes in the Bible ….right?

…and it doesn't seem possible that God would make such a thing as a cute little baby grizzly cub, then allow it's loving mother to rip my head off for wanting to play with it, though I've been warned not to.

…that mother grizzly is loving …of her own …but wrathful on any who interfere.

…the Bible repeatedly warns that God is like that also.

(Matt. 11: 15) …the Bible says "He that hath ears to hear, let him hear."

…maybe if God came down and ripped just one person's head off their shoulders and it was covered by the media …then maybe we would use our ears to hear what the Lord saith.

(….good thing I'm a happy fells and not inclined towards doom and gloom ….right?)

…I made the mistake the other night of turning on the television and was intrigued by a movie scene that showed a beautiful mermaid (very realistic) …beautiful to look at …only, she ate people! …I grappled in horror with the clicker …but before I could get rid of her, she transformed into a giant lizard!

…that show was probably even more scary than C.N.N.!

(now that I know I'm weak …I might even try "quiche"!)

…anyways …I'm reminded that people and things may not be as they appear and that I'm probably better off being in bed, asleep, after 9 p.m.

…as the mother grizzly …God lovingly provides bountifully …to those that are of Him …and as the Bible says, is wrathful in the extreme to those who aren't.

…and us …being somewhat clever or resourceful can bandy about words like "awe" or "respect" or "fear". …I don't have a problem with "fear and trembling" if that's what the Bible says …and when I consider that the Bible also says that many will say "Lord, Lord, we did what you asked …so let us in!" …I don't want to be amongst those to whom He responds "I never knew you: depart from me."

…if a forty or sixty hour weekly schedule keeps me from discerning His will and applying myself to pleasing Him …than I'd better alter my schedule ….right?

…what's the gain, if I lose my head? …"eternity" is a long, long time to be regretting and tormenting over lost opportunity.

…church message tonight was on the fruit of the Spirit, "Joy"

…and how joy is often preceded by sorrow or pain or trial. …our own natures will rebel against giving any ground to anything that won't feed it …much less, actually, encourage it's demise.

…our nature is willfulness vs. Christ's nature of unselfish giving …and to know (experience) His joy, then our self-will must sacrificed.

…on returning home from papers this morning, I saw a new lighted sign on the back of a city bus that just said "yield". …a long forgotten church song from my youth came to mind ….but the song says "Yield not ….to temptation" …for yielding is sin. Each victory will help some other to win." …sounds like something the Apostle Paul would have written! …"victory" is more than our final reward, it's also a perpetual overcoming or worldly influence and the only means of Spiritual growth in Christ.

…as regards God's viewing our hearts, perhaps all He sees is either "victory" or defeat in our efforts for His cause and His will.

…"it's a long and winding road" (Beatles) …that leads, to His door …with a million things to look at, then choose if they're "of faith" or "of other" before we reject them or adopt them.

…if we read our Bibles, then we know which of those things are pleasing in God's eyes …and through His Spirit we know there are "no maybes".

...I know the game of golf isn't "of faith" except I use that game exclusively to advance His Kingdom. ...and I suppose the joy of sex isn't "of sin" ...but only provided I enter into that joy, according to the admonition given in His word.

...I assure you ...my own nature doesn't like that part! ...but my experience in having maybe even just a little of His righteousness and His inner joy, sustains me in a victory over something that my own nature wouldn't mind a little defeat.

...is there "something" more important than "victory in Jesus? ...No!

...there's no friend or experience like the lowly Jesus ...no, not one.

..."my nature" says I want to be of great "importance" to someone or something

...be it a spouse or father or where I work or team I play on ...except for what I do to promote God's Kingdom on earth ...I'm pretty much just a "bag of dirt.

...but I'd rather be a "bag of dirt with the hope of eternal salvation"...than to be adored by the world, yet spend eternity having my fingernails painfully extracted!

...I faintly hear that (idiot) satan say "hey man ...just be cool ...that stuff is never going to happen ...don't worry – be happy!"

...to heck with him ...his fate is sealed ....mine isn't ...yet.

...our children's fates aren't sealed but that's largely contingent upon their parents' teaching and their parents' "apparent" treasures.

...the Bible calls children to honor their parents ...not teach them ...but it does direct parents to ensure that their children are raised to know and fear God.

...if we (for "whatever" reasons) expose our children to the bright lights (city) and it's temptations, then we are accountable ...no excuses.

...if we're not sufficiently blessed, it's because we haven't "positioned" ourselves to be sufficiently blessed.

...I doubt there's much "Spiritual" merit in trying to understand our worldly natures.

...the time we spend in worldliness, just distracts us from God's truth in His word.

...if we're Christian, then why would the Holy Spirit in us encourage any surrender to

...or justification in "worldly appetites"??? ...what has that to do with holiness?

...except it convict ourselves "against" worldliness.

(James 4: 2) …the Bible says "….count it all joy" when we fall into various temptations …not to succumb, but rather to learn patience and hence gain the victory over them. …what thanks or praise have we to bring to God should our Spiritual journey (experience) show defeat after defeat? …more likely, as with Cain, it'll cause us to hide from God …having given satan the victory.

…a Bible study leader said he was angry at God for a long time after his first wife died. …it wasn't the presence of the Holy Spirit in him that directed the anger towards God …it was some other spirit that he allowed to squash (defeat) the Holy Spirit's comfort in him. …maybe we think it's some great sacrifice to, on occasion, profess ourselves to be Christian …but if we have not the "peace" of the Spirit, though under duress, then is it not a form of faith? …void of any power therein to sustain us?

…that study leader proposed that it's okay to be angry at God …but I don't know which "fruit of the Spirit" anger qualifies for. …surely, one wouldn't approach "faith" as a venue for complaint …would they???

(Heb. 10: 25) …when the Bible says for us "not to forsake the assembly of ourselves …that means for the purpose of exhortation to "hold fast"

…not to whine and complain …right? …to see bickering, backbiting and petty sensitivities between church member …it's a sure indication that we're in the wrong church and I don't see how that conduct can fly under the radar of church leaders.

…maybe it's just "the new church life" and "some" just haven't gotten with the program yet. …do we simply concede that we're human and that negative thought and comments are a part of life? ….even a part of "Christian life"?

…it will be a part of even "Christian" life if no effort is made to stop it.

…probably for every effort made to attract people to church, there is a greater spiritual ambivalence that's pushing them away.

…except for rhetoric, Christians seem very secular …when we're suppose to

…(James 1: 27) "Keep ourselves unspotted from the world."

...it's not our desire for greater faith that sends us to blockbuster movies, sporting events or best selling novels ...rather it's our turning our backs on faith that plants us on the couch or compels us to seek out the latest toys on the shelf.

...the cost of fun and secular gain is eventual Spiritual death. ...everything has a cost ...even the air we breathe carries the cost of vigilance in caring for it ...if we allow it to become unclean it can kill us or kill those we love. ...we even have to pay for the dirt to cover us when we die! ...the Bible verse about "unspotted from the world" is the cost of receiving Christ's Spirit and all His Spirit makes available.

(James 4: 2) ...we perhaps ask, yet receive not, because we ask from the basis of our own natures, which are self-serving. (sinful) ...though our "lips" be of God, yet if our hearts are elsewhere, will God deny His own word and accommodate us???

...can God love satan??? ....or have we devised a "medium" that is neither of God nor satan ...but rather a flexible state of spirituality that lies somewhere in between whereby satan doesn't exactly bother us nor does God exactly condemn our choices? ...sounds a bit convenient ....but it has no validation in scripture.

...what's convenient ...is that satan hasn't published, or had published, his own instruction book wherein are cited all those things "of our own desires" that will lead us into his own fold and add us to his number.

...and so each of us is given license to determine (discern) for ourselves whether any thing other than "of faith" is to be our treasure and to what degree.

(Rom. 12: 2) "And be not conformed to this world but be ye transformed by the renewing of your mind, that ye may prove what is that good and acceptable and perfect will of God." ...that chapter continues in sharing that different aspects of faith will find predominance in different people ...but all will endeavor to promote the "good and acceptable and perfect will of God."

(...I just now see that "exhortation" is listed as a "gift" ...I don't think I knew that ...it's probably much the same as extortion ....right? ...so maybe I do have a spiritual (gift!) ...whatever our spiritual gift, others will have it also ...and that gift will be upheld by God's word (Bible) and encourage the upholding of His word....

though I may not be a prime player in any area of gifts …I can at least be an encourager of those whose desire is the "renewing of their mind" to become Christ's church here on earth.

…to wear sackcloth or giant crucifixes is unlikely to avail Christ's cause so much as our simply and pleasantly saying "no thank you" to those things presented us which can't possibly be tied to an area of faith in Christ.

…truth is that the smokin' and drinkin' that's probably frowned on by many churches, interferes less with our availing ourselves to hear from God, than do many of the leisure activities that those same churches condone and participate in.

…the Bible doesn't list a hundred things not to do …it just tells those who are interested, what to do …like "meditate on God's word day and night" …'overcome temptation"…"bring every thought into captivity of Christ" …"judge not – be merciful" …"hold fast to that which is good" …"lean not to thine own understanding" …"put on the armor of God" …"take heed unto thyself" …"do those things which are pleasing in His sight" …"be content with food and raiment" …stuff like that! …right? …so then …knowing what the Bible says to do …we either do it …or we do other stuff instead …right? …and that's what makes us practicing Christians …or some other derivative thereof ….right?

…it's pretty dumb, even in our own wisdom, to "claim" status as an oak tree …despite our looking down at our base and seeing the ground littered with figs. …an oak tree doesn't give a fig ….right? (Matt. 7: 16) …the Bible says "Ye shall know them by their fruits. …and (Matt. 7: 20) …calling out God's name in our distress, avails us nothing, unless we do the will of God and prove ourselves faithful.

…nobody "needs" God to pretend to be Christian and nobody "needs" God to do those things that are not "of faith" …but "His will done on earth as it is in Heaven" is entirely dependant on His Spirit in His people, so that His will might be accomplished. …I've been long blessed by God with His goodness but have long been largely unawares …and over the years that has been my greatest loss …and also greatest risk re: eternity. ...and I have for years, even with good intent, been a poor example for encouraging my son Richard and others down dead-end roads.

..."loose faith" or lukewarm Christianity is such a road. ...better a bumpy road that leads to utopia, than accept the smoother road that leads to an invisible precipice.

...the "world" must needs sell us on all it's trappings, as it's dependant on our support and our money to sustain it. ...it's the "way of the world" ...to convince us to sample the "minimum package" for just a few dollars ...and if we all just buy into that, then "somebody" can make a lot of money and even provide jobs for us as well! ...and so we "become" world dependant and the rest of our lives is history.

...wayward tributary, after wayward tributary away from (rather than towards) our only salvation from darkness. ...until we're so deeply imbedded in the world that we exclaim "the Bible can't possibly mean what it says!" ...and so we modify what it says ...what other option have we, if we choose not to be "transformed by the renewing of our minds"? (Rom. 12: 2) (Matt. 7: 24) "Therefore whosoever heareth these sayings of mine and doeth them, I will liken him (them) unto a wise man which built his house upon a rock. ...if not ...great will be our fall ...(Matt. 7: 13) "and broad is the way that leadeth to destruction" ...to be weak in spirit, is satan's secret way to allow us to embrace (accept) the "broad way" ...by encouraging our pride and piety over minute self denial yet still consider ourselves favored by God.

...unfortunately, other devout faiths find this "sketchy Christianity" repugnant and untrustworthy and deceitful to the point where they don't want our worldly faith polluting their own people or countries.

...do radical elements of other faiths kill innocent people, believing perhaps, that the end result justifies the means? ...the civilized western world has itself given that method validity. (Hiroshima?) ...we seldom believe that we reap what we sow ...yet "innocent life" for innocent life taken, one single choice in the past (whatever the intent) ...the math bodes poorly for the west.

...this is the weekend of which I'm missing a big family reunion in Ontario ...the first since 6 years ago (which surrounded a memorial service for my folks) ...and despite the deep roots in faith from which we all came …I don't suppose even 25% of the family would, today, claim to be practicing Christians nor attend a church regularly. …it's often said, that opposites attract and now I wonder how many of us married outside the family of devout faith from which we came …and how that has impacted our personal Spiritual walk and the Spiritual walk of our children.

…compromise often seems "best" when considered in the light of our own wisdom …yet "compromise" carries a high cost …and not just to ourselves. …I wonder if I could have attended that reunion and bridled my tongue, as to not offend anyone? (1 Cor. 10: 32) …the Bible says "Give none offense" …"seeking the profit of many, that they might be saved" …it's hard to know "what" might cause offense in those folk who we're unfamiliar with. …that verse …in (1 Cor. 10) gives some validity to another verse …(2 Cor. 6: 17) …"Come out from among them and be ye separate." …it doesn't mention exceptions.

…my dad was a preacher …and I wonder if anyone ever asked him to please not cite scripture in any particular conversation …lest it offend someone. …not our own advice or instruction …but rather God's advice and instruction is the only "good" we can contribute to a given situation …and the Bible says (James 4: 17) "therefore to him that knoweth to do good and doeth it not, to him it is sin."

…I doubt my dad could bridle his tongue for the sake of "socially acceptable" conduct.

…though we find ourselves living in a smaller envelope than we wish …can we ever adopt "socially acceptability" over sharing Christ? ….without inviting darkness on ourselves and on those we profess to love? …we can never, totally, keep darkness (satan) from either our doorstep nor from our loved one's doorstep …even Job couldn't do that …but in, daily and faithfully, putting on the armor that God readily makes available to those whose hearts desire it …so then are we able to overcome satan through Christ's Spirit …Amen!

…what's the use …should we partake of what God liberally gives in armor against sin and wrongdoing …then just walk around with it, as though in a parade!?!

…sharing with some ….yet holding back with others! …that's not "faithful"

…it's more like Spiritual schizophrenia. …faith that hinges on another's over sensitivity, is questionable faith. …I used to dodge any challenge of my own "personal" religious walk …thus choosing the realm of darkness and fear …not wanting my dirty laundry aired, when that's exactly what was needed! …and is still needed …and always will be needed!

…water doesn't make things whiter …strong bleach is required. …many churches have an abundance of water but strong bleach is the gift only of Christ.

…as I look about this apartment, it's clear that I can live in a dirty place

…Christ can't …the Bible says so. …other spirits probably can live in dirty houses

…but not Christ's Spirit. …good thing too! …else how would we know His peace, rather than satan's sporadic "cheesecake??? …doubt and weakness, is always of "ourselves" and never of "faith". (James 1: 5) ….the Bible says "if any of you lack wisdom, let him ask of God, that giveth to all men (mankind) liberally …."

(James 1: 6) …But let him ask in faith, nothing wavering for he that wavereth is like a wave of the sea driven with the wind and tossed."

…our every activity and thought, as Christian …ought be verified in God's word

…no matter the 1st century or 21st century. ……go figure

…or don't we each get to choose. …can the Christian actually knowingly wish to enjoy doing things which are possibly contrary to God's word?

…what "form" of Christianity is that? …and what "imitation of hope" have we for salvation? …it sure can't be the "sure hope" presented in the Bible, for the obedient and the faithful.

…could I be duped by satan …into professing my own confirmed salvation? …and is it with a humble and contrite heart that I might suggest my having such a status?

…it's certainly preferential to my nature …to set aside all inner debate …especially when I know "what is the only alternative" to salvation! …and so I claim, of course, I'm saved! …and I always will be saved! …and while Christ said "many are called, but few are chosen" …He must have been warning "others" and certainly not me!

…right? …and of course, not you either …you and I are likeminded …but I'm not so sure of the others …right? …faithfulness to "a church" …or "a denomination" can be just as damning as no faith at all …if the church departs the expressed word of God.

…while man thinks in terms of "I don't like it but it doesn't bother me too much" …it doesn't appear that God ever thinks that way. …the Bible calls us to encourage one another …but it's not for the sake of mere encouragement or to just help put each other at ease. …it probably bugs me a bit that we often cite how we're to "not forsake the assembling of ourselves together …."

(Heb. 10: 25) …in efforts to encourage church attendance …when, in context, that verse is preceded by (verse 23) "Let us hold fast the profession of our faith without wavering" …and is also followed by "exhorting one another."

…no doubt dozens of false teachings or false churches can take root by isolating a single verse of scripture yet ignoring it's context. …"of ourselves together" is useless (or even worse than useless) …without considering the "let us hold fast the profession of our faith without wavering" …imagine the damnation we invite should we support and advance a cause which displeases God! …our own nature, for sure, seeks a church body

of "don't worry …be happy"

…but that church body is the antithesis of taking up Christ's burden.

…it's, for sure, not our nature to find that to "continue to work out our salvation" (Phil. 2: 12) …means also to ever live in a state of friction

…though the Bible says to count that as "all joy"! (James 1: 2) …the "joy" isn't in the struggle …it's in the "overcoming" …it's in the putting to rest the temptations of the world …and favoring Christ …and in the so-doing we are able to receive His light on our lives ….and how can we expect it otherwise??? …if the Bible says our nature is sinful, then we must shun our nature, else deny God's word and deny our hope of His presence in good times and bad. …to what extent can we cloud what the Bible says or concede to accepting a reasonable facsimile? ...is "patience" (NIV) a reasonable facsimile of "long suffering" (KJV)

...is "happiness" the same as joy? etc. etc. etc. ...is "holiness" the same as "probably harmless" or "lawful" the same as "edifying"?

...I don't think there's scripture to back the premise that we're each to establish our own version of a Christian walk, else why "the Bible" to "hold fast" to? ...is the Bible just a general guideline for us to take license of our capacity to overrule? ...and yet imagine ourselves followers of Christ? ...if Christians and churches would just more aggressively let it be known to the secular world, that all options are open ...and that the admonishment and legalism in the Bible is passé' for the 21st century Christian ...then I expect much of the secular world would attend and support the churches! ...especially as the baby boom generation ages ...so, 10% admission for the hope of salvation is a gamble worth taking ....right? ...circumstance will dictate that the "price is right".

...for many, the Bible is tedious and very time consuming to read ...it needs to "be made" more user friendly ....right? ...or ...bypass the Bible reading and let "a" church that is "more in line with our own thinking" be our guide.

...a church can do what the Bible fails to do. ...the Bible states that there is only our own sinful nature, against God's Holy nature ...but a "church" can sway us towards believing in a third "newly discovered nature" afore to unmentioned in the Bible

...although some newer translations allude to the presence of a third moderate nature, wherein the Spirit of Christ, actually being in us, isn't so much of an issue.

...this new and improved third nature in the new and improved Christian opens many doors as regards what is and what isn't acceptable to faithfulness in Christ.

...and while it blurs the fruits of the Spirit and our accountability therein

...it also allows us the freedom to question the legalism of the ten commandments, beatitudes and suchlike. ...when it comes to "just what is it" that God expects from us, in return for Christ's death? ....this "third nature" will ease our burden of guilt. ...I guess that's why the Holy Spirit is also our "Comforter" ....right?

...provided "whatever we do" has some remote chance of leading another to our belief, then it's fair game.

...I heard recently, of some Christian folk who attend church on Sunday, then invite newcomers (I guess) to fun in their pool, afterwards. ...maybe "Christianity" can be a lot more "fun" than what my dad led me to believe ...although with dad, one always had the somewhat uneasy premonition that "exhortation" would immediately follow "fun". ...though often unpopular, his conduct closely adhered to his honest assessment of what pleased God according to scripture ...while the majority of us were ever looking for wiggle room or escape from the confines of holiness.

...perhaps in many respects ....we're no less lost, than the "lost" whom we're suppose to be drawing to "need of Christ".

...has the Bible perhaps "overstated" the importance of Christ's crucifixion??

...and (given the many distractions of today) has God become even more merciful for us? ...in that we (being smarter than the previous generations) are now able to (at last) decipher, even in the glaring absence of the Holy Spirit, God's more true (and more liberal) meaning?

...in church...or out ...in garb ...or out ...the priest, the pastor, the elder, the Christian ...is a follower of Christ and having put worldliness behind, is "reborn" to henceforth seek a continuing and deeper presence of Christ's Spirit in their daily lives.

...can we continue our Sunday pool-parties of fun and laughter, just as our secular neighbor does? ...maybe we can!

...and maybe the Sabbath need not "appear" holy in order to "be" holy. ...maybe our newfound "moderate" nature, being neither of faith nor of sin, will quell any pangs of doubt ...but is that a good thing? ...and how does it differ from "lukewarm" faith?

...it seems we don't get the ideal weather like we used to ...in the 60s.

...the Lovin' Spoonful had a hit song "what a day for a Daydream" ...and there's a part of our nature that desires to make "everyday" a day for a daydream ...though the Bible says (used to say) we are to endure long suffering (patience) on behalf of others

...if we are "of faith". ..."little faith" prepares us for little patience when chips are down or if tragedy strikes us. ..."little faith" probably causes more confusion for the (lukewarm) professed Christian than is the confusion of the non believer because we so easily perceive "little faith" to be "great and abiding faith" ...hence when tribulation comes to us, then we're often confused ...even angry that God would fail us in providing His comfort. ...though in truth, our greater faith has been in the world and it's offerings.

...I hear people claim having been "born again" when they were a little child, although there's nothing in the Bible to suggest that possibility. ...that seems paramount to denying the Bible's claim that we do in fact have a sinful nature until we, in a willful and immature manner and through Christ's Spirit, slowly starve and try to put that nature away from us ...to be replaced and nourished by the nature (word) of Christ.

...being "in" the world, we have become accustomed to the "instant mentality" ...fast food, microwaves, television clickers, instant pudding, etc. ...anything but a "discerning" mentality. ..."born again" seems of a gradual but growing "discerning" mentality.

...thinking back over recent years, my own experience in faith is one of "steps" as opposed to the "flick of a switch". ...much of what I was once "attracted to" in the world, I became "ambivalent to", that I might favor Christ. ...after which I gradually became "oblivious to" in favor of Christ ...now, much of what I was once attracted to ...I'm repulsed by ...and it hasn't detracted one iota from my enjoying life ...but has rather been a "requirement" to my "knowing" life! ......go figure!

...I don't recall which "dumb" straw "broke the camel's back" ...I'm just thankful it did!...like Tums, "pop-pop-fizz-fizz, oh what a relief it is". ...we need to "pop" these worldly distractions (attractions) and more and more closely "turn our eyes upon Jesus ...that "these things of earth" might grow strangely dim.

...God can overcome the "existence" of our "sinful" nature but only if we determine and discipline ourselves to not nourish (feed) it with what is contrary to His will.

…my Spiritual growth isn't impeded or derailed because I don't want it …it's impeded because I want other stuff more! …there's nothing "of God" that He doesn't want to share with me …(but then …there's probably nothing "of satan" which satan doesn't want to share with me either.)

…what's the point of my mouth saying "I want more of God in my life" …if my eyes and ears are elsewhere? …do I think God is going to interrupt my "television watching" or "golden oldies" to share something of holiness with me?

…my lips can pray and ask 'til my face turns blue …but if I'm doing it during brief commercial breaks or when my walk is generally "of the world" …then I ask amiss and am spinning my tires to no avail.

(James 4: 3) …the Bible says "Ye ask and receive not, because ye ask amiss"

…we ask, seeking our own pleasure or to seek our own return to contentment

…yet remain impervious to God's will. …I used to pray "some prayer of contrition" which a pastor might invite me to recite after him and although I was hurting and felt very humble in the sanctuary …God could see that "my life" did not reflect my onerous words. …He was having none of my "monkey business".

…of the many things I have to be thankful for, God's ignoring my feeble self-serving rantings, is a most precious blessing to me today. …I don't "know" that I'm entirely honest today …but I know I wasn't back then.

(1 Cor. 13: 12) …do I "see through a glass less darkly?" …I hope so

…even though I'm aware of satan's deceitful nature in every breath I draw.

(James 4: 6) "wherefore he saith, God resisteth the proud, but giveth grace unto the humble"

(James 4: 7) "submit yourselves to God. Resist the devil and he will flee from you.

…most of us aren't "bad" people …most just want "peace" (absence of conflict)

…and having a reasonable peace in a community or country, we then want a reasonable amount of "ease" in which to enjoy the "peace".

…the Bible holds a blueprint (plan) …and we (mankind) have a different plan that diverges greatly from God's plan. …we may think "our" plan is very similar to God's plan, though we bypass the details. ...the best of mankind looks to a "peaceful compromise" ...and with immigration, it becomes an ever expanding compromise which doesn't bode well for God's plan through Christ.

...we know that in "diet" to neither refrain nor restrain ourselves leads to poor (compromised) health ....and so likewise in all areas including our natural desires.

...we're aware that our choices aren't the best but we hope the penalty won't be too severe. ...it's our nature to not mind too much if another is disadvantages by our personal gain. ...we live in a society of "survival of the most clever" ...naturally preferring (as good people) to stay within the confines of the law, if possible.

(Gal. 6: 7) the Bible says "...for whatsoever a man soweth, that shall he also reap".

...unlike our own natures ...God's nature is into details. ...I doubt that any of men's law, for "whatever" good makes the least impression on God, except it comply with His instruction (His word). ...the popular "laws" are the one's that depart "God's word". ...it's our nature (only natural) to want freedom from censorship and uphold (encourage) freedom of "personal" choice ...provided that if there's a cost ...that it be paid by future generations (or at least someone other than us!). ...even for Christians, there's much of scripture we may not like or much that we wish said somewhat different (more "user friendly"). ...nevertheless ....just like in public school where we would have preferred to just "play", we "have to learn" to like God's word just as it is. ...don't be conformed to "play" but rather be transformed to righteousness.

(Rom. 12: 2)　(not "our right" ...but rather His right-eousness, which is available to us only through Christ's Spirit in us.)

..."our own best efforts" will wash away overtime, like sand on a beach ...history has shown that to be true ...but "His" love and countenance and wisdom endures forever.

...whether or not we sincerely tap into it, is the most important choice we'll ever make, I guess, because it's that choice that determines our potentially divergent focus towards what will be a "lasting" light which is free from the winds of change.

(Psa. 34: 8) ...the Bible says　"taste and wee that God is good"　...in Him is the only good we will ever need ...and it's best to count all other good as suspect.

…just as it's difficult for me, as a would be Christian, to see moral good in abortion or same sex marriage or capital punishment which is often endorsed by the secular world …so also can I see the secular world having difficulty finding credence in the Christian lifestyle and conduct that so closely resembles their own.

…it's one thing to "not claim" any distinct belief and so be double minded about issues …but to claim faith in Christ's Holy Spirit to direct and empower us and suffice for us …yet continue to drive all over the road (both lanes!) while claiming "faith" is dishonest at best …perhaps even abominable.

…I suppose it's true that the less we know and study of God's word, then the more we can honestly err without guilt …but if we know the Bible says to meditate on God's word day and night …(Psa. 1: 2) …among other things …and yet we choose television or romance novels or sports or whatever …then we breach "ignorant of" and enter into "so what". …I'm 100% positive that God will judge us "justly" whenever our "days end" here on earth comes.

(1 Cor. 14: 33) God is "not the author of confusion" …nor is His word ambiguous.

…if we have ears to hear …yet choose not to hear Him, the Bible says our eventual doom is sealed and our present life is void of His inner peace meanwhile.

…good message at church this morning on the route to being "Spirit filled" in the Christian's walk through this life" vs. "simply believing in God". …he displayed a glass half full of water (Spirit) and half air (sin) …the simplest way to displace (draw out) the air is to fill the glass with water.

(James 4: 7) …the Bible says "resist the devil and he will flee from you" ….but except we replace the sin with things of faith, sin will naturally return to refill any temporary void or vacuum. …the things we do for fun or pleasure that are not "of faith" lead us away from faith and are for sure not directed by Christ's Spirit in us.

…satan will avail every subjective justification to us to depart from faith …and every straying will lead us further from God's light.

…a multitude of minor departures from scripture can cause the glass through which we look to become darker and darker to where we content ourselves with a "form of

Godliness" with low Spirit and low power. ...hence we have to not step sideways but rather actually "back up" and mend our errors before we can once again walk in God's light. ...if we don't highly value "life more abundant in Christ" then our daily walk is towards ever increasing darkness .....right?

...is there a part of Christ's love or Christ light in abortion or capital punishment? ...or even in the many demands for freedoms in the secular world? ...can we, in good faith, look to the Bible and cite when the Bible favors these things? ...if so, then these things are pleasing to God ....right? and if not then these things are pleasing to satan ....right? ...it's a "lukewarm" faith that pretends or manufactures pastimes of our own natures and desires ...then claims them as pleasing to God.

(James 1: 27) ...the Bible says that a characteristic of pure religion is that we remain "unspotted" from the world" ...not "hardly" spotted ...but "unspotted" ....right? ...one's walk in faith is probably in direct correlation to the burdens they themselves carry and visa versa.

(Matt. 11: 29) ...Christ said "Take my yoke upon you and learn of me ...and ye shall find rest for your souls (verse. 30) For my yoke is easy and my burden is light".

...our heaviness is usually attributable to ourselves, through our straying from Christ to embrace the world. (James 4: 2) ...when the Bible says, we have not because we ask not ....I don't think it's speaking to "tangible things" ...but rather to those things the "world" can never supply ...yet things we so desperately need in order to realize even a taste of honesty or "completeness" in our lives.

...that the "world" may say that our own natures are not "sinful" is best to be dismissed. ...we can't accept both the praise of the world ...and the word of God which disputes it.

...the pastor, Sunday morning, was saying that if we believe (in Christ) then we are of the Spirit" ....yet perhaps just a little of the Spirit, as opposed to Spirit filled.

...and so, in us may be displayed some of the fruits of the Spirit (Gal. 5: 22-23) to varying degrees.

…only if we (through surrendering our "old" selves) provide a nurturing environment can that Spirit take root and grow …that we might become Spirit "filled".

…it's probably not "what we do" but rather "what we permit God to do through us" that defines "lukewarm" vs. "devout" Christian.

…I can't believe there is any Christian whom God doesn't wish to use to fulfill His will on Earth….and I suppose the question is "are we available?

…in golf, one can take up the game and enjoy a lukewarm leaning towards it

…and most remain there …content with their "pre-golf" lives yet adding golf to the mix …happy to add the "fruits" of golf to their lives. …but if their hearts are "for" golf, then golf takes predominance and that becomes obvious to all who know us.

…if near a conversation on, say, "missile defense" …we might interject "right!

…just like in golf' …." …after a while, people might avoid us …except those who are likeminded …they probably just figure we're "bugs". …we're not "bugs"

…we just have a passion for something that is relative to everything else!

…through that passion, it will be revealed if we have not only the "fruit" of that interest …but further have "a gift" of that interest.

…to realize any tangible return on our professed passion, we might be required to attend a qualifying school and there prove ourselves worthy of the big return …being "fun" plus "something in the bank" to draw on. …the PGA! (personal-Godly-attributes) …as with golf, the "big return" seldom comes to the casual devotee of the game or the weekend golfer but once it's in the blood, the "golf-life" is the only life!

…so for the Christian, the "big return" comes from their passion being "in the blood" …as in "washed in blood."

(Psa. 34: 8) …to "taste and see that God is good" …isn't washed in the blood …it's an invitation to taste and "better than before" isn't "life more abundant".

…"better than before" can just be our old life with a "taste" of Christ tossed in while we continue in old ways.

(Rom. 12: 2) …the Bible warns us to "not conform to the world …" but by the time we understand what that means, we've already been conformed!

…unlike many other countries, the western world of democratic freedoms has a weak handle on keeping our young people from harms (satan's) way …hence, by the time they reach the age of accountability, devout faith and what that entails seems a preposterous impossibility…nor can any adult shun the role they've played in allowing our prevailing moral and religious decay.

…to wash our hands and hold them up as "clean" is equally preposterous …yet it's our nature to quickly do so. …satan's high card is that "the world" is a "package deal" and many of it's attractions seem harmless.

…a "seeking" friend asked me yesterday "you mean I cant smoke? …or watch television!?!? …I said it doesn't matter what "I mean" …rather it's up to her to read the Bible and discern (give strong thought to) what pleases God and what pleases God's Spirit in her. …I can no more "pronounce" another's Christian conduct than can a pastor or priest or friend "pronounce" me "saved". …convenient and pleasing as another's tangible words may be …it's "the Bible" and only the Bible's truth that will confirm what pleases God's Spirit. ("hearsay" is inadmissible.)

…Sunday's church message on "Spirit filled" got me thinking about "fruits of the Spirit" vs. "Spiritual gifts". …I might occasionally display some of the fruits of the Spirit

(Gal. 5: 22-23) and that's a start …but I'll never be fulfilled until I've surrendered to the point of finding what part of His church (body) I am to be, then act on it.

…it won't be something I have to "work" at …but rather something I'm "unable to resist doing" through His presence in me …whereby my focus is to bring glory to Him and Him alone.

…my No. 1 mentor and also a retired pastor, has shared how, having displayed fruits of the Spirit and having graduated Bible college …even began preaching! …was nevertheless convicted (personally) of retaining his own agenda of "self".

…only through the blessing of several severe "whacks" by God did he push the world away and his own plans away in order to have revealed to him the Spiritual gift whereby he lovingly and enthusiastically was to be a part of God's will for him on Earth to devotedly encourage others to Christ.

…though "retired" in the "world" sense, he can never retire from the Spiritual gift (or gifts) until he's no longer able.

…to Richard, or any professing Christian …always question it, when you hear what you "want" to hear. …our "natural" reaction is to be pleased …whereas a discerned reaction may be otherwise. …it's nice to be "social" …but I don't think that word is in the Bible. (…I think "sober" is the closest in the Bible concordance) (as in watchful, vigilant, sound minded, etc.) …maybe "sociable" is something we've devised to stave off loneliness …yet no number of friends or acquaintances or family members can supplant an emptiness which only Christ can fill. (Psa. 84: 10) …better one day with Christ, than a thousand elsewhere. (..that's about 2 ¾ years! …so between, say, age 10 and age 80 …that's 70 years …if we can "be transformed" (2 Cor. 10: 5) "to bring every thought into captivity" for about 25 ½ days over our average life span, then that's better than 25,567 ½ days, if we're away from Christ …sobering thought …right?) …even so, we continue to roll the dice …spending much of our lives elsewhere, sampling the dangling carrot of "other than faith – yet seemingly harmless" …and ever wondering "when" our Spiritual "gift" will "arrive" at our door. …maybe, in this sense, our perception of "gift" needs to be aligned more with "reward" for surrender" …lest we imagine it's our due (…as with "Christmas gifts" or "birthday gifts"). …I think the Bible holds that there is a gift of the Spirit, which has been exercised (applied, for God's use and glory) by every Christian who hopes to attain Heaven. …perhaps that opens up another verse

(Matt. 20: 16) "…for many be called, but few chosen.:

…I don't think we need to panic and scramble to secure an acceptable Spiritual gift …that's more likely to lead to further self-deceit …but the Bible says that there is "something" that the Spirit will empower us to do, which we will also "want to do", whereby we will turn from world pursuits in favor of focusing joyfully on the things of God and of what use we can be to His body and His church.

…we don't have to "chase down" a "Spiritual gift" …but we have to have a sincere desire to know more of God, no matter our personal loss of social status (pride) or social circle (family and friends).

(Luke 12: 48) "…For unto whomsoever much is given of him shall be much required….." …here in the west, simply having access to the Bible, qualifies us as being those to whom "much is given" …and so likewise is no much required of us in service to God? …the world may squander what is given us of God with little or no regard for Spiritual life in Christ …but the professing Christian, if sincere …has chosen the narrow road of "paying forward" what he is blessed with …to the glory and honor of God …from whom all blessings come.

…the secular world chooses to differ from the Bible's teachings ….why is that?

…and what about professing Christians who choose to differ from scripture or make exceptions and concessions? …where do we suppose the "differing" comes from?

…is it just in the air??? …is it just our nature??? …is there a "giant" satan who directs serial killers and child molesters …yet a "mini" satan, who encourages doubt and self deception in the hearts of believers? …I'd be surprised if most "devout" Christians didn't start out being "lukewarm" …to "taste" is "lukewarm". …unfortunately, "lukewarm" can be somewhat "cool" (okay) …it's certainly, "better than before"!

(John 10: 10) …but is it "life more abundantly".

…"better than before" is for a reason …and "lukewarm" is an opportunity.

…I get up at 4:00 am every morning to deliver 120 newspapers by 6:30 am. for about 15 cents each. ….on occasion, we're given maybe a dozen sample papers to deliver …but are only paid 6 cents each for the samples …but it's an opportunity to "grow" the route at $15 for each new "subscription." …I, personally would prefer a few less rather than a few more, so I sometimes decline the opportunity to "grow" the route.

…I'm "lukewarm" about "opportunity" if it means getting up at 3:30 or 3:45 am.

…the "cost" vs. "gain" is too much. …the meager pay I get, pales, …when compared to my using this time, primarily to hum or whistle a few hymns and my hope that God will share something of Him with me.

…it's a time of the day that I am undistracted and "open" to Him.

…"ironic" that I deliver the "word of the world" …during which I receive (usually) something "of God" ….go figure.

…my son, Richard, whom I used to do the route with, has moved on to a "real" job. …and I miss his writing down some of these early morning thoughts en-route .

…most people have many many years of opportunity to grow beyond lukewarm faith …some people get very little time …but through trusting God, we don't have to understand or explain why apparent unfairness exists. …He's the potter …we're the clay.   (Rom. 9: 21) "Hath not the potter power over the clay?"

…maybe we just get to be "influences" …we "influence" our children's values and encourage them in one direction or another …even zero influence is an influence also. ….neglect can be a very harmful influence.

…the Bible says we "each" have "opportunity" to be useful material to God's will and purposes and that we're either demonstrably with Him (a part of His force) or otherwise we're with His foe (enemy, adversary) …Christ left no wiggle room by saying … (Matt. 12: 30) we're either with Him or against Him. …the Bible is loaded with exhortations and warnings against our devising "forms of Godliness" (2 Tim. 3: 5) which may look fine, but are void of His Spirit …ergo, His power.

…doesn't "His power" come through "His" Spiritual gifts?

…I wonder how often I'm taking tenuous comfort in attending church or a Bible study …as though paying alms …then immediately distance myself from whatsoever is of faith! (Rom. 14: 23)

…surely "immensely gifted" people as Pavarotti or Bocceli or van Gogh or Lansdowne or Buddy Holly or the Beatles or Randy Johnston or Tiger Woods or Howard Trump or Bill Gates …these gifts are "of God" ….right?   …so should we not attempt to follow in their footsteps? …"wait a minute …what if these "gifts" are "of someone" other than God??? …how are we simple peons to know???

…my own nature says "it doesn't really matter …because those guys are "doing" way better than me!   …did JFK really sleep with Marilyn Monroe???

(1 Tim. 6: 8) ...the Bible says "And having food and raiment let us be therewith content. (...yes but ...what about all this interesting juicy stuff!?!?) ...food and raiment isn't exactly "fun" ...right??

...unless we're all maybe suppose to be chefs and clothes designers. ...while we need food and clothing, it's our nature to quickly expand that list to include "fun".

...if we love our children then we like to see them laughing and harmlessly enjoying life. (in my son Richard's 19 years, I hardly ever pointed my finger and said "with food and raiment, be content."

...if only the Bible would say "don't do anything you don't like to do." ...or even just emphasize "the importance of having fun"!!

...I've recently picked up a good sized analytical Bible concordance (Young's)

...it's a treat to have but I can't find the word "fun" or "funny" in it anywhere.

...I appreciate that times were much tougher a couple thousand years ago

...but "fun" must have happened at some points, somewhere in the Bible times

....right? ...there must be a Greek or Hebrew word that comes close to "fun"

...I wonder what it is? ...and where to find it? ...I don't think "fun" is the same as "joy". I think "mirth" might be "fun" ?

...if I checked, I think I'd find that the wise men brought gifts of gold, frankincense and mirth.

...anyway ..."content with food and raiment"

...it speaks to me of being thankful and considering those who are frequently (no fault of their own) without even the basic needs. ...and how much blessing (Spiritual filling) am I missing through my having food and raiment, yet then looking for fun or entertainment ...nearly all of which requires "money".

...it's not enough to say "who can go without fun and entertainment!?!" ...why compare ourselves to either "monks" at the one end ...or "jet setters" at the other?

...is there fun and entertainment in Heaven (which is to be our focus)?

...Christ's Spirit will "lead" our thoughts to things "above" where neither moth nor rust will corrupt ...." (also James 5: 3)

...probably to live more simply here on Earth would far better position ourselves to receive and appreciate first God's blessings, then any particular "Spiritual gift" for us to earnestly apply to His Kingdom and His will on Earth being done (Lord's prayer)

...I believe, that through His Spirit, Christ can enable us to live everyday completely and to love others merely for the joy of loving ...but it's dependant on our being attentive to His leading and turning from every distractive temptation of satan.

...if we allow satan to become a vague concept of "bad" then we deceive ourselves of the power over us that the Bible says satan is trying to hold.

...every prayer (private or corporate (public)) should probably mention satan so that we're constantly aware of his sly appealing to our sinful and weak natures.

...if not for ourselves, then at least for our children and loved ones.

(Psa. 23) ...though we walk through the dark canyons, we need not "fear" satan's evil ...if our hearts and focus are on Christ. (Isa. 26: 3) ...the Bible says "Thou will keep him in perfect peace, whose mind is stayed on Thee."

...can I honestly say "How can I better serve Thee Lord?" ...and then immediately turn on the television? ...can I be a "let the chips fall where they may, Christian"? ...yet continue wondering what my Spiritual gift might be? ...seems a bit sketchy. ...no one can live without fun and entertainment ...or even "sin" ...if it's only in our own power.

..."rhema" (God's revealing to a receptive heart) doesn't happen unless we position ourselves for it. ...yet it's necessary for Spiritual growth ...and Spiritual growth is necessary for Spiritual gifts. ...I think I'd like to never again profess to another that "I'm Christian" ...and visa-versa.

..."Christ's nature of righteousness" is so different from "my own nature of sinfulness" that no one could mistake one for the other. ...my lofty claims are of no account.

(Luke 12: 34) ...where my treasure is, there my heart is also ...and what tumbles from my lips can easily mislead. ...and for me to "claim" salvation in advance of "judgment" is equally of no account …and is potentially even of "harm" to another's Spiritual walk.

…if I'm infallibly saved once and for all …then others need only look to the likes of me and if similarly disposed …well then, they're likewise saved …..right?

…could I possibly finagle Christ into my image??? …even sufficiently to suggest to my son Richard, that if he were to just emulate me …then he too is saved???

…perish the thought of it!!!

(1 Cor. 14: 33) …"God is not the author of confusion …"

…and if we have banished our sinful nature …to be wholly reliant on Christ

…then …and only then are we also not the source of confusion.

…I don't, deep down, believe that any here on Earth have quite yet arrived at such holiness so as to pronounce ourselves "saved"

…and no one of us is Christ's equal or example. …He and only He is the benchmark …even though many (appear to me) to have fought the good fight or run the good race, on behalf of Christ …my opinion on their being wholly, partially or not at all, of God's flock means nothing. …I mostly just care that they be hungry for more of "Him".

…I even enjoy that they not prefer the same distractions that I prefer

…for what is my Spiritual gain from that???

…I'm never at my "best" when "I'm" in control …only when God is in control.

….when He's in control "He leadeth me" towards things "of Him" (faith)

…if there's still a big chunk of "me" that wants to be in control, then my nature looks to whatsoever things that are "not of faith"

…and because of my freedom to choose, so also can I be my own worst enemy …warring against the righteousness of the Holy Spirit. …and I succumb to doing what I don't want (know I'm not suppose) to do.

(Rom. 7: 15) "…for what I would, that I do not; but what I hate, that I do.

…whatsoever is acceptable (lawful) to sin, is never acceptable to God …right?

…and no amount of conniving or mitigating can make it "somewhat so".

...do we find comfort in our Christian friends who are likewise inclined towards the same areas of Spiritual weakness? ...ought we find comfort there??

...the Bible says for us to abhor sin ...and we may well do so ...except it be found close to home (subjective) as in family or friends ...wherein we might put off "exhortation ...preferring "peace". ...but won't it be a tight-knit peace, like the wraps on a noose which forebode a grim eventuality???

...I think that "whatsoever not of faith" is far easier to grow than is "whatsoever is of faith" ...and that frequently gives me reason to pause.

...I was considering "mentors" while delivering papers earlier this morning ...and concluded that a mentor ought not be one who is "just like us" ...nor necessarily one with whom we're even comfortable! ....but rather one who has somehow advanced further towards the goal which we seek.   ...musicians and movie stars often cite early idols, who pointed the way for them, on their journey.

..."mentors" aren't perfect ...they're just further along the path ...and are people from whom we can take council in some areas ...and through whom we find encouragement.   ...I might add ....being over 55 years on this ball ...no one has ever "asked" or even suggested that I be a mentor. ...which is just as well, on account of my being so humble ...I'd have to decline anyway.

(....although I did have concerns a year or so ago about my nephew Kyle ...but he got married, which put a quick end to his calls from back east)

...it's not enough to be encouraged or supported by a church nor anyone closely associated with a church, unless they adhere to the stringent doctrines n the Bible. ...never mind if that church or person not "appear" overly cordial or joyous or accommodating or fun. ...I think anyone who hungers and thirsts after "those things which are of God" will come to "know" inner joy and inner peace.

...the "world" can supply dozens of venues for "fun" yet nothing of "inner joy" ...it can supply peace in the good times but nothing to sustain us in the darkness which is "even now already in the world." (1 John 4: 3)

…it's no small challenge to be in the world, yet not of the world …it's hard for a person and harder yet for a group of people (a church).

…for me to accept that my nature is sinful (just as it's the benign house cat's nature to pounce) and that I always will be sinful …is disconcerting, challenging and time consuming to assess and counter. …none of which is exactly "fun" …but neither is it without pleasantness. …getting up in the morning when my body would rather sleep, isn't fun either but the rewards far outweigh the alternative.

…bedsores or to become weakly or sickly doesn't happen overnight and we're lucky to know the causes of our own demise so that we can effactually make efforts to avoid ills.

…the Bible says our sinful nature is a given …it's not "optional".

…only through Christ can we avoid the growing emptiness and boredom this world offers …which leads to sickness, then even much, much worse. …though the world offers "candy" …it leads to cavities and decay.

…how much "candy" do we allow our children or those we care about ….without warning and exhortation.

…the message at church yesterday was on Phil. 4 and those things we allow our minds to take in. …better to deny ourselves rather than risk our not being able to "get rid of" the dirt our minds (sponges) absorb.

…I'm not Mennonite or Amish …but I am still leery of technology.

…I don't have a computer, despite much encouragement (well meaning) to get one.

…but I do, for the first time and thankfully, have an air conditioner.

(Eph. 6: 11-13) …like the armor of God …I'm learning to put it on "in advance" of the heat …lest I perish unprepared.…if I leave off putting it on until the heat is already upon me, then I'm far less protected, if at all. …negligence can be very costly.

…if I'm weak in faith and not vigilant …I may doze off in sleep at the worst possible time …and never awaken! …or perhaps even jeopardize others who my be weak!

…then "woe is me" big time! …sounds as though I live in constant fear …yet "fear" has never been further from me. …as I sit here now, my greatest fear is for my old friend (and my dad's good friend) Milford …who is undergoing radiation treatment for cancer and that he might forget that he never walks alone…no matter how dark the alley.

(Psa. 1: 2) …the Bible says "Blessed is he who meditates on God's word day and night."   ….what with the many demands on our time, we can overlook the comforts that are confirmed in God's word, which, like an established bank account, are there for us to draw on, provided we've invested there. …over the years, I've had ample time to invest there …but invested elsewhere instead …thus establishing a plethora of resistance, which even now (years later) interferes with my grasp of God's truth …negating old habits and influences, then establishing new ones, will probably be my path here on

…maybe forever!?! (I have decided …….no turning back.)

…Sunday's message from church, was a good reminder that where we focus our time and effort, is where we choose to build our lives and is then what defines the strengths and the weaknesses we contribute to

(Matt. 7: 26) ….the Bible speaks to our building on rock or else on sand; whereby we either stand or fall (live or die) by the culmination of our choices.

 …we may choose Christ, yet err in further choices

….but we cannot choose Christ, yet have no desire to grow in His Spirit …nor can we continue to walk in ways other than what He has prescribed (sin). …we can of course, choose to modify God's instruction or attempt to dodge portions of it and congratulate ourselves quietly at our cleverness.   (don't read Psalm 139)

…but in so doing, we sever ourselves from realistic hope through His Spirit.

…millstone or not …lukewarm faith will land us in the "depths" with no escape.

…there's a literary character (probably not historical) named Don Quixote, who seems pretty much insane …though his cause be noble.

(Gal. 5: 22-23) was cited in church Sunday and I was reminded that the fruits of the Spirit are not the fruits of the world or of our own natures.

(Gal. 5: 25) says "If we live in the Spirit, let us also walk in the Spirit."

...if Christ's Spirit lives in us, then what am I doing walking where His Spirit would never walk? ...do I fear being labeled "demented" by the world? ...by my family? ...my friends? ...my co-workers? ...maybe I'm "special" above everyone else in God's eyes ...do ya think?(Acts 10: 34) ...drat! ...I just remembered a "rhema" verse "Of a truth I perceive that God in no respecter of persons: But in every nation he that feareth Him and worketh righteousness is accepted with Him." ...so much for my having special status!

...Don Quixote had a "friend" (servant) Sancho, who cared for his well being ...and did so at considerable personal sacrifice.

...do I care for another's well being in a likewise manner??? ...or do I shy away from the "devoted" ...to encourage those more aligned with my own "less devoted" walk?

...do I revel eagerly and boldly, through His power in me? (Eph. 3: 20)

...what, exactly, am I doing ...that others without faith aren't also doing??? ...charitable works? ...kindly attitude? ...patient demeanor? ...joyous laughter? ...loving feeling? ...quiet times? ...believing in good or justice?

...I've met many people who openly profess no faith, yet uphold fine values ...just as I've met professed Christians who are self-centered and display little evidence of the fruit of Christ. (Gal. 4: 25) "If we live in the Spirit, let us also walk in the Spirit."

...is Christ's Holy Spirit impotent? ....could we be led by His Spirit and yet others be unaware that we march to the beat of a "different" drummer???

...it's okay to be labeled "hypocritical" if our conduct appears to vary from what we profess. ..."critical" isn't one of the "fruits of the Spirit" cited in Galatians ...and neither is "discernment" ...I don't think there's any profit in criticizing a "person" but if discernment reveals a straying from truth or doctrine, can we not (hands behind our back) kindly question another's basis of belief?

…when we buy something, do we not question the change returned, if the math doesn't work? …the secular world (and perhaps the lukewarm Christian) probably neither has nor wants much grasp of the Bible …if that's "us", then we're probably of two minds (double minded) on many issues …even issues of grave importance. (James 1: 8) "…..unstable in all his ways" …if so, then why don't we just say so!?! …why pretend we're something we're not? …or that we adhere to a belief which we don't adhere to? …are we just lonely and want to liked or admired? …"what's that all about??? …how can we feel good about nothing??? …all "good" of man's own creating will evaporate like the morning's dew …whereas whatsoever is "of God" …is of His love …and the Bible says, will endure forever. …man can't "create so much as a single piece of dirt and claim "it's of God" because man "says" it's so.

…adroitly, the "joy of sex" is of God …but only as prescribed by Him …all else is the fleeting result of our sinful nature and desires …having little concern for the pleasing of others over our own ill bent satisfaction. …there's good reason why Mick Jagger and The Rolling Stones could "get no satisfaction" in the 60s or 70s though he tried and tried and tried and tried.

…the Bible says (not a quote) that whatsoever "not of faith, is a no win situation

…it doesn't say "not of faith is no fun" just …"no long term win."

…through Christ …what is prescribed in the Bible may cost us a penny or a dime

…but through parting with (giving away) what He gives us …our account is replenished two and threefold. …the apostle Paul was a "bad penny" who was transformed into a "goldmine" though his "secular world" saw him only as a "loonie". (I wonder what he did for fun???)

…on papers this morning I was reflecting on my recently being told that the divorce rate for Christians has now exceeded the rate for secular marriages. …maybe even Christians "have not" good marriages "because they ask amiss" (James 4: 3)

…while churchy "weddings are popular or nostalgic, not many, I fear, are of couples with a "tried and true" focus to comply with the fine letter of scripture.

...that, in addition to churches which have grown tolerant, accepting or lenient towards inviting worldliness into their midst ...how can we not expect a relaxation in efforts to work out differences via the Bible's teachings. ...maybe marriages have become "negative latching onto" rather than "positive mutual support of God's intent." ....pretty hard to attain a "good" marriage (or life) built on a "negative" need or want.

...I guess every church has their own definition as to what "holding fast" means. ...and I expect that "Christian divorce increase was inevitable in churches, unless the churches divorce themselves from worldliness.

...Christianity is not a democracy ...it's a Monarchy ...and must remain so ...else it's just another "social club" only with religious overtones. ...subjects of this Monarchy are free to leave ...but not free to change it's doctrine, without paying the severest of price. ...I don't think I'm "devout" in faith ...so am somewhat "lukewarm"

...and even so, I was raised under strict doctrine and in a strict church ...so today ...what hope is there for my son ...or your son, should doctrine and church accommodate a base of lukewarm ness???

(Rev. 3: 16) ...Christ spoke to the early churches ...encouraging their "holding fast" ...and exhorting against their "lukewarm ness."

...to profess faith, yet neglect adherence to strict doctrine is no different (in my view) than leading our next generation astray.

(Matt. 18: 6) ...whereby, "gills and razor sharp teeth" might give us brief respite.

...we're a people determined to have our own way ...and get away with it.

...but what about the children??? ...are we "getting away with something" at a "deferred" cost to the next generation?...the church ...nor the fellowship is not to be seeking or allowing a means to weaken faith. ...we don't need "user friendly" Bibles and churches ...we need "Bible minded and God mindful" churches.

(John 8: 47) ...the Bible says "He that is of God heareth God's words: ye therefore hear them not, because ye are not of God."

…a church cannot reasonably lead a body of believers over treacherous ground if it is weighted down and unstable with double mindedness.

…can a church be forthright in presenting the word of God, yet be sensitive to the emotional complications of those not yet strong in their faith?

…maybe there could be "beginner" churches …or "progressive" churches???

…good Bible study here at the apartment building last night.

…the pastor shared some valuable insight on the trinity of the Godhead and how the Father, Son and Spirit are inseparable and vital to us now, just as in the beginning of creation (John 1: 1)

(Rom. 1: 19) …he shared how that as we are created in His image, so we have (are born with) a portion (measure) of His Spirit in us.

…what becomes of that "portion" (despite satan's draw and our own sinful nature) is starved or nourished first by our parents …then by ourselves and consequently grows or diminishes accordingly.

…he said we can even memorize the Bible cover to cover …be believers of what the Bible says …yet unless we surrender our own will (nature) to Christ and be "reborn" in submissiveness to Christ's will …then, though believers, we are not Christians.

…not without the "experience" of flushing our inner toilets (my words, not his) and endeavoring daily to increasingly purify the clean water that is newly available to us.

…the pastor's own stated experience of "incremental growth" according to his gradual surrender and his increased filling of the Spirit …was very encouraging. …I know I could never deny my own nature (sinful) in my own strength. …nobody can!

(2 Cor. 11: 14) …"And no marvel; for satan himself is transformed into an angel of light." …if satan can appear as light (truth) in our spouse or parents or church or loved ones ….then what hope have we, without Christ's combative and discerning Spirit (nature) in us to reveal (through His Spirit) what is confirmed in "the word" (Bible).

(Eph. 6: 11-13) ….."do I take seriously, every morning, before facing the world, my need to don the armor or God? ….or is it only when I'm desperate???

…"maybe" I'm stalwart and upstanding in faith …but don't I need to don the armor of God regardless? …what if I need to protect my son or spouse or friend or co-worker? …did you ever misplace your wallet …or keys? …then need them in a hurry???

…quiet desperation is a poor excuse for neglect …right? …it's through our personal experiences we learn to be more careful about important things …like wallets or keys.

…in our walk of faith, we learn the quiet desperation of being without God's armor …and that we need it all times, lest abject darkness present itself when we least expect it. …it's not a case of "will it?" …but rather a continual case of "when will it? …and "how frequently?". …not …are we safe" in Him but rather is He (His church) "safe" in us???

(Matt. 16: 18) …the Bible tells us that "He" will build His church" …through using those who are of Him (God)

…but there's also a force (which is also powerful) that is (without ceasing) trying to weaken and dismantle God's church …both from without and from within.

…if the Bible is the foundation and benchmark of growth, then we're good to be discerning of anyone bringing little tiny hammers and chisels into His church

…even though they wear a pleasant smile or give warm handshakes.

(Matt. 7: 15) "Beware of false prophets, which come to you (before you?) in sheep's clothing ………."

(Matt. 7: 22) …so look only to those who "doeth the will of the Father which is in Heaven."

…a "believer" may not necessarily hunger to know the will of God …but it seems the "Christian (desiring to grow in Spirit) will more and more have revealed to him or her, through surrender and prayer …what it is the Lord desires of them.

…I imagine it's somewhat complicated, should a "believer" wish to pass as Christian …if there is little or no Spirit within to support it.

…the Bible says there's joy and peace and life abundant through the Spirit …but "hoping" I have Christ's Spirit in me isn't much "life" if I don't "experience" Him.

…a friend at Bible study became upset at realizing they might be a believer only, though they prayed to receive the Spirit.   …I can relate to that because I've "been there – done that" …I've done the "church – Bible study – pray" route …maybe everyone does!?!

…I wanted to "keep" the old things and just "add" faith to my life. …the Bible says old things are to die (passed away) that now, all things become new (reborn). …my mouth prayed things that weren't reflected in my daily life. …in church I prayed "whatever it takes, Lord" …but my nature (sinful) reneged my prayer shortly afterwards when I left church. …"did I have to live in a church? …and hangout with just religious people!?!"

…satan doesn't mind my believing the Bible might be true (…and he doesn't mind me believing in the tooth fairy) …but he'll raise havoc if I turn away from his temptations in surrender to his adversary, God. …and I think he pretty much leaves the secular world alone …there's no threat to him there.   …it's the people in churches that he wants to deceive and weaken. …just as God seeks people through whom He can build His church …so too does satan seek those through whom he can weaken God's church. …don't we all have weak moments??? …what if it's a family spat on a Saturday evening that carries over , unresolved, to Sunday and then goes to church with us???

….satan likes that stuff!

…maybe issues preoccupy us so that we're not open to what God has to say to us, through His messenger?? …are many in our churches "without oil in our lamps" with which to see or to hear what the Lord has for us? …how many times did Christ say "Your faith has made you whole"??? …medicines …and perhaps even mediums can do some things …but they can't make us "whole" (complete).

…I don't think we have to "say" a single word, in order to "receive" from God.

…do the dumb (speech impaired) use "signing" to pray? …or the deaf, "brail"?

…we look for things to make sense in our own eyes …but we "see through a glass darkly" (1 Cor. 13: 12) …God hears our "hearts" …and sees the treasures of our hearts ….regardless of what comes out of our mouths. …Christ didn't "teach" the blind to see or the deaf to hear or the lame to walk …He "made" them to …according to their faith. …we're all broken and are all in need of being made "whole". …I don't "know" that Donald Trump or Bill Gates or President Bush or "whoever" isn't a humble servant of God. …I only know that they, also, "are not whole" except they be transformed …it's their choice.

…there are people in this apartment building, with huge challenges, who I believe are closer to "wholeness" …than are the healthy and affluent and proud.

…"believing" is the first of several progressive steps to salvation …but if "believing" is only where you're at, then I would suggest one not worry about further progress, until our heart is sufficiently humbled to accept God's further sharing with us.

…if Christ's Spirit is not in me …then there's a valid reason why not …and it's me who has to change. …it's always better to trust God than to trust ourselves.…when I completed grade six or grade seven …I envied those who completed grade eight, as they to go to a different (grownup) school. …I wasn't a lesser person than them …I just hadn't put in the time yet to qualify for the (grownup) greater learning.

…as in faith, we are given more of God's truth by Him, only as we apply what He has already given us. …if a bank squanders what we put in their care …then we won't put much more in their care …..right? (parable of the talents)

…the simplest of minds can "believe" that Christ is the risen savior, based on the Bible saying so …but if that same mind chooses not to believe that satan (anti-Christ) is "even now already in the world" (John 4: 3) …then of what merit is their "selective" belief?

…the Bible says our nature (inclination) is sinful (easily swayed by satan)

…"subjective (personal preference) belief" will lead us to darkness

…whereas "every word of God" belief will enlighten us.

…Christ's "light" has the power to push satan's "darkness" out of our lives

…but that has to be our hearts (not lips) desire …and only when that's our desire, will Christ's Spirit grown in us to "comfort" us, in the battle and "strengthen" us in the struggle. …what good is it to "wish" things were better, yet do little or nothing to avail ourselves of the "better" that's offered. …do we just want a "free" better?

…those things that we ask (wish) others to do …would we ask Christ to do them also? …if not …why not? …has our "21st" century conscience" exceeded the scope of the Bible? …do we revert to milk …no long able to digest strong meat prepared for us?

(Heb. 5: 12) …better to fight and fail …rather than flounder about in weakness and double mindedness, willfully choosing the mild over the strong meat.

…I still do a fair amount of that floundering in weakness" stuff …years of habit is not easy to separate from. …a good self discipline is in the exhorting others to do what we ourselves are suppose to be doing. …better to "invite" another's judgment than fear it ….right? …questions or doubts, ever from our brothers and sister in faith, aren't a patch on the judgment to come …what if today or tomorrow is the conclusion of our "working out our own salvation"? (Phil. 2: 12)

…the secular world largely avoids church (other than weddings or funerals) probably because of "having more important things to do" or "of not wanting to feel bad about themselves." …whereas the Christian (practicing student of a stated doctrine) has much to answer for …no matter the source of the questions. …I don't know about other faiths …but the Bible says there is but one God and one mediator between God and man … that mediator being Christ Jesus. …I guess a "believer" could potentially believe every faith in every book …thus avoiding controversy entirely. …I had a friend like that but I would never describe him as being stable …and when he got cancer, I don't think he knew where to turn or who to pray to. …when I first met him, he said he was Christian and I believed him. (…he knew the Bible fairly well, sponsored a foster child, said he prayed for good things, etc. etc.) …but as I got to know him better and saw him converse with others …I found he was not only

Christian …but also Muslim and Buddhist …he was even a Catholic Protestant! (he's the only one of those I ever knew).

…I guess if we have no "tried and true" master, then we're just free agents …(jack of all faiths …"mastered by" none.) …so then we can ascribe to all beliefs …but must denounce any that say we can't have the others …else alter those that require singular loyalty …such as the Bible based faith.

…a favorite Bible verse says "For God so loved the world that He gave His only begotten son, that whosoever believeth in Him should not perish but have everlasting life." (John 3: 16) …I would read what precedes and what follows that one verse …before I got too excited about my "salvation". (Acts 19: 1-6) …even certain disciples at Ephesus, though believers, were yet without the Holy Spirit. …it's good to share with others or proclaim God's word …but without His Spirit in us and charging our batteries …it's sharing His good news …but we're bereft of "His power" through His Spirit. …as His Spirit grows in us, so too can we discern what in our daily lives is of "His" nature vs. what remains of our "own" nature.

…our sinful nature compels us to vagueness …whereas His Spirit compels us to seek and find clarity. …the simplicity of Mennonite or Amish ways have long puzzled me as appearing weird or empty of fun and excitement but I'm warming to their concept of remaining at least somewhat separated from the rat-race world around them. …all the more so, as I see the more popular denominations adopting worldly ways into their own doctrines. …there's a big difference between "what pleases God" vs. "what probably doesn't bug God too much." …we're not to support and sustain "a" church but rather "His" church. …the early churches (Revelations) were reprimanded for their "letting things slide" to lukewarm ness or false teachings. …they too, probably perceived themselves as being kindly tolerant or patient or well meaning …which of course is the easier road for ourselves and for our churches. …it's disturbing to see us purée' God's word to make it easier to digest. …church last night was based on the fruit of the Spirit called "goodness". …much can appear "good"…even satan can appear good…but does "our perceived good" bear resemblance to the character of

Christ? …and is it entirely born out (confirmed) in God's word? …our being raised amongst worldly trappings is probably a poor initiation into a discerning and faithful walk with God.

…on papers this morning I was thinking about the effects of habits on our "character" …our habits don't have to be "bad habits" to be "ungodly habits." …they just have to be things we do "other than" those things which the Bible says pleases God. ..there are many things, by my nature, that I want to do …and ask "how can there be anything wrong with my doing this!?!" …and if I discount the Bible, then there's nothing at all "wrong" with my going ahead and doing it! …yet they are things that I would never ask Christ to oversee me doing.

…I really wish Christ would "physically" be with me to deliver papers in the morning …then I could just "ask" …rather than "wonder' about things. …but for now, the best I can hope for, is that the Bible and His Spiritual presence will give me "His truth" over time. (…hopefully, after I die ….things will be more to my liking.) (and when I think of the "alternative" …I wish I hadn't had that thought.)

…when Richard and I first took on this paper route thing, it was slow going …
(about 120 papers) …with each of us regularly asking the other "did you remember this one or that one?" …it was far from relaxing …especially in the morning darkness (5:00 am) …but as it slowly became "habit" …it also became "second nature" …
(less doubt, more surety.) …"in the world" …we can become comfortable in a "rut" …but "in faith" there is no comfort, except in the discomfort of "further seeking" …and I think God sees that in the blink of His eye. …if we're seeking, God reveals …but if we're distracted (as by "our" nature we often are) then we cut ourselves off from what He wishes to share with us.   ……it's up to us.

…God knows a lot of worldly stuff seems fine to our own selves (our own nature) …but He sees past what we see …and whatever we taste of the world, He see it's conclusion. …if it's conclusion pleased Him, then He would have told us to pursue "the seeds of it" in the Bible. …that He didn't is not an oversight on His part

…it's an "unawares" on our part, despite His relatively austere directions, we continue to override what the Bible says is pleasing to God and venture into what man has created to please himself. …maybe not full blown violence, pornography or obscenity …but perhaps the seeds of it.

…while the "believer" of the Bible may have limited qualms about the "seeds" of unpleasant stuff …the Christian, housing Christ's "Spirit, must be repulsed, as even the seed of that stuff is of darkness …and would any measure of Christ's Spirit have to do with darkness? …"our" nature is to be double minded …Christ's nature will have none of that "monkey business". …even the believer, must have a good grasp of the Bible …unless they are semi-believers. …what sincere and seeking Christian, propelled by Christ's Spirit, would choose to seek potential seeds of darkness …whether in books or television viewing …movies …friendships …whatever? …when to do so, closes the door to anything of God except remorseful conviction?

…do we "like" to feel bad about what we do??? …maybe that's a real possibility??? …maybe some have become so complicated that the only good they experience is the absence of bad??? …(not the kind from sickness or physical pain …but rather from choice.) …to greater or lesser extent …that's the "rut" it appears many (even in church) have allowed themselves to descend to.

…from our youth, we're allowed, or even encouraged to explore and expand our natural inclinations …most of which lead us far from establishing "habits of faith believing". …we have opportunity to develop and grow spiritually but instead we adopt habits of peer compatibility and peer relationships rather than a relationship of trusting Christ.

…rather than build our house on Christ, the solid rock …we've found an ample supply of crushed stone, which, for our lack of vigilance, we've tried to glue together "a rock".

…that's tenuous at best but nevertheless, probably better than "sand"

…but it won't free us from worry and fret and fear of what might change.

…I've personally lost a lot of years and a lot of ground to the world around me.

…I didn't invite fear and instability into my life …any more than I invite dust to settle on my desk …but it's pervasive and I know it's ever present …and I know that to ignore it, invites sickness. …sin is like dust …in that I can ignore it but God can see it …and others, who care for my well being can see the dust on my desk and perhaps my sin also. …if someone warns me they're coming to visit …I can clean this little place in relatively short order.

…a true Christian friend will exhort (warn) me at some point, that surface "cleaning" probably isn't sufficient and that "stripping" this desk and then "refinishing" is required on account of my past negligence.

…I'm a busy guy and I don't want to hear that …it may even negatively impact our friendship …but to be a true Christian friend, they don't have a choice.

…my occasional sensitivities must take second place to their being blunt in their sharing what the Bible says. …it's the Bible and not them that is blunt.

…no Christian has to "sell" people on God's word …they just "have to" proclaim God's word …after which it's between the hearer and God. …just like a good book or movie or restaurant or golf course, etc. …we proclaim (share) what we find of high value to us.

(…unless we've encountered nothing of high value.)

…a young bald headed lady had a hit song (in the 90s, I think) …"Nothing Compares to You" …it wasn't about God …and even if we stumble in our conceiving God as Spirit …we can nevertheless comprehend that nothing compares to "unconditional or ideal love" …and "love" is in truth, unconditional and without knowing more about God, we'll never know more about the source or demonstration of true, uncomplicated love.

…I think many people have quietly been offered love and friendship

…yet (for whatever reasons) have spit on it. …kid's do it everyday

…I bet I did it to some extent

…and that's a problem with being raised in the "bright lights" and the fast lanes.

…too many peers, bringing cosmopolitan backgrounds.

…what youth can bridle their taste to meat and potatoes, while their peers are offering chocolate and cheesecake? …how can the "family" not become dysfunctional?

…even parents put the "goodies" on the table, yet say "don't touch it while we're away."

…maybe that's why I used to put my son Richard on the golf course, shine …or rain. (on the other hand …I recall him yelling …not too many years ago, that if I was a Christian …then he didn't want to be one!) (…in my own youth, I never said that to my dad…out loud.) …my dad was "hard line big time", while my mom was the "soft touch"

…and as I read the Bible …Christ was both. …but He was never compromising!

…growth in Spirit requires we be "locked" onto a course unwaveringly, though our speed may vary from time to time.

…my friend Greg is, in my opinion, a bright guy …both financially and also in assessing human character. (managing 20 – 30 subordinate union workers, year after year, must be an education in itself!) …I perceive him as quietly astute …he listens to what others say and observes their conduct as regards what they profess …."talk the talk – or – walk the walk".

…dreams and hopes can be good things …my personal hope of eternal salvation is valid …provided my "walk" aligns with my "talk".

…for years I chose "worldly treasures" yet claimed a "lofty hope" which the Bible says is not available to those who "choose" worldly treasure.

(Micah 6: 8) …do justly, lover mercy, walk humbly with God

…sounds straightforward …but is "sketchy" in practice …yet it's a good point to access our "honesty" from. …without honest assessment, we're left to our own subjective deceit, which is only natural (our nature)… what's natural (the Bible says) is not to be trusted in seeking faith in Christ.

(1 Tim. 4: 16) ….the Bible says "take heed unto thyself and unto doctrine "

….worldly treasures can have us walking in a rut, yet our sinful natures will have us "claim" to be walking on "higher ground."

(James 1: 27) ….while the Bible says "pure religion and undefiled before God and the Father is this …"To visit the fatherless and widows in their affliction and to keep himself unspotted from the world."…"my nature" is to visit the "well disciplined" fatherless and the "more good looking" widows …which isn't exactly what the Bible intends as "pure" religion …but it's rather my preferred (natural) interpretation …whereby I can "honestly" see that I have much of my own nature yet to be displeased with.

(I'm nowhere even near ready to touch "unspotted" from the world!!)

(my not having red hair or freckles, is slim comfort of "unspotted ness")

…anyways, the Bible is pretty clear on how we aren't to be trusted, even by ourselves …except (as Christians) in "whatsoever is of faith."

…what we "believe" is the same as what determines our "walk" in this life. …as shared at Bible study …we are born with the seed of God in us and that seed desires to grow …but it can grow to fulfillment only by our preparing the conditions for growth.

…is it an oxymoron to want whatever we want, yet not be interested in fulfillment??

…there a reason why "our nature" doesn't like God's prescription for our fulfillment. …that being, that we have "another nature" in us which is nothing of God, but rather of His enemy. (….sorta like "cops and robbers" only far more serious.) …we are the jewels or treasure and God and satan vie to possess us.

…halfway through papers this morning I found myself singing a tune by Elton John called Circle of Life …(might be from a movies "Lion King")

…anyways, the line came up "the circle of life, is a wheel of fortune" …and it's got me thinking of all the risks we take, courtesy of the lives we choose to lead and are we at all vigilant (give much thought to) of the impact on others of our every roll of the dice. …as I recall "monopoly" is a game where I try to get all of the houses, hotels and money …and to heck with everybody else! …I don't think it's God who encourages us to adopt a complex lifestyle, yet confusion can sure wreak havoc with God's will that we be fulfilled through His Spirit (seed) in us. ...faith (our focus being on God) draws us near to God ...but other stuff??...probably, no.

...the Christian may use all sorts of venues to share their faith ...but can they do so without becoming "...spotted by the world"? ...and thus be presenting a form of "impure religion"? ...has "walking the walk" changed stride over time? .....maybe become more of a "skip and a hop"?

...it's possible for "lukewarm faith" to become sufficiently prevalent, that I wouldn't know it if I saw it ...maybe that time is here already!?!

...apart from my son (maybe a few times in the past and understandably so) I'm not aware of anyone "reviling me or persecuting me or speaking wrongly against me

...for my speaking out for Christ ...why not??? ...am I not speaking out? ...or is my speaking out "lukewarm" and of no account!??? (there's so much rubber and plastic in the world now ....I hope I haven't ingested so much of it that it's infected my faith.)

...although I may not exactly be in "sin" ...nevertheless, I'm a long way from "meditating on God's law day and night" as He repeatedly asks in His word

...nor am I applying His counsel to every daily interaction.

...we don't have to know the Bible implicitly to be accountable for our partaking of the world and thus choosing to belittle God's grace, mercy and sacrifice.

...to be aware of even the Lord's Prayer, yet no seek it's inherent truth, is sufficient to ascribe us to satan's camp. ...to "say" ..."...thy will be done on Earth...." ...yet do nothing or little about it, is in truth our honest effort expressed before God.

...our "own" natures crave "companionship with the world" or to be liked and respected and accepted ...none of which holds (the Bible says) the least credibility with God.

...it's that mindset which, in fact, casts our lot with sinners and with satan.

(John 9: 21) "Now we know that God heareth not sinners but if any man be a worshipper of God and doeth His will, him He heareth." (John 9: 39) ...Christ said "For judgment I am come into this world, that they which see not might see (His truth) and that they which see (choose not His truth) might be made blind." (cut off?)

...life is filled with indecision and resulting consequences ...university or work ...marry or not ...children or not ...if God and prayer are not the determining factor, then we are left our "treasures" (idols) to look to, should things go awry.

...how much darkness we abide or endure, is up to us ...the Bible says God gives sight and takes away sight, according to our hearts desires ...if they be for Him ...or against Him (undecided). ...if we wish to "quickly" pick up a few "spots" from the world, then, the Bible tells us it's displeasing to God ...maybe even "abomination"! ...that's a big roll of the dice!   ...am I immature? ...desperate? ...both!?! ...I've had about 40 years now of opportunity to distinguish between what's of the "world" vs. what's of God

...do I need another 40 years to narrow the gap!????   ("woe is me!")

...the pastor at church Sunday evening was reassuring that "we don't have to do anything to be accepted of Christ."...I didn't find that comforting...nor scriptural

...I think the Bible says we have to profess Him as Lord over our lives and live accordingly ...which is "huge"!

...that particular pastor is young ...seems easy going (accepting) ...and is quite popular. ...which, to an older codger like me, presents red flags on all fronts!   ...but that's my son's church of choice when he goes ..."and no marvel......."

(2 Cor. 11: 14) ...if satan is "transformed into an angel of light"

....then where do lukewarm churches stand? ...are pastors or priests, deemed to be free from deceit or self motivation or a sinful nature?

...couldn't a pastor, who is given free reign (without prior viewing of his message by church elders, re: adherence to doctrine) ....couldn't that priest or pastor gently lead a congregation "away" from God's truth? ...are there no lukewarm churches?

...if there are, how did they come to be lukewarm if not by a softening (moderation) of the word of God??? ...if the "head" speaks for the "body" then the body ought to know how best to prepare (shoe, gloves, raingear, etc.) their parts for the arduous journey ahead ....unless the head says "no worries, mate! ...be happy!"

(Matt. 7: 13) "wide is the gate that leadeth to destruction," ...

(this is beginning to sound a bit negative …I'd better, "watch-it" ….right.

…Good Bible study last night.   (John 1: 25) …about how God's light was all but lost, through Adam and Eve's defiance …yet through Christ alone, is now (again) made available through faith.   …and how powerful our sinful nature is at repelling God's light by our choices that distance ourselves from His truth.   …the Bible says "our own wisdom is as foolishness ….even harmful foolishness.

(…I think it may have been Einstein who agreed with that conclusion after Hiroshima and Nagasaki)

…the intellectual and proud have the greater barrier to overcome in order to do just, love mercy and walk humbly with God.   (Micah 6: 8)

…much good (debatable?) is done, in the here and now, in support of various causes …just maybe not God's cause. …some groups collect toys for children at the front door …yet sell drugs out the back door. …some pastors give sermons on morality while in the midst of adulterous relationships.

…it's "our" nature to justify that which we want, though the Bible speaks against it.

…I think it's a weakness of ours, that "image" over "substance" prevails …

("talk the talk" over "walk the walk")   …the comedy line "the devil made me do it" (Skip Wilson) has thrived since the beginning.

(Gen. 3: 13)   (:the serpent beguiled me and I did eat.") ……even the Apostle Paul, said, the devil made him do it.

(Rom. 7: 20) "…..it is no more I that do it, but sin that dwelleth in me."

…it's both "revealing" and (unfortunately) "convenient" …both "truth" and "cop-out". …maybe it lead us to think that if the Apostle Paul was just like us …then Christ was probably also just like us, hence we're just like Him! ….right?

…I sort-of wish Pastor Dave hadn't gone to Rom. 7 …if I was ever baffled by a dozen or so consecutive Bible verses, which I deem highly valued to my daily walk in faith, then Romans 7 takes the cake. …I find it mind boggling and continually pray for clarity and rest as to what Paul's talking about there.   (I could probably write several pages just on my swerving thoughts as to where the Apostle Paul is leading us! ….yet end right where I started.)

(Rom. 7: 15)   "For that which I do I allow not; for what I would, that do I not; but what I hate, that I do."   …sound very unnatural …was there something he did …that he wouldn't do?? …or maybe something he didn't do, which he must have done???

…though we believe the Bible (to varying degrees) we believe the world also.

…we believe we'll get paid …provided we do the job given us …likewise in faith, we have the "hope" of receiving according to our efforts.

…if we're continually looking for "meaning" (purpose, fun, excitement) away from God's light …then through our being distracted, so are we unavailable to God.

…even though He has for us "life" and life more abundant, unless we're in a state of preparedness, how then can we receive? …God never "force feeds" …and unless we are "hungry" our eyes and ears are not open. …in our homes, we may build our house (lives) on Christ the solid rock …but if we don't …then venture out each morning into a world built on sand, then we have no strength or base support (armor) from which to repel the world's instability and double mindedness. (lost souls in a lost world.)

…only as we stave off the devil, can we position ourselves (be prepared) to receive from Christ. (James 4: 7) …the Bible says "….Resist the devil, and he will flee from you (verse 8) Draw nigh unto God, and He will draw nigh to you."

…in the book of Job, there took place a conversation between God and satan but Job had no say …a similar conversation may be taking place right now concerning me or you …and we, also, have no say. …it's not our call "is it fair or not" …only "are we obedient and faithful or not." …God didn't make available to Job anything special that He doesn't make available to you or me.

…it was Job's "devotion to God" which made him "of use" to God in this world.

…as a "believer" can I look at God's word and point out where I am of any "credible use to God"? …in the sense that Job was? …not just showing up at church

…or helping the needy …but rather learning God's will, then doing it?

(Luke 11: 2-4) …why commit to memory "Our Father which art in Heaven …Thy will be done on Earth …" ….then fold my hands over my fat tummy and wait for it to somehow happen!?! …am I "really" in the game? ….or am I merely a spectator? ….what's my response?

(Luke 12: 34) …where my treasure is, there my heart (will) is also …am I dishonest? …can I enjoy (treasure) worldly stuff, then when tragedy or cancer strikes …suddenly pray "Hey God …remember me? …apart from all the worldly stuff I'm enjoying (maybe of satan and maybe not) I need a favor just now on account of this tumor or this wound …I know it may not "appear" that I'm of your flock, but I am, so help me out of this mess." …may as well pray to a cause which I honestly and actually "have been tending, …like the vegetable garden …or my television or radio, which "I have" actually been "listening" to and have "actually treasured"!

(Gal. 6: 7) …the Bible says "Be not deceived, God is not mocked" …but the Bible didn't know "me", when it was written …right?

…we've come a long way ….right? …we're way smarter than those "peasants" from years and years ago ….right?   …and we have concerns that they couldn't begin to fathom …right?   (I jest)

…our socially advanced and complex mode of life is perhaps our greatest barrier to a closer walk with God. …we're born into it and thereby see ourselves as faultless when worldliness eats up our souls and our children's souls.

…we become sensitive and defensive and exclaim "what could I do?" or "what could we have done?" when we in fact simply allowed Godlessness to prevail.

…we "could" have been more vigilant …we "could" have spoken out more when wrong or apathy presented itself.

…maybe we were busy or working or not feeling our best …maybe we're shy …or just quiet …maybe we like peacefulness and prefer to no make waves or think we can present Godliness as fun and laughter.

…we "may be born a raised in a world of immense social freedoms but we're probably poor stewards of those freedoms. …some countries treasure "discipline" to core values above social "freedoms" and we see it as unfortunate that they don't laugh as much as we do. …"unfortunate" …is when fun and laughs become the criteria for anything! …especially if it supplants our seeking life more abundant through faith in Christ.

…if fun and laughing is "of faith" then it might be pleasing to God …but if "not of faith" …then what of???

…I heard a Bible study leader say that Christ laughed at weddings etc. …but as the Bible doesn't cite that He did, so then I guess we might just imagine that He did because there was probably joy in those weddings …right? (not that laughter and fun need always accompany joy …right?) …I guess there' just no fun or laughter we're to enjoy except that which we would enjoy were Christ actually present with us physically, right?

…interesting message at church tonight on the fruit of the Spirit "faithfulness".

(good message despite this speaker also!, stating "patience" as "long suffering".)

(maybe "long suffering" has too many syllables …or maybe sounds negative

…or maybe we're unfaithful to original doctrine?)

…that speaker last night (sorry – don't recall his name) …spoke on how many lesser things distract us from faithfulness to guarding our treasure …and of our justification for it …and our deceit in allowing distraction.

…only of our hope in the Lord, will we hunger to nourish His seed in us to take root and produce fruit "of Him".   (Jer. 17: 8) …else we are double minded and fickle.

…right or wrong …I know I'm not overly ambitious …and for argument's sake I claim this characteristic to be …not lazy …but rather "efficient!"   …and so, being relatively content (hassle free) in my "efficiency" I'm better able to share with others the errors of their ways.   (Rom. 12: 8) …voila! …the Spiritual gift of exhortation!

…I guess I'm blessed to be given a Spiritual gift so close to "my own worldly character", hence I've had to "surrender" much less of my "old self" to be counted among those "of God's flock." …I would guess there's many of us Christians who have found "Spiritual gifts" at the tips of our fingers ...thus avoiding any great "uprooting" ....right?

...and don't we pray (privately, not publicly) that our close family and close friends be likewise blessed???

...I asked a mentor yesterday ...if given the warnings in (1 Cor. 11: 29) "believers" can partake in communion equally with "Christians" ...yet dodge the bullet of "unworthily" ...and he advised "yes ...if they have fully surrendered to Christ"

...as previously mentioned ...my friend Tissa was a believer of Christianity ...but also a believer of Islam and Buddhism also. ...it can get confusing

...so the best advice to myself is not "go figure" ...but rather "don't worry" ...yet "care greatly" for the souls of others.

...on the paper route, early this morning, I was thinking on a favorite "rhema" Bible verse (1 Cor. 13: 55) "O death, where is thy sting? O grave, where is thy victory?" ...that's a comfort ...but even more immediate, is "O fear, where is thy foothold?" (not a quote)

...I need not worry about another's "worthy or unworthy" ...I need only share what God shares with me, whether in agreement or disagreement. ...we know there is nothing of Christ in idle grumbling about another's walk in faith. ...it's not "judging" to ask another, as to where their daily steps are leading them

...and it's good and healthy to be concerned that it be upwards and not downwards.

...any one of us can "say" the Holy Spirit is working in us ...directing our paths

...priests, pastors and cult leaders have all shown themselves fallible ...and so there's no harm in our asking that, especially leaders ...adhere to Bible doctrine.

...God is constantly speaking to each of us, but are we taking time to listen?

...is the "truth" we "want" to hear, the same as the "truth" in God's word??? ...if not ...we're probably not "Christians" ....rather, "cultists". ...cultists don't utilize "God's truth" to "God's glory" ...they use "Bible words" to advance their own ends

...then encourage others to think as they themselves think, irregardless of the greater truth found in God's "complete" instruction for salvation. ...it ought to be of concern ...how frequently church members (through personal sensitivities) shy away at the hint of exhortation ...for which we're to "not forsake the assembly of ourselves."

...if I advance even "benign" interests (like golf?) rather than Godly doctrine, am I then not seeking separation from what is "of faith"? ...or have I been given special liberty, as a Christian, to incorporate what is of my personal inclination or nature, into whatever part of Christ's body I claim to be: i.e. ...if I am the "hand" of Christ, then cannot this hand of Christ hold a golf club?? ...I don't think this "hand" of Christ could hold a playboy magazine but a golf club ...or maybe a boxing glove might be okay ...right? ...or a television clicker? ...can I just let "my" conscience be my guide??

..."my" conscience is determined by "my" nature. ...Christ's nature wants nothing to do with "my own" (sinful) nature, therefore ...except I surrender "my" nature and be transformed ...then I remain at the mercy of myself and "my own created" world. ...that's a grim prospect if you've had a taste of something far greater.

...whether in calm, in storms, we each master our own ships and report to the authority of our own choosing.

...for a friend or mentor or brother or sister to question my conduct based on scripture, is not a judging thing but rather a caring thing

...and once I don't mind "their" questions ...then I can learn to not mind questions or criticism from more secular people or even possibly, enemies!

...and yet respond with "calm and caring" rather than "over sensitivity, hurt and venom".

...the portion of our lives that is "of faith" will seek greater faith ...whereas the portion that is of "other than faith" will seek avoidance of greater faith and also deception in our present faith....darkness doesn't like light ...and light can't like darkness.

...I had a humbling experience on papers this morning when confronted unexpectedly by a scene of God's beauty, so much so, that I immediately wished I had turned away, lest I offend. (Isa. 6: 5) (....a bit of "woe is me, I am undone" moment)

...we're blessed to live amidst what God has created, yet we're determined to spoil it with our own strife and stress.

...I hear that even camping has now been invaded by man's toys and noise.

...a reminder that our social freedoms can quickly create our personal prisons.

...throughout time, the fruit of "unfaithfulness" to God has led to the search for alternate loves and alternate purpose or worth.

...deep inside we seek (even demand) self validation and respect for our choices and values, though there be little virtue or note worthiness

...plus we demand the freedom to change our minds as suits us.

...a lady at work shared that she's seriously considering changing churches and cited the increased price of gas as her reason.

(I don't honestly think "gasoline" if the prime reason ...but it may be a factor.)

...just as faithfulness to a spouse will only come through unselfish love and putting "them" ahead of ourselves ...so faithfulness to any gathering in Christ's name will come through putting Christ's will (per His word) ahead of all social implications.

..."social faithfulness" could well prove to be the death of us "spiritually" though it appear the opposite. ...the judgment (view) of our peers is futile, except it encourage us to ongoing Spiritual growth in Christ.

...as Christ brought to us the light of God through the word, then no matter how "almost faithful" our friends and peers, if they choose "almost" to hunger for more of God, yet "almost" to also hunger for more of satan's goodies ...then there's a problem. ...being born with sinful natures into a sinful world is an unavoidable problem and in our own strength we can't overcome the darkness (death) that ensues.

..."this world" is like the stony ground or thorns in Christ's parable of the sower

(Mark 4: 16) ….the onus is on each of us to establish strong roots and vigilance for ourselves and for our children, so that we not become offended at (verse 18) God's instruction nor distracted into choking out His instruction. (verse 19)

…I'm not aware of any instance in the Bible where God has drawn near to those who ignored Him …except to exhort them about mending their ways.

…another good Bible study tonight …..(John 1: 5 – 10)

…Pastor Dave shared how, despite all prophesy of Christ's coming …yet God's people were looking for someone more like themselves to perhaps revenge the wrongs done them and turn the tables to their own worldly favor or advantage. …that sort of thing is never "of God's love" …God's love compels us to do good to those that push us down, otherwise our motives are as theirs.

…His love, which is to be growing in us, is a love of unity "oneness" in Him) without class or caste status ….and without fear. (1 John 4: 18) …"perfect love casteth out fear"

…one of my favorite Bible verses is (Micah 6: 8) …do justly, love mercy, walk humbly with God …it's not only a humbly with God …it's not only a full time job

…it's a full time life. …and I'm made aware just now that it doesn't tell me to "seek" justice but rather to simply "do" justly.

…to "be" considerate need not be complicated by "expecting" consideration from others. …our ungodly nature (sinful) soaks up every source to support our self-centeredness and "me first" attitudes.

…when I lazily fail to overcome temptations, I wallow in self pity and bask in the appeasing sympathy of others, through which caring for others or being thankful to God can hardly break through …and whereby "darkness" becomes my lot.

…as Christians, we may ascribe to desiring "Christ-likeness" in our talk …but our "walk" is what determines the state of our hearts …and the Bible says that except our prayers align with our hearts …then God hears none of it.

 …and why would He? ….are we so weak as to hope God will compromise His Holiness and Righteousness to accommodate even a mild form of deceit?

...or that God might look kindly on the fruit of satan? ...rather pray it never happen and by so doing assert our faithfulness. ...for sure, our sinful nature, desires a righteousness akin to our won ....and for sure, that is to be avoided!

(Matt. 6: 33) ...the Bible says "But seek ye first the kingdom of God and His righteousness" ...i.e.: then will contentment be added to us ...not our own determination of desire or need but rather a desire to be concerned for others.

...it's not unusual for us to seek self-importance from our spouse or family or employer or church ...where one may compromise another ...yet in our "seeking first the Kingdom of God ...then all else will be added to us, even though it may not appear as such ....our trust in God's word must supercede all other trusts that impact our lives.

...Christ is the "prince of peace" ...but only to those who choose Him ...otherwise He is strife and division. (Luke 16: 51) ...and gladly so ...that we might know such conviction as to change our ways. ..."division" will, no doubt, also be a portion of our choosing closeness with Christ, as there are family and friends who would have us continue in darkness to support their own lifestyle choices, not of His light. ...most of us seek an acceptable balance with a foot in both camps, yet wish "they" might seek Christ so that "we" might more greatly experience our being filled by His Spirit ...and so we again find that we're being kind to ourselves in direct violation of scripture.

...a friend recently asked if I thought suicide was sin. ...I would say so.

...the Bible says there is a measure (spark of light) of God, which lighteth every person that cometh into the world. (John 1: 9) ...that bit of light is His though in our care to grow it and return the interest gained to Him.

...as in the parable of the talents, to bury that light is sin (many of us do just that) and so to extinguish that light (and that little light's potential) must be grievous sin.

...no one, led by Christ's Spirit, is led to suicide but rather it is the leading of satan.

...my guess is that suicide is a culmination (compounding) of past choices which have been against God ...as probably is depression even. ...as we ignore God's word, then so we "establish" our own sense of what's right and what's good based on our own natures …which the Bible says is "as filthy rags." (Isa. 64: 6)

…if we believe not that God created us, then we may come to think we've created ourselves and so can do whatever we want with ourselves …even "end" ourselves!

…if I accept (Roman 14: 23) "wherefore whatever is not of faith, is sin" …then many loopholes are closed as regards what I might "prefer" to believe …especially "subjectively believe."

…only God can judge the circumstances of a particular suicide …I don't have His wisdom …but the "Bible" has His wisdom …so I can at least maybe help someone a little by suggesting they look "there" for answers to questions not only around suicide but as pertains anything! …and through my knowing the Bible a bit, I can maybe save them some time by citing applicable scriptures for "them" to look up.

…I just now see the wisdom of Christ's using "parables" to breach subjective sensitivities. …through parables, Christ's followers were able to apply God's light (no matter how much of that light they had nourished and matured) to ascertain themselves, God's will and what pleased Him. …we are so blessed to have His word close at hand to guide us and nourish us, to life more abundant.

…those who love the Lord with their all (whatever that measure) are free from concerns about suicide …but if we choose not to resist satan, then we will endure the anguish and hopeless desperation that he endures …even unto the taking of our own lives through wretched despair. (Rev. 14: 10) "The same shall drink of the wrath of the wine of God, which is poured out without mixture into the cup of His indignation….."

…we each …without excuse have the option to choose for Christ or choose to allow ourselves to be swallowed up by a force (anti-Christ) (1 John 4: 3) "even now already is in the world". …we can choose to make light (laugh at) of God's word …or choose to take it seriously. (I doubt God has ever led anyone to not take His word too seriously!) …(but for sure, satan led Adam and Eve to.)

…if we believe …and with a contrite heart, ask the Spirit to indwell us …then we Know "His" truth, despite satan's whisperings.

…in that we hunger and thirst for more of His truth …so we know His Spirit is in us. ……otherwise …I would say, no.

…maybe we're busy …maybe we have demands on us …maybe we'd sooner be fishing or golfing or watching television …whatever …if His Spirit is in us, then whatever is "not of faith" will grow strangely dim. …and it may be only in retrospect that we're even aware of it. …best to be suspicious of our hearts if we think we're acquiring faith at no expense to worldly attractions. …the Bible defines those worldly attractions in general terms …like "things" …I expect "His" Spirit will guide us to treasure those "things" which are of faith. (2 Cor. 5: 17) …the Bible says "Therefore if any be in Christ they are a new creature (being): old things are passed away; behold, all things are become new."

…I doubt that means we are to get a "new" and greater enjoyment of the "old things of our own natures" …rather that those old things (attractions) are to depart and be replaced by new light in faith …new hunger …new thirst, etc.

…I acknowledge that I'm moderately cynical (I prefer "discerning") but it must have been a news cast I've recently seen that left me, this morning, with the thought of "illegal immigrants in faith".

…I figure I either "belong" to Christ, whereby I'm adopted by Him …or I'm an illegitimate imposter in His fold, hopeful that my deceit won't be discovered by other sheep or the Shepherd.

…that, of course, is a pipe dream, as the Bible clearly states that I can't have my feet in Christ's camp while my heart is elsewhere. …for sure I can dress up to look Christian …and I can carry a Bible around …and smile away like something's not right upstairs …but I'll know, for sure, that truth known …something actually isn't "right upstairs".

…so, will I humbly, with head down, back out of the fold and clean myself of deceit??? …or will I hang around in disguise until I earn "the boot" when the accounting comes???

…like most every believer or Christian, I enjoy the encouragement or comfort of another's steady hand on my shoulder and hearing that I'm doing fine in my Christian walk …but that's more hindrance than help if my walk is not one of hunger and thirsting after God's righteousness and not that of church or friend.

(Gal. 1: 10) "For do I now persuade men, or God? Or do I seek to please men? For if I yet pleased men, I should not be the Servant of Christ." …it's futile to believe the Bible "in part" …or "as suits our comfort level" (conscience) but so great is God's love, that even without hope of Heaven or fear of hell, yet is the wisdom in God's word, so abundant, that it maintains His creation (this world) in harmony, if we deny our own nature.

…even death is not an end, any more than our evenings sleep is an end

…someone said "the rest of our days depends upon the rest of our nights."

…so it ought be well to believe that we each have an eternity and that whether that eternity be good or heinous, depends on the rest of our lives supporting God's word …or defying God's word.

…we are servants …or we demand service. …I think scripture said "we reap what we sow" long before we called it "the golden rule".

…we don't seem to mind the struggle to keep dandelions and weeds from our cultured lawns and gardens …yet struggle hardly any to save and maintain our souls.

…I see how people speak to those who they don't like …and assume it's how they would speak to me also, should I ever cross them.

…invoking "subjective emotion: is a poor filler for "just principle".

…it's wrong! …and whether I embrace it, allow it or fight it, is what determines the quality of my life and the lives of those I care for.

…not only what we encourage but also what we silently allow, is what contributes to our light or our darkness. …the protests of 60s - 70s created great unity of focus for youth, but maybe it was mostly a "we want" focus. …those days may hold great memories but probably at considerable cost morally and Spiritually.

...the next generation also reaps what we sow. ...to go from mother's milk to strong meat in short order is bound to cause indigestion and now we have that "in spades".

...it's not that today's society doesn't utilize some wisdom from the Bible

...it's just that we attribute it to ourselves! ...we may sing "Praise God from whom all blessings flow ..." ...but we don't really mean "all" ...we probably mean "some" or "a few". ....we see the majority of our "good stuff" from ourselves and our own natures ...so if our own natures are sinful, when what we produce (fruit) is of satan.

...Christ ...was a "fish out of water" (John 1: 11) ..."He came unto His own and His own received Him not." ...that's the "bad news" ...the "good new" is ...(verse 12) "But as many as receive Him, to them He gives power to overcome darkness" ...not just on Sundays but everyday, when we look to Him to guide us through our own chaos.

...if we don't have much time to "look to Him" ...that's not God's fault.

...I wonder if we sometimes thank God for things that satan gives us ...like maybe a promotion at work that gives us more money ...but takes another ten hours from our family or devotions every week. ...the man who needs a "worldly challenge probably doesn't need a "Godly challenge" .....right??? ...yet all mankind needs constant Godly challenge to grow and as one grows in faith, so are they empowered by faith and are emboldened to profess Christ. ...to be "plugged into" Christ lessens every worldly burden and increases every rest and every joy.

...believer and non-believer alike benefit from God's blessings but only seeking believer (Christian) will know the added blessing of faith whereby in our pleasing God (verifiable through His word) we also please that portion of us which belongs to Him.

...the hymn says "T'is so sweet to trust in Jesus ...just to take Him at His word...." ...good stuff !!

...the alternative is to be left to the mercy of our own natures, which, despite our "perceived "good intent" is sinful (offensive to God).

...to pursue "pleasing" God, is the "race" set before the seeking Christian ...not the settling for what "probably doesn't bug God too much".

…"apathy" is indifference and the world is largely content to settle for it. …there's no passion there …and no life more abundant there. …we can consider even that we have life, is "the luck of some draw" …or that we weren't aborted prior to drawing breath …but that mindset is a bit stifling and limiting …like arriving at 2nd base but not knowing how we got there!?

(Matt. 7: 26) …that's a "house built on sand" and how ever much we add to it, when we look back or look down …it's still going to be sand and it's always going to be "unstable."

…my Grandmother, Edith Gifford, often used to say "imagine that" when confronted with something beyond her personal comprehension …to my knowledge, she lived a full, Christian, productive life …yet never once left the confines of the province of Ontario.

…maybe I've been to the other side of the world and seen both palaces and great depravity …my grandmother's footing in faith gave her a more sure base from which to live her life. …Nannie Gifford died maybe 25 years ago but her "faith" lives yet in all those who once knew her.

…what is truly "of God" never dies …it only grows greater somewhere else

…maybe a pinch in me …but several pinches in others who, in any number of ways, encountered Christ through the brief life of my Grandmother …and then my Mother likewise. …as I reflect on the Godliness of my Grandmother …so will my son Richard …one day, reflect on my Mom …seed produces the fruit thereof.

(…somebody, write that down !)

…but fruit also produces seed ….right? …and seed is subject to many, many influences …which for man, many years are within the parent's control. …if fruit and seed of the Spirit is allowed to spoil, then what hope has mankind.

…we may appear to be a country at peace but Spiritually, we're at war and worse yet, at war and "off guard". …where there is no Christ …there can be no peace or lasting rest …rather only the fruit of our own natures which will always war against Christ.

…whether the Middle East or our own backyards …where people of God do nothing to proclaim Him, there will be self interest and bitterness.

…only through Christ is the comfort of lasting peace made available to some, who (Rev. 3: 13) "have an ear to hear what His Spirit saith."

…Christ said (Luke 12: 51) "Suppose ye that I am come to give peace on earth? I tell you, Nay; but rather division:…."

(…Richard, ….don't ever, ever, …disagree with Christ.) …if ever God's word doesn't quite make sense to us …the failing of that "sense" will always be ours

…and to our own limited vision, God's love is unfathomable and satan will persuade us that, what we ourselves determine in our darkness, is of utmost importance.

…if we choose to believe that …then no amount of negotiation or compromise will bring rest …to any situation …not work situations nor marital nor family nor church nor community nor national …all these will have an unstable foundation apart from Christ.

(Rom. 8: 9) …the Bible says that without Christ's Spirit in us …we're not even Christians! …and that it's through the Spirit that Christ can intercede between ourselves and God. …through the Holy Spirit only, does God hear our prayers …all else is but our own selfish wishful thinking wherein God may as well be Santa Claus. (James 4: 2) …"we have not because we ask not."

…maybe it's as though God has a language of love and humility

…whereas satan's (sins) language is different and the Bible says (John 9: 31) "God hears not sinners!"

(James 4: 3) ….we ask "amiss" when we ask from a proud heart for personal (subjective) peace on an issue over and above what the Bible states is to be the Christian standard (pleasing to God).

…I suppose it's possible to proclaim Christ as our treasure and humbly share His burden for the lost …yet, remain unscathed or unscarred by the world …but that never happened to any sincere followers of Christ in the Bible.

…that, of itself, gives me reason to pause and reflect on my Spiritual walk today.

(I guess I'm just really "blessed" that I seem to be getting off so lightly!)

…would my "walk" differ much, if I "liked" the presumed experience of faith and His pure love …but also liked worldly stuff? …not "dirty" worldly stuff

…just the fine, cultured, civilized worldly stuff. …I suppose we're all servants of our treasures ….Christian or no.

…the longer we live, the more loved ones we have in unfortunate circumstances …whether in hospital (or the likes) or maybe in third world countries.

…I sometimes pray for healing or comfort for those friends or family

…I do that because I particularly treasure those people …that's only normal ……right?

…but if truly Christian …I'm to treasure Christ and His cause above what is normal in the world.

…it's not "wrong" that I pray for those with whom I have a special connection but if Christ be my "all in all" then I more earnestly will pray that those in dubious circumstances share their treasure and hope (Christ) with the "lost" nearby them….those gravely sick or persecuted, who have Christ …are far better off than those who have health or ease but are without Christ.

(…would my viewpoint change ….were I both sickly and persecuted? ….probably.)

…the Bible says " whatsoever we ask in Christ's name" that He will do.

…many seem to have the "gift of gab" (not a Spiritual gift)

…idle talk comes natural and I fear we may bring that "gift" to our prayer life.

(1 Thes. 5: 17) …to "pray without ceasing" I don't think means to talk incessantly without "earnest and effectual" (discerning) consideration beforehand.(James 5: 16)

…I have a good, Christian friend who sees much of the public (corporate) prayer he hears, as likened unto chartering a big sport fishing boat capable of 10 or 20 rods

…then he goes out alone casting out line after line

…hoping for a "bite" on at least one presentation!

…there's a reason why the Bible says (James 5: 16) "The fervent and effectual prayers of the righteous availeth much."

…if we pray "Thy will be done " Then the Bible will confirm that we're not "asking amiss" (James 4: 3) …but rather giving thought to just "what it is" that is His will."

…interestingly, the Bible says "Likewise the Spirit also helpeth our infirmities (limitations) for we know not what we should pray for as we ought ….."

…that description sure fits me …I have no trouble asking for things that suit me

…but that's not what we are to pray for, is it?

…aren't we to seek God's will, as stated in His word, then pray for just that

…whether it suits our natures or not.

…the saying "be careful what you ask for because you just might get it"

…that should apply to prayer more so than anything because it reveals our heart's treasures and if what we pray for isn't in the Bible then we shouldn't, as Christians, be praying for it. …maybe it's not God's will that we have great health and fantastic fun!

…maybe He wants us positioned to "share His sufficiency" during illness or weakness or difficult times …or something where evidence of faith in Him is brought to bear.

…we seldom pray that a loved one be sufficiently broken that their need of Christ become paramount ….even though we know (either from experience or from the Bible) that it's "our own" nature that deplores weakness, brokenness or humble surrender.

…how many times did Christ say "your faith" has made you "whole"?

…we need only pray that another find such faith and leave it to God to deal sufficient blows to be effectual. (1 John 5: 14) ….the Bible says "And this is the confidence that we have in Him, that, if we ask anything "according to His will" , He heareth us.

…"other than" His will ….I would say ….no.

…we are born with a sinful nature and deceptive nature …and a Godly nature is available through faith, believing …but only if we crucify (put to death) our worldly nature and seek what is of the Kingdom of God.

…whatever is "of God" is sufficient to serve His purposes …earth, sun, stars, trees, water, animals, us, etc. etc.

…all exist and all pass away only at His will and in His season.

> "When you get where you are going
> where will you be?"
> What will you be?

The above inscription is the scanned page from the back of Mom's Bible ...in her own hand writing (no reason given) God's works in mysterious ways ......right?

Also see:

Into Captivity
Series
052, 061, 062, 071 etc.

Author -born 1948 – Ontario

strict Protestant upbringing

fled Christianity at first opportunity

roamed wilderness for about 40 years

married 1981 – son, Richard 1986 – divorced 2004

began writing 2004 – became Christian 2004

Notes/Comments

Notes/Comments

Printed in the United States
83768LV00002B/3-20/A